W9-BQI-748

CARS OF THE SIZZLING '60s

A DECADE OF GREAT RIDES AND GOOD VIBRATIONS

Publications International, Ltd.

Louis Weber, CEO
Publications International, Ltd.
7373 North Cicero Avenue
Lincolnwood, Illinois 60712

Manufactured in China.

8 7 6 5 4 3 2 1

ISBN: 0-7853-4487-X

Library of Congress Catalog Card Number: 97-67074

Acknowledgements

PHOTOGRAPHY

The editors gratefully acknowledge the cooperation of the following for supplying photography that helped make this book possible:

Jerry Cizek, Chicago Automobile Dealers Association; AAA-Chicago Motor Club; David Temple; Vince Manocchi; Doug Mitchel; Miles Arsenault; Nicky Wright; Rob Reaser; Jeff Rose; Milton Gene Kieft; Roger Servick, Sid Mead Corp.; Thomas Glatch; Sam Griffith; D. Randy Riggs; Mike Mueller; Mark A. Patrick, The National Automotive History Collection, Detroit Public Library; Peggy Dusman,American Automobile Manufactures Association; Bud Juneau; Mitch Frumkin; Des Plaines, IL Historical Society; NHRA; Lincolnwood, IL Police Dept.; Richard Spiegelman; Dan Lyons; David Talbot; Jerry Heasley; Texas Dept. of Transportation; Ken Beebee; Nina Padgett; Scott Baxter; Illinois State Police; Steen Fleron; Mirco DeCet; Ron McQueeney, Indianapolis Motor Speedway; Illustrations: Dick Nesbitt; Jairus Watson.

OWNERS

Special thanks to the owners of the cars featured in this book for their enthusiastic cooperation. They are listed below:

1960: James R. Cunningham; Roy Hawkins; Roy Sklarin; George T. Mason; Al Houghton; Lill & Joseph Mutschinszky; Ian J. Smale; Larry Stumpf; Charles E.Jenkins; Joseph E. Medeiros; Dave & Norma Wasilewski; The Behring Auto Museum/University of California-Berkeley; Jim Perrault; Charlie Wells; Mike Spaziano; Scott A. Kennedy; Bob Newman; Rick J. Santelli; Joyce & Jim Wickel; Jim Mueller; Norval Northcott; Rick Shick; Garth Higgins; Rear Admiral Thomas J. Patterson; Rodger Eberenz; Joe Sutter; Robert & Gene Fattore; Fred Engel; Beth, Pro Team Corvette Sales, Napoleon, Ohio; Terry Lucas; Vivian Riley; Greg Englin; Gary Almeida; George Kling; Barry & Barb Bales; M.J. Shelton; Janet Carter Wright; Rudy & Bonnie Patane; Mini Motors Classic; Paul Sable.

1961: Steve Nye & Ken Leighton; Ben Gipson, Speciality Sales; Jack Driesenga; Lloyd W. Hill; Ken M. Hustvet; Howard A. Moore; Steve Thompson; Frank Spittle; Blaine Jenkins; Sam H. Scole; Harold Lee Lockhart; Dave Ritchie; Dean Stansfield; Larry Hills; Bill Clement, Chevy Craft Inc.; Jack Gratzianna; Jack West; Bill Jones; Jim Davidson; Alan Ranz; Joseph Smiesko; Robert & Karen Christanell; Robert Thornton; John Brichetto, Studebaker National Museum, Inc.; Tom Buttling; Harrah Natonal Auto Museum; Larry K. & Susanne G. Knudsen; CC Classic Car; Tony Perrett; Tony Mozynew; Larry Claypool.

1962: Burt Carlson; Ken Havekost; Michael Porto; George Dalinis; Phil Fair; Patt & J.R. Buxman; Mike Elward, Nostalgia Motors; Richard Carpenter; Bob Burroughs; Ken Boorsma; Westley Myrick; Eldon T. Anson; Robert Dowd; Rex Harris; Doug Scott; Larry E. Driscoll; Dean J. Moroni; Mark & Carolyn Badamo; John T. Finster; Virgil K. Cooper; Douglas & Beverly Finch; Bobby Wiggins; Rusty Symmes; Gary A. Girt; Henry M. Iseksen; Richard Yech; Mitchell Corp. of Owasso; Michael Kelso; Melvin Lewis; Greg Minor; Bill & Kathy Berks; Henry Hart; Ronald A. Smith; Stephen Gottfried; Brooks Stevens Museum; James Herman; Raymond Pablo; John Weinberger.

1963: Myron Davis; Richard Carpenter; Amos Minter; Bob Burroughs; Bill Blair; Ward Hartsock; Ron Kendall; Kieth Thompson; William L. Finney III; Guy Mabee; Charles Ziska; Arnie Addison; Barry Norman; Bill Jackson; John P. Vetter; John W. DeVed; Ken Kowalk; Ron and Claudia Bjerke; Joseph Bartera; Les Raye; Nick Schafsnitz; Tom West; John Wacha; Garth Higgins; Robert Hallada; Phillip and Sandy Lopiccolo; Dave Bristol; Jeff Logan; Donald Lambert; Rich Antonacci; Jerry Coffee; John W. Sieble; Wanda Habenicht; Mike Congelose; Edwin and Vivian Pettitt; Dave and Cindy Keetch; Doug Anderson; Harold VonBrocken; Jon B. Myer; Harold C. Lichty; Bob Montgomery; Mike Coleman; Ken Dedic; Philippa Newnham; Mark Clark.

1964: John Fobair; Donnie Carr; Fred Huck; Ralph M. Hartsock; Ed DeWitt; Greg and Rhonda Meredyk; Frank Spittle; Fred E. Williams; Joseph Pieroni; Ron Stewart; Ray and Gil Elias, Tom Schlitter; Gladys Duzell; Vince Manocchi; Mike and Marge Tanzer; Michael Tesauro, Jr.; Scott R. Koeshall; Les Raye; Paul D. Pierce; Lee Pankratz; Jade McCall; Jerry Hammer; Pete Henneberger; Patricia J. Feutz; Sam Pierce; Bob Painter; Howard L. Baker; Carlos and Sherry Vivas; Owen Sessions; Dennis A. Urban; Charles and Jan Peck; Jim Behrendt; Joe Kelly; Ed Raden; Ralph M. Mathiot; Stu Chapman; Bonnie Patane; Gerry Layer; Richard Simmons; George Raterink.

1965: Mick Cohen; Richard Carpenter; Connie Davis; Larry Barnett; Tom Devers; Scott Brubaker; Aaron Kahlenberg; Walter Schenk; David L. Griebling; William W. Kramer; Vince and Helen Springer; Ronald E. Miller; Vince Cesena; J. W. And Barbara Silveira; Rocky D'Orio; John Breda; Gary Dickenson; Christopher M. Krueger; Sherman Williams; Frank J. Mohart III; Ron Russ; Dave Fink; Horace and Susan Mennella; Steve and Sally Kuss; Ed Oberhaus; Ron Kendall; Jim MacDonald; John T. Finster; Earl F. Hansen; Robert G. Finley; Frank Spittle; Charles E. Stinson; Bill Worthington; Steve Sydell; Keith Duncan; Phil Trifaro; Robert Kleckauskas; David Yordi; Austin Fray; Neil and Amber Matranga; Michael Vacik; David and Cindy Keetch; Don Guskey; Mike and Jim Schaudek; Alan N. Basile; Herman Seymour; Mark Ward; Stu Chapman; D. Herning.

1966: Ken Havekost; Karl W. Smith; Don Rook; Ed Catricala; Robert Simpson; Duane L. Dodds; William E. Wetherholt; Richard Hanley; Manny Montgomery; Ross Wolldridge; Charles P. Geissler; John and Shirlee Rasin; Nick Juliano; Harry and Virginia Demenge; Richard A. Emry; Alice Greunke; James Harris; Jerry Buczkowski; Glenn Eisenhamer; J.W. And Barbara Silveira; Lawrence Keck; Vince and Norma Rhodes; Volo Auto Museum; Robert Yonker; Thomas and Christine Payne; Howard S. Engerman; Tom West; Barney Smith; C.C. Barnette; Ed Oberhaus; Jim Bowersox; Tom McGann; Richard Dollmeyer; Michael P. McFarland; Leigh Scott; Roger A. James; General Motors; Gary Jimenez; Earl F. Hansen; John T. Finster; Ken Nelson; John Baritel; Tom Korbas; Howard Von Pressentin; James and Mary Engle; Hans Schumacher; Richard and Madeline Martindale; Thomas M. Nicholson; Richard Witek; Chris Terry; Jeff Hare; Brad and Bev Taffs.

1967: Ken Carmack; Lee Pontius; Owen Schumacher; Allan Shroer; Tony and Suzanne George; Bill Barnes; Nate Struder; Ralph Hartsock; Duane and Carol Silvius; Dave Bartholomew; Jeff and Trish Holmes; David Hooten; Rich Neubauer; Ron Wold; Tom and Katherine Stanley; David Temple; Charles Montano; Roger Holdaway; Jim Labertew, RPM Motors; Larry Simek; Larry and Karen Miller; M. Randall Mytar; Eugene Fattore, Jr.; Ed Oberhaus; Paul McGuire; Rich and Joan Young; Dan Tessner; Allen Cummins; Gary Mills; Bill Hoff; Roy L. Spencer; Gary A. Cameron; Classic Auto Showplace; David Snodgrass; Jeffrey L. Hill; Mike Grippo; Dave Diedrics;

1968: John L. Maciejewski; James Lojewski; Robert Lojewski; Duane and Carol Silvius; Lou Schultz, Jr.; Don Rook; Ramshead Auto Collection; Jeffrey Baker; Robert Costa; Don and Becky Galeziewski; Nick Van DeWater; Dennis V. Guest; Allan S. Murray; Fred Elliott; The Beechy Family; Leon Bosquet; Mark Kuykendall; Dave Bartholomew; Louise and Jerry Gambino; John Infinger; Samuel Pampenella, Jr.; Edward J. Wey; Charles Plylar; Gary Emerson; Robert and Mary Lu Secondi; Donald F. and Chris Dunn; David and Phyllis Knuth; John Adamek; Jim Ashworth; William G. Lajeunesse; Howard Schoen; Bill Woodman; Norman Andrews; Ed DeCamp; Gerri Randalph; Barry L. Klinkel; Thomas and Mae Crockatt; Robert A. Lotito; D.R. Ogsberger; Robert and Esther Seeley; David A. Ulrich; Donald R. Crile; Michael Morocco; Doug and Judy Badgley; Si Rogers; Jon F. Havens; Steve Maysonet; Bill Pearson.

1969: Rodney Brumbaugh; C.L. Zinn; Samuel and Wanda Roth; Brian McGilvray; Volo Auto Museum; Larry Bell; Al Fraser; Kieth Rohm; Michael Leone; Mason-Dixon; Mary Lee Capriano; Browney L. Mascow; The Beechy Family; Tony Lengacher; Mike Waite; Richard Goble; Tom Hasse; Greg Turley; Biff and Donna Hitzeman; Nelson Cardadeiro; Jeff Knoll; Gary Pahee; Charles and Marie Cobb; Lewis L. Hunter; Edwin Putz; Glenn Moist; Mark E. Figliozzi; Vanetta Wilkerson; Gary D. Robely; Michael Mennella; Ron Voyles; John Cook; Carl Beck; Dennis Roboletti; Charley Lillard; Steven Knutsen; Ed Cunneen; Dolores Banuls; Jay T. Nolan; Jack Gersh; Corvette Mike; M.G. Pinky Randall; Bill Borland; James E. Collins; Ron Johnson; Robert and Ann Klein; Linda L. Naeger; Fred Engers; Tim Dunlop; David Snodgrass; Ron Robinson.

SPECIAL THANKS:

Barbara Fronczak, Chrysler Historical Collection; Skip Marketti, The Behring Auto Museum; Mark A. Patrick, The National Automotive History Collection, Detroit Public Library; Chevrolet Public Relations; Floyd C. Joliet, General Motors Design; Texas Dept. of Transportation; AAA-Chicago Motor Club; Norman Currie, Globe Photo; UPI/Corbis-Bettman; Howard Eskanazi, FPG; Michael Grubb, Shooting Star; Howard Frank, Personality Photos, Inc.; Ron Mandelbaum, Photofest; Ron Harvey, The Everett Collection; Sergeant Joe McCue, California Highway Patrol; Richard Quinn.

Contents

Foreword

We cruised the 1960s in some of the most exciting cars Detroit ever built, while around us the cultural and political landscape changed in ways we still don't fully understand.

Our most trusted institutions seemed betrayed. Assassins violated the presidency, derailed the electoral process, and desecrated the struggle for civil rights. A military that promised victory in Southeast Asia earned the contempt of millions. College campuses were turned into battlegrounds by anti-war demonstrations. When entire city blocks went up in flames much of America was bewildered, but not those who struggled daily amidst the volatile mix of poverty and inequality.

Pillars of industry shook under pressure to add environmental protection and product safety to their agendas. Not even sports was immune: the charismatic world heavyweight boxing champion was dethroned because of his political and religious beliefs. And finally, families were tested, as generations and the sexes clashed over new ways of looking at America, and of living in it.

But in change there was vitality. It was as if the nation were invigorated by a wave of youthful energy. A new sense of freedom coursed through art, fashion and music, politics, public discourse and personal behavior. Some of it turned out to be ill-considered, even frivolous. But it was kinetic. It was American.

In 1967, cold-war Communists sniped from Moscow that the "capitalist, free market response to the automobile has been unscientific, even irrational." The Reds were right about that one. What American truly saw the automobile in terms of rational transportation? It

meant freedom and personal expression. Sure, some of our cars were ill-considered. But they all were part of a national dynamic that was never more animated than in the 1960s.

Just look at the decade's definitive American automobiles. Rejecting the chrome and fins of the 1950s for technology that stretched Detroit's boundaries, Chevrolet gave us the rear-engine Corvair, Oldsmobile the front-wheel-drive Toronado, Pontiac a LeMans with a rear-transaxle and an overhead-cam six.

And in contrast to the bunker mentality of the fuel-crises 1970s, Detroit's product planners seemed invigorated. Ford's Mustang put the country's youthful ideal on wheels. Feeling energetic? Strap on a Pontiac GTO, the original muscle car. Exploring a new sense of liberation? Slip into the personal/luxury Buick Riviera.

Independent automakers who couldn't keep pace were sunk, Studebaker foremost. When there was a niche even the Big 3 couldn't fill, in stepped the imports. Rational little cars from Toyota and Datsun formed Japan's beachhead, but the decade's import story was Germany's Volkswagen Beetle, which struck a chord and became an American icon.

If it is safe to say the meaning and consequences of the '60s continue to confound us, it's also arguable that the automobile was among the few institutions that made good on its promise.

A note: Car prices quoted in the text are start-of-the-model year base prices without options, and production and sales figures are for the model year, not calendar year.

1960

Wobbled by a serious economic recession in 1958 and mindful of growing consumer interest in small cars, Detroit entered 1960 committed to the development of compacts. It was a road that would lead to some of the American auto industry's most interesting products ever.

Detroit's 1960 game plan was more focused than that of Washington, which dedicated itself mainly to containing communism—a laudable, if rather amorphous, goal. The Cold War was getting chillier: Soviet premier Nikita Khrushchev became apoplectic when an American U-2 spy plane was shot down over Sverdlovsk in May, and in an August appearance before the United Nations he angrily banged his shoe on the podium while denouncing Capitalism.

Washington took halting steps toward racial equality this year, but state and local governments didn't necessarily salute just because D.C. said desegregate. In May, President Eisenhower signed the heavily compromised Civil Rights Act of 1960, which did nothing to prevent the arrest five months later of the Rev. Martin Luther King, Jr., at a peaceful sit-in he had organized in Atlanta.

The GOP ticket of Richard Nixon and Henry Cabot Lodge faced off against Democrats John Kennedy and Lyndon Johnson in November's presidential contest. Kennedy won by a hair's breadth: a margin of 113,000 votes out of 68.3 million cast.

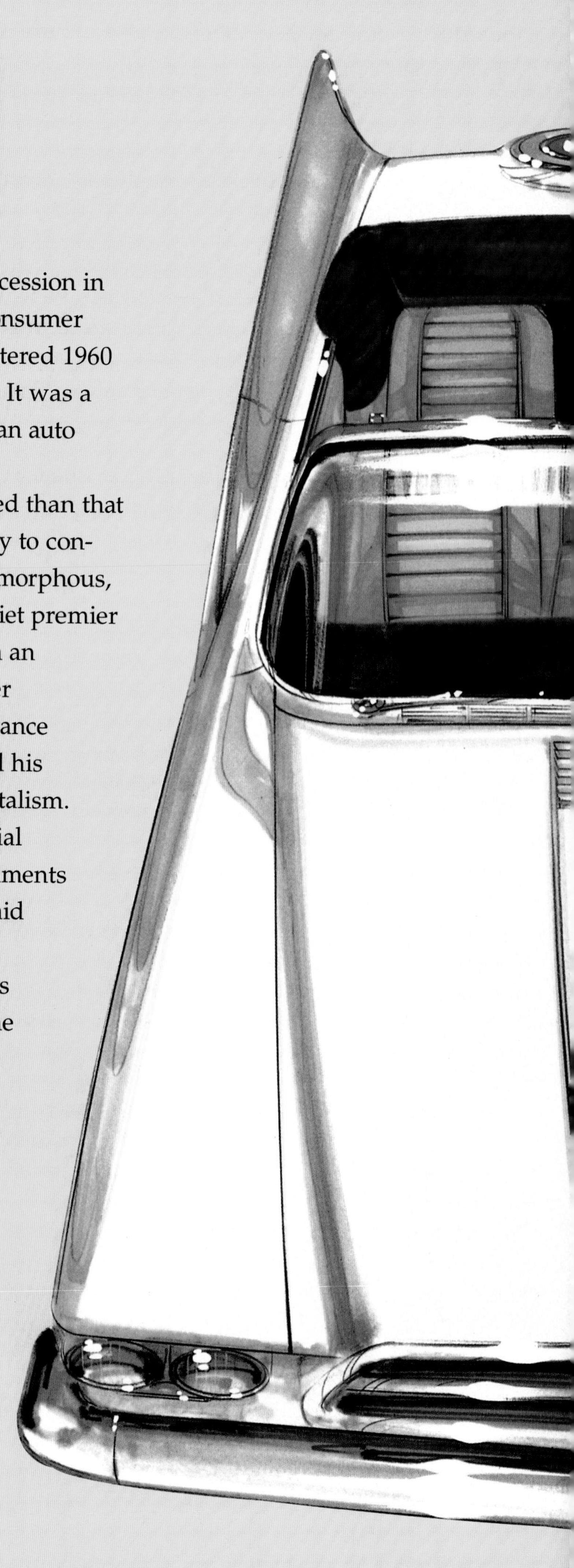

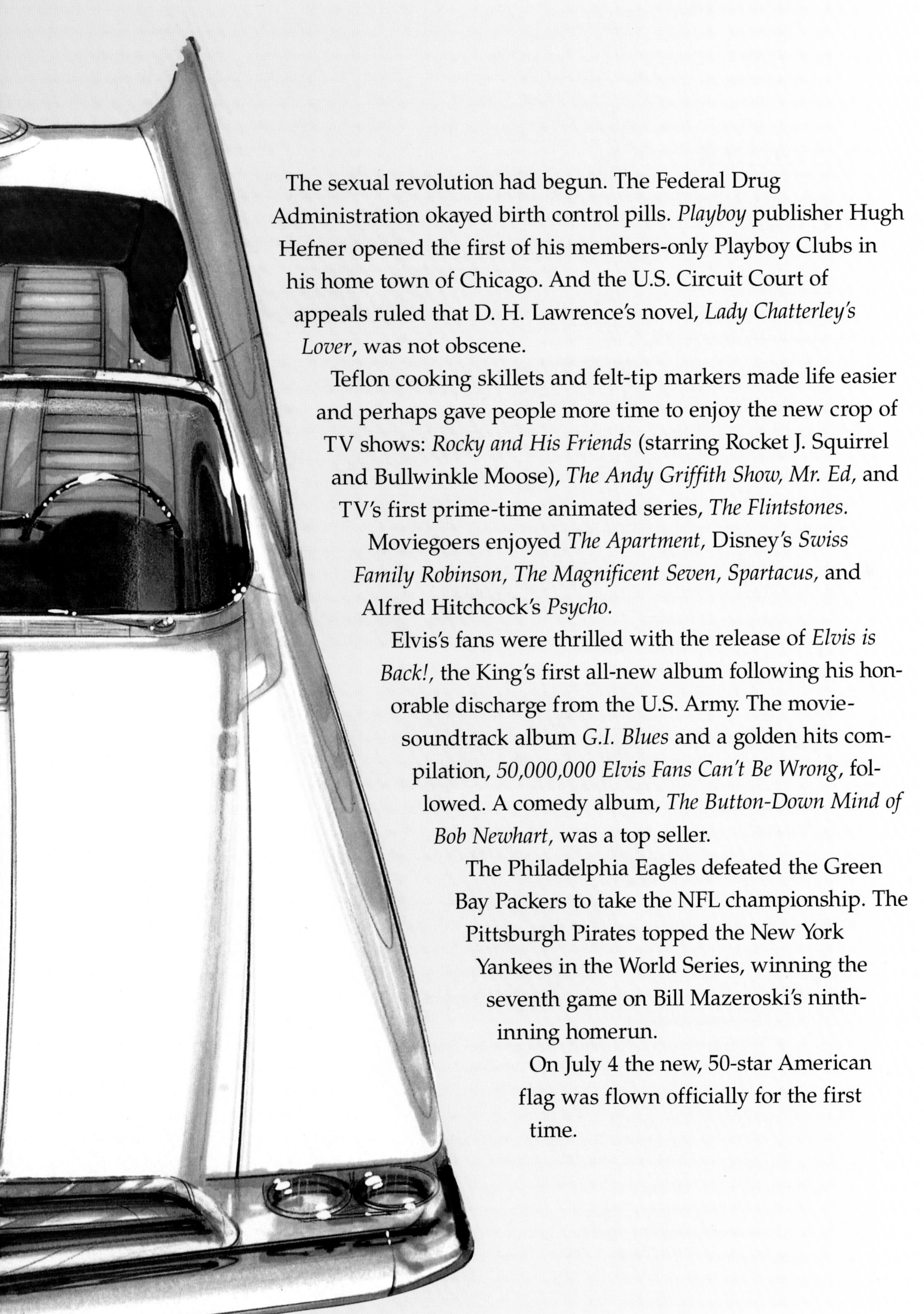

The sexual revolution had begun. The Federal Drug Administration okayed birth control pills. *Playboy* publisher Hugh Hefner opened the first of his members-only Playboy Clubs in his home town of Chicago. And the U.S. Circuit Court of appeals ruled that D. H. Lawrence's novel, *Lady Chatterley's Lover*, was not obscene.

Teflon cooking skillets and felt-tip markers made life easier and perhaps gave people more time to enjoy the new crop of TV shows: *Rocky and His Friends* (starring Rocket J. Squirrel and Bullwinkle Moose), *The Andy Griffith Show, Mr. Ed,* and TV's first prime-time animated series, *The Flintstones.*

Moviegoers enjoyed *The Apartment,* Disney's *Swiss Family Robinson, The Magnificent Seven, Spartacus,* and Alfred Hitchcock's *Psycho.*

Elvis's fans were thrilled with the release of *Elvis is Back!*, the King's first all-new album following his honorable discharge from the U.S. Army. The movie-soundtrack album *G.I. Blues* and a golden hits compilation, *50,000,000 Elvis Fans Can't Be Wrong*, followed. A comedy album, *The Button-Down Mind of Bob Newhart*, was a top seller.

The Philadelphia Eagles defeated the Green Bay Packers to take the NFL championship. The Pittsburgh Pirates topped the New York Yankees in the World Series, winning the seventh game on Bill Mazeroski's ninth-inning homerun.

On July 4 the new, 50-star American flag was flown officially for the first time.

American Motors Corporation

Created with the 1954 merger of Nash and Hudson, American Motors, which markets its cars as Ramblers, enters the 1960s well-positioned to take advantage of the nation's new affinity for compact-size cars

Production for 1960 reaches 458,841, the highest annual total ever for an independent automaker; Rambler finishes fourth in sales among U.S. makes

A major restyling brings smoother lines and full-width grilles

A new assembly plant opens in Brampton, Ontario, Canada

The 3-seat Rambler station wagon bows

Rambler American adds 4-door sedan and new Custom series

All models have ceramic-armored muffler and tailpipe

Production is increased 35 percent after purchase of a 2-million square-foot steel-furniture plant in Kenosha, Wisc.

Bonded brake linings are new

Top-opening rear trunklid is added to Metropolitan

Production of ¼-ton Mighty Mite Marine vehicle begins

1

2

3

1. A facelift and curved Scena-Ramic windshield were new on the line-topping Ambassador. This Custom hardtop, AMC's priciest non-wagon, cost $2822. A 250-bhp 327-cid V-8 was standard. **2.** At $3116, AMC sold just 435 Ambassador Custom Cross Country hardtop wagons. **3.** Compact cars were the rage, and even with a 117-inch wheelbase, Ambassador qualified. "Rambler—The Car That Made The Word 'Compact' Famous" was an AMC tag line. **4.** Ambassadors were versatile. This is the "Rambulance."

4

1

2

3

4

1. America's first subcompact, the 4-cylinder, 3-passenger Metropolitan, was built by Austin in England from a Pinin Farina design. Production ended in 1960, but leftovers were available. **2.** Rambler's mid-line Six and Rebel wagons could seat nine. **3.** A 4-door sedan joined the compact American series in '60. This is the $2059 Custom. **4.** The $2185 American Super 2-door wagon had a Nomad flair. **5.** Plain and simple: the American 2-door sedan.

5

Chrysler Corporation

Chrysler Corp., No. 3 among Detroit's Big 3 automakers, celebrates its 35th birthday

L. L. "Tex" Colbert steps aside after 10 years as Chrysler Corp. president to be suceeded by William C. Newberg, who holds the position 64 days before Colbert reassumes the post; stockholders assail Colbert's leadership

"Unibody" construction replaces body-on-frame assembly for all Chrysler Corp. cars except Imperial

Copying Ford, Chrysler Corp. introduces 12,000-mile/12-month warranty

Classic Slant Six engine debuts at 170- and 225-cid; the dependable workhorse would survive into the 1980s

Big V-8s get Ram Induction

Alternator is made standard on Imperials and Chryslers

Dodge divides lineup into compact "junior" and full-size "senior" models

Plymouth whittles its dealer network from 6800 to 4000

Compact Valiant debuts on a new 106.5-inch wheelbase

Flagship Imperial is restyled

DeSoto lineup is trimmed from 18 models to 6; rumors mount about the division's demise

1

2

1. Hurt by poor quality and pale styling after the classic '57s, Chrysler rebounded for '60 with a crisp, finned look from Virgil M. Exner, its vice president of design. It also switched to unibody construction for all Chrysler Corp. cars except Imperial. Engineering studies used ⅜-scale body models of clear plastic, shown off here by Chrysler Corp. president Tex Colbert. **2.** The entry-level Chrysler was the 122-inch wheelbase Windsor; the hardtop coupe cost $3279.

3. In unitized construction, floorpan and body panels form the car's "frame." Chrysler claimed structural twisting was reduced by 100 percent and bending by 40 percent compared to traditional body-on-frame designs. Unibody would eventually become the industry standard. **4.** Saratogas were a rung up from Windsor, rode the big 126-inch wheelbase, and used a 325-bhp 383-cid V-8. Most Saratoga buyers favored 4-door hardtops or sedans, leaving this pretty $3989 coupe the slowest seller in the series. **5.** The most-popular Chrysler was the Windsor 4-door sedan; 25,152 sold starting at $3194. **6.** Windsor hardtop wagons cost $3733 with six seats, $3814 with nine. **7.** New Yorker was the top Chrysler model and came as a coupe, sedan, wagon, or convertible. A 350-bhp 413 V-8 was standard. The 4-door hardtop listed for $4518 and weighed 4175 lbs.

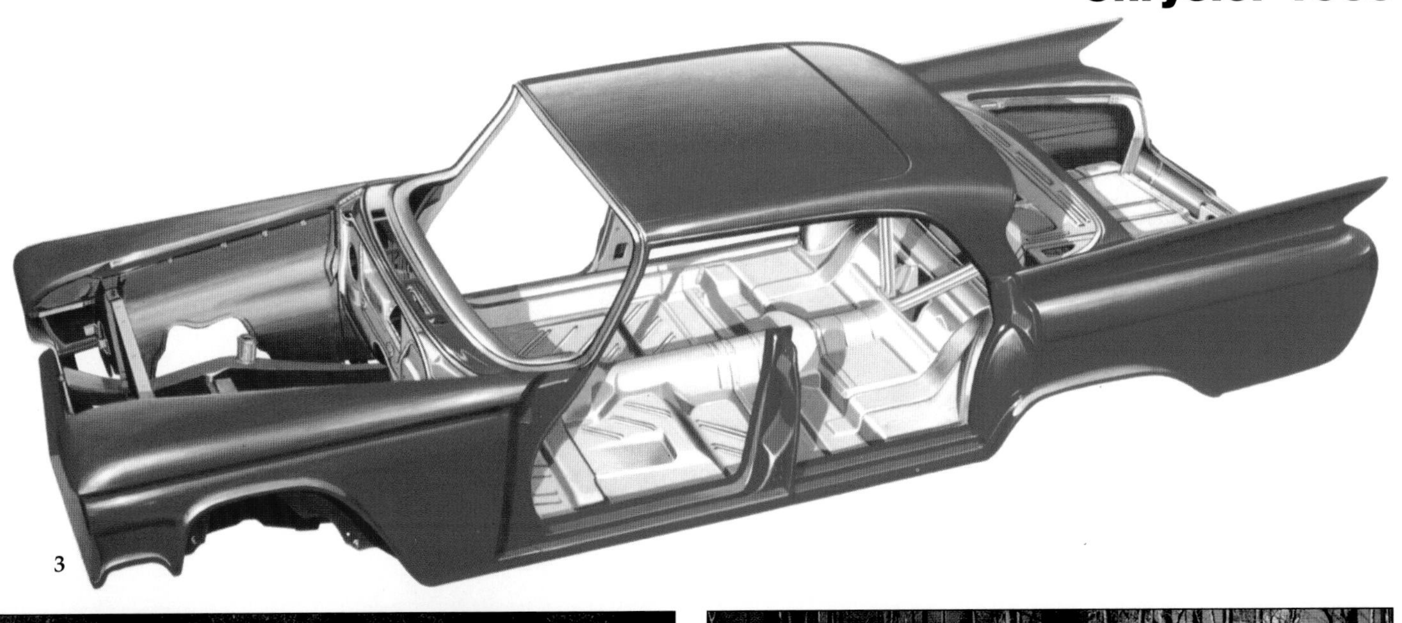

3

4

5

6

7

1960 Chrysler

1-2. Nowhere did the flowing lines of the fresh bodywork look prettier than on a New Yorker ragtop, all 219.6-inches of it. Note the deftly integrated "boomerang" taillamps within the very-tasteful-for-the-day fins. New Yorker buyers got a unique grille design, plus a deluxe two-tone interior. Chrysler never sold convertibles in large volume, but the redesign helped boost production of the New Yorker version to 556, from just 286 in 1959. Still, this $4875 soft top was the lowest-production '60 Chrysler model. By comparison, the Cadillac Sixty-Two convertible cost $5455, had 325 bhp, and sold 14,000 copies.

1

2

3

4

3. This New Yorker has the Flight Sweep Deck Lid with its stamped pseudo spare-tire doughnut. This was standard on the 300-F and Imperial, optional on New Yorker, Windsor, and Saratoga. **4.** At $5131 and 4535 lbs, the 9-passenger New Yorker Town & Country wagon was the most-expensive and heaviest '60 Chrysler.
5. Chrysler's 1960 auto show layout aimed for elegance, with performance symbolized by a strategically placed checkered-flag display. The division built 77,285 cars that model year, 12th highest production total among U.S. automakers.

5

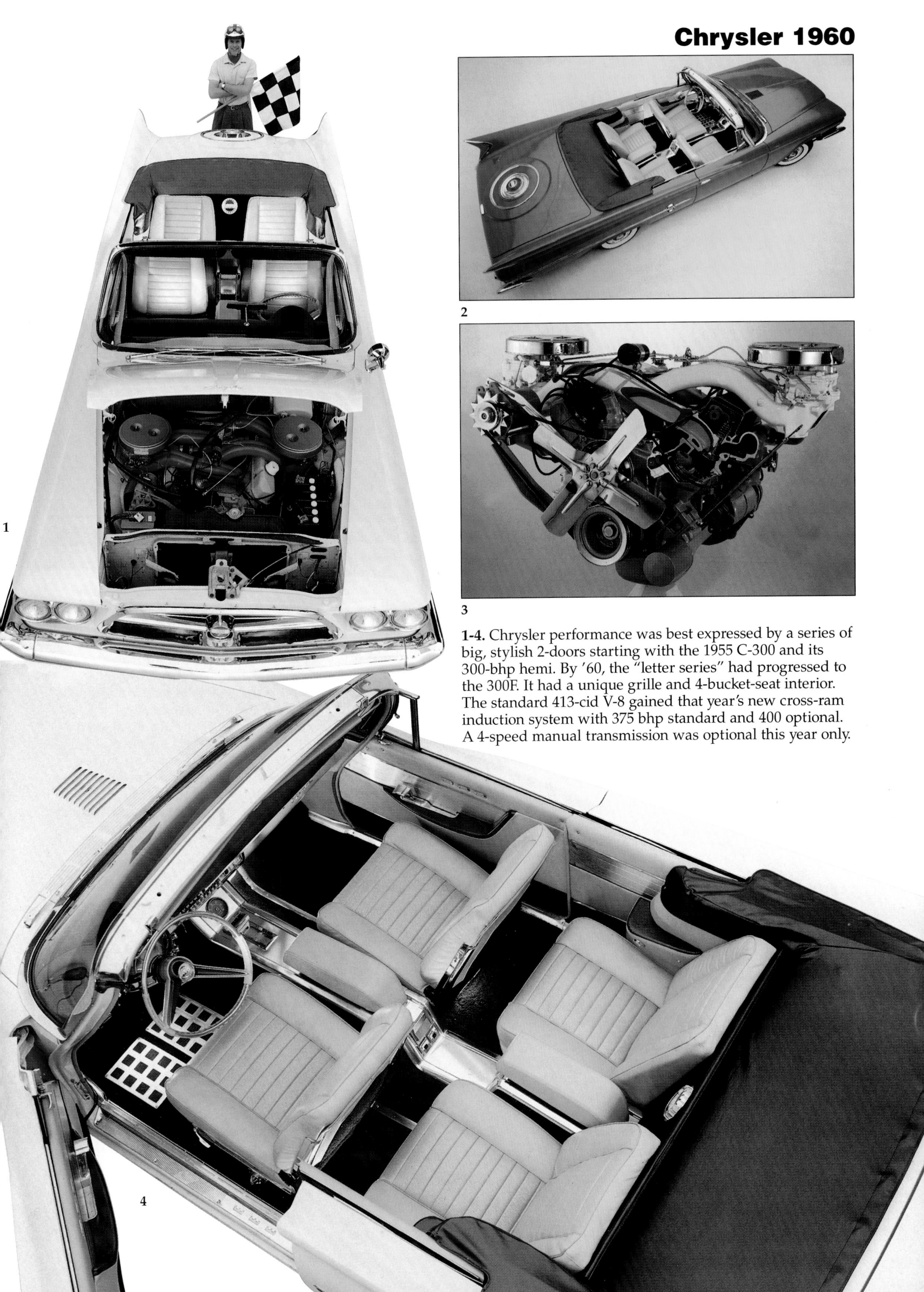

1

2

3

4

1-4. Chrysler performance was best expressed by a series of big, stylish 2-doors starting with the 1955 C-300 and its 300-bhp hemi. By '60, the "letter series" had progressed to the 300F. It had a unique grille and 4-bucket-seat interior. The standard 413-cid V-8 gained that year's new cross-ram induction system with 375 bhp standard and 400 optional. A 4-speed manual transmission was optional this year only.

1960 DeSoto

1

2 Nothing says Quality like the 1960 De Soto

Chrysler denied it, but by the start of the 1960 model year, the fate of its proud DeSoto division was all but sealed. Sales had declined steadily under poor marketing and a lack of distinction against similar-looking Chrysler division models. **1, 3.** Adventurer had been DeSoto's flagship, an only-slightly tamer version of the mighty Chrysler letter-series coupes and convertibles, in fact. But for '60, a desperate DeSoto applied the Adventurer name to all its top-trim-level models. Adventurers used a 383-cid V-8 with a 2-barrel carburetor rated at 305 bhp. A 4-barrel version was a $54 option and had 325 bhp. In a final bow to its high-performance past, it could be ordered with the dual-4-barrel ram-induction system, a $283 option good for 330 bhp at 4800 rpm. **2.** Even DeSoto's advertising slogan seemed tired and without focus as production fell to just 26,081 units, of which 11,597 were Adventurers.

3

1

2

3

4

1-3. DeSoto showed some spirit on the auto-show circuit, with the same gaudy displays and gown-draped models as virtually every other carmaker. These Adventurer hardtop coupes started at $3663; 4-door hardtops and sedans also were offered. But DeSoto was losing its independence. In 1959, Chrysler Corp. had relieved DeSoto of its own headquarters and plant; now all DeSotos were built at a Chrysler factory on the same 122-inch wheelbase as the Chrysler Windsor and big Dodge. For '60, DeSoto lost its stand-alone status and was folded into the new Chrysler-DeSoto-Plymouth Division. **4.** DeSoto's entry-level model was the Fireflite; it came with a 295-bhp 361 V-8 and was priced from $3017 to $3167.

1960 Dodge

1

1. Responding to the growing market for more sensible cars, Dodge fielded a much broader 1960 lineup highlighted by a new 118-inch wheelbase "junior" series called the Dart. It was offered in Seneca, Pioneer, and Phoenix trim, the last being reserved for the hardtop coupe and convertible body styles. Dart wagons rode the 122-inch wheelbase used by the "senior" Matador and Polara series. Shown on the move at Chrysler's Chelsea, Mich., proving grounds are (clockwise from top left) the Matador hardtop coupe, Dart Pioneer wagon, Dart Phoenix 4-door hardtop, and Polara 4-door hardtop. **2-3.** Popularly priced between $2300 and $3000 and carrying new unibody styling similar to the big Dodges, Dart was a success, accounting for an amazing 87 percent of the division's 367,804-unit production. Overall, Dodge was up nearly 200,000 units.

2

3

"Can't continue fishing without bait. Send more cars."

—Richmond, Calif., Dodge dealer Reese F. Starr, pleading for more of the popular new 1960 Dodge Dart; October 1959

1

2

1-2. Dodge billed its Darts as low-priced economy cars, but fulsome styling made even the entry-level Dart Seneca 4-door look more expensive than its attractive $2330 base price. This was the best-selling Dart; Dodge built 93,167 of them with 6-cylinder engines and 45,737 with the 230-bhp 318-cid V-8. Despite appearances, most '60 Dodges were relatively light and offered good performance with reasonable gas mileage. **3.** Dart's base engine was the new 145-bhp 225-cid Slant Six, here on the right of the Dart Phoenix convertible. To the left is the hot D-500 383 with ram induction and 330 bhp. That engine was an option on the $2988 ragtop and gave the 3690-lb convertible some real get-up-and-go.

3

1960 Dodge

"Our design and engineering advances in the light-tonnage field have been made with one primary thought in mind. This is to provide passenger-car styling, comfort, convenience, and ride in trucks capable of fulfilling nearly every hauling need."

—Dodge Truck General Manager M. C. Patterson, on the upgraded qualities of the 1960 truck line; September 1959

1

2

3

4

1-2. The rangy Polara topped Dodge's 35-model roster; the 4-door hardtop started at $3275. **3.** Assembly lines ran at capacity as Dodge sales soared. **4.** At $3621, the 9-seat Polara hardtop wagon was the costliest model. It weighed 4220 lb. This one looks pretty in pink but hides a D-500 punch. **5.** Former President Harry S. Truman (center) takes delivery of a Polara in Kansas City, Mo. **6.** M. C. Patterson, Dodge general manager, and J. B. Neal, Dodge assembly plant manager, link up as the 151,852nd '60 model rolls off the line. With this car, production topped the output of '59 Dodges. **7.** The panoramic Polara wagon was well suited to demonstrating a silicon glass treatment.

5

6

7

1960 Imperial

1

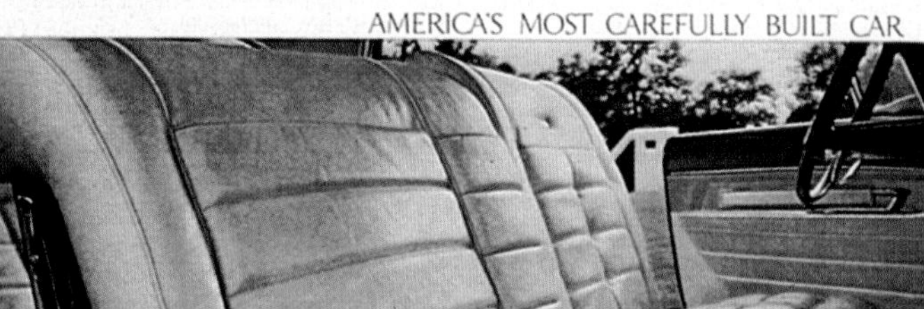

2

3

Imperial became a distinct make in 1955, but never quite severed its Chrysler link. **1.** Custom, Crown, LeBaron, and the limousine Crown Imperial were offered. Here's a Crown Southampton ragtop. **2-3.** Imperial resisted unibody construction, turning body-on-frame craftsmanship into an advertising slogan. **4.** The limo rode a 149.5-inch wheelbase, all other Imperials a 129.

4

1

2

3

4

The '60 Imperials carried on Exner's finned '57 look while integrating the make's trademark "gunsight" taillamps. With curb weights between 4650 and 4900 lb, these cars were heavy and looked it, but Chrysler's torsion-bar suspension and their standard 350-bhp 413-cid V-8 made them the performance equal of any rival. **1.** To presidential candidate John Kennedy, the convertible made a fine campaign car; he's in the middle-rear seat. **2.** Dancer/actor Fred Astaire (left) found that the Imperial suited his elegant style. **3.** All ragtops were Crowns, started at $5774, and weighed 4820 lb. Air conditioning, 6-way power seat, Auto-Pilot cruise control, and automatic headlamp dimmer were among Imperial's standard features. **4.** Custom sedans like this one, along with Crown models, had a body-colored roof; LeBarons got a stainless steel panel and a slightly smaller backlight.

1960 Plymouth

1

2

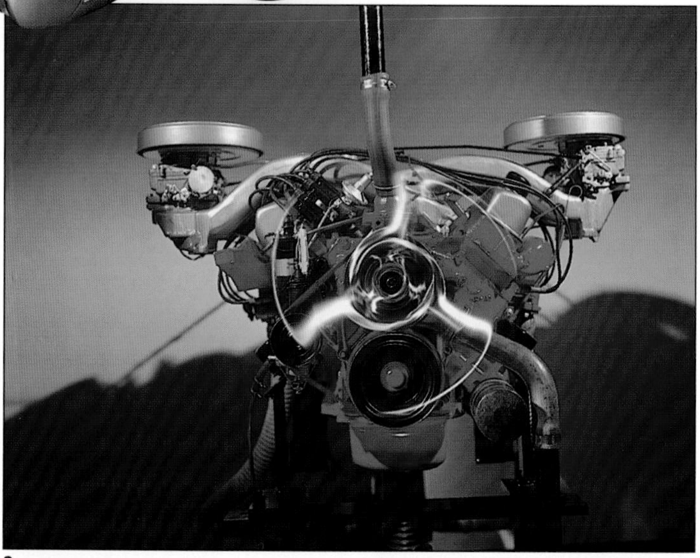

3

4

Plymouth ended the 1950s in third place in sales, but wouldn't match that again in the '60s. Trouble started with 1960's misshapen restyle. **1.** Fury led the line; here's its 4-door hardtop. **2-3.** Popular with cops, Plymouths with the 330-SonoRamic Commando 383 were hot rides. **4-5.** This Fury ragtop has optional mirrors and two-toning, but all had a wild dashboard. Note transmission buttons left of wheel.

5

1

2

3

1. All wagons were Suburbans. Top model was the Sport with its standard 325-bhp 383 V-8. At $3134 and 4020 lb, the 9-seat version was Plymouth's costliest and heaviest car. **2.** This Fury has the accessory grille bar. **3.** Fury Jr. was a ¼-scale fiberglass promotional item driven by an electric motor. **4-5.** Chrysler started experimenting with gas-turbine-power in 1954. George J. Heubner, Jr., executive research engineer, looks at the '60 Plymouth test car.

4

5

1960 Valiant

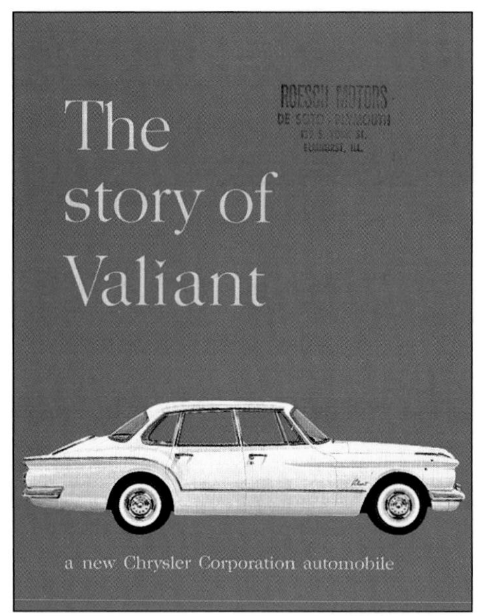

1

2

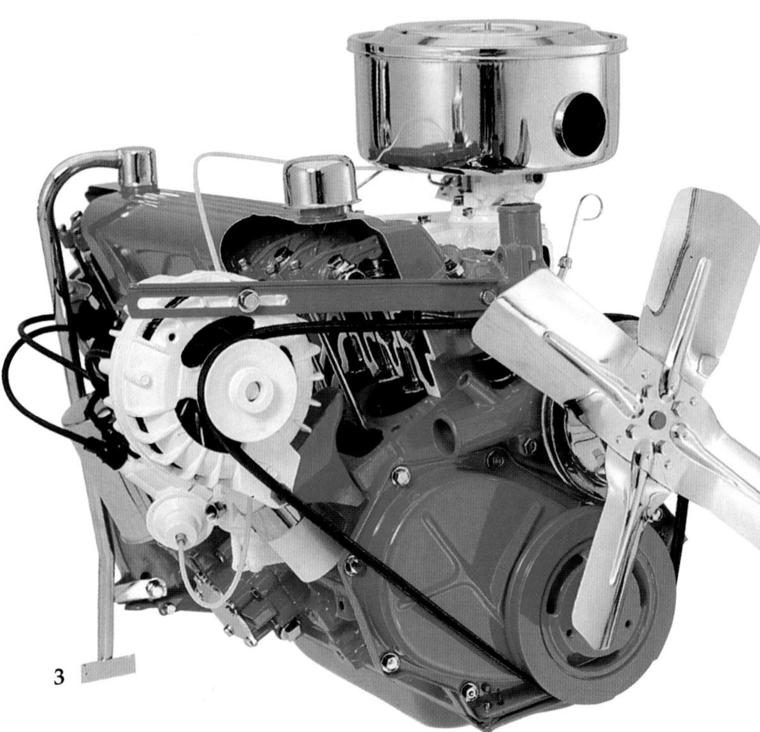
3

4

5

6

1. Built by Dodge and sold mainly by Plymouth, Valiant debuted as its own brand and was quickly recognized as the best engineered—and oddest looking—Big 3 compact. With its unitized body and torsion-bar front suspension, it was the best handler, too. **2.** Stylist Exner's stamp was evident from any angle. **3.** The 2700-lb car worked great with the new Slant Six, named for its hoodline-lowering canted block and angled head. Valiant's 170-cid version had 101 bhp. A Hyper-Pak ram-induction 4-barrel option gave it 148. **4.** Development began in 1957 and included many disguised prototypes. **5.** The line started with the $2053 V-100 sedan. **6.** Valiant beat Falcon and Corvair in a compact-class stock-car exhibition race. That's Lee Petty aboard.

1

2

1. Chrome bodyside trim identifies this sedan as an uplevel V-200 model. It retailed for $2130. The "spare-tire" outline was on all Valiants. **2.** Valiant formed the basis for the Asimmetrica idea car built by Ghia of Italy. It violated car-design symmetry with an offset driver-side bulge running the length of the hood. **3.** Both the V-100 and V-200 were offered as 6-passenger sedans and wagons. Wagons started at $2815 and could be ordered with a third seat for 9-passenger capacity.

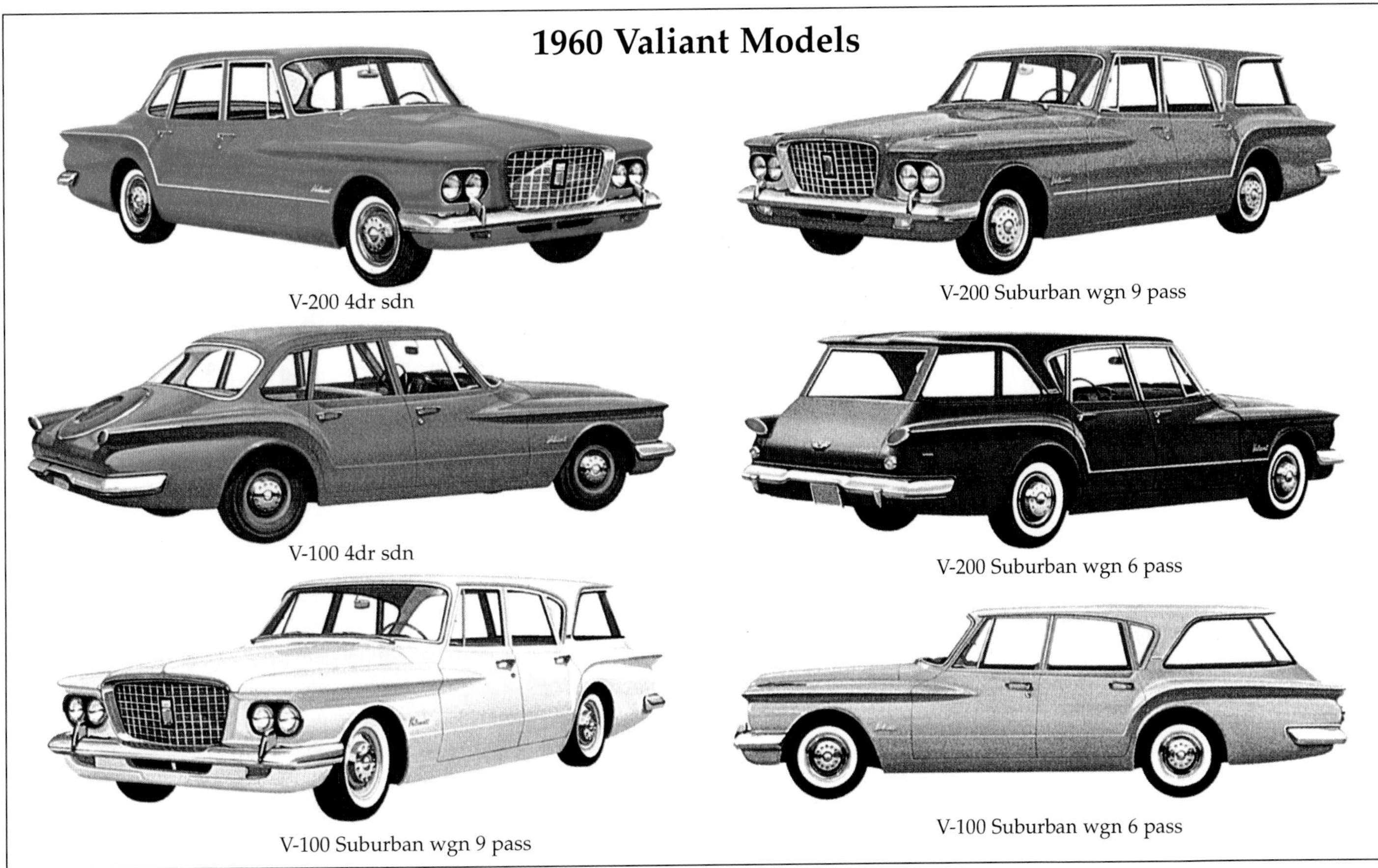

3

Ford Motor Company

FoMoCo board chairman Ernie Breech is forced to resign in July; company president Henry Ford II takes his place

Robert S. McNamara is named to succeed Henry Ford II as FoMoCo president in November but resigns in December to become Secretary of Defense in the new Kennedy administration

In the third big management shuffle of the year, tempestuous Lee Iacocca is named general manager of Ford Division

Compact Falcon debuts and is a blockbuster success, with model-year sales of more than 430,000; it rides a 109.5-inch wheelbase and has unitized construction; lineup includes 2- and 4-door sedans, a wagon, and a Ranchero car/pickup hybrid

Big Fords get their first new body since 1957; they are longer, lower, and wider but gain little interior room

The saga of troubled Edsel draws to a painful conclusion; the 1960 edition drops the trademark horse-collar grille for a generic split-horizontal affair and dies after production of just 2846 cars

Mercury introduces its compact; it uses a Falcon platform stretched into a 114-inch wheelbase and is called the Comet

Thunderbird gains new grille and an optional sliding metal sunroof, a first among postwar American cars

1

2

3

Edsel bowed for 1958 as its own make positioned between Ford and Mercury. Ranger and Pacer models were built on a 118-inch Ford wheelbase, Corsair and Citation on a 124-inch Mercury chassis. But bad timing, poor quality, and that lemon-sucking grille spelled their doom. **1.** For Edsel's '60 swan song, the grille was conventional and all used a 120-inch Ford wheelbase. **2.** Station wagons were called Villagers and held up to nine passengers. FoMoCo ended 2-piece tailgates after this year. **3.** Ranger was the only other series and offered hardtops, sedans, and the $3000 convertible; its fender skirts cost extra. A 185-bhp 292-cid V-8 was standard; a 223-cid six and a 300-bhp 352 V-8 were options.

1

See "FORD STARTIME" in living color Tuesdays on NBC

Ford Falcon: easiest car in the world to own

Introducing a wonderful new world of savings in the new-size 1960 Ford *Falcon*

Look at the price tag for big news! For all its big-car comfort, styling and power, the Falcon delivers *for less* than many imported economy cars.

Honest-to-goodness six-passenger comfort. Plenty of room for six . . . *and all their luggage!*

New 6-cylinder engine . . . up front for greater safety and stability. A brand-new power plant specifically designed to power the Falcon over America's hills and highways with "big car" performance and safety.

World's most experienced new car. The Falcon was proven over every mile of numbered Federal Highway in Experience Run, U.S.A., a grueling demonstration climaxing Ford's 3 years and 3 million miles of testing and development.

Up to 30 miles a gallon on regular gas. Experience Run, U.S.A., proved the Falcon's exceptional gas mileage and oil economy.

Made in U.S.A. . . . serviced everywhere. The Falcon is a product of Dearborn, Michigan, automotive capital of the world. Every part of the Falcon has been designed for maximum durability and dependable performance. Falcon service is available at over 7,000 Ford Dealers across the country.

FORD DIVISION Ford Motor Company

FORD BUILDS THE WORLD'S MOST BEAUTIFULLY PROPORTIONED CARS

FORD – The Finest Fords of a Lifetime FALCON – The New-Size Ford THUNDERBIRD – The World's Most Wanted Car

2

3

The original Falcon recalled the Model A: cheap but cheerful, simple but not spartan. A conventional suspension and mandatory 90-bhp inline 6-cylinder engine looked dull next to Corvair engineering, but they made for a roomy little car that rode well, was easy to fix, and got 20–25-mpg. Falcon was an immediate hit, and turned out to be Ford's most-popular 1960 car. **1.** The 4-door sedan listed for just $1974. **2.** Its 2-door counterpart was the entry-level Falcon at $1912 and was the line's best-seller, attracting 193,470 customers. **3.** Lop off the 2-door wagon's rear roof section and you have the Ranchero pickup/car. **4-5.** Wagons had two or four doors and seating for six. They shared the sedan's wheelbase and running gear but were eight inches longer overall.

4

5

1960 Ford

1 2 3 4 5

Big Fords got a 1-inch wheelbase stretch, to 119 inches, and distinctive new bodies that rejected round taillamps. **1.** Galaxie was the most popular series, accounting for 289,000 of the 910,851 full-size Fords built for '60. Custom and Fairlane models also were featured; wagons came in Ranch and Country Squire series. **2.** All ragtops were Galaxie Sunliners; they cost $2860 and weighed 3791 lb. This one has optional hood trim. **3.** The Galaxie Victoria hardtop cost $2675. **4.** Despite the new Falcon and fresh big cars, total Ford production was down by 11,600 from 1959. **5.** Besides the convertible, the new fastback Starliner coupe was the flashiest Galaxie.

1

2

3

4

5

1. The $2388 Fairlane 500 Town Sedan was the best-selling big Ford, at 153,234 units. **2.** The 2-door version of the base Fairlane was the "club sedan" and its starting price was $2257. Standard on all full-size Fords was a 145-bhp 223-cid inline 6-cylinder engine. A 185-bhp 292-cid V-8 added $113. A 352-cid V-8 could be ordered in 235-bhp form for $148 and in 300-bhp tune for $177. A 360-bhp variant also was available. Ford-O-Matic automatic transmission was a $180 option with the 6-cylinder engine and a $190 item with the V-8. Heaters also were optional; the basic system cost $59. **3.** An offshoot of the Galaxie Sunliner was the Meteor Montcalm, a specially trimmed Ford sold by Canadian Lincoln-Mercury dealers. It featured a unique grille, triple round taillights, and distinctive side trim and badging. **4.** Wagons were a popular stop for auto showgoers in the early '60s. Ford wagon production was 171,824 full-size and 74,310 Falcons this year. At $2967, the 4072-lb Country Squire was the costliest non-Thunderbird model. **5.** Main Street retailing hadn't surrendered to shopping malls in '60.

1

2

3

4

1. Thunderbird was in the third and last year of its original 4-seat configuration. The convertible cost $4222 and tipped the scales at 4130 lb. Its decklid was hinged at the rear to accept the power folding soft top, a system similar to Ford's 1957–1959 retractable hardtops. **2.** T-Bird coupes could be equipped with Detroit's first manual sunroof, a $212 option. This car has aftermarket chrome trim around its taillamp housings. **3.** The hardtop started at $4172 and weighed 3958 lb. **4.** Ford built 62,535 Thunderbird coupes and 10,516 ragtops for '60. All used a 300-bhp 380-cid V-8.

1

2

3

Lincoln was in the third and final year of its distinctive "cat's-eye" styling period, an undistinguished time that saw sales of Ford's prestige marque decline. This design bowed for 1958 on an imposing 131-inch wheelbase, 1.5 inches longer than Cadillac's and an inch longer than Imperial's. These cars were styled to look big, and they were big, at more than 19 feet bumper to bumper. Curb weights were 4917 lb to 5272 lb, depending on model, and to cope, Lincoln created a 430-cid V-8, the largest American-car engine of the day. It made 375 bhp initially but returned just 10 mpg, so for 1960, the 4-barrel carb was discarded resulting in a 315-bhp rating and only nominal gas savings. **1.** Base, Premiere, and Continental Mark V series were offered. This is the Mark V convertible. It cost $7056. **2.** All but the Continental series got a formal rear roof-pillar shape for '60, but it wasn't as popular as the Mark's reverse-angle design with its retractable backlight. This is the $6845 Mark V sedan. **3.** A distinguished-looking bunch eyes a $10,230 Lincoln limo at an auto show display.

1960 Mercury

1

Mercury in 1960 was being asked to shoulder the premium aspirations of the dying Edsel while building volume against the likes of Pontiac. It didn't entirely succeed at either but did offer some handsome and well-built cars in Monterey, Montclair, and top-line Park Lane series, with Commuter and Colony Park wagons. Montclair, Park Lane, and Colony Park used a 310-bhp 430-cid V-8, the others either a 280-bhp 383 V-8 or a 205-bhp 312. **1.** Here's the $3077 Monterey ragtop. **2.** At $2631, the Monterey 2-door sedan was the least-expensive big Merc. **3.** WGN-TV's Jack Brickhouse interviews a Mercury honcho at the Chicago Auto Show. **4.** Cocktail dresses, the $3794 Park Lane Cruiser hardtop coupe, and an Andy Frain usher—that's show biz!

2

3

4

1

2

4

3

5

1. The 4380-lb Park Lane 4-door hardtop cost $4380. This color is Polynesian Beige. **2.** Colony Park wagons had fake wood siding and a Stow-Away forward-facing rear seat for 9-passenger capacity. **3.** Top-line Mercs battled Oldsmobiles while the $2781 Monterey Cruiser hardtop coupe fought Plymouths and Chevys. **4-5.** Mercury dipped into compact territory for '60 with the Comet, basically the new Ford Falcon with a squared roof, more-elaborate grille, and tailfins. Wheelbase was 114 inches on 2- and 4-door sedans, while wagons used Falcon's 109.5-inch span. It wasn't exciting but sold over 116,000 units despite a midyear introduction. Standard was Falcon's 144-cid 6-cylinder, but unlike the Ford, Comets could be ordered with a 101-bhp 170-cid six. Prices were around $2100.

General Motors

Biggest of the Big 3 is hit by a steel strike and temporarily suspends Pontiac, Cadillac, Buick, and Olds production; but Chevrolet output tops 1.6 million, beating second-place Ford by more than 200,000 units and establishing new industry sales record

Chevy introduces its compact, the radical Corvair with a rear-mounted flat 6-cylinder engine; model-year production is 250,000

Full-size Chevys tone down "batwing" tailfins introduced for 1959

Corvette sales exceed 10,000 for the first time

Cadillac, whose 1959 tailfins represented the pinnacle of Detroit's styling flamboyance, tones things down slightly with a more mature new look

Buick subdues its front-end styling but finishes in ninth place in sales, its poorest showing since 1905, when it built just 750 cars

Oldsmobile stands pat with its model lineup but flatens its tailfins and downgrades the horsepower of two of its three 371-cid V-8s; slips from fifth to seventh in the sales race

Pontiac builds on the momentum of 1959, when it was rejuvinated by a line of fast, good-looking cars; body is restyled and returns, momentarily, to a full-width grille; division relinquishes fourth place in sales to Rambler

1

2

Turn-of-the-decade Buicks were big and flashy while the marketplace was thinking smaller and more economical. Plus, Buick buyers were taken aback by the daring delta-wing styling. Sales were soft, but performance and style were high. **1.** Electras rode a 126.3-inch wheelbase and were topped by the Electra 225 series, so named for its 225-inch long body. Buick built 6746 "deuce-and-a-quarter" ragtops at $4192 each. **2.** The 225 hardtop cost $4300 and weighed 4650 lb. This one has optional two-tone paint. All Electras and Electra 225s sported four decorative Ventiports; lesser models had three. **3.** Buicks used coil springs all around for good ride, fine handling. **4.** Off to the showroom via a GMC hauler.

3

4

1

3

2

1. LeSabre was the base series, but the $3145 convertible model didn't look like a cost-cutter. **2.** Buick's a prop in this posed safety-lesson shot. **3.** The hot Invicta rode LeSabre's 123-inch wheelbase but used Electra's 325-bhp 401-cid V-8 instead of the 235– 250-bhp 364. **4.** With Mirrormagic, the reflected speedometer image could be adjusted to suit the driver's height. **5.** Cheapest Buick was the $2756 LeSabre 2-door sedan. This one has manual steering and brakes.

4

5

1960 Cadillac

1

2

Cadillac retreated from 1959's styling excesses—a bit. It still represented America's grandest automotive statement. Bottom to top, the lineups went Series 62, DeVille, Eldorado, and Series 60 Special. All had a 390-cid V-8; Eldos had three 2-barrel carbs and 345 bhp; the others came with a single 4-barrel and 325. **1-2.** Each Eldo body style got its own name. The Biarritz convertible cost $7401 and hid its power top under a fiberglass tonneau. **3.** The lap of luxury. Atop the dashboard is the Autronic Eye automatic headlight dimmer.

3

1

2

3

4

5

1-3. Cadillac was a GM jewel, outselling Lincoln, Chrysler, and Imperial combined. **4.** What car's name was more melodic than Coupe De Ville? It weighed 4705 lb and cost $5252, same as in 1959 because Cadillac didn't increase any model's price for '60. **5.** The 2-door hardtop Eldorado was the Seville. Fender skirts were standard on all Caddys, but only Seville got a fabric-covered top. **6.** The Eldo 4-door, or Brougham, was the priciest Caddy at $13,075; just 101 were built. **7.** Some of those brochures are worth a lot today. **8.** The Cyclone was the division's auto-show dream car of the day.

6

7

8

1960 Chevrolet

1

NOW!
THE REVOLUTIONARY
Corvair
BY CHEVROLET
WITH THE ENGINE IN THE
REAR WHERE IT BELONGS
IN A COMPACT CAR! ★ ★ ★

You have your choice of two Corvairs—this one's the de luxe Corvair 700.

The only American car with an airplane-type horizontal engine!
The only American car with independent suspension at all 4 wheels!
The only American car with an air-cooled aluminum engine!

The rumors about this one were right—but they didn't go far enough. Because here, for the first time, is a truly compact, economical American car that retains the ride and 6-passenger comfort you're used to in a big one. The key to this small miracle: America's first and only *rear-mounted aluminum engine*—a revolutionary 6-cylinder power plant that combines compactly with the transmission and drive gears in one lightweight package. You'll get up to 30% more miles to a gallon and—because this engine is *air cooled*—you'll never have to fuss with antifreeze.

Floor is practically flat for more foot room. Corvair's size—almost 5 inches lower, 2½ feet shorter, 1,300 pounds lighter than conventional sedans—makes it a joy to jockey through traffic and park in tight spots. Yet its unique Unistrut Body by Fisher offers plenty of room for 6 broad-shouldered passengers. And, thanks to Corvair's rear engine, the floor is practically flat, front and rear, so there's generous foot room for everybody. *Easy handling without power assists.* Shifting engine weight to the rear also adds extra ground-gripping traction and gives better compact car handling and braking. And with *independent suspension at all 4 wheels,* Corvair rivals much more costly cars in the poised, unruffled way it rides.

A price your budget will appreciate. Wonderfully practical as all these advances sound, you'll find the most practical thing about this new Corvair is its price. Make it a point to visit your Chevrolet dealer soon—and see what a wealth of engineering a modest amount of your money buys! . . . *Chevrolet Division of General Motors, Detroit 2, Michigan.*

THE FLOOR IS PRACTICALLY FLAT for more foot room. Trunk's up front—and you can also have a handy folding rear seat (optional at extra cost) for added storage space. Lightweight rear engine, compactly combined with transmission and drive gears, is world's first production 6 with ultra-smooth power of horizontally opposed pistons. And wrapping up all these brilliant features is Corvair's brilliant new styling—pure and simple as modern architecture. THERE'S NOTHING LIKE A NEW CAR—AND NO COMPACT CAR LIKE THE CORVAIR . . . by CHEVROLET!

2

3

1. Corvair was Chevrolet's first compact. Edward N. Cole, the division's brilliant former chief engineer and now general manager, liked the design of the Volkswagen Beetle. **2-3.** Corvair emerged with a rear-mounted air-cooled horizontally opposed 6-cylinder engine and a swing-axle rear suspension. It boasted a flat floor, room for six passengers, and good cargo space on a 108-inch wheelbase, much shorter than the big Chevy's 119 inches. **4.** No grille was needed, making for a distinctive look. **5.** It was cute, but a rear weight bias and swing axles gave Corvair tricky handling.

4

5

"No one will know what the full effects of a car like the Corvair will have on the market. It all depends on the economy and how good a sales job our dealers do. . . ."

—Chevrolet General Manager Edward N. Cole; September 1959

2

1

3

4

1. Ed Cole, father of Chevy's small-block V-8 and Cadillac's milestone overhead-valve V-8, was a champion of the Corvair. **2.** Top Corvair sedan was the $2103 model 700. **3.** The 500 was the entry-level series starting at $1984 for the 2-door. A sporty $2238 Monza coupe also was offered. **4.** Corvette, America's one true sports car, was Chevy's excitement machine. **5.** In the last year of its round-tail styling, the fiberglass 2-seater used a 283-cid V-8 of up to 270 bhp with a 4-barrel carb, or as much as 315 with fuel injection.

5

1960 Chevrolet

1

3

2

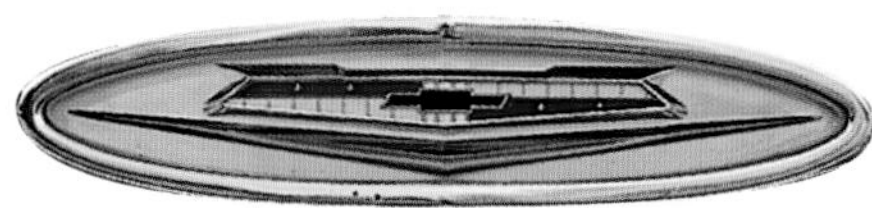

Styling of America's most-popular cars was calmer after '59's wild redesign. "Eyebrow" air ducts were plucked from above the headlamps, and full bat-wing fins and teardrop taillamps gave way to a cleaner stern with round lamps. Biscayne, Bel Air, and Impala were familiar model names, with wagons in Brookwood, Parkwood, Kingswood, and Nomad trim. Six-cylinder cars had a 135-bhp 235.5-cid engine; V-8s came with a 170-bhp 283. Optional on any model was a 348-cid V-8 of up to 335 bhp. **1-2.** The only convertible was in the Impala series and at $2954 was the costliest non-wagon. Ragtop sales hit a model-year record 79,903. A fancier bodyside jet complete with vapor trail and three taillamps instead of two identified Impalas. **3.** With prices starting as low as $2175, Chevy did offer elegance with economy. **4.** Some 1.3 million big Chevys were built for '60. **5.** That Parkwood in the background is one of 212,700 wagons.

4

5

1

2

3

4

1. Presidential candidate John F. Kennedy rode an Impala toward Camelot. **2.** With 28 percent of the U.S. auto market, Chevy dealerships were happy places in 1960. **3.** This Impala Sport Hardtop Sedan is done in Suntan Copper. **4.** At a relatively light 3500 lb, the Biscayne pillared coupe was a good home for the hot 348 V-8. On the left is drag racer Terry Prince, whose car covered the quarter-mile in 13.50 sec at 103 mph. **5.** Horsepower-minded engineer Vincent W. Piggins was Chevy's performance guru. **6.** Sporting Impala-level trim, the Nomad was Chevy's lushest wagon and, at $2996 with a V-8, its costliest car. **7.** An unmarked black sedan delivery had a cool demeanor.

5

6

7

1960 Oldsmobile

1

2

3

4

5

1. The flagship Ninety-Eight used a 126.3-inch wheelbase. That's a $4159, 4431-lb Holiday 4-door hardtop, the series' best seller at 27,257 units, and a SceniCoupe 2-door hardtop. **2.** Base Dynamic 88 and mid-line Super 88 had a 123-inch wheelbase. This is the popular $3402 Super 88 Holiday Sport Sedan. **3.** All three lines offered ragtops. This is the Super 88. **4.** Olds was a Miss America pageant sponsor; here's '60's winner, Lynda Lee Mead, of Natchez, Miss. **5.** Anthony Eisely as Tracy Steel, Connie Stevens as Cricket Blake, Robert Conrad as Tom Lopaka, and Poncie Ponce as Kim, enjoyed Oldsmobiles in the *Hawaiian Eye* TV series.

1 2 3 4 5 6

1. Olds dealers saw sales fall 10 percent in a compact-minded market. **2.** Crash! Bang! Ouch! A '60 Olds meets its fate. No word on that of the driver. **3.** Ninety-Eights had a 315-bhp 394-cid V-8, 88s a 371 V-8 of 240 or 260 bhp. **4.** Best-selling Ninety-Eight? This 4364 lb, $4159 SportSedan, at 27,257 units **5.** Most-popular Olds of all was the Dynamic 88 Celebrity 4-door sedan. Smartly priced at $2900, its sales increased 9 percent, to 76,377. **6.** The Super 88 Holiday SportSedan epitomized Oldsmobile style, size, and comfort.

1960 Pontiac

1

4

2

5

3

6

A youthful 1959 redesign, including a 5-inch widening of its track, helped establish Pontiac as GM's excitement division. **1-3.** Part of the image remake was the award-winning series of brochure and advertising art by renowned automotive illustrators Van Kaufman and Arthur Fitzpatrick. Emphasizing the wide-track theme amid settings that conveyed a sense of casual taste, the illustrations became collector's items. **4.** Discarding 1959's split grille didn't prove popular, but shaving off the tailfins was a modern move. Catalina and Ventura models used a 122-inch wheelbase, Star Chief and Bonneville a 124-inch platform. This is the Bonneville Sport hardtop. **5.** Overall production increased by 13,239 units, to 396,179, and Pontiac fit in nicely with America's move to suburbia. **6.** All models used Pontiac's 389-cid V-8 and would have had no problem towing a boat. Horsepower ranged from 215 to a robust 348 courtesy of three 2-barrel carbs. The tri-power setup was optional on any model and made for a potent Poncho.

1. The $3476 Bonneville ragtop was the priciest non-wagon. 2. The $2932 Star Chief Sport sedan was the rarest non-wagon with just 5797 built. 3. A Star Chief body by Fisher is about to mate with a chassis by Pontiac. 4. One of 35,402 Catalina Safari wagons nears completion. 5. Conveyors slid cars through 228 feet of ovens, drying the Magic-Mirror acrylic lacquer paint via infra-red lights in 10 minutes.

Studebaker-Packard Corporation

This historic old South Bend, Ind., automaker peaked in the late 1940s by being "first by far with a postwar car," but by 1954 it was desperate enough to merge with another troubled-but-proud marque, Packard

It enters the 1960s with just two model lines, but one is the compact Lark, whose introduction in 1959 previewed the country's turn to smaller cars, giving Studebaker its first profit in five years and saving the company from extinction

For '60, Lark retains its basic design but adds a convertible body style, some new trim, and different grille inserts

With the Big 3 fielding compacts for 1960, Lark's advantage is diminished and production dips from 131,078 to 127,715

Studebaker's second model was the Hawk "family sports car," evolved from the dashing 1953 coupe designed by Raymond Loewy

Steadily falling demand had pared the initial four-model flock to a single Silver Hawk by 1959, and for '60, it was now simply the Hawk

Hawk remains a pillared coupe on a 120.5-inch wheelbase

South Bend assembly plant gains a new $1.5 million paint system

1

2

3

4

Lark came in two series, the VI and VIII, each with DeLuxe and step-up Regal models in 2- and 4-door sedans and wagons and 2-door hardtops. **1.** The new convertible was offered as a Regal and was America's only domestically built compact ragtop in 1960. At $2621 for the series VI and $135 more for the VIII, it proved reasonably popular, finding 8571 buyers. **2.** The 4-door Lark wagon easily outsold the 2-door. Wagons rode a 113-inch wheelbase, other models a 108.5. **3.** The usefully sized 4-door sedan was the line's biggest seller, at 54,946. This is the $2331 Regal VIII. Larks came with a 90-bhp inline-6. With the optional 259.2-cid V-8 of 180 or 195 bhp, they could do 0–60 mph in under 10 sec. **4.** The Hawk's glory days were fading, but Studebaker wasn't admitting it. For '60, the 6-cylinder version was dropped and a new 289-cid V-8 of 210 or 225 bhp was standard. Price was $2650, weight 3207 lb. Still, sales fell 43 percent, to 4507.

1-2. Lark meant utility with a bit of flair, and its marketing reflected it. Compared to the chromed monsters of its rivals, the styling was clean, with a somewhat European attitude. A consistent Mobilgas Economy Run winner, even V-8 Larks averaged 22 mpg. **3.** Studebaker built its first truck in 1902. It launched its last, the Champ, in 1960. **4.** The company published this "guide" to the new compacts. Guess which make came out on top? **5.** With no funds for restyle, Hawk was dated by its '50s-look fins.

1

3

2

4

5

Etc.

Los Angeles Studebaker dealers sponsor Project Survival, a TV special that explains how to live through a nuclear attack

Construction is completed on 20 percent of the U.S. interstate highway system

Auto dealers in Cuba believe the new Castro government will create a larger, wealthier middle class and an increase in potential new-car buyers

TV personality Arthur Godfrey is a backer of a plan to build the Rollsmobile, a two-thirds-scale replica of the 1901 Ford runabout; the $1195 curiosity goes 25 mph

Willys introduces the Jeep Surrey, and a restyled Jeep Wagon

263-bhp Aston Martin DB-4 goes 0–100–0 mph in 27 sec

British Motor Corp.'s new Austin and Morris 850 forecast the front-wheel-drive future; get surprising interior room from 10-foot-long cars by mounting 4-cylinder engine crossways in front

Sold through East Coast dealers, Holland's compact DAF 2-door sedan comes with built-in electric shaver

Toyota Toyopet Tiara sedan takes aim at import-car market ruled by Germany's VW and France's Renault

Dealers in 11 western states offer the Datsun Bluebird line: a sedan, sports car, station wagon, and pickup truck; prices start at $1595

1

2

3

4

5

1. The Electric Shopper, made by the Electric Car Co. of Long Beach, Calif., came with a fiberglass or metal body. **2.** A Triumph TR-3 looks sharp at the 1960 Chicago Auto Show. **3.** At the same show, prospects check out a Toyota Toyopet; is the lady on the left happy or just embarrassed? **4.** The Saviano Scat was a heavy-gauge steel, go-anywhere vehicle manufactured in Warren, Michigan. **5.** The Crofton Bug came from San Diego; it listed at $1350. **6.** Datsun entered the U.S. in 1958 with the tiny Bluebird sedan and by 1960, was also offering this appealing Fair Lady roadster. It cost $1996 and had a 48-bhp 72.5-cid 4-cylinder.

6

1

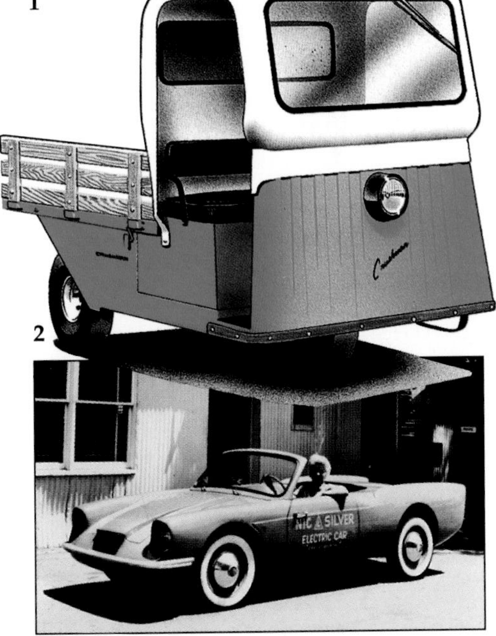

2

3

4

1. Ferrari's 250 GT Cabriolet cost $12,600, had a 260-bhp V-12, and went 120 mph. 2. Cushman's 3-wheel carry-all. 3. Nic-L-Silver's sporty Pioneer roadster. 4. Upright and boxy best describe Checker's Superba. 5. Gallic style and a Chrysler V-8 came together in the fabulous French-built $12,800 Facel Vega Excellence. 6. Jim Rathmann won the Indy 500 in this Offenhauser-powered Watson racer.

5

6

Etc.

Renault revamps its U.S. distribution system, opens a Kansas City headquarters, and introduces the "beach wagon," a doorless, wicker-seat variant of the 4CV

At Squaw Valley, California, 26 4-wheel-drive British Land Rovers come to the rescue when impassable, rain-swollen roads threaten to delay the opening of the 1960 Winter Olympics

Los Angeles-area dealers take delivery of Israeli-made Sabra station wagons, sedans, hardtops, and panel trucks

The Taunus 12-M Super, a compact sedan built by Ford of Germany, goes on sale at about 200 U.S. dealerships

Volkswagen dealers in Grand Rapids, Mich., offer local Republican and Democratic parties free use of VW station wagons (vans) with which to transport voters to the polls

Porsche unveils the 356B; costs $4000, weighs 1950 lbs

Top 10 Selling Imports

1. Volkswagen	159,995
2. Renault	62,772
3. Opel	25,533
4. English Ford	23,602
5. Fiat	20,773
6. Triumph	17,720
7. Simca	17,077
8. Austin-Healey	16,322
9. Mercedes-Benz	14,435
10. Volvo	13,926

Total import-car share of the U.S. market: 7.58 percent

1961

Compact cars gained in popularity this year, with four of them—Ford Falcon, AMC Rambler, Chevy Corvair, and Mercury Comet—among the ten top-selling models. Although imports lost ground in the American market, it was clear that the small-car idea was not going to go away.

Those pesky Communists weren't going to go away, either, at least not anytime soon. The USSR ignored American and European pleas to suspend atmospheric nuclear testing, and exploded some whoppers. And in the most galling act of all, the Soviets masterminded the construction of a concrete wall separating Communist East Berlin from democratic West Berlin. JFK ordered a 1500-man battle group to West Berlin, and by October, U.S. and Soviet tank troops were glowering at each other on the Friedrichstrasse. In this tense atmosphere, millions of Americans built backyard fallout shelters.

In April, anti-Castro Cuban revolutionaries bankrolled by the U.S. government mounted an embarrassingly unsuccessful invasion of the island at the Bay of Pigs.

Soviet cosmonaut Yuri Gagarin became the first human in space, launched into orbit in April; America's first space traveler was astronaut Alan Shepard, who completed a sub-orbital flight in May.

Kids around the country went bonkers for backyard trampolines, but parents had second thoughts when Junior and Sis began flying off and breaking their heads. A popular grown-up

diversion was *The Executive Coloring Book,* which gently satirized the Kennedy Administration and First Family. Although expensive at $9.98, more than 1 million copies were sold.

American TV viewers filled up on *The Andy Griffith Show, My Three Sons, Candid Camera,* and a pair of new medical dramas, *Dr. Kildare* and *Ben Casey.* ABC's *Wide World of Sports* premiered, but the brightest new series was *The Dick Van Dyke Show.* Jack Paar began his last year as host of the *Tonight Show;* Johnny Carson was still a year away.

Meanwhile, FCC chairman Newton Minow, addressing a National Association of Broadcasters Convention, decried commercial TV programming as a "vast wasteland."

Popular music produced Chubby Checker's "The Twist," Del Shannon's "Runaway," Connie Francis's "Where the Boys Are," and Jimmy Dean's "Big Bad John." *His Hand in Mine* was Elvis Presley's first full album of sacred songs. Adults tapped their toes to that "Sing Along" guy, Mitch Miller, who released four albums.

Top movies included *West Side Story, The Parent Trap, The Hustler, 101 Dalmatians,* and *A Raisin in the Sun.*

In sports, Roger Maris of the New York Yankees clubbed a record 61 regular-season home runs; the Yankees went on to beat the Cincinnati Reds in a five-game World Series. The Green Bay Packers knocked off the New York Giants 37–0 to take the NFL championship.

American Motors Corporation

Rambler records its all-time high finish in the U.S. sales race, passing Plymouth by 20,400 units to capture third place; this despite a '61 volume of 370,700 that's actually down 12 percent from '60

After an expenditure of $31 million on new tooling, production capacity at AMC's factory in Kenosha, Wisc., reaches 600,000 cars annually, making it the largest single auto plant in the United States

George Romney begins exploring the idea of running for governor of Michigan; the former Nash executive had been named chairman of the board of the newly formed American Motors Corporation in 1954; Romney stood out among auto execs of the day—he neither smoked nor drank

Following Ford's lead, AMC introduces 12,000-mile/24-month warranty

Rambler's entry-level American is restyled inside and out, gains convertible and 4-door wagon bodies

"Classic" badging debuts on the mid-priced model

Top-of-the-line Ambassador gets "Euro" style grille

Roy Abernethy promoted to corporate general manager

1

2

3

1. An odd shovel-nose restyling cost Ambassador some sales; volume fell 21 percent. The Custom 4-door was the top seller at 9269 units. **2.** Priciest Rambler was the $3111 Ambassador Custom 8-seat wagon. **3.** Every Ambassador was a V-8; the 327 had 250 bhp standard, 270 optional. **4.** All '61 Ramblers could be ordered with Airliner Reclining Seats, a splitback-front bench that folded flush with the rear-seat cushion. AMC called this setup the Nap Couch. Both seatbacks folded to create the Twin Travel Bed.

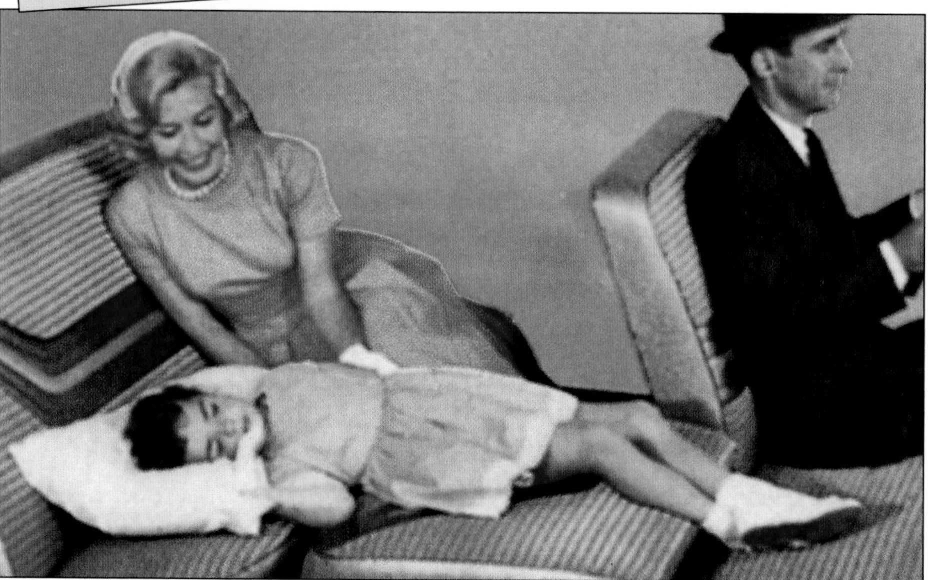

4

1

2

3

4

5

6

7

1. Rambler Six and Rebel series were restyled and consolidated under new Classic Six and Classic V-8 model families for '61. Wagon tailgates opened to the side. **2.** Squared sheetmetal replaced soft contours on the 1961 American. **3.** American wagons came in 2- and new 4-door styles. **4-6.** The most-exciting new American was the line's first convertible. AMC hyped it at auto-show displays and in ads. The spunky ragtop came only in uplevel Custom trim, cost $2369, and found 12,918 buyers. **7.** AMC continued to import—and promote—the lame-duck Metropolitan; 969 were sold in '61. Its 73-cid Austin 4-cylinder made 55 bhp.

1961 Chrysler

Chrysler Corporation

Amid falling sales and allegations of mismanagement, "Tex" Colbert is forced out as Chrysler Corp. president, to be succeeded by Lynn A. Townsend; turmoil within the company boils over

A reorganization of top-level management and division alignment is undertaken; includes the most-structured and largest layoff of salaried and white-collar workers in Chrysler history

DeSoto is killed after a run of 3034 '61 models; rumors that the name will resurface on a new car never come true

Chrysler-Imperial and Plymouth divisions are merged

Management vows never to build a compact Chrysler model, instead introducing the Newport as an entry-level Chrysler model; it's a sales success

Dodge gets a compact, a clone of the Plymouth Valiant badged the Lancer; a taxicab variant is part of the line

Lancer and Valiant gain hardtop and 2-door sedan body styles

Dodge offers rebates to dealers to spur sales of Dart and Lancer

Chrysler Corp. gets contract to build and test Saturn S-1 booster rocket

1

2

3

4

5

6

7

8

9

10

1. A Golden Lion 413-cid V-8 powered the $4175 Chrysler New Yorker hardtop coupe, here in Tuscany Bronze over Sierra Sand. **2.** The canopy and turbine engine of the Turboflite show car never made it to production, but something similar to that big rear wing would. **3.** Newport was the new entry-level Chrysler. **4.** A child seat wasn't necessarily a safety seat in 1961. **5.** Every Chrysler Corp. make is here. **6.** Canted headlamps were new for Chrysler and its new value-leader, Newport. **7.** Embattled Chrysler Corp. president Lynn A. Townsend. **8-10.** Now basically just a retrimmed Newport, DeSoto entered '61 as a 2- and 4-door hardtop without specific model designations. Chrysler killed the marque after fewer than 3100 were built.

1 2 3 4

1. Dodge dropped the Matador series, leaving the 122-inch wheelbase to the top-line Polara. Dart filled out the 118-inch-wheelbase platform (122 on wagons) with Seneca, Pioneer, and Phoenix models. **2.** At 3555 lb, the Phoenix 4-door hardtop belied its "junior" Dodge tag. Prices started at $2677 for the 145-bhp 6-cylinder model and $2796 with the 230-bhp 318-cid V-8. Any Dart was also available with a 375-bhp 413 V-8, which Polara didn't get. **3.** Dodge mildly reworked a Phoenix ragtop for show car duty. **4.** Quirky "reverse-slant" tailfins were new. On Polara, they had integrated taillamps. Darts got this similar fixture at midyear to supplement their initial lower lens.

1

2

3

4

5

1. Dodge built 183,561 Darts for '61 and the $2796 Phoenix 2-door hardtop was a sharp one. As on all Darts, a 3-speed manual transmission was standard with the 3-speed Torqueflite automatic a $211 option. 2. Polaras came with a 265-bhp 361-cid V-8; here's the $3110 4-door hardtop. 3. The Seneca wagon with an ancestor, a Dodge Brothers Depot Hack, circa 1918. 4. The tough 145-bhp 225-cid Slant Six made Senecas a wise fleet choice. 5. The new Lancer compact was a rebadged Valiant and sold well at 74,776 units. The base 170 series started at $1979 and with its 170-cid Slant Six, made a fine taxi. 6. Costliest of the the up-level 770 Lancer series was the $2449 wagon.

LOOK WHAT DODGE HAS DONE FOR COMPACTS

LANCER

6

1961 Imperial

Chrysler could already boast that every Imperial was road tested before delivery, that interior fabrics were shrink-fitted, even that medallions on the flagship LeBaron were considered by the Internal Revenue Service to be jewelry—and taxed as such. But more was needed to fight Cadillac and the fresh Lincoln. **1.** If Chrysler thought new free-standing headlamps was the elusive ingredient, it was wrong. **2.** The sedan body style was dropped, leaving 2- and 4-door hardtops and a convertible. Custom, Crown, and LeBaron series returned on a 129-inch wheelbase. The Crown Imperial limousine had a 149.5-inch span. It cost $16,500 and just nine were built. **3-4.** At $4923, the Custom Southampton coupe was Imperial's price leader. Only 889 were produced.

1

2

3

4

1

2

3

4

1-2. Chrysler Corp.'s most-expensive and heaviest regular-production automobile was the Imperial LeBaron Southampton hardtop. Offered as a 4-door only, it cost $6426 and tipped the scales at 4875 lb. It accounted for 1026 of the 12,258 Imperials built for '61, a decrease of 21 percent in overall production compared to model-year '60. Exclusive to this model was a new "town car" style rear roof treatment with a smaller backlight designed to give back seaters more privacy. **3.** As his eponymous character on TV's *The Adventures of Ozzie & Harriet*, Ozzie Nelson had no visible means of income. In real life, the guy could easily afford a $5774 Imperial Crown convertible. The program ran on ABC from 1952 to 1966. **4.** Imperial's best-seller, with 4769 deliveries, was the $5647 Crown 4-door hardtop. Like all Imperials, it used a 350-bhp 413 V-8.

1961 Plymouth

1

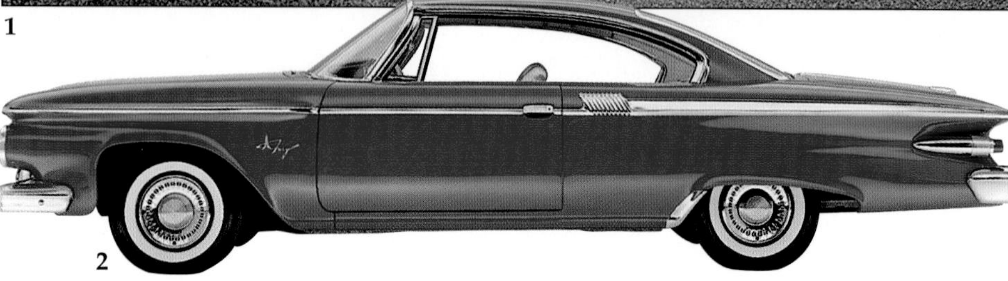

2

A facelift cost Plymouth its fins, but sales still fell. **1.** Sportone two-toning for the top-line Fury didn't help. Note the high driver's seatback. **2.** The Fury coupe. **3.** A mid-line Belvedere hardtop cost $2580 with the 318 V-8, $119 less with a 225-cid Slant Six. **4.** The $3134, 3995-lb 9-seat Sport Suburban.

3

4

1

1. Valiant joined the Plymouth line and gained a 2-door hardtop. Here it is with three Chrysler Corp. show cars: from left, Imperial D'Elegance; Valiant-based Plymouth XNR; and Plymouth Cabana. **2.** At 59,056 units, the $2110 V-200 Valiant 4-door sedan was the best-selling '61 Plymouth. The 225-cid Slant Six was a new Valiant option this year in place of the base 170-cid six. **3-4.** Valiant station wagons could now be dealer-outfitted with a factory-built third seat.

3

2

4

Plymouths were hot stockcars in the hands of drivers like Lee Petty, father of "King" Richard and a racing hero in his own right. In a famous sequence, Lee's No. 42 and Johnny Beauchamp's No. 73 Chevy tangle in a Daytona 500 qualifying race. Petty goes over the wall and is seriously hurt. He'd return to race briefly during 1963.

Ford Motor Company

Ford division edges Chevy by 20,776 in model-year production; first of only two times in decade it will finish ahead of its arch rival

John Dykstra takes over as FoMoCo president

FoMoCo Chairman Henry Ford II announces Ford will no longer abide by industry policy and will begin again to support sanctioned racing

Ford joins horsepower war, enlarges its 352-cid V-8 to 390 cid; top version has 401 bhp

Thunderbird is redesigned; gets "projectile-look" styling and the new 390 V-8

Lincoln Continental gets a classic new body; 4-door sedan and 4-door convertible are offered, both with back doors hinged to open at the rear

Falcon answers sporty Corvair Monza with "1961½" Futura 2-door hardtop with bucket seats and console

Ford adds compact Econoline van; mounts 6-cylinder engine between front seats

Mercury offers first 6-cylinder engine; adds bucket-seat S-22 2-door sedan to its Comet line

Low-priced Meteor version of full-size Mercury debuts

Ford and Mercury get 12,000-mile/12-month warranty; Lincolns get 24/24 coverage

1

After outselling Chevy's Corvair by 186,000 units and Plymouth's Valiant by 241,000, Falcon's styling was little changed for '61. But underhood, the 101-bhp 170-cid 6-cylinder was a new option. With the base 85-bhp 144-cid six, a Falcon could average 30 mpg on the highway. **1.** Price of the entry-level 2-door sedan was up just $2, to $1976. It was the line's best-seller, at 159,761 units. **2.** Futura bowed as the bucket-seat answer to the Corvair Monza. The 2-door coupe cost $2162 and found 44,470 buyers. **3.** Ranchero returned based on the 2-door wagon and billed as a small pickup truck. It had an 800-lb payload capacity. **4.** Aarrgh! Peanuts characters shill for the Falcon.

2

3

4

1

2

3

4

The Square Bird fell to the rocket ship on the 1961 Thunderbird. Wheelbase remained 113 inches and overall length 205, but a 300-bhp 390-cid V-8 replaced the 300-bhp 352 and the 350-bhp 430. **1.** Bookends: a base Falcon and the $4639 T-Bird ragtop. **2.** Pacing the Indy 500 boosted its profile, but sales of the '61 still slipped by 20,000, to 62,535. **3.** The coupe now cost $4172. It weighed 3858 lb, up 159 lb; the ragtop gained 233 lb, to 4130. **4-5.** Easy-ingress Swing-Away steering was new and standard.

5

1961 Ford

1

2

3

4

5

6

Facelifted big Fords were shorter by four inches and narrower by two, on the same 119-inch wheelbase. **1.** A Continental-kit-clad Galaxie Sunliner. **2.** The "Thunderbird" 390 was the new hot V-8. **3.** Fred Lorenzen and his ragtop racer. **4.** Heaviest and costliest non-Thunderbird was the 4015-lb, $3013 9-seat Country Squire. **5.** A Galaxie stops to launch. **6.** A Fairlane stops for lunch.

1

2

3

4

5

1-2. Promotion city: Flora, Ill., became "Ford Town" as its 1500 vehicle owners got a new '61 Ford car or truck to drive for a week. **3.** At nearly 200,000, Fairlane 4-doors were best-sellers. **4.** The new 390 made up to 375 bhp with a 4-barrel carb (shown) and 401 on three 2-barrels. **5.** Ford's redesigned pickups were lower and wider. This is the F-100. **6.** Econoline vans debuted in cargo, passenger, and open-bed form. A 6-cylinder between the front seats drove the compact's rear wheels.

6

1961 Lincoln

1

2

3

4

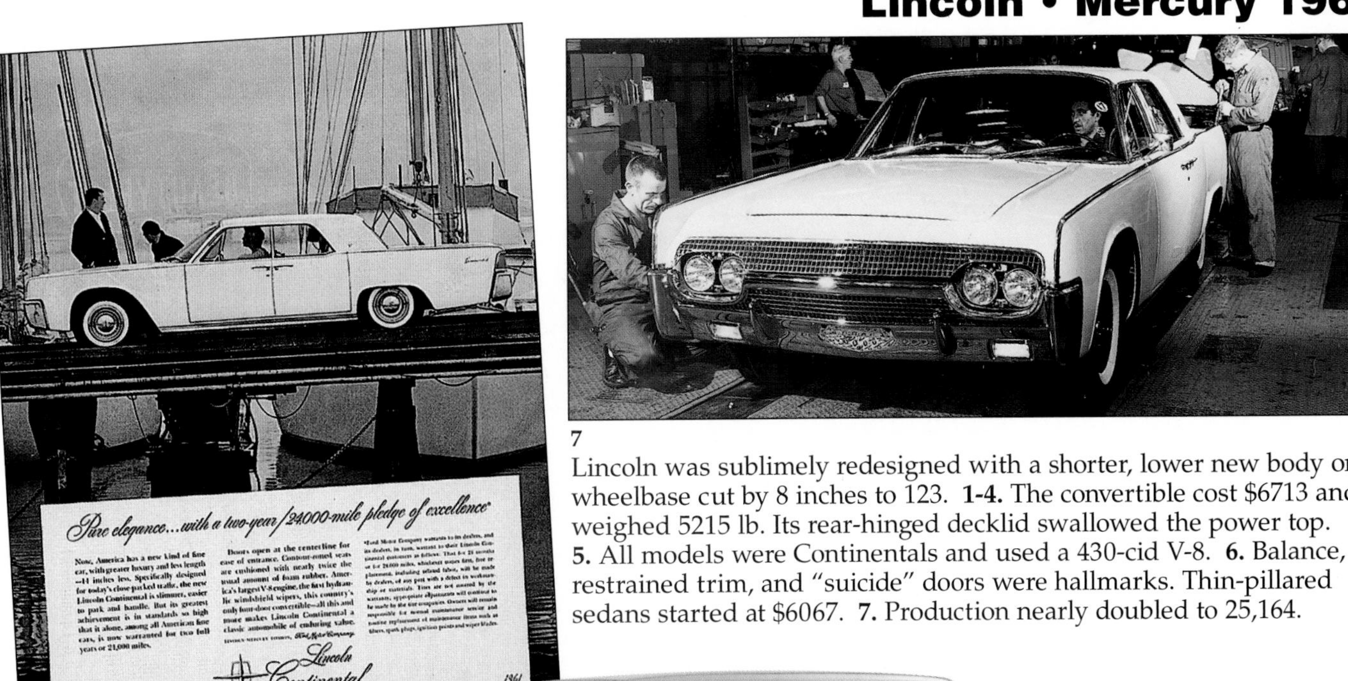

5

7

Lincoln was sublimely redesigned with a shorter, lower new body on a wheelbase cut by 8 inches to 123. **1-4.** The convertible cost $6713 and weighed 5215 lb. Its rear-hinged decklid swallowed the power top. **5.** All models were Continentals and used a 430-cid V-8. **6.** Balance, restrained trim, and "suicide" doors were hallmarks. Thin-pillared sedans started at $6067. **7.** Production nearly doubled to 25,164.

6

1961 Mercury

1

2

Comet got a new grille and an optional 101-bhp 170-cid 6-cylinder mate for the 85-bhp 144-cid Thrift-Power Six. A new S-22 model brought bucket seats. **1.** This 2-door sedan has the popular Fashion Group, which added whitewalls and wheelcovers. **2.** Top seller, at 85,332, was the 4-door.

1961 Mercury

1

3

Mercury was taken down a notch for '61, relinquishing its upper-middle market slot for "the popular price range." **1.** The 126-inch wheelbase Montclair and Park Lane models were dropped, leaving a downsized Monterey as the flagship. Like other '61 Mercurys, Monterey borrowed from Ford its running gear and 120-inch wheelbase chassis but got unique nose and tail styling. **2.** The convertible was the costliest Monterey, at $3128, some $1000 less than the '60 Park Lane ragtop. **3.** Wagons retained the Colony Park and Commuter badges but also dropped from a 126- to a 120-inch chassis. The 9-seat Colony Park listed for $3191, $646 less than its larger '60 counterpart.

2

1

2

1. Mercury mocked-up but never produced a '61 Montclair. Its Ford origins are evident in the shape of the roof, bodysides, and front fender. **2.** Comet was again part of Mercury's orbit. Production of the compact surged to 197,263, best for any Mercury model since 1957. That helped push division sales to nearly 320,000, almost 50,000 above model-year 1960. The new popular-price strategy evidently worked. **3-4.** A new Mercury name for '61, Meteor took over Monterey's old role as the entry-level big car. It was unremarkable except that it alone could be ordered with the 330-bhp version of the 390 V-8, Mercury's hottest engine.

3

4

1961 Mercury colors

Turquois Mist

Sultana White

Palm Springs Rose

Sheffield Gray Metallic

Signal Red

Tawny Beige

Columbia Blue Metallic

Saxon Green Metallic

General Motors

Restyling all its big cars and launching a line of compacts gives GM the busiest new-product year in its history

Oldsmobile's compact is called F-85, Buick's is the Special; both are of conventional design with dowdy styling but standard V-8 power (the new 215-cid aluminum engine)

Pontiac's new small car, the Tempest, introduces a radical flexible driveshaft and rear-mount transaxle with independent rear suspension, plus the first postwar U.S. 4-cylinder engine

Big Chevys lose tailfins and at midyear gain optional Super Sport trim and historic 409-cid V-8

Corvair gains a station wagon and serves as the foundation for a new compact van

Corvette gets redesigned tail

Following Ford's lead, GM introduces 12,000-mile/12-month warranty

An automatic transmission becomes standard on all Buick models

Semon E. (Bunkie) Knudsen is new Chevy general manager

E. M. (Pete) Estes is named general manager of Pontiac Division

John Z. DeLorean is appointed chief engineer of Pontiac

1

After entering the entry-level compact field with the go-its-own-way 1960 Corvair, General Motors broke into the mainstream small-car market with a trio of more-conventional Buicks, Pontiacs, and Oldsmobiles. **1.** Buick's compact was the Special. It bowed in 2- and 4-door sedan and 4-door wagon body styles priced between $2330 and $2816. Like the other new GM compacts, Specials were designed as a step up from small cars such as the Ford Falcon and Plymouth Valiant. Styling was similar to that of the big Buicks and included the brand's trademark front-fender Ventiports. But Specials used a 112-inch wheelbase and averaged 2700 lb, compared to a 123-inch wheelbase and as much as 3700 lb for the next-larger Buicks. **2.** All three body styles came in base trim, with the 4-door sedan and wagon also offered in Deluxe form. This is the Deluxe sedan, which started at $2519 and was the line's best-seller, at 32,986 units.

2

1

2

1-2. Special was similar in size to its Pontiac and Olds cousins. It had conventional body-on-frame construction and its only engine was a new 155-bhp 215-cid aluminum V-8. Also used in the other compacts, this new V-8 was developed by GM engineering but designed for production by Buick and assembled at a Buick plant. **3.** Special wagons could have two or three rows of seats. **4.** Introduced at midyear, the Skylark was a sporty Special coupe with a distinct grille and taillamp treatment, a vinyl top, and a 185-bhp version of the 215 V-8. The $2621 model snared 12,683 buyers, to become the third-best-selling Special.

3

4

1961 Buick

1

Big Buicks got a modern restyle for '61. **1.** Flagships Electra and Electra 225 had a new 126-inch chassis but retained a 401-cid V-8. The costliest Buick was this Electra 225 Riviera hardtop; 13,719 were sold, not bad, given its $4350 price. **2.** LeSabre was the cheapest ragtop, at $3382. **3.** Least expensive big Buick? The $2993 LeSabre 2-door sedan. **4.** LeSabres and Invictas used a 123-inch wheelbase. Here's a LeSabre. **5.** Cool ride: a fenderskirted LeSabre convertible.

2

3

4

5

1

2

One reason Cadillac outsold Chrysler, Imperial, and Lincoln was that it offered a far broader model range. For '61, there were seven body styles, including a new sedan with seven inches sliced off its tail. The "short deck model" was still an imposing 215 inches long overall, but was a little easier to parallel park. **1-2.** Regaining its flagship status with the demise of the Eldorado Brougham was the Series 60 Special, a formal-roof hardtop costing $6233. A sumptuous cabin upholstered in fine cloths and leather with a pull-down front armrest awaited. **3.** Cleaned-up styling included paired-down tailfins now mimicked by lower-body "skeg" fins. Two convertibles were available, this $5455 Series 62 (15,500 sold), and the $6477 Eldorado Biarritz (1450 sold).

3

1961 Cadillac

1

2

1-2. Two-door hardtops came either as this Coupe De Ville, starting at $5252, or as the Series 62, beginning at $4892. They shared their thin-pillared roof with the Buick Electra and Olds Ninety-Eight. Some within Cadillac thought the new grille had too much Chevy in it, but nobody said it was ugly. At the rear, oval pods held taillamps and backup lights. Despite a bigger slice of the luxury market going to the striking new Lincoln, Cadillac production declined by just a modest 3805 units in '61, to 138,379. **3.** The sole engine was again a 390-cid V-8, though now it came only as a 325-bhp 4-barrel. The 345-bhp tri-carb version was retired.

1

2

4

3

Chevrolet forgot the '50s with new sheetmetal and the introduction of two bow-tie icons, the Super Sport package and the 409-cid V-8. **1-2.** Bowing on hardtop and convertible Impalas, the $54 SS option added special trim and upgrades to suspension, chassis, and brakes. **3.** The SS dashboard gained a passenger grab bar and a steering-column tachometer. **4.** The new 409, a heavily reworked 348-cid V-8, had 360 bhp in introductory trim and was the stuff of legend.

1961 Chevrolet

1

2

3

4

5

A 119-inch wheelbase returned under new, shorter bodies. Engines spanned a 135-bhp 235.5-cid six to V-8s of 283 cid (170–230 bhp) and 348 cid (250–350), with the 409 reserved for Impala Super Sports. **1.** The $2769 Impala Sport Sedan was the 4-door style leader. **2.** Coupes got a new "bubble roof" shape; this one has the SS option. **3.** The sedan in the ad is a Biscayne from the $2175 to $2423 entry-level series. **4.** Wagon output hit 169,000; here's the top-line $3099 Nomad **5.** Chevy dealers closed fewer deals than they wished in the first of only two model years in the '60s that Ford's production outpaced Chevy's.

1

2

3

4

5

6

7

1. This 700 Series was the best-selling 4-door Corvair, at 51,948 units. **2.** Best-seller overall: the Monza coupe at the top of this ad. It cost $2201 and found 109,945 buyers. **3.** The entry-level 500 sedan retired after '61. **4.** A wagon was new to the line. Called Lakewood, it had 4 doors, came in 500 and 700 trim, and sold 26,402 units. **5-7.** Corvair also debuted a "truck" line using the cars' rear-engine running gear but a wheelbase of 95 inches, 13 inches less than the car's. Called the Corvair 95, it came as a pickup with an available side ramp door and as a window or panel van.

1961 Chevrolet

1

1-2. The '61 Corvette blended a '50s-style nose with a tapered new tail that suggested the excitement of the decade ahead. This was the last year it would use a 283-cid V-8; 230 bhp was standard and up to 315 was available with optional fuel injection. Base price on this, Chevy's most-expensive car, was $3934. **3.** Tiny Corvettes with electric motors were a popular dealer promotion. **4.** Chief GM stylist Bill Mitchell's Stingray Special was not only a genuine race car, but its look forecast the next-generation Corvette. No. 111 in this shot, it's behind a Lister-Jaguar and leading a Birdcage Maserati at California's Laguna Seca track.

2

3

4

1

2

3

Olds remade its image in '61, shifting from performance to premium-car luxury. Its big cars looked crisper, more mature, and made better use of space. Dynamic and Super 88s were 5.6 inches shorter, 3 inches lower, and 3.8 inches narrower on the same 123-inch wheelbase. Ninety-Eights kept a 126.3-inch span but lost two inches of body length. Curb weights were down as much as 100 lb. All used a 394-cid V-8 of 250- to 325-bhp, with 330 for the new Super 88-based Starfire convertible. **1-2.** This clear-top Dynamic 88 was built for First Lady Jacqueline Kennedy. **3.** The 4-door hardtop was the most-popular Ninety-Eight body style. This is the top-line Sport Sedan. It sold for $4159 and weighed 4319 lb. **4.** A Super 88 Holiday hardtop sedan, which listed for $3402, poses with a $3773, 4370-lb 9-passenger Super 88 Fiesta wagon. In all, Olds built 317,548 cars for '61, a slight drop from '60 in an overall slow car market, but enough to move up a notch to sixth in the industry.

4

1961 Oldsmobile

1

2

4

3

5

6

1. Even the cheapest hardtop, the $2956 Dynamic 88 coupe, cut a sharp figure. **2-3.** Olds ads conveyed a feeling of upscale leisure. **4-6.** Starfire was created for the emerging personal-luxury field. It was a Super 88 ragtop with the Ninety-Eight grille, rear panel trim, and wheel covers, plus front bucket seats with console, brushed bodyside panel, and 330 bhp. At $4647, it was the costliest '61 Olds.

Oldsmobile 1961

The Olds member of GM's new compact family was the F-85. It shared a 112-inch wheelbase with its Buick and Pontiac counterparts, but unlike the adventurous Pontiac Tempest, had an orthodox powertrain layout. GM's new 155-bhp 215-cid V-8 was the sole engine. The V-8's aluminum construction saved weight, but the alloy contaminated the heater cores, causing lots of warranty headaches. With sales just topping 76,000, the F-85 trailed the Tempest by some 25,000 units and the Buick Special by 10,000. But it was a boon to Oldsmobile's bottom line. **1.** The 4-door sedan and wagon were unveiled first, each offered in base form priced from $2384 to $2762, and Deluxe trim from $2519 to $2897. The Deluxe 4-door sedan was the best-seller, at 26,311 units. Wagons came with two or three rows of seats. **2.** The pillared coupe bowed at midyear in base form for $2330 or as this $2621 Deluxe-level Cutlass, the first Olds to wear that badge. **3.** The F-85 (right) was two feet shorter than a big Olds, but had a roomy and rather well-appointed cabin.

1

2

3

1961 Pontiac

1

Pontiac's redesigned fleet of big cars revived the split-grille theme on shorter and lower but roomier bodies. **1.** Bonneville returned as the top model on a new 123-inch chassis. Here's the Sport hardtop coupe. **2.** Catalina and Ventura shared a new 119-inch wheelbase platform. This is one of 13,297 Ventura Sport hardtops built for '61. **3.** Among its options are Pontiac's 8-lug aluminum rims that combined wheel hub and brake drum. **4.** Comfort, style, and aftermarket air conditioning—nice. **5.** Lighter- weight new cars and stronger engines made Pontiac drag racers tough to beat on street or strip.

2

3

5

4

Pontiac 1961

1

1. Pontiac 2-door hardtops shared the new "bubble roof" with Chevy and Olds. Here's the Bonneville again; it listed for $3255. The track width of the '61s was reduced by 1½ inches, but it didn't dent the "wide-track" advertising slogan. **2.** The Ventura hardtop coupe cost $2971, same as in '60, but weighed 3685 lb, 180 lb less. All big Pontiacs used the 389-cid V-8, which could be ordered with as much as 348 bhp. Late in the year, the 373-bhp special-order Super Duty 421-cid debuted. **3.** If cars lead a parade in Pontiac, Mich., they'd better be Pontiacs. **4.** New Pontiacs won 21 of 52 NASCAR Grand National stock-car races. Junior Johnson's Catalina ended this one early.

2

3

4

1961 Pontiac

1

"Compact was taken to mean a car that was downgraded in just about everything—price, size, power, performance. The new cars being introduced by Buick-Oldsmobile-Pontiac may be smaller, but they will outperform many larger models."

—General Motors Vice President Nelson C. Dezendorf, on GM's interpretation of "compact car"; October 1960

Christmas tree shoppers are busy from Maine to California . . . joining in the fun are Pontiac's stunning new Safari Wagon and Tempest 4-Door Sedan.

THERE'S NOTHING LIKE A NEW CAR FOR

FESTIVITY

Watch your family's spirits shift into high gear and leave winter doldrums far behind when a sparkling new General Motors car enters the scene—making Christmas complete.

A dazzling new General Motors car keeps family excitement at Christmas morning peak the whole year around! Why, even a trip to the corner store is a festive occasion . . . and you're sure to find more places to go and wonderful things to do, just because it's so much more fun getting there.

GM adds an extra measure of pleasure to motoring—and you'll find many reasons why. One is the handsome coachwork by Fisher Body. You'll like the looks, the lines, and the colors. You'll appreciate the wonderfully wide interiors that offer leg room, shoulder room, and wiggly-kid-room. On the road you will be impressed with the traditional General Motors reliability, which means confident and comfortable traveling. And you'll mentally tip your hat to GM engineers when you thrill to the exciting performance of these '61's—General Motors' finest by far.

Don't forget! There's sure to be a new car for *your* family in the GM line . . . just look at all the models, sizes, colors, engines, transmissions and power options! It pays to do your Christmas shopping early—it pays more to start your Christmas shopping at your General Motors dealer's showroom.

For the car of your choice, GO GM GENERAL MOTORS

Chevrolet • Pontiac • Oldsmobile • Buick • Cadillac • All with Body by Fisher

2

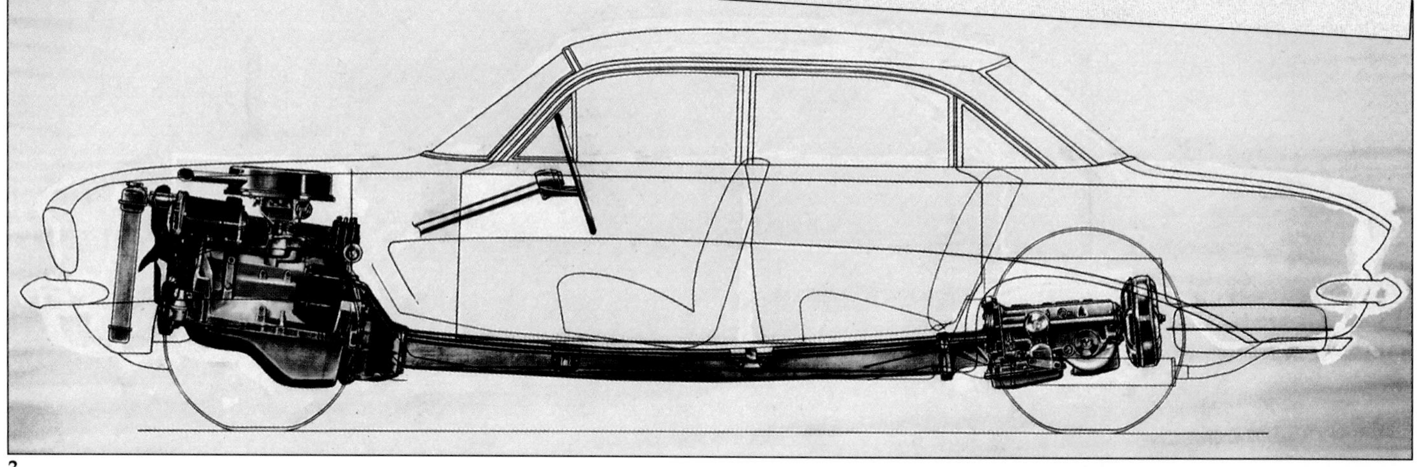

3

4

1-2. Pontiac's interpretation of GM's middle-market compact looked conventional on the outside, and echoed the big cars' styling, down to the split grille. **3.** Beneath the skin, Tempest went its own way. While the Buick and Olds compacts came only with the new 215-cid V-8, Pontiac used half a 389-cid V-8 to create for Tempest a 194.5-cid inline-4 cylinder engine with 110 bhp, or 130 with 4-barrel carb. About 2 percent were fitted with the optional 215 V-8. Both engines were linked to a rear transaxle via a flexible-cable driveshaft. Front suspension was independent, and swing axles made the rear independent, too. **4.** Tempest came as a sedan, wagon, and coupe and sold 100,783 units, easily more than the Buick and Olds compacts.

Studebaker-Packard Corporation

Ominously, production falls by more than half, from 120,465 in 1960 to 59,713; aging design is a big part of the problem

Sherwood Egbert, executive vice president of a California manufacturing firm and a man with no automotive experience, is named Studebaker-Packard president and CEO; he's 6-foot-4, handsome, 40 years old, and he believes S-P's future hinges on cars with style and performance

In March, Studebaker buys the company that manufactures and distributes STP oil treatment

Lark gets first completely new dashboard design since 1956; includes an oval steering wheel without a horn ring

Exterior styling is marked by a new rear roofline and, in an effort to make the Lark look lower, relocation of side trim to above the natural body line

The side-valve Champion six, which dates from 1939, is converted to an overhead-valve design and power increases from 90 bhp to 112

Bucket seats are made standard on the Hawk and a 4-speed manual is offered

Following Ford's lead, Stude introduces a 12,000-mile/12-month warranty on all its models

1

"We've a hell of a lot of good dealers in the Studebaker-Packard family....my job is to lead and help them."

—Studebaker-Packard President Sherwood Egbert; January 1961

2

Lark was threatened by more compact competition than ever. **1.** It tried relocated bodyside trim, seen here on a series VI convertible. **2.** It touted performance but was no longer the only compact to offer a V-8. **3.** Price was competitive, but modern, roomier, and fuel-stingier GM rivals were better values. **4.** The Hawk gained a 4-speed manual gearbox, the same as used in the Corvette, but sales fell 40 percent. **5.** The Champ pickup was utilitarian—and rust-prone. **6.** A few taxi firms turned to Stude for a Lark.

3

4

5

6

Etc.

American LaFrance Corp. produces the first gas turbine-powered fire-engine and delivers it to the San Francisco Fire Department; the 1000-gal-per-minute pumper weighs 31,500 lb and accelerates 0–50 mph in 45 sec

Liberty Mutual Insurance Co. shows cutaway drawings of a "Safety Car" with protective "capsule chairs," flexible steering shaft, telescoping steering tube, reduced-diameter steering wheel for added visibility, and an Alert-O-Matic signal system that sounds if the driver falls asleep or stops the car if the driver does not awaken

Checker changes the name of its Superba Special "consumer" series to Marathon.

GEMs (Ground Effect Machines) that traverse land and water by riding atop a low-pressure bubble of air are developed independently by Princeton University, Curtiss-Wright, and a triumvirate of Creative Industries/Molded Fiber Glass Body Co./Bertelsen Mfg. Co.

Willys's new Jeep Fleetvan is introduced for mail delivery

Datsun Bluebird delivers overhead valves, a 3-speed manual, and full foam seats for $1616

Two Simcas, a Special convertible and an Etoile sedan, are displayed in St. Petersburg, Fla., not at an auto show but at the Fine Arts Festival

1

2

3

4

1. Jaguar E-Type—XK-E in America—debuts. The 150-mph, $5595 sports car is an instant classic. **2.** International-Harvester Scout debuts; included in the model line are a compact pickup and a topless runabout. **3.** "CHECK YOUR SPEED," cautioned the Illinois State Police on their Chevy Biscaynes (left) and Plymouth Savoys. **4.** VW's Beetle was surprisingly roomy. **5.** Elegance and sportiness: the Mercedes-Benz 280SE Cabrio. **6.** The Rootes Group's hardy, smooth-cruising Humber Super Snipe. **7.** Chrysler's Ghia coupe show car was a one-off.

5

6

7

1

2

3

4

5

6

7

1. The compact Seagrave was proposed by a fire-equipment manufacturer. **2-3.** Anglo-Americans: Ford Zephyr Mark II Saloon and GM Vauxhall Victor. **4.** Triumph's Herald convertible. **5.** American-style tailfins adorned Sunbeam's Rapier Series III. **6.** Auto Union of Germany sold more than 2000 DKWs in the U.S. in '61; this is a 1000S 2-door hardtop. **7.** The French Facel Vega HK500 used a 383-cid Chrysler V-8. **8.** Before the Indy 500, a young driver saw his mother admiring the sleek Ford Thunderbird pace car, which would be awarded the race winner. A.J. Foyt promised his mother the car, then kept his pledge by taking his Offy-powered Trevis to the checkered flag at a 139.1 mph average speed.

8

Etc.

Britain's Humber Super Snipe 4-door sedan is the first import with four headlamps; other features of the $3995 car are disc brakes and leather upholstery

English-built Jensen 541-R arrives in the U.S. with pigskin upholstery and a $7750 price

Austin-Healey "Bugeye" Sprite comes to the U.S. from England with an 80-inch wheelbase, 48 bhp, and a $1795 tab

The Mercedes-Benz 220S 4-door sedan has 124 bhp and offers optional fuel injection; M-B of America establishes a parts and service organization independent of the parent company

Foreign cars banned from the 8th annual Japanese Auto Show

Toyota brings Jeep-like Land Cruiser to 11 western states; the utility wagon has a 135-bhp 6-cylinder and comes in hardtop and canvas-top versions

Top 10 Import Registrations

1. Volkswagen	177,308
2. Renault	44,122
3. Mercedes-Benz	12,903
4. Volvo	12,787
5. Fiat	11,839
6. Triumph	11,683
7. Austin-Healey	8935
8. MG	8806
9. English Ford	8660
10. Metropolitan	8657

Total import-car share of U.S. market: 6.47 percent

Compacts continued to sell well this year, even as some buyers looked for added luxury and increased size. Ford accommodated them with a new segment, the mid-size, or intermediate, car. Meanwhile, Pontiac's introduction of the sporty, powerful, and plush Grand Prix would accelerate growth of the "personal-luxury" segment pioneered by the Thunderbird.

That anybody was able to think about luxury at all was amazing because the world was trembling on the brink of nuclear war. In October, President Kennedy ordered Soviet premier Nikita Khrushchev to remove Russian ballistic missiles that had been sneaked into Cuba, just 90 miles off the Florida coast. Khrushchev came back with ominous threats, but JFK called his bluff. The missiles were removed and shipped back to the Soviet Union, ending what came to be known as the Cuban Missile Crisis.

The Kennedy administration grew increasingly preoccupied with Southeast Asia. In January, JFK announced a program of economic and social aid for South Vietnam, and in March, the U.S. State Department confirmed that American fliers were training South Vietnamese pilots.

Astronauts John Glenn, M. Scott Carpenter, and Wally Schirra made successful space flights as America geared up to meet JFK's goal of landing a man on the moon by decade's end.

Folk music was evolving into "protest music," thanks to such young artists as Bob Dylan, Joan Baez, and Peter, Paul & Mary; the last-mentioned trio had a No. 10 chart hit with "If I Had a Hammer." The Beach Boys made waves with their debut album, *Surfin' Safari,* while a quite different group, the Four Seasons, scored with their first LP, *Sherry & 11 Others;* the title cut was a No.1 single. Tony Bennett had what would be his biggest hit, "I Left My Heart in San Francisco." But the year's most-successful record was Vaughan Meader's *The First Family,* an album that affectionately spoofed the Kennedy Administration.

The Beverly Hillbillies premiered on CBS-TV in September and became wildly popular. Other hits were *The Defenders, Hazel, The Red Skelton Show,* and *To Tell the Truth.*

Popular movies included *Dr. No* (the first James Bond feature), *The Manchurian Candidate, Lawrence of Arabia, Whatever Happened to Baby Jane?,* and *The Three Stooges in Orbit.* Marilyn Monroe began shooting a film, *Something's Got to Give,* but completed only a few minutes of footage before her death in August.

Facing off against the New York Knicks on March 2, Philadelphia Warriors star Wilt Chamberlain became the first pro basketball player to score 100 points in a single game. The Warriors won, 169 to 147.

The National League added two baseball teams this year, the New York Mets and the Houston Colt .45s. Bad weather stretched a seven-game World Series to 13 days; when it was over, the New York Yankees had defeated the San Francisco Giants, winning their second Series in a row, and 20th in 27 appearances.

American Motors Corporation

AMC president and chairman George Romney resigns to seek Michigan Republican gubernatorial nomination, and is subsequently nominated and elected

Roy Abernethy succeeds Romney as president and CEO; he's less loyal to sensible compact cars and begins an ambitious model expansion

Richard E. Cross is named AMC chairman

Richard A. Teague named director of styling

Sales of Metropolitan are halted; production of the English-built subcompact actually ceased in 1960, but it took nearly two years for AMC to get rid of the unsold inventory

AMC restyles its flagship Ambassador and drops its 117-inch wheelbase for the 108-inch span of the mid-size Classic; few customers notice

E-Stick, a manual transmission with "automatic" clutch is introduced as a $60 option on Classic and American

William M. Schmidt is hired as styling consultant

Model-year production increases 12 percent, to 423,104, but Pontiac and Oldsmobile, with their new compacts, overtake Rambler in the sales race

1

2

3

4

1. AMC president George Romney was elected governor of Michigan in '62 with 51.4 percent of the vote. Seven Republicans ran for statewide office that year; he was the only winner. Here, Gov.-elect Romney (center) announces his resignation from AMC. It took two men to replace him: Richard E. Cross (left) as chairman, and Roy Abernethy (right) as CEO. **2.** The American got a new grille, as seen on the $2344 convertible. **3.** Here's the top-trim 2-door, badged the 400 and listing for $2040. American sales slipped 8 percent, to 125,679. Overall, Rambler's model-year output rose about 12 percent, to 423,104, but the make fell from third to fifth in the industry. **4.** Goodyear promised better road-hazard protection with its new "inner spare" technology.

1

2

3

4

5

1. After a fling with European-inspired styling, Ambassador reverted to a no-risk look and the chassis of the compact Classic, losing nine inches of wheelbase but no interior space. It also became the only Rambler with a V-8, the 327 cid with 250 or 270 bhp. **2.** Classics used the 195.6-cid six of 127 or 138 bhp. This is the new top-line 400 sedan, which listed for $2605. **3.** Here's the $2492 Classic Custom wagon. **4.** A production milestone was reached in '62. **5.** The Classic made a tidy ambulance.

Chrysler Corporation

Chrysler institutes sweeping changes to the look and size of mainstream Dodges and Plymouths, an ill-timed move to compact dimensions that sets the divisions back years

A full redesign of the Chrysler models is scrapped in favor of a finless last-minute restyling of the 1961 cars

With options like the 413-cid V-8, center console, and front bucket seats, a new line of "non-letter" Chrysler 300s steals the sporty beat from the 300H; sales of the true letter-series model falls from 1530 to 558

Mainstream Dodge models receive oddly styled new bodies and lose much bulk; all are built on a 116-inch wheelbase instead of the Dart's previous 118 and Polara's 122; sales plummet

At midyear, a panicky Dodge retrims a Chrysler to create a genuine full-size model, the Custom 880

Plymouth, with its narrower model mix than Dodge, suffers even more from the downsizing; falls to eighth place in model-year production, its lowest ranking ever

Imperial styling is cleaned up; fins are replaced by conventional rear fenders topped by freestanding "gunsight" taillamps

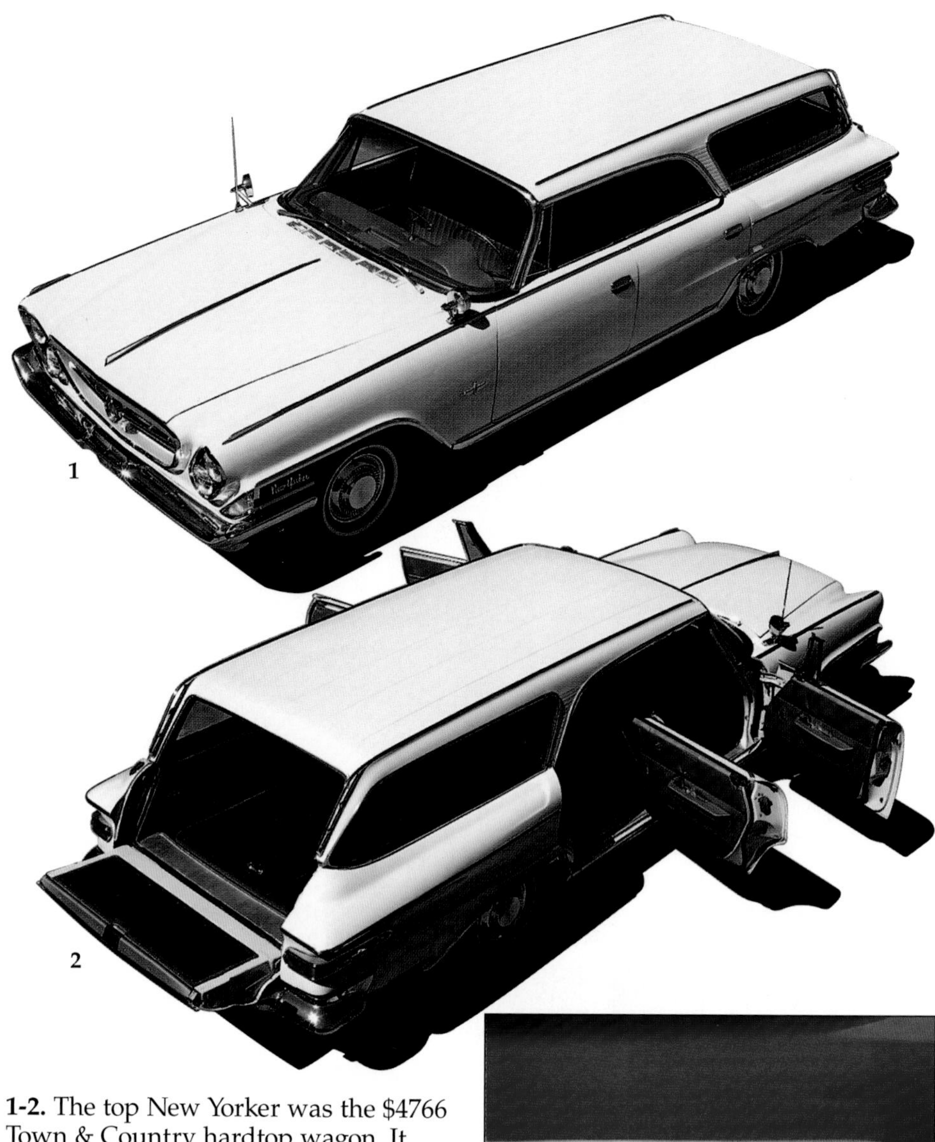

1-2. The top New Yorker was the $4766 Town & Country hardtop wagon. It boasted a carpeted cargo floor. **3.** Sales hit 128,921, the Chrysler brand's best model year since '55. **4.** Chryslers were getting rare on the drag strip, but this 300H was an exception. A stock 380-bhp 300H did 0–60 mph in 7.7 sec.

1

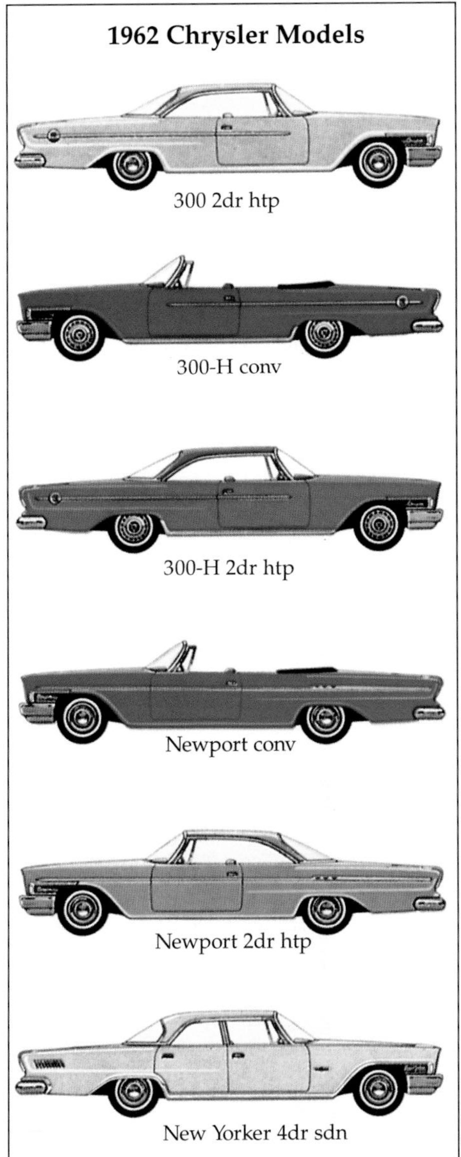

2

The hastily revamped '62 Chryslers used '61 Dodge Polara body shells with new finless rear quarters and carried-over '61 Chrysler noses. The trim-looking result pleased the public. **1.** In this photo, a '62 Imperial LeBaron (right) stands aloof from a New Yorker (from left), a new 300 Sport 4-door hardtop, and a Newport Town & Country wagon. **2-3.** New Yorker was the only Chrysler nameplate to retain the 126-inch wheelbase (others were at 122). It shelved its coupes and convertibles for 4-door sedans, wagons, and this $4263 hardtop. The brand's sales leader was the entry-level Newport series, priced from $2964 to $3586.

3

1962 Dodge

1

Erroneously believing Chevy was downsizing its big cars for '62, Dodge adapted styling meant for a wheelbase of 119 inches to one of 116. The result was a weird-looking sales dud in Dart and up-trim Polara 500 series. **1.** Polara came in three body styles. The 4-door hardtop cost $2960. **2.** The 2-door hardtop started at $3019. **3.** The Polara convertible listed for $3268. **4.** Dart's 440 ragtop started at $2945. **5.** Production fell 21,933 against equivalent '61s, forcing Dodge sales down as rival makes were increasing.

4

2

3

5

1

2

3

4

1-2. The upside of downsizing was lighter cars, making this basic Dart with its 410-bhp 413-cid V-8 a rocket. **3-4.** Cops liked the newfound go, too. **5-6.** Dart's top trim line was the 440; the 4-door hardtop cost $2763 and the ragtop $2945. **7.** Lancer was ending its two-year life. The new GT, a 2-door hardtop, used the 145-bhp Slant Six.

6

1962 DODGE DART 440 SPORTS-SWEEP

5

7

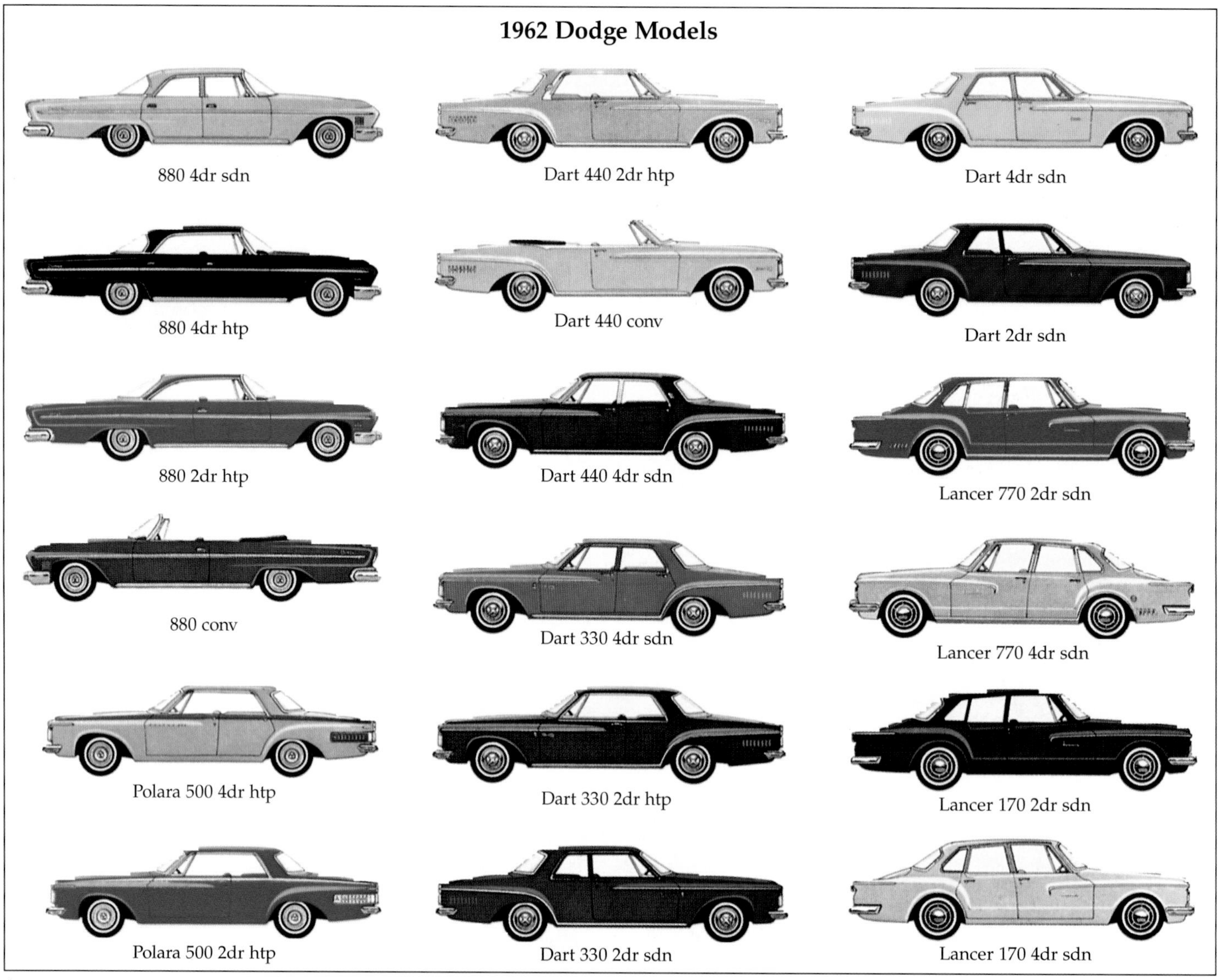

1962 Dodge

1962 Dodge Models

880 4dr sdn

Dart 440 2dr htp

Dart 4dr sdn

880 4dr htp

Dart 440 conv

Dart 2dr sdn

880 2dr htp

Dart 440 4dr sdn

Lancer 770 2dr sdn

880 conv

Dart 330 4dr sdn

Lancer 770 4dr sdn

Polara 500 4dr htp

Dart 330 2dr htp

Lancer 170 2dr sdn

Polara 500 2dr htp

Dart 330 2dr sdn

Lancer 170 4dr sdn

1

2

3

With DeSoto gone, Dodge was happy at midyear to field a full-size model as the corporation's entry in the upper-medium market. **1.** The result is visible in the chart above as the Custom 880 series. This was nothing more than a 122-inch-wheelbase Chrysler wearing a '61 Dodge grille, but it ended up outselling the Polara, 17,505 to 12,268. Prices ranged from $2964 to $3407. **2.** Dodge Turbo Dart (left) and Plymouth Turbo Fury were turbine-powered research cars for '62. **3.** Engineer George J. Heubner (center) and product planner Robert Anderson (right) gas about the turbine engine.

1

2

Imperial retained freestanding headlamps, but its gunsight taillights now floated on fin-shorn fenders. **1-3.** The line's sole ragtop cost $5774 and weighed 4865 lb. **4.** A dash fit for Captain Video. Transmission buttons were in the left pod, heater controls in the right. **5-6.** Available only as a 4-door hardtop, the Imperial LeBaron Southampton was Chrysler's priciest regular-production car, at $6426.

3

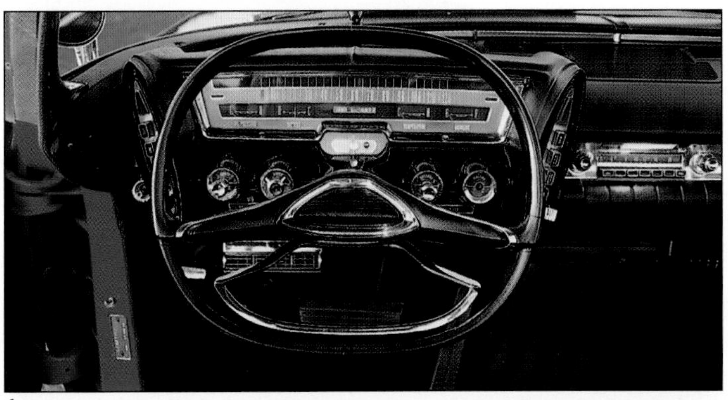

4

5

6

1962 Plymouth

1

2

Subjected to the same downsized remake as Dodge, Plymouth emerged less-odd-looking, though hardly more successful. Its sales dropped, too. **1-3.** Its costliest car was also its sharpest: the $3082 Sport Fury convertible. Just 1516 were built. **4-5.** This Savoy looked harmless, but with its 410-bhp dual-4-barrel 413-cid V-8, the 3200-lb sedan was a threat to anything on wheels. Slotting between this and the Sport Fury were Belvedere and Fury models. Savoys got one taillamp per side, Sport Furys three, others two.

3

4

5

1

2

3

4

1. Valiant was among Chrysler Corp.'s few bright spots, with a 10-percent jump in sales, to 157,294. **2.** Starting at just $1930, Valiant was at home in Florida's Briny Breezes retirement park. **3.** Dodge would kill the Lancer, but Valiant became a fixture as the entry-level Plymouth. **4.** At any temperature, the Slant Six was a reliable friend. **5.** Valiant gained a bucket-seat coupe for '62. The $2230 Signet 200 turned out to be the line's third-best-selling model, at 25,586 units. **6.** Two-toning was also new. **7.** Most-popular '62 Plymouth of all was the V-200 sedan, with 55,789 sold.

5

6

7

Ford Motor Company

Historic Ford Rotunda building in Dearborn is destroyed by fire, a $15 million loss

Ford shows experimental 2-seat sports car, calls it Mustang

30 millionth Ford V-8 is built

"Senior" compact Ford Fairlane debuts; introduces new small-block V-8, sized initially at 221 cid

Galaxie 500 and 500XL series added to full-size Ford line

Thunderbird adds Sports Roadster and Landau hardtop

Mercury gets version of new Fairlane; pulls a name off full-size model and badges its new senior compact the Meteor

Full-size Mercury Monterey Custom series adds bucket-seat S-55 convertible and 2-door hardtop at midyear

Ford enlarges the 390 to 406 cid; offers 405 bhp

Heaters and defrosters made standard on all FoMoCo cars

Two-way radio offered as a dealer-installed option on all Ford cars and trucks

Consul Capri coupe, built mainly for British and European market, comes to Ford dealerships in the U.S.

FoMoCo considers marketing sub-compact Cardinal for '63; later calls off U.S. production before it begins

1

2

1. Ford appropriated one of its familiar big-car names for its new "senior" compact. Fairlane debuted as a 2- and 4-door sedan in base and uplevel 500 trim. All were built on a new 115.5-inch wheelbase platform that slotted neatly between the Falcon's 109.5 and the Galaxie's 119. **2.** A 138-bhp 223-cid inline-6 was standard. Shown is the optional 145-bhp 221-cid V-8, a new Ford engine. At midyear, a 164-bhp 260-cid version became available. **3.** Sales of 297,116 made Fairlane a first-year hit. The 500 models, such as this sedan, took 73 percent of production.

3

1. Ford gave its big cars a full restyle and celebrated by officially re-entering racing, to the delight of stock-car drivers like Fred Lorenzen. **2-3.** The standard roofline wasn't very aerodynamic on racetracks so Ford tried to sneak the removable Starlift top past rules makers. NASCAR nixed it after one race. **4-7.** The top-line Galaxie 500 series was named for the big 500-mile races. Arriving at midyear was the 500XL. Along with it came a 406-cid V-8, Ford's first 400-plus-cid engine. At $3518, this XL Sunliner was the costliest non-T-bird. **8-9.** A basic "500" 2-door hardtop cost $2674, but this one's got the optional 390-cid V-8; it made up to 401 bhp.

1

2

3

5

4

6

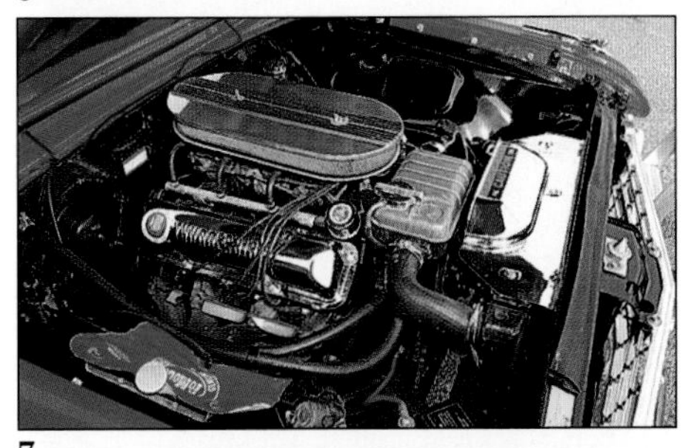

7

8

9

1962 Ford

1

2

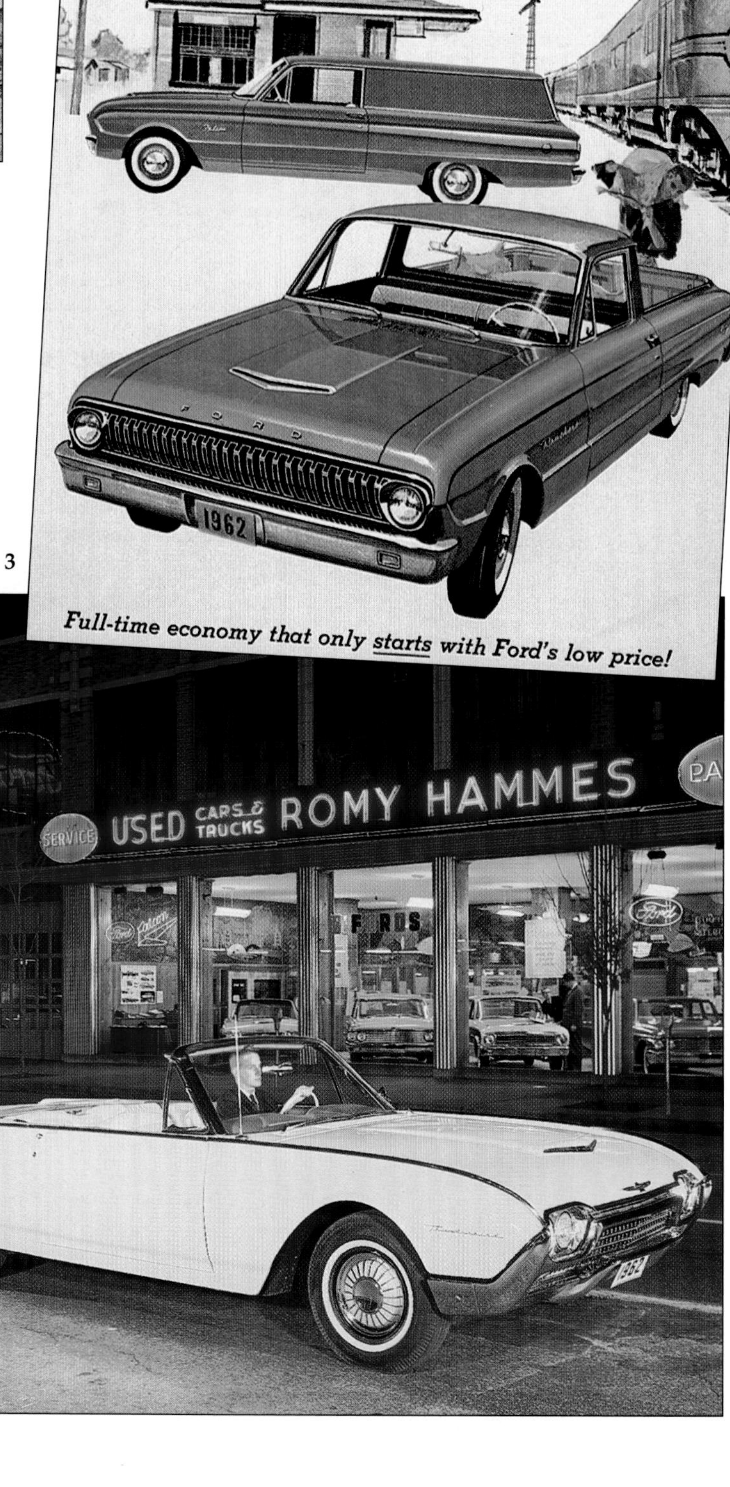

3

1. Falcon production topped 414,000, despite competiton from the popular new Fairlane. This is the sporty Futura 2-door as it started 1962. **2.** At midyear, Futura got a formal new roofline and an optional 4-speed manual gearbox. **3.** The Falcon wagon-based Sedan Delivery and Ranchero were marketed as trucks. **4.** Gyroscopes balanced the Gyron idea car on one front wheel and one rear. **5.** Ford's other '62 show car was a tube-frame 2-seater on a 90-inch wheelbase with a mid-mounted 90-bhp 1927-cc V-4 engine. It was called Mustang. **6** Leaving the dealership in that shiny new car, here a T-Bird ragtop, then driving around with no particular place to go—the stuff of dreams.

4

5

6

1

2

COUNT THE DOORS

Four doors mean you walk into the rear seat compartment of a Lincoln Continental convertible instead of climbing around the front seat. Please notice, too, how the rear doors open—from the center—to provide you with a wider entrance. This is one of the reasons the Lincoln Continental may be called the only luxury convertible in America.

On the Lincoln Continental the convertible top disappears beneath the rear deck without stealing a single inch of seating room. This, therefore, is the one convertible that has a rear seat large enough for three large passengers.

Luxury is only one of many qualities you find in this great motorcar—others are: timeless, classic styling, and unsurpassed quality of manufacture. As a matter of fact, special gages and test equipment had to be developed to meet the exacting quality standards. The result is America's finest automobile, the Lincoln Continental for 1962. It is your wisest investment in tomorrow, warranted for twice as long as any other American car (two full years or 24,000 miles).*

LINCOLN CONTINENTAL
Product of Ford Motor Company Lincoln-Mercury Division

3

4

5

6

The Industrial Design Institute rarely honored cars, but it cited Continental's "simplicity and design elegance." Buyers liked it, too: Sales doubled in '61, then jumped 19 percent, to 31,061, in '62. A recast grille was the main change. **1-2.** The sedan listed for $6074 and remained the best-selling body style, at 27,849 units. **3-5.** The classy convertible cost $6720 and weighed 5370 lb. **6.** This armored limo was built on a production 113-inch wheelbase for Vice President Lyndon Johnson. It was similar to the '62 Presidential Continental, which had a 156-inch wheelbase. That car's removable plastic roof was not in place in Dallas on November 22, 1963, when Lee Harvey Oswald assassinated President Kennedy, who was riding in the rear seat.

1962 Mercury

1

Like Ford's, Mercury's big-car line was rebodied for '62. Monterey and Monterey Custom were the trim levels, with wagons under Commuter and Colony Park headings. **1.** At midyear, Mercury launched its sport/luxury S-55. These were Monterey Custom 2-door hardtops and convertibles with special trim and a standard 300-bhp 390-cid V-8. **2.** The S-55 was most noted for its bucket-seat interior. It included a full-length console with integrated shift lever.

2

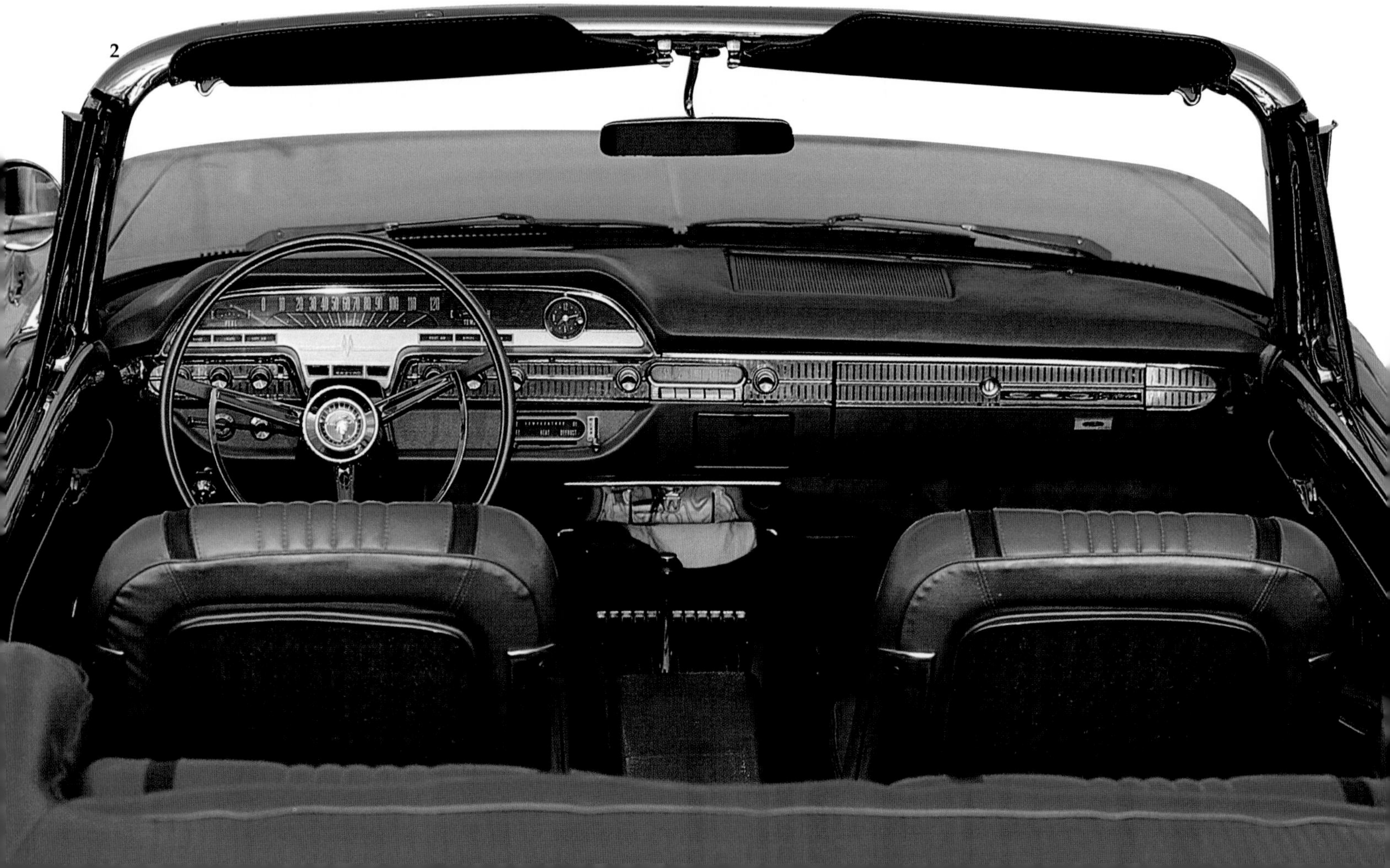

1

2

3

4

1. Named for the Mt. Palomar observatory, this dream wagon had a roll-back rear-roof section over an elevated third seat. **2.** Piggybacking on the new Fairlane was the Meteor, which used an inch-longer wheelbase than its Ford cousin, but shared chassis and running gear. These 2- and 4-door sedans effectively invented the mid-size car category. **3.** Midyear saw introduction of the S-33, a 2-door Meteor with bucket seats and console. **4.** At 4198-lb, the 9-passenger Colony Park was Mercury's heaviest car, but the S-55s were more expensive. **5-6.** Slot-car racing was the latest fad, with plastic scale models soaring in popularity, as well.

5

6

General Motors

Building on 1961's momentum, all five GM divisions register higher sales in '62

Buick production jumps 38 percent; division adds Skylark convertible and a bucket-seat luxury coupe called Wildcat

After one-year hiatus, Buick resumes importation of Opel

Cadillac introduces 4-window Series '62 sedan and dual-braking system with separate front and rear hydraulic lines

Chevy notches its first 2-million-unit production run, another new record and nearly 600,000 ahead of Ford

Chevy fights the Falcon by unveiling Chevy II compact

Corvair gets a convertible

Oldsmobile moves up two spots to fourth place in model-year production

Olds F-85 gets Jetfire sports coupe with a turbocharged 215-cid V-8 of 215 bhp

Pontiac moves into third place in sales and will stay there through the rest of the '60s

Pontiac adds Grand Prix sport coupe, Tempest convertible

Power steering offered on GMC Suburban and pickups

Chuck Jordan named chief of GM automotive design

GM promotes seatbelt usage

"I believe the industry always will have small cars with luxurious appointments."

—Buick General Manager Edward D. Rollert; 1962

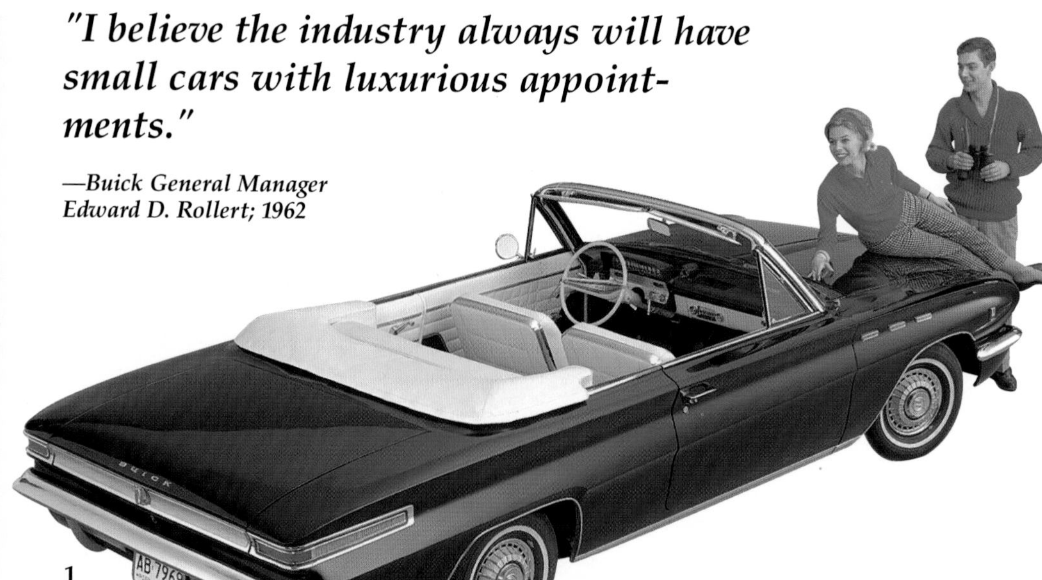

1

2

3

While big Buicks were restyled, the Special retained the pointed-fender theme from '61. But there was change afoot. **1.** The premium Skylark model expanded from a single 2-door pillared coupe to add a genuine 2-door hardtop and this flashy convertible. The ragtop was the most-expensive in the line, listing for $3012 and like other Skylarks, came with a flashy bucket-seat interior and unique exterior trim. **2.** The new convertible also was available in base and Deluxe levels; this is the $2879 Deluxe. **3.** Buick debuted a new engine for '62, making Special the first high-volume American car with a V-6. The 198-cid unit made 135 bhp and was standard in the base series. Deluxe Specials continued with the 155-bhp 215-cid V-8, while Skylarks got a 190-bhp version of the V-8.

1

2

3

4

5

6

7

1. A fresh name to Buick, Wildcat was a sporty new $3927 2-door hardtop. **2.** The Electra series was dropped, leaving the Electra 225 alone atop the line. This is the $4366, 4396-lb deuce-and-a-quarter convertible. **3.** Ohio's Flxible Co. built Buick-based ambulances and hearses and in '62 created this Electra 225 8-passenger limo. **4.** Summer fun: ice cream, beer, a boat, and a Buick convertible. **5.** Gone was the 364-cid V-8, so Invictas, 225s, and LeSabres like this one got the 401. **6.** LeSabre lost its convertible model, leaving the Invicta as the sole mid-priced Buick ragtop. **7.** Curb service was super.

1962 Cadillac

1

2

3

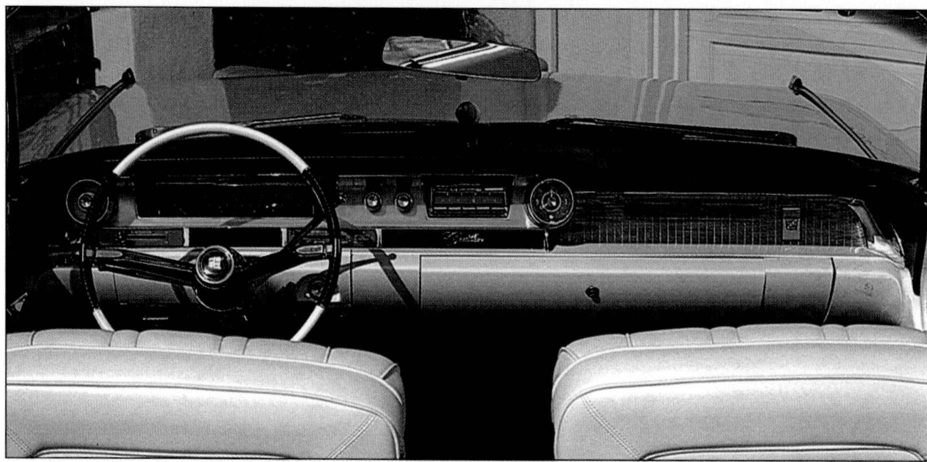

4

5

6

7

1. Cadillac didn't prove its claim that millions would rather drive one of its cars, but it didn't have to. A Coupe de Ville is in the ad. **2.** The $5631 4-window Sedan de Ville wasn't inexpensive, but Caddy still could tout its value against "less eminent" makes. **3.** Fins continued to shrink and were no longer chrome-lined. Lower pods got vertical. Here's the "entry-level" Series 62 convertible. It cost $5588. **4.** The 1962 62 was a great place from which to view the world. This was the first year a heater was standard in all Caddys! **5.** Eldorados all were ragtops for '62. They wore the Biarritz name, started at $6610, and weighed 4620 lb. **6.** That year's Eldo show car had a radiused rear-wheel opening and fins that were real. **7.** May as well go in style: the Cadillac ambulance.

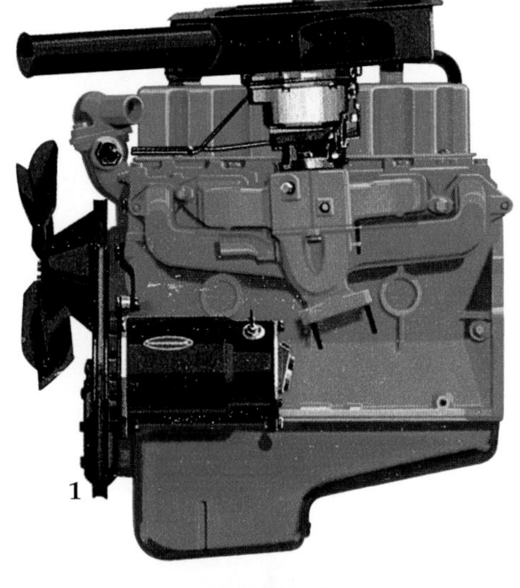
1

3

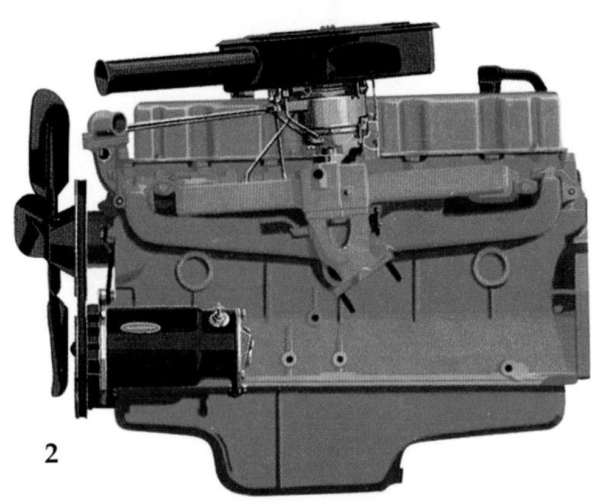
2

4

5

6

Chevy II was Chevrolet's back-to-basics Falcon fighter. **1.** A new 90-bhp 4-cylinder was the basic engine. **2.** A 120-bhp six was available. **3.** The wagon could seat nine. **4.** This $2003 sedan was the entry-level model. **5-6.** The $2475 Nova ragtop topped the line. **7.** Interiors were quite roomy for the car's 110-inch wheelbase and Nova's was snazziest. **8.** Sales of 326,600 made Chevy II a hit.

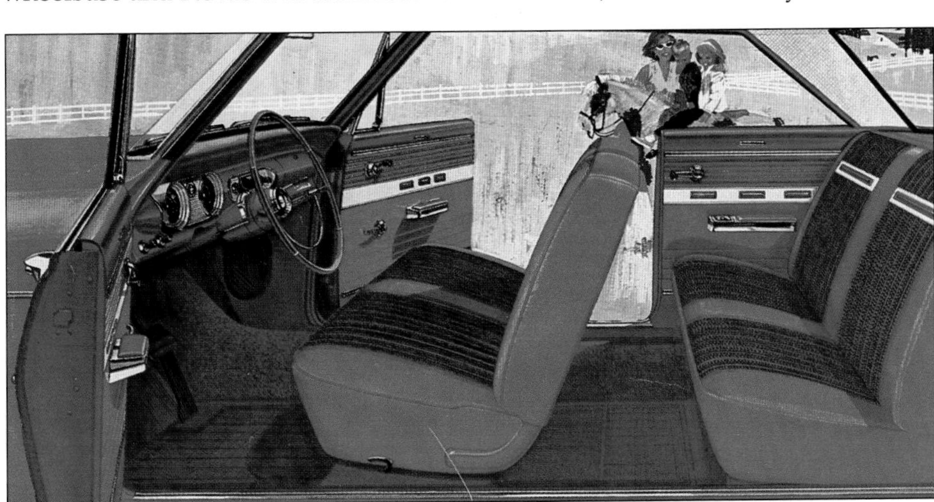
7

8

1962 Chevrolet

1

2

The Sporty Car in Chevrolet's New World of Worth

CHEVROLET **'62 Corvair**

Built for budget-minded people who go for sports car driving

Here, with saucier styling, tasteful new interiors and bigger new brakes, is the latest version of the car that proved itself in the fiercest rally competition going. Read on and get to know this new Corvair better.

You'll like what we changed—and what we *didn't* change—about this new '62 Corvair. We've spruced up the interiors, sparked up the styling and included a bundle of goodies (a cigaret lighter, front door armrests, dual sunshades, an automatic choke—even a forced-air heater and defroster!) as standard in sedans, coupes and station wagons. You also get bigger, more efficient brakes that team up with Corvair's rear-engine traction to give you just about the surest-footed car that ever latched onto a road.
But here's what we haven't changed. Corvair's quicksilver steering. Its jigsaw agility. Its gutty air-cooled engine. Your dealer's is the place to see it. Chevrolet Division of General Motors, Detroit 2, Mich.

Corvair Monza

This is the one that started the bucket seat brigade—the Monza Club Coupe.

'62 CORVETTE

New go—for the goingest car in America!

Dramatic styling refinements and a smooth new 327-cubic-inch V8 make this the sweetest Corvette yet. See America's only true sports car at your dealer's. He's got just the one to convert you to a wind-in-the-face sports car enthusiast.

3

1. A Corvair for every need. Monza gained a wagon, plus an inviting Spyder convertible. **2.** This Corvair rampside pickup wears non-factory paint and wheels. **3.** Corvair was pitched as a budget sports car, and indeed, the 150-bhp Monza Spyder was lively. **4.** Real power lie with the 409-cid V-8, now at 409 bhp in dual-quad form. **5-6.** The twin 4-barrel 409 and rare aluminum body parts turned this Bel Air sports coupe into a restless sleeper. **7.** Hayden Proffitt's 4-speed 409 Bel Air won Top Stock at the U.S. Nationals, running the quarter-mile in 12.8 sec at 114 mph. **8.** "Dyno" Don Nicholson's 409 Impala SS got the Stock Eliminator crown. **9.** Speeders feared cops in big-block Biscaynes.

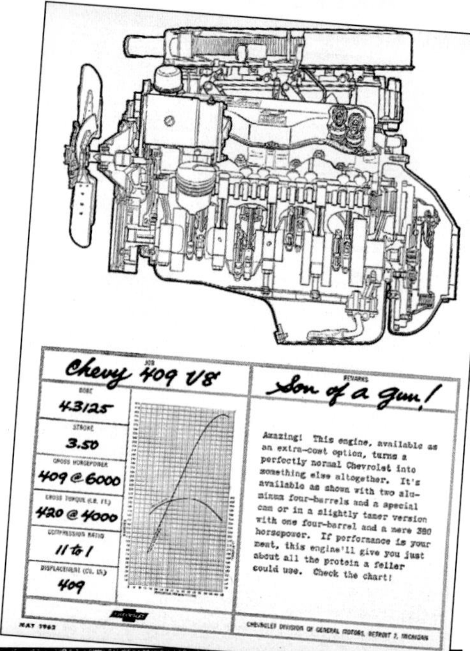

JOB: *Chevy 409 V8*

BORE	4.3125
STROKE	3.50
GROSS HORSEPOWER	409 @ 6000
GROSS TORQUE (LB. FT.)	420 @ 4000
COMPRESSION RATIO	11 to 1
DISPLACEMENT (CU. IN.)	409

REMARKS: *Son of a gun!*

Amazing! This engine, available as an extra-cost option, turns a perfectly normal Chevrolet into something else altogether. It's available as shown with two aluminum four-barrels and a special cam or in a slightly tamer version with one four-barrel and a mere 380 horsepower. If performance is your meat, this engine'll give you just about all the protein a feller could use. Check the chart!

MAY 1962

CHEVROLET DIVISION OF GENERAL MOTORS, DETROIT 2, MICHIGAN

27

4

5

6

7

8

9

1

2

3

Of the 2 million Chevys built for '62, 1.4 million were full-size models and of those, half were Impalas. The only 2-door Impalas were the Sport coupe and the convertible. **1.** The coupe listed for $2776 and came with a V-8. **2.** The ragtop was the only Impala to start above $3000. This one has the $54 SS option. **3-4.** Corvette's base price topped $4000 for the first time, and the side cove was no longer available in a contrasting color. It used Chevy's new 327-cid V-8. This example has the 340-bhp version. **5.** The XP-755 did double duty as a show car and a test bed for future Corvettes. **6.** On the race track, No. 10 Don Yenko and No. 11 Dr. Dick Thompson ran 'Vettes; No. 0 is Jim Rathmann's Chevy-engine Chaparral. **7.** Betty Skelton was a professional aerobatic pilot and an expert driver. She set land speed records at Daytona and Bonneville, and promoted Corvette.

4

5

6

7

1962 Oldsmobile

1

2 3 4

1-2. Olds broke from the pack with a new F-85 coupe, the Jetfire. Its 215-cid V-8 was fortified with a turbocharger to make 215 bhp. **3.** A turbo was radical technology for the day and a source of pride for development engineer Gilbert Burrel (left) and chief engineer Harold Metzel, here with the Turbo Rocket engine. **4.** Olds General Manager Jack Wolfram (left) and Metzel with the Jetfire, which was the most expensive F-85, at $3049. Available with manual or automatic transmission, the Jetfire could do 0–60 mph in a credible 8.5 sec but was not a great all-around performance car. It found 3765 buyers after its midyear introduction. **5.** The turbo V-8 had 60 bhp more than the ordinary version of the aluminum engine. To insure complete detonation, a mixture of distilled water and methyl alcohol was injected into the fuel/air charge to cool the combustion chamber. **6.** Here she is, Miss America 1962, Maria Fletcher, from Asheville, N.C., with the pageant's "official car." **7.** On Jan. 11, 1962, Oldsmobile built its 7,500,000th car since being founded in 1897. The milestone machine was a Starfire.

5

6

7

1

2

3

New nose and tail styling for its big cars helped Olds to its best sales year since 1956 and a jump from sixth to fourth place in industry production. **1.** The line started with the Dynamic 88, ascended through the Super 88 and Starfire, and peaked with the Ninety-Eight. This is the $4118 Ninety-Eight Sport Sedan, the series' top-seller, at 33,095 units. **2-3.** The bucket-seat Starfire became its own series and added a coupe. The $4131 hardtop outsold the convertible—at $4774, the priciest Olds—34,839 to 7149. All big Oldsmobiles again used a 394-cid V-8, and Starfire's 345-bhp again was the most-powerful version. **4.** A Ninety-Eight looks at home in the new American cultural vortex, the shopping mall. **5.** Yup, all six cars are aboard. **6.** Sales of just 3693 made the $4459, 4298-lb Ninety-Eight convertible the rarest full-size model for '62.

4

5

6

1

2

1. Pontiac's new Grand Prix coupe would help define the personal-luxury field. Sales of 30,195 made it a hit. **2.** Grand Prix's $3490 base price included bucket seats and this 303-bhp 389-cid V-8. **3-4.** To the sedan, pillared coupe, and wagon, Tempest added a convertible. It cost $2564. **5.** Royal Pontiac of Royal Oak, Mich., got factory help to build some quick Pontiacs. **6.** Call me a Tempest.

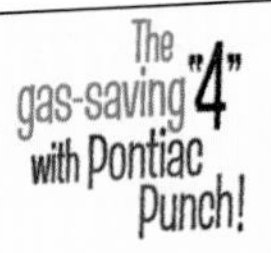

3

4

5

6

Pontiac 1962

1. Pontiac's big-car foundation was the broad Catalina line. Here's the $3172 ragtop. **2.** Bonneville topped the range and included the $3349 Sport hardtop coupe. **3.** The 9-seat Catalina Safari wagon started at $3301 and weighed 4220 lb. **4-6.** Tri-tone vinyl spiced the Catalina. With its 405-bhp dual-quad 421-cid Super Duty V-8, a special-order $2550 option, this one did 0–60 mph in 5.4 sec and the quarter-mile in 13.9 at 107 mph. **7.** Racing Super Duty Catalinas ran the quarter-mile in 12.8 sec at 111 mph. **8.** Pontiac built GM's 75 millionth car in March. Division boss E.M. "Pete" Estes and a junior spaceman mark the astronomical feat.

1

2

3

4

5

6

7

8

Studebaker-Packard Corporation

The last year in which "Packard" would be a part of the Studebaker-Packard corporate name

S-P president Sherwood Egbert enlists his friend, industrial designer Brooks Stevens, to modernize the Hawk and Lark on a shoestring budget

Stevens replaces Raymond Loewy's flowing lines with squared-up shapes to create a more formal coupe renamed the Gran Turismo Hawk

Lark gets not only new styling but a new image, with longer bodies and a grill appearance similar to that of a Mercedes-Benz

A new top-line Daytona series of 2-door hardtop and convertible join the Lark line

Prototypes of a striking new Studebaker sports coupe are shown at the New York International Auto Show; the fiberglass-bodied car is the work of stylist Loewy and is called Avanti; it's slated for introduction as a 1963 model

A pre-production Avanti fitted with a 299-cid V-8 and a Paxton supercharger breaks 29 national stock-car speed records at Bonneville Salt Flats; Studebaker earlier in the year had acquired Paxton Products and in the process snared its president, Andy Granatelli

1

2

4

1. Brooks Stevens' fin-shearing restyle turned the Hawk into the modern-looking Hawk GT. Sales nearly tripled, to 8388. 2. Alan Young as Wilbur Post, Connie Hines as his wife, Carol, and the horse, of course, is the famous Mr. Ed. The popular talking-equine sitcom was sponsored by Studebaker for the '62 and '63 seasons. The car is the revamped Lark, its new Mercedes-inspired grille and relocated bodyside crease more evidence of Stevens' talent. **3.** The new Daytona series, here in hardtop form, was Lark's sporty entry. **4-5.** Four-door Larks adopted a 113-inch wheelbase. This Regal has the Skytop roll-back fabric sunroof option.

5

6

1

2

Designer Stevens not only executed a crash revamp of the existing Stude line, he also envisioned future models. Working on a shoestring with the obscure Italian coachbuilder, Sibona-Bassano, he built three one-off prototypes. All would have used the 289-cid V-8 set further back in the chassis and made liberal use of supercharging. **1-3.** Projected for 1965, this low-cut sedan offered large-car interior room on a compact-class 116-inch wheelbase. The doors could be swapped diagonally as a cost-saving measure. Note the rectangular headlamps. **4-5.** Stevens called this 1966 Hawk replacement the Sceptre. Its left-side trim illustrated the "deluxe" version. **6-7.** The proposed '64 Lark wagon also used interchanging doors and showed a sliding rear roof, which was the only facet of these cars to make it to production.

3

4

6

5

7

Etc.

New-car sales at some Miami dealerships increased during the Cuban Missile Crisis because, as one dealer put it, "people remember how difficult it was to buy cars during the last war"

70,000 spectators watch 14-year-old David Mann win the Akron Soap Box Derby

The Amphicar, a German dual-use vehicle that travels on land or in water, has an electrically welded steel hull and twin propellers; in the water, the front wheels act as twin rudders. Price is $3395

The first Austin Cooper sedan arrives in Los Angeles, and is given to the Rev. Mildred Poole, Lincoln heights Foursquare Church, by her parishioners

Austin-Healey's redesigned Sprite sports car dispenses with the "bug-eyed" look for a smoother, more integrated front-end design. A racy new version of the A-H 3000 also makes its U.S. debut

The English-made Bristol 407 luxury car stores its spare tire behind the left-front wheel, and the battery compartment behind the right-front wheel; access to either is gained by lifting a hinged flap sited just behind the wheel

The sporty Consul Capri coupe, manufactured by English Ford, comes to America with hardtop styling, front disc brakes, and bucket seats

1

2

3

1. Rodger Ward won the Indy 500 in this Offy-powered Watson racer; he was the first to top 150 mph at the Brickyard. **2.** A Thunderbird looks good on the stars of ABC-TV's *77 Sunset Strip* (from left): Edd "Kookie" Byrnes, Efrem Zimbalist, Jr., and Roger Smith. **3.** A visitor from Italy checks out an American beehive as he takes delivery of a Hertz Chevy Impala. **4.** The Stuart Electric battery-powered, fiberglass-bodied 2-seater had a range of 40 miles when driven at 35 mph.

4

1

2

3

4

5

1. British Motor Corp.'s Jeep-like Mini Moke cost $1270. **2.** Into the British AC Ace roadster Carroll Shelby put first a 260-cid Ford V-8, then a 289, to create the original AC/Shelby Cobra. Price: $5995. **3.** The fetching Giulietta was the first Alfa Romeo to make a mark in America. **4.** Maserati's 3500 GT cost $11,400. **5.** From Britain, Ford imported its 4-cylinder Consul. **6.** The perky MG Midget. **7.** Dick Shawn leaps into his Dodge Dart in the madcap movie comedy *It's a Mad Mad Mad Mad World*. **8.** A $3300 German import, the dual-purpose Amphicar.

6

7

8

Etc.

Datsun's SPL-310 roadster debuts and is joined in West Coast dealerships by the Bluebird sedan; number of Datsun dealers in the western U.S. increases by 100; sales increase 115 percent

Peugeot's 404 sedan goes on sale at import dealerships on East Coast and Gulf Coast; the Pininfarina-bodied car is priced at $2575

One of the largest-volume Renault dealers in the U.S. is Snuffy Smith Motors, Dallas, Texas; pearl of the Renault line is the Dauphine Deluxe, which has a unitized body, synchronized 3-speed transmission, and a 32-bhp rear-mounted, water-cooled engine

Lucky winner of the Miss NBC-TV Teen Contest drives home a new Simca

VW introduces Model 1500 "Squareback" wagon and sedan; the popular "Beetle" continues, with torsion-bar suspension, a unitized body, and, now, a gasoline gauge

Top 10 Selling Imports

1. Volkswagen 192,570
2. Renault 29,763
3. Triumph 15,967
4. Volvo 13,157
5. Mercedes-Benz ... 11,075
6. Austin-Healey 10,019
7. Fiat 9762
8. MG 9319
9. Peugeot 4926
10. Jaguar 4442

Total import-car share of U.S. market: 4.89 percent

1963

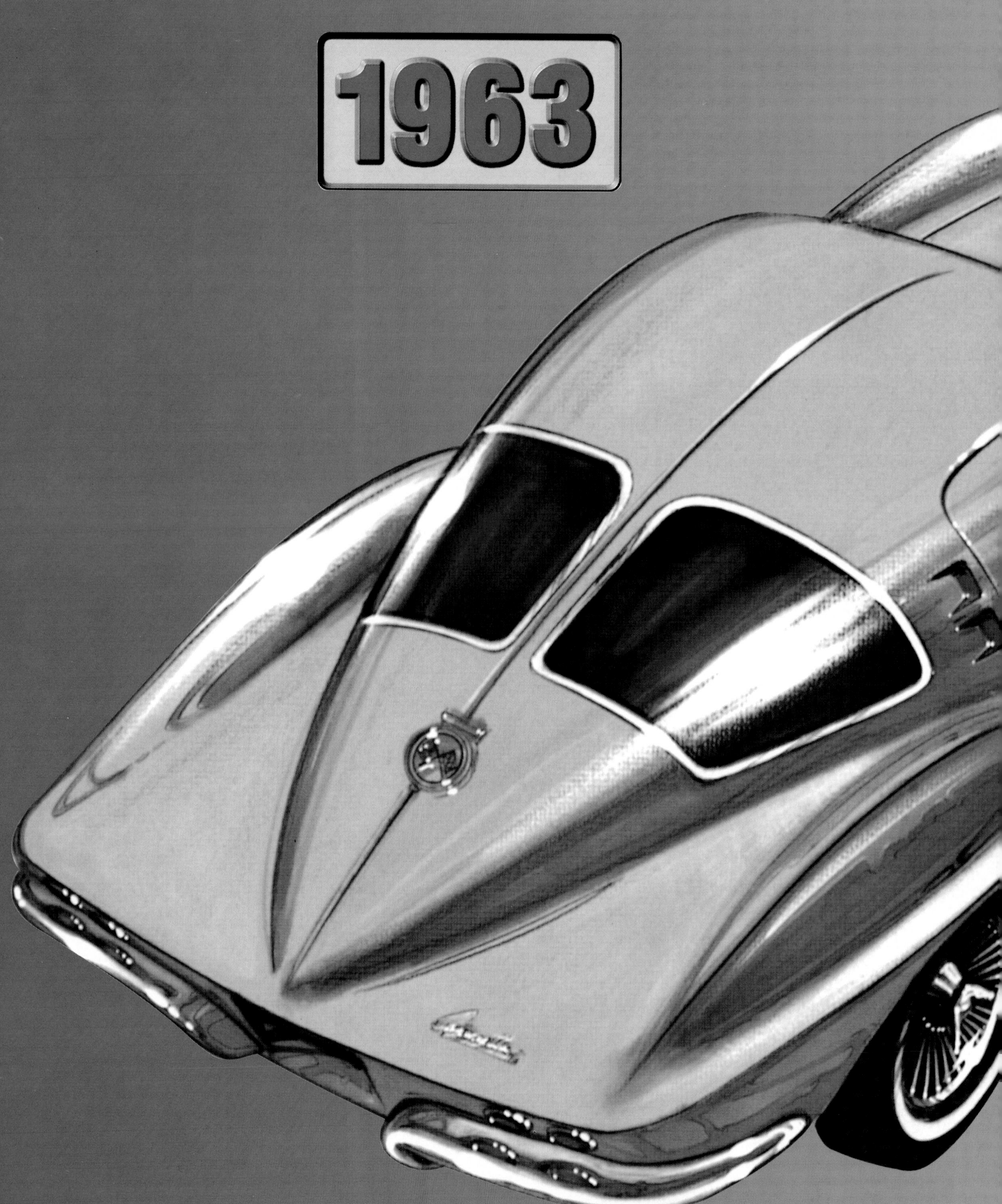

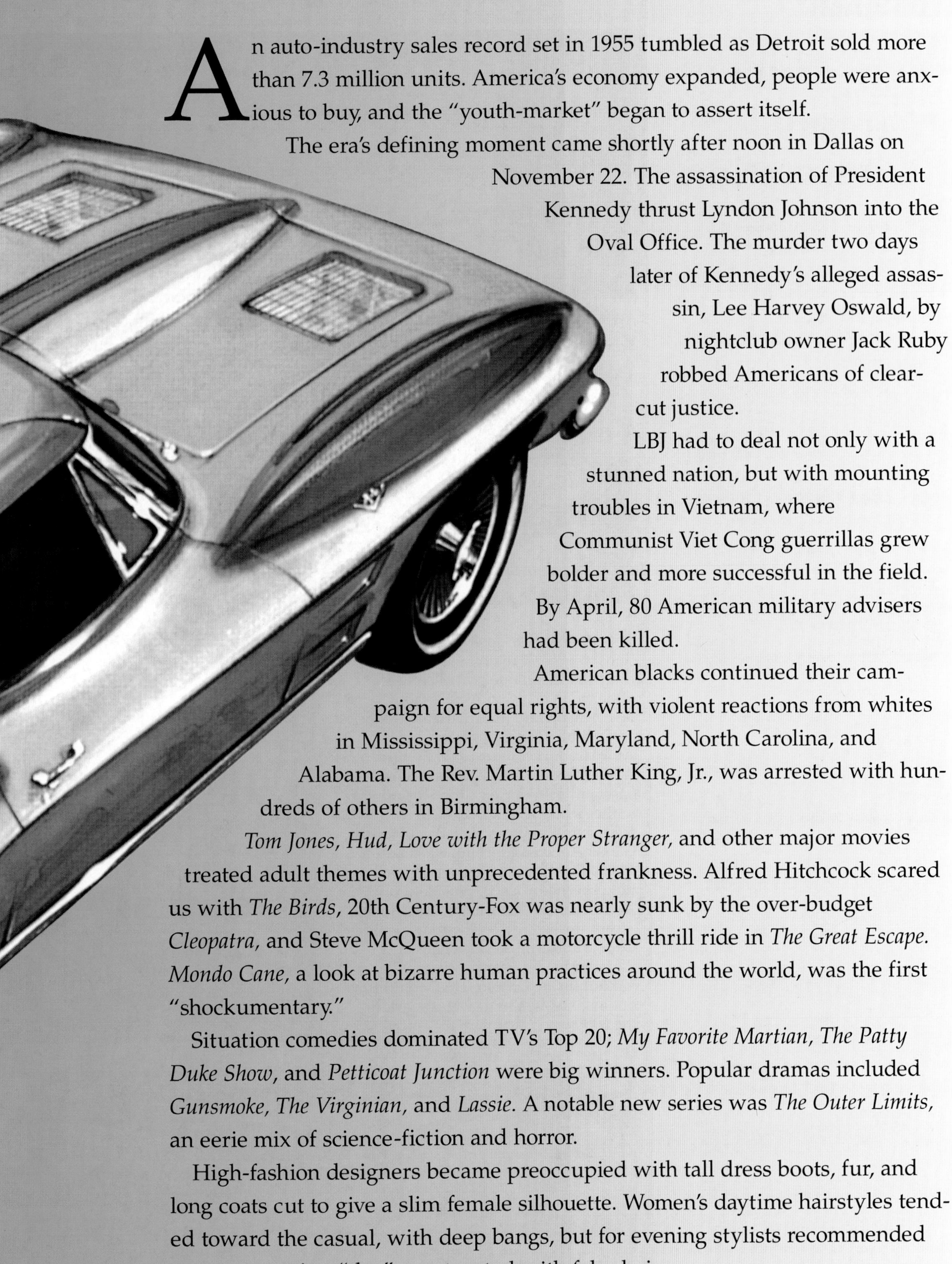

An auto-industry sales record set in 1955 tumbled as Detroit sold more than 7.3 million units. America's economy expanded, people were anxious to buy, and the "youth-market" began to assert itself.

The era's defining moment came shortly after noon in Dallas on November 22. The assassination of President Kennedy thrust Lyndon Johnson into the Oval Office. The murder two days later of Kennedy's alleged assassin, Lee Harvey Oswald, by nightclub owner Jack Ruby robbed Americans of clear-cut justice.

LBJ had to deal not only with a stunned nation, but with mounting troubles in Vietnam, where Communist Viet Cong guerrillas grew bolder and more successful in the field. By April, 80 American military advisers had been killed.

American blacks continued their campaign for equal rights, with violent reactions from whites in Mississippi, Virginia, Maryland, North Carolina, and Alabama. The Rev. Martin Luther King, Jr., was arrested with hundreds of others in Birmingham.

Tom Jones, Hud, Love with the Proper Stranger, and other major movies treated adult themes with unprecedented frankness. Alfred Hitchcock scared us with *The Birds*, 20th Century-Fox was nearly sunk by the over-budget *Cleopatra,* and Steve McQueen took a motorcycle thrill ride in *The Great Escape. Mondo Cane,* a look at bizarre human practices around the world, was the first "shockumentary."

Situation comedies dominated TV's Top 20; *My Favorite Martian, The Patty Duke Show,* and *Petticoat Junction* were big winners. Popular dramas included *Gunsmoke, The Virginian,* and *Lassie.* A notable new series was *The Outer Limits,* an eerie mix of science-fiction and horror.

High-fashion designers became preoccupied with tall dress boots, fur, and long coats cut to give a slim female silhouette. Women's daytime hairstyles tended toward the casual, with deep bangs, but for evening stylists recommended ornate, towering "dos" constructed with false hair.

The Los Angeles Dodgers swept the New York Yankees in a four-game World Series. Dodger pitcher Sandy Koufax struck out 15 in Game One, a new Series record. The Chicago Bears beat the New York Giants in the NFL title game.

American Motors Corporation

"Full-size" Ramblers—the Classic and top-line Ambassador—are redesigned, moving from a body-on-frame 108-inch wheelbase to a new unibody platform on a 112-inch span

Styling, the work of departing designer Edmund A. Anderson, casts a lower silhouette, features smoothly rounded bodysides, and—a Detroit first—one-piece door-frame structures

An impressed *Motor Trend* magazine bestows upon the Rambler line its coveted "Car of the Year" honors; cites "engineering excellence and outstanding design achievement"

Classics get first V-8 option, a new 198-bhp 287-cid unit; previous top engine was a 138-bhp 196-cid 6-cylinder

Entry-level American adds a hardtop model

American wins the Mobilgas Economy Run with best fuel economy of any U.S. car for second straight year

AMC begins a $42 million expansion of its Kenosha plant; capacity increases to nearly 700,000 cars per year

Despite more excitement than AMC has seen in years, production increases only slightly and Rambler slides from fifth to eighth in volume among U.S. makes

1

Though Rambler listed 35 model variations in 1963, it really offered only three distinct models. **1.** The Classic 4-door sedan leads an Ambassador 4-door wagon and an American 2-door convertible. The Classic and Ambassador were restyled by Ed Anderson on a new 112-inch wheelbase and a 2-door hardtop was added to the American line. **2.** With its new styling and unibody construction, the Classic/Ambassador line was chosen *Motor Trend*'s car of the year for '63. Roy Abernethy (left), president of American Motors, was on hand to accept the award. **3.** The redesigned Classic and Ambassador help boost Rambler model-year production by 5242 units, to 428,346. This would turn out to be AMC's high-water mark of the 1960s.

2

3

1

New to the Classic and Ambassador were Uni-side door openings. With Uni-side, two large stampings replaced the 50 or so pieces that usually made up the door frame. These inner and outer stampings greatly reduced water leaks, tightened tolerances, and cut down on rattles. **1-2.** The Ambassador lineup featured 2- and 4-door sedans and a 4-door wagon. All were available in three trim levels—800, 880, and 990—and all used AMC's 250-bhp 327-cid V-8. **3-4.** The 990 4-door sedan tipped the scales at 3158 lb and started at $2660.

2

3

4

1

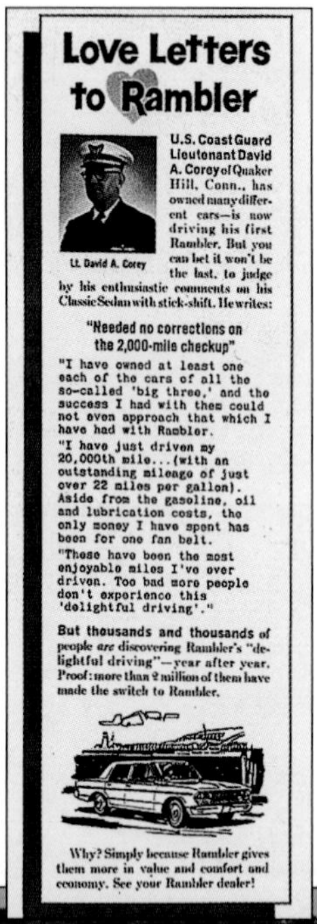

Love Letters to Rambler

U.S. Coast Guard Lieutenant David A. Corey of Quaker Hill, Conn., has owned many different cars—is now driving his first Rambler. But you can bet it won't be the last, to judge by his enthusiastic comments on his Classic Sedan with stick-shift. He writes:

Lt. David A. Corey

"Needed no corrections on the 2,000-mile checkup"

"I have owned at least one each of the cars of all the so-called 'big three,' and the success I had with them could not even approach that which I have had with Rambler.

"I have just driven my 20,000th mile...(with an outstanding mileage of just over 22 miles per gallon). Aside from the gasoline, oil and lubrication costs, the only money I have spent has been for one fan belt.

"These have been the most enjoyable miles I've ever driven. Too bad more people don't experience this 'delightful driving'."

But thousands and thousands of people *are* discovering Rambler's "delightful driving"—year after year. Proof: more than 2 million of them have made the switch to Rambler.

Why? Simply because Rambler gives them more in value and comfort and economy. See your Rambler dealer!

2

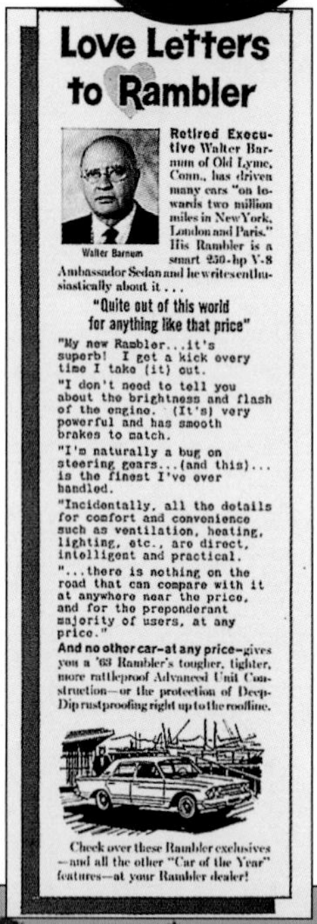

Love Letters to Rambler

Retired Executive Walter Barnum of Old Lyme, Conn., has driven many cars "on towards two million miles in New York, London and Paris." His Rambler is a smart 250-hp V-8 Ambassador Sedan and he writes enthusiastically about it . . .

Walter Barnum

"Quite out of this world for anything like that price"

"My new Rambler...it's superb! I get a kick every time I take (it) out.

"I don't need to tell you about the brightness and flash of the engine. (It's) very powerful and has smooth brakes to match.

"I'm naturally a bug on steering gears...(and this)... is the finest I've ever handled.

"Incidentally, all the details for comfort and convenience such as ventilation, heating, lighting, etc., are direct, intelligent and practical.

"...there is nothing on the road that can compare with it at anywhere near the price, and for the preponderant majority of users, at any price."

And no other car–at any price–gives you a '63 Rambler's tougher, tighter, more rattleproof Advanced Unit Construction—or the protection of Deep-Dip rustproofing right up to the roofline.

Check over these Rambler exclusives—and all the other "Car of the Year" features—at your Rambler dealer!

3

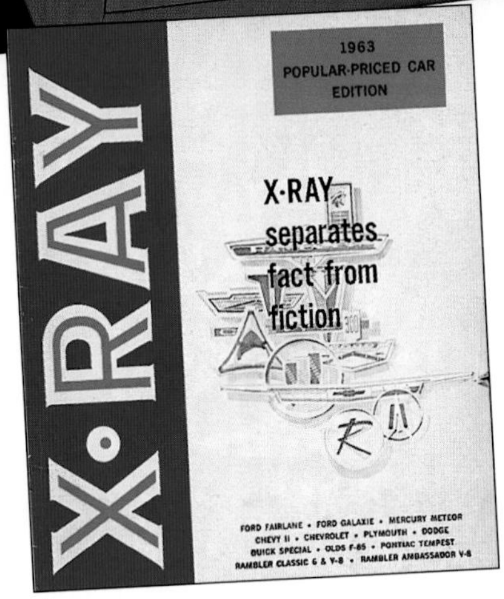

X·RAY

1963 POPULAR-PRICED CAR EDITION

X·RAY separates fact from fiction

FORD FAIRLANE • FORD GALAXIE • MERCURY METEOR
CHEVY II • CHEVROLET • PLYMOUTH • DODGE
BUICK SPECIAL • OLDS F-85 • PONTIAC TEMPEST
RAMBLER CLASSIC 6 & V-8 • RAMBLER AMBASSADOR V-8

4

The New Shape of Quality

RAMBLER FOR 1963

CLASSIC 6 • AMBASSADOR V-8

5

1. The new Classic came as a 2- and 4-door sedan and 4-door wagon in 550, 660, and 770 trim. Here's the 770 sedan at $2349. All were available with a 127- or 138-bhp 6-cylinder and, for the first time, with AMC's 198-bhp 287-cid V-8. **2-5.** Rambler tried to woo customers through traditional family-oriented channels as well as "fact-based" publications such as *X-Ray*. **6.** The 770 wagon cost $2640. **7.** Its 660 counterpart went for $2537 with six seats, $2609 with nine. **8-9.** Sleepin' or eatin', Rambler was a sensible choice.

6

7

8

9

1

2

1-2. American carried over mostly unchanged. The base-level 220 and mid-level 330 were available as 2- and 4-door sedans and wagons. **3.** Like 1962, top-line 440s came in sedan, wagon, and convertible body styles, as well as this 2-door hardtop that was added for '63. **4-6.** Available with either a front bench seat (440) or two buckets with a floor-mounted console (440H), the hardtop added 14,850 sales to the American lineup. Also new was the 138-bhp 6-cylinder found in the Classic. It was optional on lesser Americans and standard on the hardtop. **7.** Here's the $2344 convertible.

3

4

'63 RAMBLER AMERICAN family-size with a flair for fun

5

6

7

Chrysler Corporation

Chrysler's "production" Turbine car grabs headlines; 50 examples of the 4-passenger hardtop coupe are assembled by Ghia of Italy and loaned to consumers for evaluation

Chrysler Corp. startles the industry by announcing a revolutionary 5-year/50,000-mile powertrain warranty on all its 1963 cars

Chrysler models are restyled, getting the "Crisp, New, Custom Look"; they're the first cars released under the direction of new of design chief Elwood Engel

Moving fast to correct 1962's sales-sapping downsize, Dodge lengthens and enlarges its standard cars; most get a 119-inch wheelbase, up by 3 inches

Dodge takes Dart name from its big-car line and applies it to its all-new compacts

Chrysler allows its dealers to sell makes other than Chrysler Corp. products

Chrysler Corp. delivers first Saturn S-1 space-vehicle booster rocket to NASA

Chrysler paces the Indy 500 with its 300 Sport and offers replicas of the car for sale to the public

Dodge and Plymouth big-block V-8 grows from 413 to 426 cid and delivers up to 425 bhp

1

1-2. At $5860, the New Yorker Salon was called "The world's most complete car." **3.** Like other '63 Chryslers, it sported the "Crisp, New, Custom Look" penned by Elwood Engel and rode on a shorter 122-inch wheelbase. **4-5.** Chrysler's letter series for '63 was designated *J—I* was not used because of possible confusion with the number one. Chrysler Chief Engineer R. M. Rodger showcases the 390-bhp version of the 413-cid V-8 that went into the J. Down 15 bhp and lacking a convertible body style, production of the letter series hit a record-low 400 units.

2

3

4

5

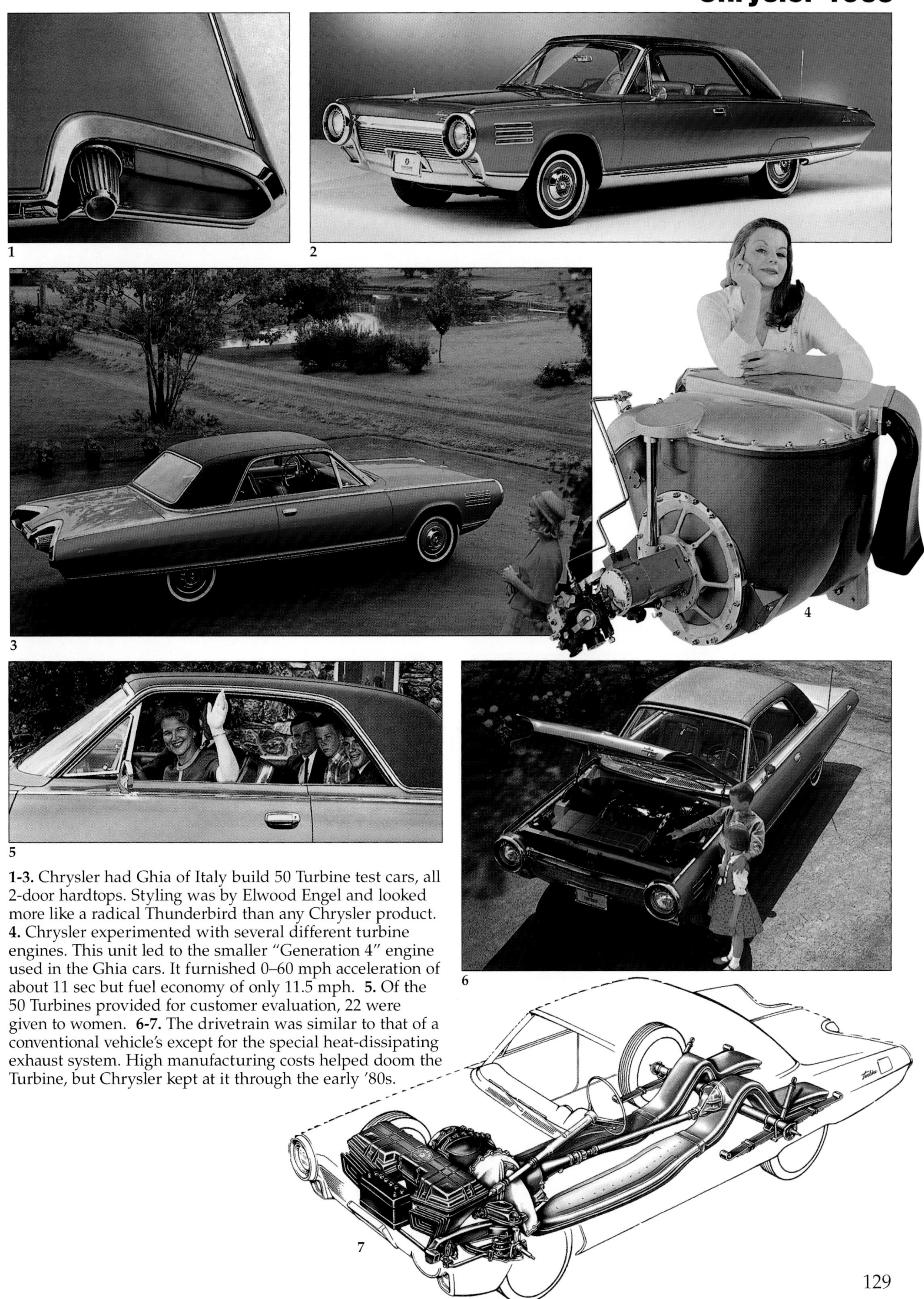

1-3. Chrysler had Ghia of Italy build 50 Turbine test cars, all 2-door hardtops. Styling was by Elwood Engel and looked more like a radical Thunderbird than any Chrysler product. 4. Chrysler experimented with several different turbine engines. This unit led to the smaller "Generation 4" engine used in the Ghia cars. It furnished 0–60 mph acceleration of about 11 sec but fuel economy of only 11.5 mph. 5. Of the 50 Turbines provided for customer evaluation, 22 were given to women. 6-7. The drivetrain was similar to that of a conventional vehicle's except for the special heat-dissipating exhaust system. High manufacturing costs helped doom the Turbine, but Chrysler kept at it through the early '80s.

1963 Dodge

1. Dodge's front-end styling was new, as seen on this Polara 500 hardtop coupe. 2. Optional on all Dodges except the Dart were three 426-cid V-8s, the most potent making 425 bhp. 3. The Ramcharger engine's provocative upswept exhaust headers were required because the engine bay was too narrow to fit conventional pipes. 4. Bucket seats were standard in the Polara 500. The dashboard supplied a clock and alternator gauge along with the speedo, gas, and temperature gauges. 5. Dodge production nearly doubled to 428,346, good enough to bump the division from ninth to seventh in overall model-year volume.

1. If you ordered the 425-bhp Stage III 426-cid V-8 you got huge hood scoops and super performance, but an engine ill at ease anywhere but a drag strip. In fact, Dodge did not recommend any version of the 426 for street use. **2-4.** On the strip, the super-powered Dodge earned instant respect. The potent 425-bhp Ramcharger blistered NHRA record books with quarter-mile times in the 12-sec range at speeds approaching 120 mph. **5-6.** Recovering from the "downsizing" fiasco, Dodge turned to cleaner, more conventional lines for its $2963 Polara ragtop and $2781 Polara hardtop.

1963 Dodge

1

2

Dart replaced the Lancer and featured crisper styling and a 111-inch wheelbase, 5 inches longer than Plymouth's compact, the Valiant. **1.** Ragtops came in this up-level 270 trim and as GTs. **2.** Dart production was 153,922, some 90,000 more than the '62 Lancer. **3.** Four-door sedans were the best-selling models and came in 170 or in this snazzier 270 trim. **4.** The $2289 hardtop came only as a GT. It featured standard bucket seats. **5.** All Darts used the Slant Six engine; a 101-bhp 170-cid unit was standard and a 145-bhp 225 was optional. This is the 270 convertible at $2385.

3

4

5

1

2

Dodge's largest car, the 880, put new front-end styling on its carried-over 122-inch wheelbase. Three base-level models were added, for a total of nine full-size offerings. **1.** The $3109 4-door hardtop car, came only in top-level Custom trim. **2.** The 880 wagon was available in either trim. The 9-passenger version was Dodge's most-expensive starting at $3407. It weighed 4186 lb. A 265-bhp 361-cid V-8 was the standard 880 engine, with the 383-, 413-, and 426-cid V-8s optional.

1963 Imperial

1

2

Ex-Ford stylist Elwood Engel took office in time to give the Imperial a minor facelift. The restyle consisted of a new grille insert with elongated rectangles, plus a crisper roofline and restyled rear deck. The 129-inch chassis lineup was unchanged, and sales were 14,121, down a fraction from '62. **1.** The Imperial Custom 4-door hardtop tipped the scales at 4690 lb and cost $5243. It was the second most popular Imperial model, with 3264 sold. **2.** The 149.5-inch wheelbase Crown Imperial limo listed for a whopping $18,500.

1963 Plymouth

1

2

3

Like Dodge, Plymouth displayed a more conservative, squared-up look for 1963. **1.** The most-expensive model in the stable was the Sport Fury convertible at $3082. **2.** Its cousin, the Sport Fury hardtop, listed for a more palatable $2851. Combined, the two sold more than 15,300 copies. **3.** Built on the same 116-inch wheelbase as the Fury, the Belvedere 4-door sedan tipped the scales at only 3020 lb when equipped with a Slant Six. The Belvedere lineup included 2- and 4-door sedans, the hardtop coupe, and 4-door wagons in 6- and 9-passenger guise.

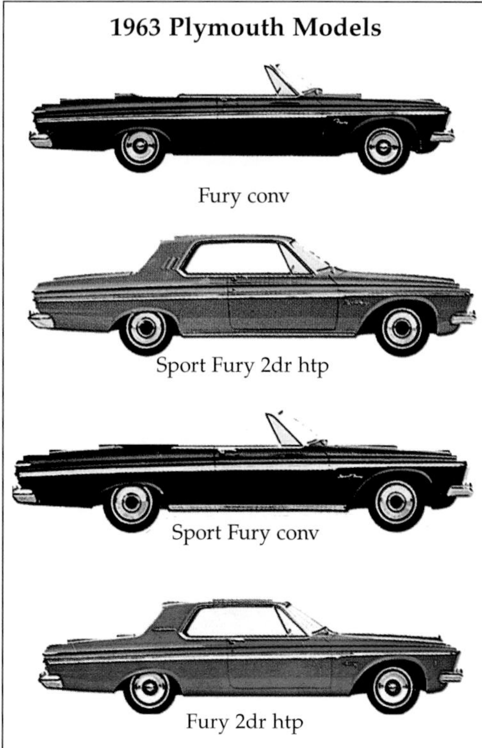

1

2

3

4

Plymouths with 426-cid Super Stock V-8s were a race-track force. **1.** Golden Commandos were the factory-sponsored drag team. **2.** The "Melrose Missile" did the quarter-mile in 12.3 sec. **3.** In oval racing, Richard Petty drove Plymouths to 14 NASCAR wins, while Plymouth won the USAC title. Here's A. J. Foyt on a USAC track in a Savoy. **4-6.** A sedate-looking Belvedere was a fearsome street racer when fitted with the dual-quad, 425-bhp 426 wedge. It had a 3-speed manual; 4-speeds hadn't arrived yet at Plymouth.

5

6

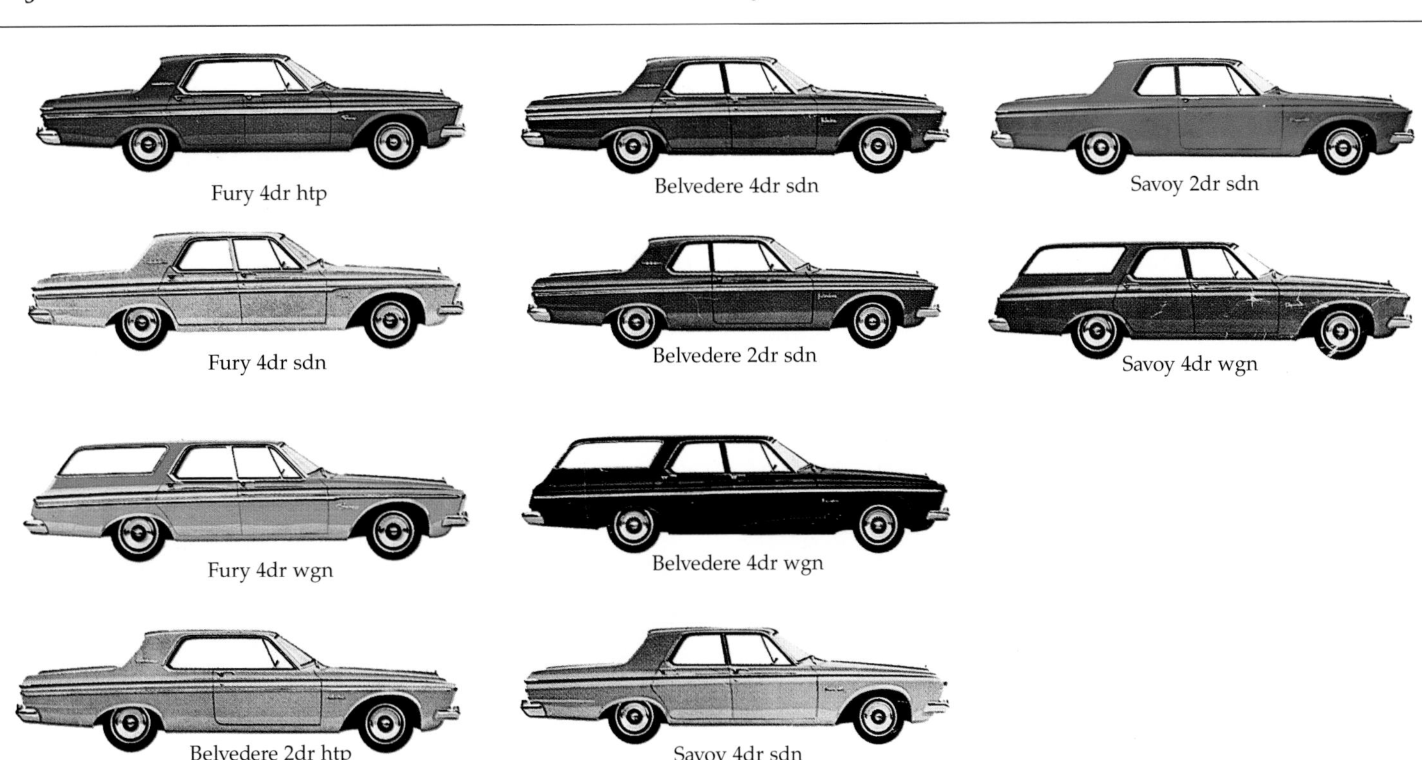

1963 Plymouth

1963 Valiant Models

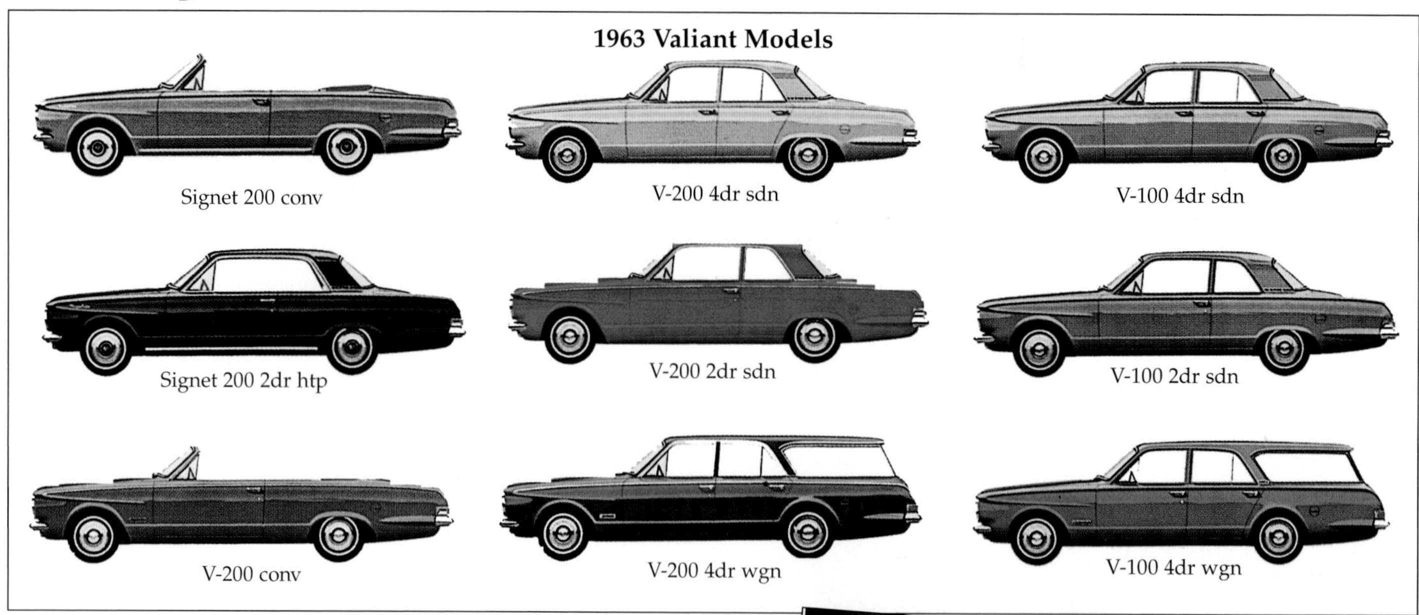

Valiant got a new body on a fractionally shorter 106-inch wheelbase. **1.** The $2454 Signet convertible was the most-expensive model. **2.** Valiant sales, which included 9154 ragtops and 30,857 hardtops, were healthy and helped pull Plymouth from eighth to fourth in industry sales. The standard engine was the 170-cid Slant Six, but buyers could again opt for the 145-bhp 225-cid version. **3.** The lineup consisted of 2- and 4-door sedans, a 4-door wagon, a 2-door convertible, and, in Signet trim only, this pert 2-door hardtop. **4.** Goodyear hyped its new Double Eagle tire with LifeGuard Safety Spare. The Safety Spare feature placed a second tire—complete with tread and bead—inside a regular tire to ensure mobility. It was not a factory-supplied tire.

1

4

2

3

Ford Motor Company

FoMoCo car production exceedes 1.5 million but still trails Chevrolet

Midyear bucket-seat editions of the Falcon, Fairlane, and Galaxie add spice to the lineup; they're marketed as "The Lively Ones" in a tie-in to a TV show of that name

Large-displacement V-8s available in all models except the Falcon and Fairlane—up to 427-cid with up to 425-bhp

Falcon, Fairlane, and Mercury Comet gain additional body styles

Ford celebrates centennial of founder Henry Ford's birth and 60th Anniversary of the company

"Whiz Kid" Arjay Miller named corporate president

Ford truck volume reaches postwar high

Ford introduces America's first fully synchronized three-speed gearbox

Rear-engine Ford-powered Lotus finishes second at the Indianapolis 500

Ford tries—and fails—to buy Italy's Ferrari sports-car company

All engines add a PCV valve—the first emissions controls

Mercury adds the Breezeway power rear window to its full-size models

1

2

1-2. Thunderbird entered the final year of its styling cycle with minimal appearance changes. Sales slipped by 5913 but were still healthy at 63,313. **3.** The Sports Roadster model was a convertible with a removable fiberglass tonneau over the rear seats. It came with Kelsey-Hayes chrome wire wheels and cost a whopping $5563. Just 455 were produced.

3

1963 Ford

1

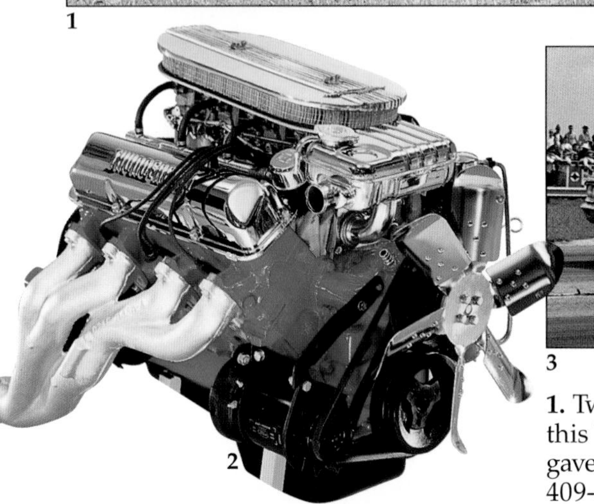

2

3

1. Two Galaxie 500 convertibles targeted the sunshine set: a plain Sunliner and this bucket-seat XL. **2-3.** Ford bored out its 406-cid V-8 to create the hot 427. That gave it an advantage on the strip—in displacement if not results—against the 409-cid Chevys. **4-5.** Model-year production of 1,525,404 represented Ford's best year since 1957 and a new record. But arch-rival Chevy widened its lead.

4

5

1

2

3

4

5

1-2. The aerodynamic "slantback" Galaxie 500 coupe bowed at midyear. Tiny Lund's version finished tenth in NASCAR. **3.** Galaxies, including this 2-door sedan, got a new grille and taillights. **4.** A 4-door hardtop was new to the Galaxie 500XL line. It attracted 12,596 shoppers. **5.** Lesser Galaxies, like the 300, were aimed at fleet buyers. **6-7.** Ford wagons shared a 119-inch wheelbase with other body styles. The County Squire got faux-wood siding. **8.** Ford's small-block V-8 powered the hot AC Shelby Cobra.

6

7

8

1963 Ford

1

2

3

4

1. Sculptured bodysides and squared-up roofs identified the '63 Falcons. The 4-door sedan was offered in base and Futura form. **2.** Wagons came in 2- and 4-door body styles and in standard and Deluxe trim. **3.** The panel-wagon was called the Sedan Delivery. **4.** A midyear addition was the bucket-seat Futura Sprint convertible and hardtop. **5-6.** Mid-size Fairlane sedans came in base and 500 trim, but the wagons were available only in base trim. **7.** The sharpest of the nine Fairlanes was the midyear Fairlane 500 Sports Coupe. It had bucket seats and cost $2504. **8.** The workhorse F-100 pickup could be fitted with the flair-fendered Flareside bed or this smooth-flanked Styleside. **9.** Ford's other pickup was the "cab-over" Econoline. It cost $1890 and, for '63, gained an upgraded interior and 5-leaf rear springs.

5

6

7

8

9

1

2

ENTER LIKE A LADY

Notice the doors. Four. This is America's only four-door convertible. And notice how they open. From the center, to make everyone's entrances graceful.

Inside, there is greater safety. All four doors lock automatically when the driver flicks a single switch. And there is luxury: in fine soft upholstery, rich looped carpeting, exquisite details like the walnut inlay on the glove box and door panels. And there is extra space. This is the only convertible whose rear seat is wide enough for three adults to ride in comfort... wider than in any other convertible.

But great engineering is equally important in the Continental concept. This car is designed and constructed to the highest standards in the world.

Of course, it is costly. But we refuse to compromise and build lower priced models as others do. Because they would not be Continentals. There is only one Continental... timeless in styling, enduring in performance, retaining its high value year after year.

For 1963, enter the private world of Lincoln Continental, the finest car in the world.

LINCOLN CONTINENTAL

SIX THOUSAND, TWO HUNDRED AND SEVENTY DOLLARS*

This is the manufacturer's suggested retail price for a 1963 Lincoln Continental sedan. Included as standard equipment are: Automatic transmission; power steering and brakes; power windows and power side vent windows; power door locks and 6-way power seat; heater and defroster; push button radio, rear seat speaker and power antenna; and, of course, white sidewall tires.

The price is probably less than you would expect. For no other car in the world is constructed to such standards of excellence and includes so many luxuries and performance features as standard equipment. We do not make lower priced models as others do, because we refuse to compromise the Continental's standards, the highest in the world. There cannot be a "second best" Lincoln Continental.

This is the Continental. Divide its original price by the years of beauty and comfort and service you can enjoy, consider its high resale value... it is truly economical. And it is the world's finest car.

LINCOLN CONTINENTAL

*Manufacturer's suggested retail price shown for a 1963 Lincoln Continental sedan equipped as described above. State and local taxes if any, license, fees, and delivery charges are not included.

3

1-2. A finely checked grille, matching back appliqué, and increased trunk space marked the '63 Continental. Retuning got another 20 bhp out of the 430-cid V-8, for a total of 320. Both the pillared sedan and convertible were 4-doors on a 123-inch wheelbase. **3.** President John F. Kennedy was riding in this Lincoln when he was assassinated in Dallas on November 22, 1963. Texas Gov. John Connally, in the seat in front of the president, was wounded. Called by Lincoln the Presidential Continental, the car was built for the White House to Secret Service specifications by Hess and Eisenhardt of Cincinnati. It rode a 156-inch wheelbase, was 21 feet long overall, and weighed 7822 lb. The car had armor plating and two removable roofs—neither of the roofs were in place on this day.

1963 Mercury

1

2

Fresh idea, fresh roof, fresh air: Mercury's Breezeway Design

MERCURY

4

Mercury's new sizzler the...

Marauder

A new breed of scat!

Note the sleek, racy design of Mercury's newest hardtop: the 1963½ Marauder. Aerodynamic styling cuts air resistance, takes full advantage of Mercury's brilliant new V-8's.

No matter which Mercury V-8 engine you choose, you get brilliant performance! A big 390V-8 is standard on the Marauder hardtop model. On S-55 bucket-seaters, the standard engine is a 4-barrel Super Marauder 390V-8. Optional engines range up to a 427 V-8.

Marauder transmission choices include multi-drive Merc-O-Matic and 3- and 4-speed fully synchronized manual shifts. Looking for a top performer? See your Mercury dealer.

FACTS ON SUPER MARAUDER 427 V-8: Displacement: 427 cu. in. • 4.23 bore x 3.78 stroke • 425 hp @ 6000 rpm • 480 lb-ft torque @ 3700 rpm • dual 4-barrel carburetors • compression ratio 11.5:1 • mechanical valve lifters • fully synchronized 4-speed stick shift transmission.

5

At the top of the Mercury lineup was the Monterey. **1-2.** Thirteen models in all, the line included the $3650 S-55 hardtop coupe. It also was available in convertible and sedan form, and bucket seats were standard. **3.** Mercury got a copy of the bored-out 406 and offered this new 427-cid V-8 in any Monterey. Up to 425 bhp was available. **4.** Mercury's Breezeway power-retracting rear window provided great ventilation. **5.** A midyear addition was the Marauder, a slantback hardtop coupe in the mold of the Galaxie 500.

3

1963 Mercury colors

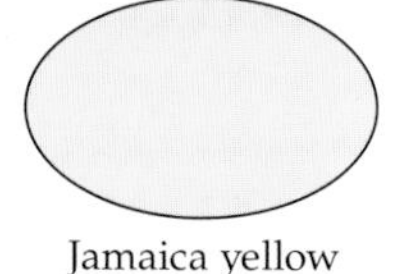

Jamaica yellow

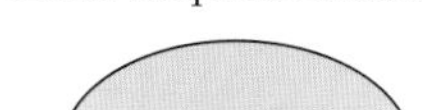

Ocean turquoise iridescent

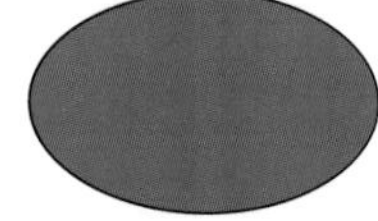

Carnival red

Blue satin iridescent

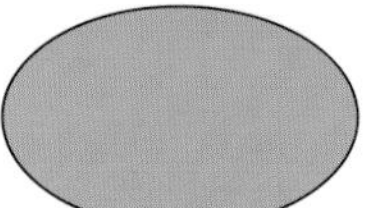

Desert frost iridescent

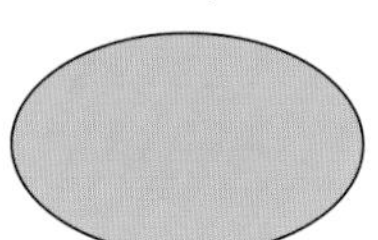

Castilian gold iridescent

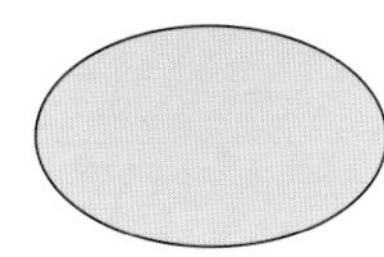

Pink lustre

Peacock turquoise

Pink frost iridescent

Cascade blue

1

2

3

4

5

Mercury's version of the Fairlane intermediate was the Meteor. Its 116.5-inch wheelbase was an inch longer than Fairlane's. Wagons used a 115.5-inch span. **1.** The S-33 hardtop coupe was Meteor's performance leader. **2.** The 4-door Custom Sedan was the sales leader, at 14,489 units. **3.** Custom Cruiser wagons were available in either 6- or 9-passenger configurations. **4-6.** Like Falcon, Comet added new front and rear styling, hardtops and convertibles, and bucket-seat S-22s. **7.** Sunoco and other gas stations let you "Dial Up" the octane level.

6

7

General Motors

GM management orders a halt to all corporate-sponsored race activity; Ford and Chrysler Corp. seize the chance to increase their performance profile, but GM remains U.S. sales leader

Buick introduces the stunning Riviera, a bold personal-luxury statement

Buick elevates the Wildcat from a trim option on the Invicta to its own model

Chevrolet redesigns the Corvette, creating the landmark Sting Ray; it's the birth of a classic sports car

'Vette gets independent rear suspension and its first coupe body style

Trusty Chevy Bel Air hardtop dropped after a 10-year model run

Cadillac builds its 2 millionth car since World War II

Oldsmobile adds four inches to the length of the F-85

Pontiac restyles full-size models; look includes trendsetting stacked headlamps

Pontiac's Tempest gains a 326-cid V-8 option, launches a separate Le Mans series

Pontiac offers optional transistorized ignition—an industry first

Alfred J. Fisher, namesake of the Fisher Body Co., a GM subsidiary, dies at age 70

1

2

The Buick Riviera was reborn for '63 as a stunning $4365 hardtop coupe artfully blending American and British style. Exactly 40,000 copies were built for the model year. This svelte personal-luxury hardtop coupe changed Buick's stodgy image almost overnight. The car was designed by GM styling chief William L. Mitchell and came to be considered among the best automotive shapes ever. Interestingly, Riviera was conceived as a LaSalle for Cadillac, but Buick sales needed a boost, so the Riviera it became. **1-2.** The Silver Arrow I show car was custom-built for Mitchell and toured the auto show circuit as a precursor to the Riviera. **3.** Inside, Riviera had an adjustable-tilt steering wheel that could be set to one of seven positions by the driver.

3

1

2

1-3. Riviera used a trim 117-inch wheelbase chassis shared by no other car, but it borrowed much of its running gear from existing Buicks, including finned aluminum brakes and its standard 325-bhp 401-cid V-8. An exclusive option on the 3988-lb coupe was a 340-bhp 425. This was the first mass-produced General Motors vehicle with frameless door glass.

3

1963 Buick

1

2

3

4

5

1-3. Buick's sporty Wildcat was promoted to its own model line and included this $3871 4-door hardtop, plus a new $3961 ragtop and $3849 2-door hardtop. The only engine was Buick's 325-bhp 401-cid V-8. **4.** Buick's largest car, Electra 225, had a 126-inch wheelbase. The convertible tipped the scales at 4297 lb. With the 425 V-8 reserved for Riviera, Electra made-do with the 325-bhp 401. **5.** Riding the same 123-inch wheelbase as the Wildcat, the lower-priced LeSabre came in convertible, hardtop, coupe, sedan, and wagon form. Hottest available LeSabre engine was a 280-bhp version of the 401. **6.** Though Buick production was up 58,292 units to 457,818, it held fast to sixth place in model-year output.

6

Buick's smallest car, the Special, kept a 112-inch wheelbase but got a new look that included slab bodysides. **1.** Atop the Special line was the Skylark series. Here's the $2857 Sports coupe. **2.** Even Wildcatters admired the $3011 Skylark ragtop. **3.** Special and Special Deluxe models used this 198-cid V-6. A 155-bhp 215-cid V-8 was optional. **4.** Skylarks got a 200-bhp 215. **5.** Prices were different in '63: milk was 69 cents a gallon and a double cheeseburger took a 59-cent bite out of your budget.

1963 Cadillac

1

2

3

Cadillac prices rose only slightly for '63, so it remained a hard-to-beat luxury value. The long-running Cadillac V-8 got its first major revision in 14 years. Cylinder size was unchanged, as were valves, rocker arms, heads, compression and connecting rods, but everything else was different. There was a lighter, stronger crankshaft, a stiffer block weighing 50 lb less, and relocated accessories. Displacement increased from 390 cid to 429. Horsepower was up a modest 15, but the engine was smoother and quieter by far. **1-2.** DeVille sat squarely in the middle of Cadillac's lineup. It came as a 2- and 4-door sedan, the latter with four or six windows, and as the top-trim Park Avenue 4-door hardtop. Cadillac's best-selling model at 31,749 units was this dashing $5386 Coupe DeVille. **3.** Cadillac advertising acknowledged without apology the "prideful" aspects of Cadillac ownership, though this one gave no explanation for the car's lights remaining on as its owner walked away.

1

2

CADILLAC OWNERS DON'T ALWAYS AGREE about why they
bought the car. A great many report that unexcelled craftsmanship and quality led them to the "car of
cars". Others say the size and solidity of the car, its silence and smoothness in motion, convinced them
to make the move. Still another group state their selection stemmed from the confidence and pride they
experience at the wheel of a Cadillac. The reasons are legion. But there is one subject upon which
Cadillac owners unanimously agree: the new 1963 car is the most rewarding possession a man can have.

1. Cadillac's marquee car, the Eldorado Biarritz, was facelifted along with the other 1963s and enjoyed the return of its Eldo name in block letters on the front fender. Caddy's other ragtop was in the Series 62 line, but it cost $1018 less than the $6608 Biarritz. **2.** Inside, all '63s put occupants behind a redesigned dashboard that brought the radio and heater controls closer to the driver. Narra wood trim was featured on Eldorado and Series 60 Special dashboards. **3.** Aftermarket suppliers were able to fit an automatic top and window-closing feature—long a dream feature of GM's Motorama shows—to the Cadillac convertibles.

3

1963 Chevrolet

1

2

The dramatic new Sting Ray, the first fully redesigned Corvette since the '53 original, was a big hit, with 21,513 sold, a 33-percent increase over 1962's record. **1.** Wheelbase was shortened 4 inches, to 98, the coupe body style debuted, and suspension was, for the first time, independent at the rear. Powertrains were carried over, with a 250-bhp 327-cid V-8 standard and up to 360 bhp available with the optional fuel injection. **2.** The '63 coupe was the only 'Vette with a "split" rear window and is coveted because of the sexy but visibility-reducing touch. **3.** Sales split evenly between the $4037 ragtop and the $4252 coupe.

3

1 2 3

4

1. *Route 66* took Tod Stiles and Buzz Murdock around America in an hour-long CBS-TV show that also was a celebration of the Corvette. For the '63 season, a Sting Ray replaced the pair's '62 convertible, and Glenn Corbett, as Lincoln Case (left), replaced George Maharis's Murdock as Tod's partner. **2.** This show car was a one-off custom 'Vette owned by former GM styling chief Harley Earl. **3.** An all-out racing car, the Grand Sport was developed by master Corvette engineer Zora Arkus-Duntov and designed to compete with the Ford Cobra. To qualify for production-class racing, 125 examples needed to be built, but GM's 1963 ban on racing forced Chevy to halt production after only five. **4.** The 6-cylinder-powered Nova 400 series was atop the Chevy II line. Flashier beltline strips and chromed rocker panel moldings set it apart from lesser models. Sadly, '63 would be the last year for the Chevy II convertible, which came only in 400 guise. **5.** News in the Corvair line included introduction of the Monza Spyder coupe and convertible with their 150-bhp turbocharged flat-6-cylinder engine and other performance features. This Monza ragtop carries the mid-level 102-bhp engine.

5

1963 Chevrolet

1. In addition to the Corvette, Chevrolet offered three different convertible lines in '63: the Impala, the Chevy II, and the Corvair Spyder. **2.** Full-size Chevys, like this Bel Air 4-door, got a clever going over for '63. With tasteful brightwork and alterations to bodyside contours, the change from the '62 models *looked* greater than it really was. **3.** Chevrolet still topped the sales charts with more than 2,148,000 sold. **4.** Car songs were all the rage in '63, and the Beach Boys immortalized Chevy's big V-8 with a bouncy little ditty called "409."

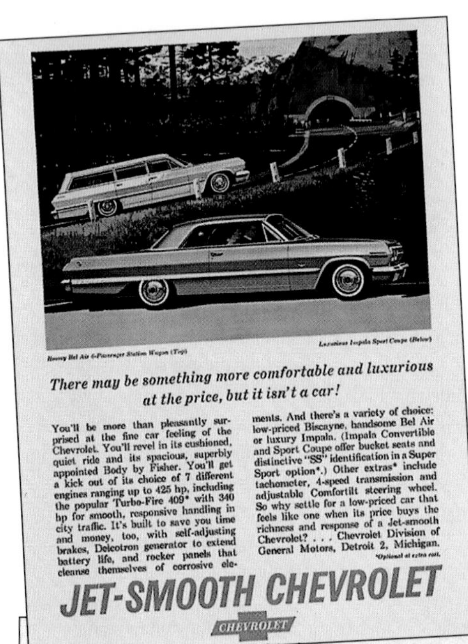

1

2

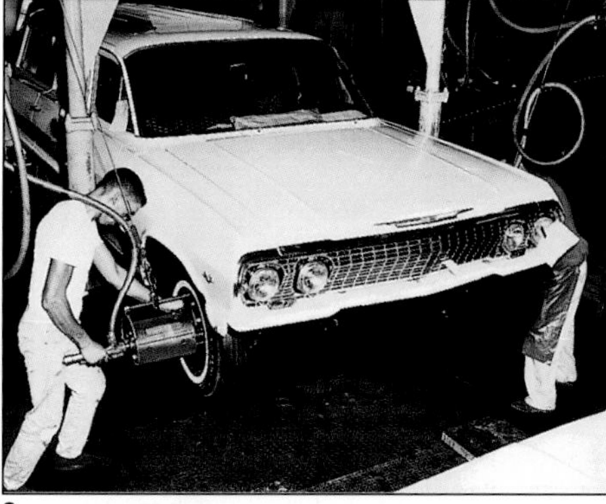

3

4

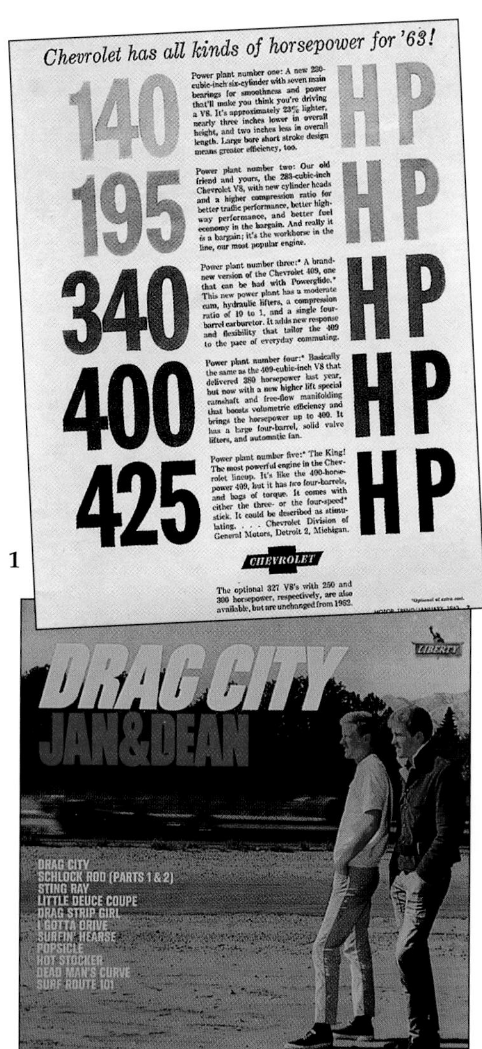

1

4

2

3

1. Chevy took a backseat to no one in its engine lineup. **2.** The 409-powered Impalas burned up drag strips. **3.** On the NASCAR circuit, however, Chevy lagged behind Ford and Chrysler. **4.** When surf-duo Jan & Dean sang about "Drag City," teens didn't think they were describing a dull burg. **5-8.** Once upon a time, moms walked their kids to school, car dealerships were clean and friendly, families relished outings to the country, and gas was 30 cents a gallon.

5

6

7

8

1963 Oldsmobile

1

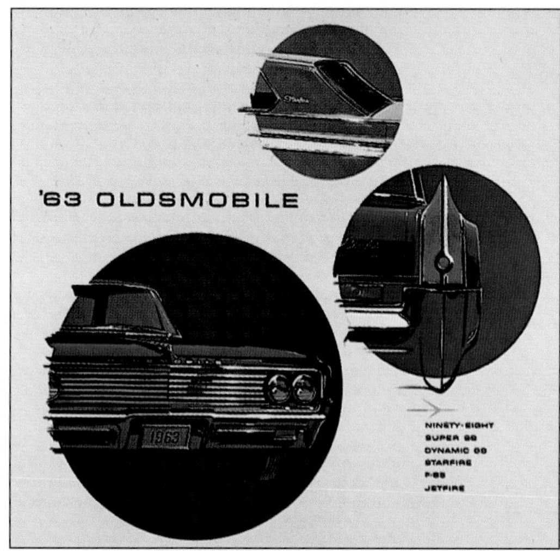

2

3

1-2. Oldsmobile's line changed little, with models still available in three distinct wheelbases. They were, clockwise from top right: the F-85 and Jetfire at 112 inches; Dynamic 88 and Starfire on a 123-inch chassis; and the top-of-the-line Ninety-Eight with a 126-inch wheelbase. All offered convertible and hardtop models, and the F-85 and 88 added wagons. **3.** Crisper styling, as on this Dynamic 88 Holiday hardtop coupe, helped boost Olds sales to 476,753. **4.** Through the '60s, Olds provided a new car for use by the winner of the Miss America Pageant. Here's 1963's victor, Jacquelyn Mayer, of Sandusky, Ohio, with her Ninety-Eight. **5.** The $3748, 4247-lb Dynamic 88 Fiesta wagon, with 3878 sold, was the rarest '63 Olds.

4

5

1

2

3

1-2. Starfires continued as hardtops and convertibles with a 345-bhp 394-cid V-8. **3.** The Ninety-Eight Holiday Sports coupe cost $4178. **4.** Olds helped welcome Americans to their new homes in the suburbs. **5.** El Torero toured the auto show circuit in '63. It was a gold Ninety-Eight convertible with gold leather and baroque trim panels. **6-7.** The "Pocket-Rocket" Jetfire continued with its hardtop styling for '63. Sales of this $3048 turbocharged coupe rose a bit to 5842 units for what would be this model's last year.

4

5

6

7

1963 Pontiac

Youthful and energetic, Pontiac's 1963 restyle was one of the era's benchmarks. **1-2.** The full-size models' stacked headlights would be copied by other cars. Here's the Bonneville in convertible and coupe form. **3.** The division saw its highest model-year production to date, 589,294, under the leadership of general manager E. M. "Pete" Estes. **4-6.** Grand Prix continued on its 120-inch wheelbase; other big Pontiacs were at 123.

2

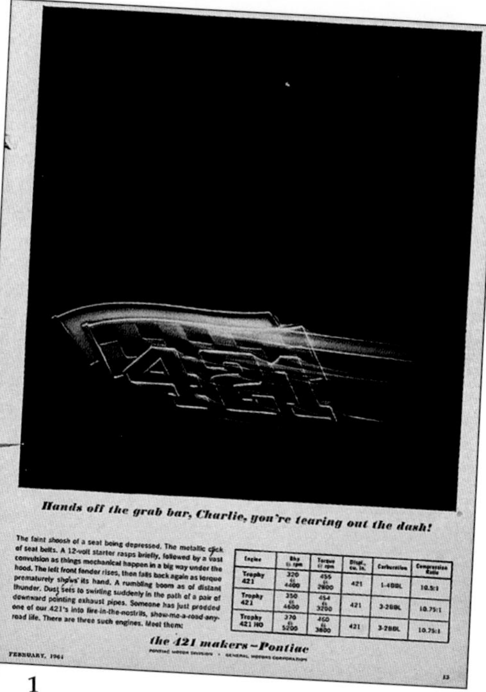

1

1-3. A 421-cid V-8 remained Pontiac's top engine. It delivered up to 410 bhp in "High Output" tune with two 4-barrel carbs. So equipped, the Catalina Sport hardtop was a terrific blend of speed and style. **4.** At 3685 lb, the Catalina 2-door sedan was the lightest full-size Pontiac. Factory-available aluminum front-body pieces, even "Swiss Cheese" frames with holes cut out, reduced weight even more. A Super Duty Catalina could do 0–60 mph in 5.2 sec and the quarter mile in 13.7 at 107 mph. **5.** Pro drag-race versions did the quarter in 12 sec at 116 mph, while Joe Weatherly won the oval-track crown in a '63 Catalina prepared by Bud Moore. **6.** The aftermarket was first with FM car radios, but the automakers were close behind.

3

4

6

5

1963 Pontiac

1

2

3

1-2. Like its Buick and Olds sisters, Pontiac's 1963 Tempest was squared up and slightly bulked up on an unchanged 112-inch wheelbase. It remained the only one of the trio with a rear transaxle. The sporty LeMans became a separate series this year with a $2418 hardtop coupe and this $2742 convertible, of which 15,957 were sold. Power options ranged from a lowly 115-bhp 195-cid 4-cylinder to a husky 260-bhp 326-cid V-8. **3.** Tempest production slumped by nearly 12,000 units, but at 131,490, sales were still healthy. **4.** Because the Tempest was nearly 1000 lb lighter than a comparable Catalina, it was also a fine choice for acceleration mavens. Roadgoing Tempests could now be ordered with the 326-cid V-8, but this specially built drag racer shoehorned in the 421. It was not legal for the public highway.

4

Studebaker Corporation

Studebaker President Sherwood Egbert, ill with cancer, steps down in November and is replaced by Byers A. Burlingame

In December, Studebaker ends U.S. automobile and truck production in South Bend, Ind., consolidating output of a reduced model range in its small Canadian plant in Hamilton, Ontario

Automotive division posts net loss for the year of approximately $28 million; production declines more than 20 percent as Studebaker sells just 69,555 cars for the model year

The stunning Avanti finally debuts—almost a year late; offers a selection of 289-cid V-8s, with or without a supercharger

Similar engines are optional in Lark V-8 and Hawk models

Four-speed automatic transmission becomes available on select V-8 Larks

Wagonaire wagon gets a rear roof panel that slides forward to accommodate tall loads

Hawk gets new front styling, but that doesn't stop sales from toppling nearly by half, to 4634 units

Studebaker begins installation of front seatbelts in March 1963; other automakers follow suit starting in '64

1

2

3

4

1-3. Shown in '62, but delayed by production problems until 1963, Studebaker's Avanti wowed with its unique Raymond Loewy styling, aircraft-inspired 4-seat interior, and ample V-8 power. It had a fiberglass body and was built on a Lark convertible frame shorted to a trim 109-inch wheelbase. Avanti—Italian for "forward"—was supposed to save Studebaker, but it was too little too late. The car was picked to pace the 1962 Indy 500, but when the Memorial Day classic rolled around, Studebaker had to replace the unfinished car with a Lark—and so went a huge publicity opportunity. Price was a reasonable $4455, but only 3834 were produced for '63. Still, the look was captivating, the performance outstanding, and the car gained a loyal following. Two versions of Studebaker's aging-but-reliable 289-cid V-8 were offered: a 240-bhp edition called the R1 and a supercharged 290-bhp edition called R2. The R2 could go 0–60 mph in 7.3 sec and topped out at 117 mph. **4.** Loewy dressed up this Avanti for his personal use.

1963 Studebaker

1

2

4

1. Sales of the Lark compact dropped 21 percent, to 74,201, despite more cosmetic tweaks. Here's the Daytona 2-door hardtop. **2-4.** The Custom 2-door was less flashy, but this one packs the 290-bhp R2 option, so it was quite fast. Avanti suspension and disc brakes, plus bucket seats were included on a midyear model called the Super Lark. **5.** Lesser Larks, like this Custom 4-door, continued as utilitarian values.

3

5

Studebaker 1963

1

1. Pride of the Lark line, the Daytona convertible, cost $2805. Only 1015 Lark ragtops were sold in 1963, making it rarer than the Avanti. 2. Studebaker's proving grounds near South Bend, Ind. 3. In Studebaker's eyes, the Cruiser was not a Lark at all. 4-6. A '63 Studebaker novelty was the Wagonaire wagon. Its keen sliding rear roof section was unfortunately prone to water leaks. This is the top-line Daytona version, which sold for $2835 with the base 180-bhp 259.2-cid V-8.

2

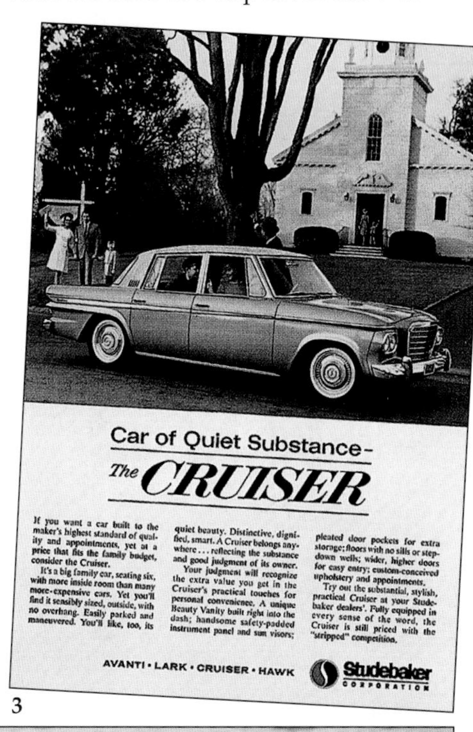

3

4

5

6

Etc.

Craig Breedlove is the first American since 1928 to hold the world land-speed record; his jet-powered Spirit of America skims across Utah's Bonneville Salt Flats at 407.45-mph

Willys Motors, Inc., changes its name to Kaiser Jeep, Corp.; Jeep introduces Wagoneer station wagon

Ford driver Fred Lorenzen is the first NASCAR competitor to win more than $100,000 in prize money in a season; he collects $122,587 but finishes third in the point standings

Formula 1 World Champion Jim Clark of Scotland serves notice that mid-engine cars are the wave of the future by finishing second in the Indy 500; his 1300-lb British-built Lotus packs a 376-bhp 255-cid Ford V-8

Seven states register more than 3 million new cars; in descending order, they are California, New York, Pennsylvania, Ohio, Texas, Illinois, and Michigan. California registrations total nearly 7.7 million

U.S. Commerce Department says no "Negro businessman" owns a new-car franchise

Service customers at Blauschild Chevrolet in Cleveland are greeted by cute "Chevyettes" serving coffee, cookies, and pastry

New-car leasing takes hold; typical monthly payments range from $100 to $200

1

1. Named for Britain's World War II fighter, the Spitfire was Triumph's small sports car; it had 63 bhp and cost $2000. **2.** Ford of England's Hooper-bodied Capri seemed an amalgam of early-'60s Dodge, Plymouth, and Olds pieces. **3.** Resembling a scaled-down '48 Ford, Volvo's PV544 helped established the Swedish marque in the U.S. **4.** Beetle sales in the U.S. topped 200,000 for the first time. The '63 had 40 bhp and cost $1595. **5.** Saab dealers sold the Quantum, a Massachusetts-made roadster powered by Saab's 42-bhp, 2-stroke 3-cylinder.

2

3

4

5

1

2

3

4

5

1. Form met function at Checker. **2.** Teamster boss Jimmy Hoffa checks out the PF Sigma safety car, designed by Italy's Pininfarina. **3.** Parnelli Jones held off Jim Clark for his only Indy 500 win. **4.** Roger Moore of TV's *The Saint*, and Volvo's P1800. **5.** *The Young Racers* was filmed at Europe's Grand Prix tracks. **6.** Dawn of the sport-utility vehicle: Jeep's Wagoneer debuted.

6

Etc.

Unscrupulous VW dealers in Los Angeles install 1963 taillight assemblies on 1959 Beetles and pass them off as new cars

Safety Council of Greater St. Louis sponsors a Safe Driving class for women

Toyota introduces the restyled Toyopet Crown De Luxe; top speed is 75 mph

The top Rolls-Royce model, the Phantom V limousine, retails for $27,617; Rolls and companion Bentley get dual headlamps for the first time

Roll-down windows are made available on the International-Harvester Scout

The Sports Car Club of America (SCCA) crowns its first woman class champion, Donna Mae Mims (H-production)

Thieves steal the safe of a Mission, Kansas, Chevy dealer, hoisting and driving it off with one of the dealership's own tow trucks

Top 10 Selling Imports

1. Volkswagen 240,143
2. Renault 22,621
3. MG 21,270
4. Triumph 20,117
5. Volvo 14,175
6. Fiat 10,805
7. Mercedes-Benz ... 10,378
8. Austin-Healy 8348
9. Jaguar 4421
10. Saab 4117

Total import-car share of U.S. market: 5.10 percent

The record-shattering sales of the 1963 model year were topped in '64, when nearly 7.9 million new cars were sold, an unprecedented gain. Beneath the consumer optimism, though, was growing trepidation about Vietnam, where increasing numbers of American servicemen were dying at the hands of Communist forces. In major policy speeches early in the year, President Johnson emphasized civil rights, anti-poverty programs, education, and the fight against Communism. He seemed confident his "Great Society" could be realized.

On July 2, barely a month after the murder of three civil-rights workers in Mississippi, LBJ signed the landmark Civil Rights Act of 1964. That didn't stem racial unrest that was beginning to erupt in violence in some American cities. In October, the Rev. Martin Luther King, Jr., won the Nobel Peace Prize.

November's presidential election saw Johnson and running mate Hubert Humphrey win in a landslide over Republicans Barry Goldwater and William Miller.

A respite from the traumas of assassination and war came on the evening of Sunday, February 9, when the Beatles made their first appearance on CBS-TV's *The Ed Sullivan Show*. The British foursome's first album, *Meet the Beatles*, rocketed to No.

1 and produced "I Want to Hold Your Hand," "All My Loving," and "I Saw Her Standing There." In short order, "Beatlemania" was in full swing while music-scene observers debated the band's talents and likely staying power. The British Invasion took off with the Rolling Stones ("It's All Over Now"), the Dave Clark Five ("Glad All Over"), the Animals ("House of the Rising Sun"), and the Searchers ("Needles and Pins").

From Detroit came The Supremes ("Baby Love"), the most successful of the new girl groups; others were the Ronettes ("Be My Baby") and the Shangri-Las ("Leader of the Pack"). Surf-sound duo Jan & Dean had hits with "Dead Man's Curve" and "The Little Old Lady from Pasadena." Bob Dylan's *The Times They Are A-Changin'* was a Top 20 album.

Fashion reflected the bold colors and patterns of Pop Art and became more self-consciously "youthful" than ever before. Millions of boys annoyed their parents by adopting shaggy Beatle haircuts.

At Miami Beach, a gifted young boxer and brilliant self-promoter snatched the World Heavyweight Championship from Sonny Liston. His name was Cassius Clay.

The St. Louis Cardinals downed the Yankees in the World Series; and the Cleveland Browns upset the Baltimore Colts to take the NFL crown. The U.S. dominated the Summer Olympic Games in Tokyo.

American Motors Corporation

Coming off its all-time-high sales year, AMC's turf is threatened by the Big 3's emerging "senior compact" class while its image clashes with America's burgeoning infatuation with youth-oriented performance machines

Digging in its heels, AMC unveils its best compact ever, the redesigned Rambler American

The new American is the work of designer Richard Teague, who discards the boxy 1961–63 look for breezier styling so good it survives until decade's end

Teague extends the American's wheelbase but keeps the body overhangs short; Rambler's smallest car is now a genuine 6-passenger automobile

The mid-line Classic gets a new engine, the Torque Command six; it's standard on a sporty midyear model called the Typhoon

Classic offers its first 2-door hardtop body style

The flagship Ambassador drops its entry 880 line for a single deluxe 990 trim level and adds a 2-door hardtop

Despite record production of the new American, total Rambler output falls 12 percent; still, the marque maintains its eighth-place standing among domestic makes

1

To create the pretty, new American, Teague cut four inches from the front structure of the 1963 Rambler Classic and got a 106-inch wheelbase chassis. That increased the wheelbase by six inches, but overall length grew by just four. **1.** A full range of body styles was offered in three levels of trim: 220, 330, and 440. All used a 195.6-cid 6-cylinder that, depending on the model, had 90, 125, or 127 bhp, peaking at 138 on the top-of-the-line 440-H hardtop. **2.** Prices started at $1964 and topped out with this $2346 ragtop that came only in 440-level trim.

2

1

2

3

4

1-2. AMC hooked a fastback roof onto the American and landed the Tarpon. This show car would shortly lead to a production model. **3.** Carrousel made the show circuit as a gilded Classic wagon. **4.** Air conditioning was still a luxury, so wagon owners often rolled down the rear window for ventilation. This optional aluminum screen kept kids from leaning out the open portal. **5.** Tough? Ask the dad who owns one.

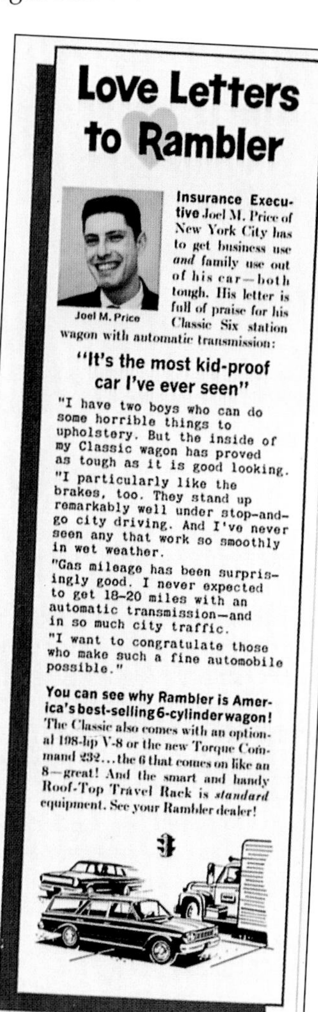

5

1964 AMC

1

2

An AMC executive once asked George Romney if he cared that Ramblers always seemed to be in the highway slow lane. "No," replied Romney, "just so long as there are a lot of them." That focus on staid, sensible cars blurred under Romney's successor, Roy Abernethy. Evidence was found in the Classic line, which, since 1956, had offered only pillared sedans and wagons with 6-cylinder engines. A V-8 was available for 1963, and for '64, a stylish 2-door hardtop made the scene. It came only in top-grade 770 trim starting at $2397. **1.** Aft of the front wheel is a badge showing that this hardtop has the 198-bhp 287-cid V-8. Bucket seats and floor console also were available. **2.** To publicize Classic's new 145-bhp 232-cid Torque Command 6-cylinder engine, AMC at mid-season unveiled this special black-over-Solar-yellow hardtop. It was called the Typhoon and started at $2509. **3.** They didn't look it, but AMC execs were excited when Rambler number 3 million, a nice Classic wagon, rolled off the Kenosha line. Classic production was 206,299 for '64.

3

1

2

3

The new Classic pushed Ambassador upmarket, eliminating the 880 series. All were now 990s powered by the 327-cid V-8. **1-3.** A 2-door hardtop joined up and was the basis for the line-topping 990-H. It had a sporty cabin and 270 bhp, up from the standard 250. **4.** In its last year on a 112-inch chassis, Ambassador production fell to 18,519, lowest of the decade. This $2985, 3350-lb 4-door was the only wagon offered.

4

Chrysler Corporation

Chrysler Corporation continues to recover from its 1962 disaster; sales increase for each of its divisions

Chief stylist Elwood Engel redoes the Imperial in the mold of the '61 Continental he created for Lincoln

Highlight at Plymouth is the springtime introduction of the Valiant-based Barracuda; it has the decade's first fastback roof

Mainstream Plymouths are restyled; 2-door hardtops get reverse-slant rear roof pillar

Going into the last season of its styling cycle, the Chrysler lineup gets only a cosmetic touch-up but continues to close the sales gap on Cadillac

Standard-size Dodges are restyled, finally shedding remnants of the Exner look; reverse-slant rear roof pillar is used on 2-door hardtops

Dodge Dart gets a mild facelift, but the division does not get a version of the fastback Barracuda

Chrysler relaunches its hemispherical combustion-chamber V-8, now as a 426-cid beast for racing only; it takes two Plymouths and a Dodge to a 1-2-3 finish in the Daytona 500

Chrysler also fashions a new V-8 from its 318-cid unit; the 273-cid V-8 would serve through the end of the '60s

1

1. Thin horizontal bars refined New Yorker's grille. Sales rose 10 percent, and this 4-door sedan, at 15,443 units, was the most-popular model. Chryslers used three V-8s. The Newport had a 265-bhp 361 and the 300 models a 305-bhp 383. The third was a 413-cid that made 340 bhp in the New Yorker and either 360 or 390 in the 300K. **2.** Chrysler was still the only manufacturer to offer a 5-year/50,000-mile warranty and attributed much of its sales increase to this coverage. **3.** The Silver 300 was a midyear special available only in silver with a black vinyl roof and leather and vinyl interior.

MOVE UP TO CHRYSLER '64

Engineered better . . . backed better than any car in its class

CHRYSLER DIVISION CHRYSLER MOTORS CORPORATION

2

3

2

1

3

1. The "regular" 300 series consisted of a 4-door sedan, 2- and 4-door hardtop, and this $3803 convertible. **2.** Non-letter 300s were not sports cars but found an SCCA event in which to shine. **3.** The genuine letter-series car for '64 was the 300K. It was a bona fide high-performance luxury machine available as a $4056 2-door hardtop or this $4522 ragtop. **4.** No wagon was more stylish than the $4828, 4395-lb 9-passenger New Yorker Town & Country. **5.** The Turbine wasn't a race car, but it played one in *The Lively Set* movie. **6.** Its 2-year run on a 122-inch wheelbase was closing, but New Yorker never felt small.

4

5

6

1964 Dodge

1

3

4

2

1. A "barbell" grille and wedgy rear-roof pillar helped identify Dodge's standard '64 models. They returned in 330, 440, and Polara series. Here's a Polara 500 hardtop. **2.** Exner's influence continued to fade as the pod-type instrument panel gave way to a full-width dashboard. The floor-shifted 4-speed manual and bucket seats were options. A column-shifted 3-speed manual was standard while the optional automatic transmission was in the final year with dash-mounted buttons. **3-4.** Dodge model-year output topped 500,000 for the first time in 1964.

1

2

3

4

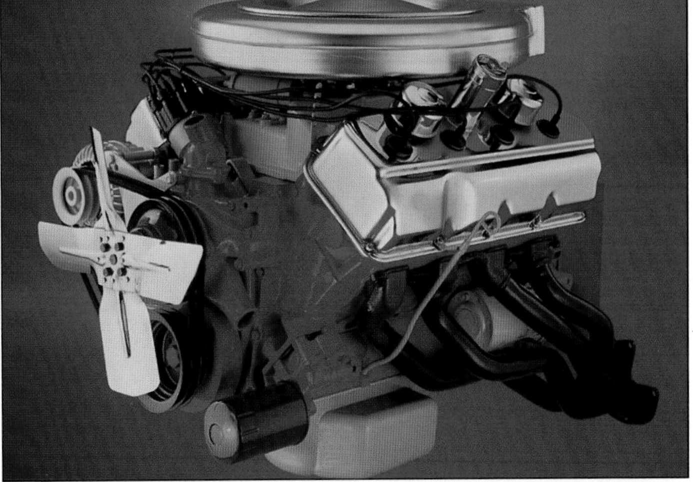

5

1-3. Factory-backed Dodges were drag strip terrors and included the Ramchargers team, Roger Lindamood's "Color Me Gone," and "Dandy Dick" Landy. **4.** The raucous 426-cid Wedge, with its rams-horn headers and up to 425 bhp, returned for its last year as an option in any standard Dodge. **5.** The mighty Hemi, a 426-cid V-8 intended for professional racing only, was rated at 425 bhp but had over 550. **6-8.** This drag-race-ready 330 has the Hemi, light-weight body panels and seats, and a trunk-mounted battery for better weight distribution. **9-10.** "The Little Old Lady from Pasadena" was a fictional street racer made real by Dodge public relations. **11-12.** When you got it, flaunt it.

6

9

10

7

8

11

12

1964 Dodge

1

2

3

1. Dodge had rushed its original 880 series into showrooms in mid-1962 and would retain it as its full-size line through '64. These final 122-inch-wheelbase models continued in base and Custom trim, all with a 265-bhp 361-cid V-8. **2.** The sole convertible came in Custom livery and retailed for $3264. **3.** For a reasonable $2977, the Custom 880 4-door sedan delivered a sense of spacious, low-key luxury. The 880s were intended to compete with lower-priced Mercurys, Oldsmobiles, Buicks, and even Chrysler Newports, with which they shared their basic design and running gear. **4.** Dart continued to do well and was for the first time available with a V-8. The new 180-bhp 273-cid engine was optional in any model—2- and 4-door sedan, 4-door wagon, and convertible—but 89 percent of Darts were still ordered with a Slant Six. Shown is the sporty GT coupe, which retailed for $2318.

4

1

2

Elwood Engel succeeded Virgil Exner in '61, and his Lincoln roots showed up in the formal lines of the '64 Imperial. Reinvigorated, its sales nearly doubled, to 23,295. **1.** The 2-door hardtop came in the "entry-level" Crown series and started at $5739. **2-3.** Crown also hosted the lone convertible, a $6003 beauty that weighed 5185 lb. All Imperials used a 340-bhp 413-cid V-8. **4.** A Crown ragtop gives some comfort to entertainer Eddie Fisher, whose wife, Elizabeth Taylor, dumped him for her *Cleopatra* co-star, Richard Burton, in '64. **5.** The $18,500, 6100-lb limo's 149.5-inch wheelbase was 20 inches longer than other Imperials'.

3

4

5

1964 Plymouth

1

2

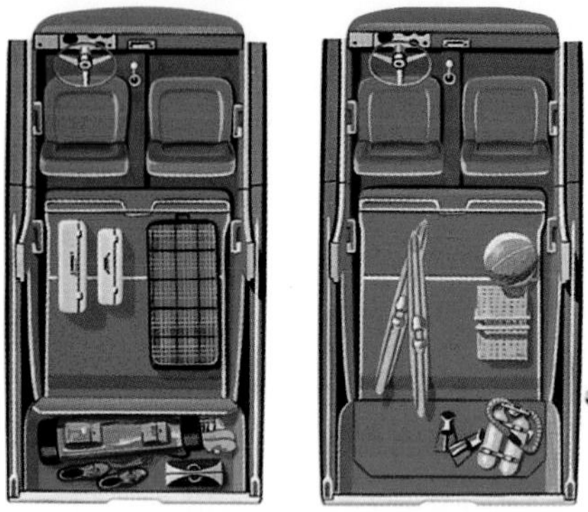

3

4

5

6

1-2. Launched on April 1, 1964, two weeks before the Mustang, Barracuda could be considered America's first pony car. It certainly was the decade's first fastback sporty model, beating the Mustang 2+2 by a number of months. What it lacked, at least initially, was the Ford's jaunty styling or performance flavor. **3-4.** Badged Plymouth Valiant Barracuda, the new car was nothing more than a Valiant compact with a new roof, though it did boast a 172.5-cubic foot cargo hold with a useful fold-down rear seat. **5-6.** It shared Valiant's assembly line, and also its running gear, including Slant Sixes of 101 and 145 bhp, and the new 180-bhp 273 V-8. **7.** Though they paraded at the Daytona speedway, Barracudas were not race-car quick; a V-8 could do 0–60 mph in an uninspiring 12.9 sec.

7

1

2

3

4

6

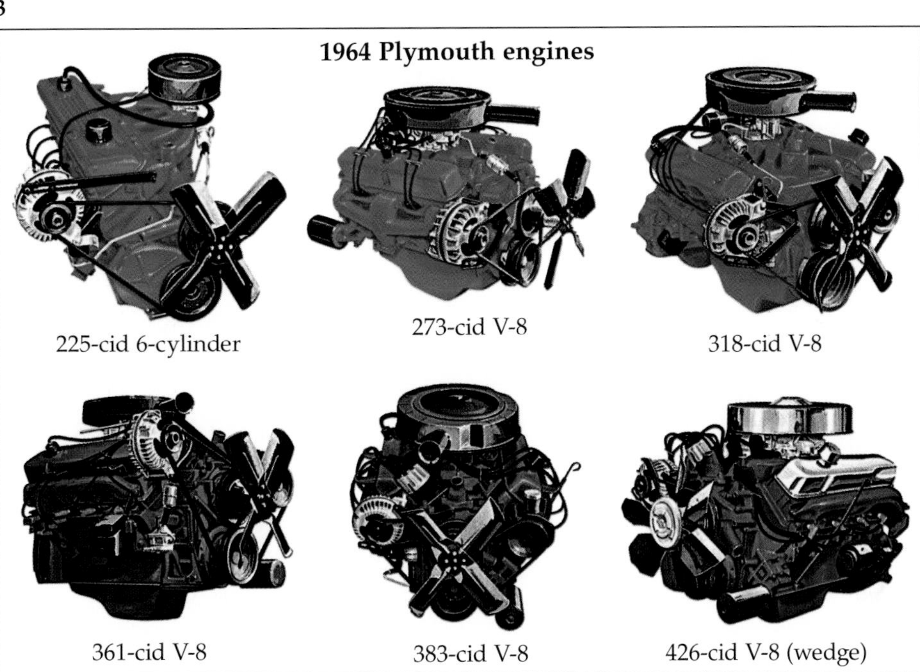

5

7

Cleaner styling helped standard-size Plymouths look a lot better on their carried-over 116-inch wheelbase. **1.** Despite a strong focus on performance, the workaday 4-door sedan was the most-popular body style, as on this Belvedere. **2.** Tough, inexpensive, smartly sized outside, large inside—Plymouth sedans made perfect urban taxis. **3.** A Dodge Polara (left) and a Plymouth Fury flank the new 426-cid Hemi. The racing V-8 took a young Plymouth driver named Richard Petty to the 1964 Daytona 500 winner's circle. **4.** Plymouth's sporting image made a fine foundation for promoting other performance products, such as Hurst transmission linkages. **5.** The regular-production engine lineup: Slant Six (101–145 bhp); 273 V-8 (180 bhp); 318 V-8 (230 bhp); 361 V-8 (265 bhp); 383 V-8 (305–330 bhp); and the tamer new version of the 426 wedge-head V-8, a 365-bhp 4-barrel called the Street Wedge. **6.** Fury coupes started at $2598 with the six, $3212 with the 318. **7.** A Street Wedge Sport Fury did 60 mph in 6.8 sec.

1964 Plymouth

1

2

3

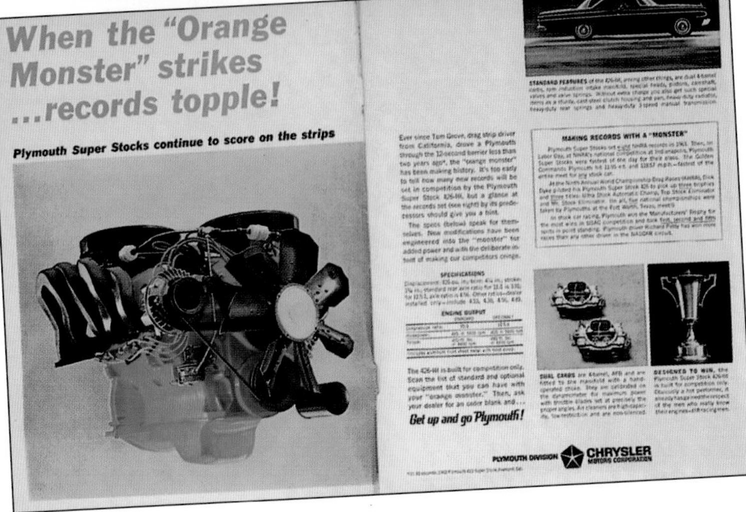

4

5

6

1-4. It was intended for competition, but anyone could order Chrysler's strongest regular-production engine, the dual 4-barrel, 425-bhp 426-cid "Maximum Performance" Wedge V-8. Matched with a 4-speed manual and bucket seats, it made the Sport Fury a stylish and swift street racer. **5.** Professionally prepared Max Wedge Plymouths shot drag racers like "Golden Commando" Bill Shirley through the quarter-mile in 11.5 sec at 116 mph. **6.** Meanwhile, Hemi Plymouths, such as Paul Goldsmith's No. 25, and Dodges, like Bobby Isaac's No. 26, were hitting 174 mph on the big NASCAR ovals. **7.** The Satellite II show car looked to the future with a sort of targa roof.

7

Ford Motor Company

Ford changed the industry with the April 1964 introduction of an inexpensive but exciting new sporty car, the Mustang; officially, it was a 1965 model, so it appears in this book under that model year

"Total Performance" theme revs up; factory-backed cars race at LeMans, Monte Carlo, Indianapolis, on drag strips, and in NASCAR

Motor Trend names the entire Ford lineup "Car of the Year" citing "engineering advancement based on high-performance testing in open competition"

Full-size Fords are fully reskinned; some consider them the prettiest Fords of the 1960s

Fourth-generation Thunderbird arrives with new sheetmetal, goes on to break the 1960 model's sales record

Ford-brand sales increase, but the make slips even further behind rampaging Chevrolet

Mercury celebrates its 25th Anniversary and reshuffles its lineup to become a clearer step-up from Ford and a more solid player in the medium-priced class

Lincolns look little different but are given a longer platform and taller body to provide more interior space

1

1. Even Ford's compact was into performance. Eight Falcon teams ran the Monte Carlo Rally; one finished second overall, another won the GT class. **2.** Falcon kept a 109.5-inch wheelbase but got its first restyling. Sporty Sprint hardtops and convertibles had a 260-cid V-8 that was optional in other Falcons in place of sixes. **3.** Base and Futura models returned. The best-selling Falcon, 38,032 units, was this Future sedan. It listed for $2165 with the V-8. **4.** Mustang meets the press in April. This book covers the Mustang starting with the 1965 Ford models.

2

3

4

1964 Ford

1

1-2. A freshened Fairlane freed of its fins remained a healthy seller at 277,586 units. 3. Fit fiberglass body pieces, gut the interior, and install a competition 427-cid V-8 estimated at 500 bhp and voila: the Thunderbolt. 4. In theory, a T-Bolt was available to anyone for $3900, but just 54 were built, all aimed at professional drag racing, where they ran the quarter-mile in the mid-11-sec range at 123 mph. 5. Theoretically, anyone with $20,000 could also buy a Ford GT40, but these too were specially built racers. With a competition small-block Ford V-8 mounted behind the 2-seat cockpit, GT40s won Daytona and Sebring in '64 but got beat at LeMans. 6. Shelby's Cobra was available to the public for about $6000 and was also a sports-car-racing champion celebrated in song. It now used the 289 V-8. 7. A winning race-track record gave Ford's 1964 advertisements credibility.

2

3

4

5

6

7

1

2

3

1. Styled with aerodynamics in mind, the '64s were among the best-looking big Fords of the decade. Jewel of the line was again the Galaxie 500XL. A 138-bhp six was standard in most full-size Fords, but XLs came with a 195-bhp 289 V-8. With the optional 300-bhp 390, the 2-ton XL did 0–60 mph in 9.3 sec; with the 425-bhp 427, it did it in 7.4 sec. **2.** Sales of 58,306 made this year's $3233 hardtop the most-popular XL ever. **3.** Thin-shell buckets were a new XL item. **4.** The 500XL hardtop continued to be paired with a convertible. It started at $3495. **5.** Galaxie sedans had an un-racy roof. **6.** Off-loading new cars was an art. Convertible tops were carefully wrapped at the factory. **7.** Ned Jarret was foiled in the Daytona 500, but Ford won 30 of 62 NASCAR contests.

4

5

6

7

1

2

3

FLIGHT PLAN CLEARED—PROCEED TO THUNDERBIRD
Move the Swing-Away steering wheel over, slide into the cockpit—
and you're ready to soar. New "shell-design" contoured front seats
cradle you in luxurious comfort—and give rear seat passengers more
foot room. On the flight deck a warning light reminds you to fasten
the retractable seat belt. Optional lights tell you when fuel is low,
when a door is ajar. A unique new Silent-Flo ventilation system controls cabin atmosphere. Try the irresistible surge of a 300-h.p.
Thunderbird V-8, the incomparable smoothness of an in-flight ride
and you'll know why...other cars you drive...this one you Thunderbird!

Thunderbird *unique in all the world*

A PRODUCT OF Ford MOTOR COMPANY

4

1. Open 'til midnight! Clean used cars! Like-new '63 Fords! Even a late-model Valiant! Clean, of course! **2.** Thunderbird kept its 103-inch wheelbase but gained a new body. The basic hardtop started at $4486 and accounted for 65 percent of sales. **3.** A vinyl roof and coach bar mark the Landau model, which cost $103 more than the basic hardtop and took 25 percent of sales. **4.** "Personal luxury" was the theme. Gone was the optional 340-bhp 390-cid V-8, leaving a 300-bhp version as the sole engine. The cabin was more opulent, with standard perks such as an automatic parking brake release, though still optional were air conditioning ($415), power windows and seats ($290), and leather ($160). It was a smart approach. Sales jumped 32 percent, to 92,465. **5.** The ragtop listed for $4953, but there was no Sports Roadster model.

5

1

2

3

4

1-2. Continental's classic lines lent themselves to custom coachwork, such as this one-of-a-kind Town Brougham. A window divided its rear cabin from the open chauffer's compartment. **3-4.** Continental underwent its biggest change since '61, but Lincoln was careful to maintain the car's look and character. The wheelbase was stretched 3 inches, to 126, improving rear-seat entry, rear leg room, and cargo space. Head room also grew, but classy curved side glass gave way to cheaper flat panes. The 320-bhp V-8 remained. Weight was up 119 lb, to 5055 on the hardtop and 53 lb, to 5393 on the convertible. Base prices rose only $22, now $6292 for the closed car, $6938 for the ragtop. It all paid off in a 14-percent jump in production to 36,297, Lincoln's best model year since 1957.

1964 Mercury

1

2

3

4

Another facelift helped disguise Ford genes, but the bigger change was in attitude. Mercury's full-size line demoted Monterey to the base series and revived the Montclair and Park Lane badges. The repositioning didn't translate into increased sales, though. **1-4.** Unique breezeway backlights returned, but the coolest Merc was the Marauder fastback, available with two or four doors in all three series. This Bittersweet Coral coupe from the Montclair family packs the 300-bhp 390-cid V-8. Top available mill was Ford's 425-bhp 427. **5.** Mercury was well represented in this "wagon train" of Ford employees who trailered to the New York World's Fair.

5

1

2

The Falcon-based Comet divided into four series: 202, 404, Caliente, and Cyclone. **1.** The 404 Villager wagon was the costliest: $2734. **2-3.** At $2126, cheapest was the 2-door 202 sedan. **4.** Comet spoke Total Performance with a version of the Fairlane Thunderbolt drag racer. **5.** All T-Bolts were sedans, but the 427-cid V-8 was installed in a Comet wagon, too. **6.** Ronnie Sox and his 427 hardtop were champs with a 11.4 sec, 123-mph quarter-mile run.

3

4

5

6

General Motors

GM accounts for 51 percent of domestic car production

This is GM's year of the intermediate; Oldsmobile-Buick-Pontiac compacts are enlarged, and Chevy introduces its first mid-size car

Every Buick except Riviera gets larger; two new engines bow, a 225-cid 6-cylinder and a 333-cid V-8

Cadillac is restyled, and for the last time has tailfins; the new climate control system maintains a set temperature regardless of the weather

Chevy's version of the new intermediate is the Chevelle; it's a first-year hit, outselling Corvair and Chevy II, as well as the Ford Fairlane

Chevy division sales top 2.3 million—380,000 more than Ford Motor Company's total

Oldsmobile sales increase slightly, but the division drops from fifth to seventh among U.S. makes in production; Jetstar debutes as a new full-size price leader; the 4-4-2 bows as the first modern Olds muscle car

Pontiac ignites the muscle-car age with the GTO, a high-performance version of its revised Tempest intermediate

Chevy and GMC introduce new compact cargo and passenger vans; they're essentially front-engine versions of the old Corvair-based rear-engine models

1

2

3

1-2. Sergio Pininfarina, of the famous Italian design house, called the original Riviera "one of the most beautiful American cars ever built." Except for revised badging and detail trim, its appearance was unchanged for its second season. Underhood, the 425-cid V-8 replaced the 401 as the standard engine. It had 340 bhp with the 4-barrel carb, or 360 with the optional dual 4-barrel setup, and provided 0–60 mph acceleration in under 7 sec. Riviera retained exclusive use of a 117-inch-wheelbase chassis. Base price was $4385. **3.** Electra 225 continued as the full-size flagship on a 126-inch wheelbase. This is the $4070 2-door hardtop.

1

2

1. Invicta retired, leaving LeSabre and Wildcat as the mainline big cars. Differing mainly in trim—and that only LeSabre had a wagon—they shared a 123-inch wheelbase and revised bodies longer by 3.2 inches, to 218.9. LeSabre's base engine was the 300-cid V-8. On Wildcats, such as the 2-door hardtop pictured, the 401 was standard and the 425 optional. **2.** Service technicians were mechanics in 1964. **3.** Just 7181 sunlovers bought the $4374, 4280-lb Electra 225 ragtop. **4.** The Special/Skylark line added 3 inches of wheelbase, to 115, and new bodies 11.4 inches longer, at 203.5. A 155-bhp six was standard, a 210-bhp 333 V-8 was a $70 option. **5.** Wagons came as Specials and the flashier Skylark Sport Wagon, which featured this novel Skyroof. **6.** Buick's least-expensive convertible was this $2605 Special.

3

5

4

6

1964 Cadillac

1

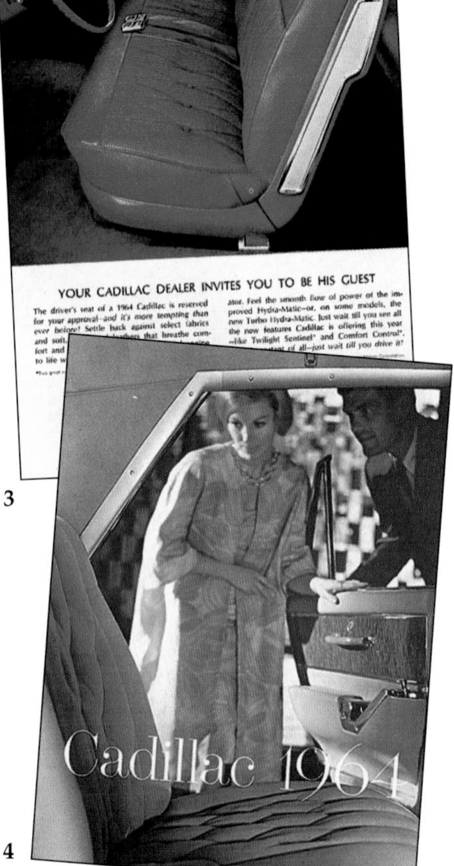

3

4

2

5

1-2. The most sober-looking Cadillacs in years had just a hint of tailfin, as seen on this $6233 Fleetwood Series 60 Special. **3-4.** Spacious rear seats were a tradition, and for '64, prospective buyers were invited to sample new features, such as Twilight Sentinel automatic headlights and Comfort Control, the industry's first fully automatic automotive heating and air conditioning system, which maintained a selected temperature year-round. **5.** Even the Standard of the World could be humbled by a Midwest winter.

1-2. Cadillac's most-prestigious 2-door, the Eldorado, abandoned the Biarritz part of its name and took up with the Fleetwood family, as evidenced by the Fleetwood rear-fender crests. And after years of looking a lot like other Caddy ragtops, the $6630, 4605-lb Eldo was individualized by full rear-wheel cutouts sans fender skirts—the only '64 so styled. More significantly, it shared with all Cadillacs a V-8 enlarged from 390 cid and 325 bhp to 429 cid and 340 bhp. Already decent performers, Cadillacs could now do 0–60 mph in an impressive 8.5 sec, though fuel economy fell from around 13 mpg to 10 mpg. **3.** If one had to inquire as to the fuel economy of the 5300-lb 9-passenger limo, one didn't really merit this $9939 automobile, now did one?

1

2

3

1

2

1-2. Chevelle answered the Ford Fairlane and was Chevy's first mid-size car. It used the new corporate 115-inch chassis and offered a convertible, which Fairlane did not. Engines ranged from a 120-bhp six to a hot 300-bhp 327-cid V-8. **3-4.** Malibu Super Sports were the performance models. **5.** The base 300-series sedan rivaled the Impala for interior room. **6.** Wagons came in Malibu trim, too. **7.** The El Camino was another body style Fairlane didn't have.

3

4

5

6

7

1

2

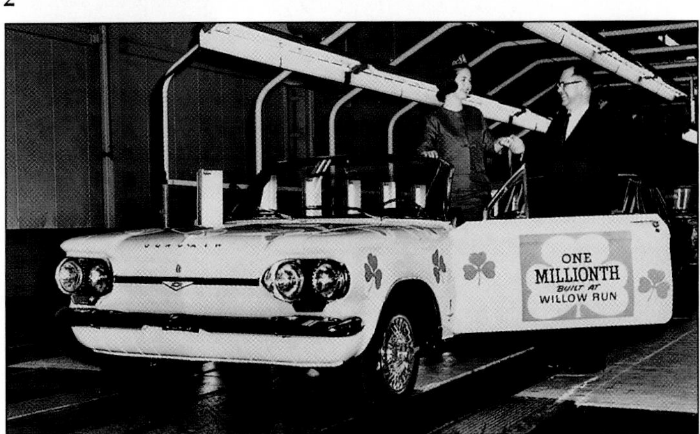

3

4

1. Corvair, Chevy II, Chevelle, and Impala gave Chevrolet a car in every high-volume market segment. **2.** Suspension changes helped tame Corvair's sometimes-odd handling, and the engine grew from 145 cid to 164. It had 95 bhp in base form, with the sporty turbocharged Monza, here in convertible form, getting 150 bhp. **3.** A Corvair inched off the Willow Run line on St. Patrick's Day as the plant's one-millionth car. **4.** Italian designer Battista Pininfarina (center) and GM styling chief Bill Mitchell (right) look over the experimental Corvair-based Super Monza. **5-6.** Sales of 333,000 Chevelles took a toll on Chevy II sales, which slid 51 percent. The convertible was gone, but the compact was for the first time offered with a V-8, the 195-bhp 283. It gave a little car some punch.

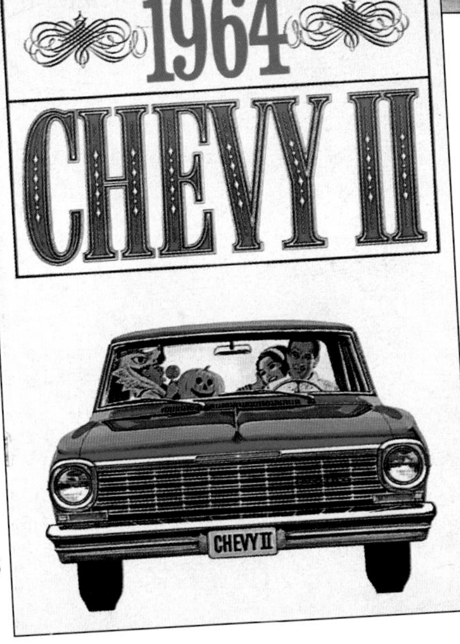

5

6

1964 Chevrolet

Go ahead and let them think you splurged

The new Chevrolet offers you more luxury, more style in the most luxurious Chevrolet ever built. Featuring famous Body by Fisher...rich and spacious interiors... seven engines to choose from and a whole line-up of options to satisfy any whim. All at a reasonable Chevrolet price!

With all the luxury the '64 Chevrolet offers, you'll wonder how we kept the price as nice as it is.

Look inside and you'll find generous foam-cushioned seating...yards and yards of attractive new fabrics and extra-soft vinyls . . . deep-twist carpeting from door to door.

Get in for a spin and you'll learn just how responsive this great highway performer can be. Chevrolet's exclusive Jet-smooth ride is mainly the result of hefty coil springs at all four wheels taking the brunt of road shocks. You have a choice of seven engines, ranging from 140 hp to 425 hp.* And this year, more optional equipment choices* help you get everything you'd like in a car. Things like: Comfortilt steering wheel, AM-FM radio, Automatic Speed and Cruise Control.

Any car this luxurious should have its price examined. See your Chevrolet dealer. He loves to have his cars examined. . . . Chevrolet Division of General Motors, Detroit, Michigan.

CHEVROLET

'64 JET-SMOOTH LUXURY CHEVROLET

1

2

3

1. Chevy built 1.6 million Biscaynes, Bel Airs, and Impalas this year. The majority were 4-doors, and the most glamorous of these was this Impala hardtop called the Sport Sedan. It cost $2742 with the base 140-bhp 6-cylinder, $2850 with the 195-bhp 283-cid V-8. **2.** Squared-up styling marked the '64s. This is an Impala. **3.** The Super Sport graduated from a trim package to a series. Its 2-door hardtops and convertibles came with sixes or V-8s and got unique SS badges, trim, and wheelcovers. **4.** At the dawn of the car-stereo age was this aftermarket item described as a "cartridge tape player." **5-6.** Chevy's bottom-feeder big car was the $2363 Biscayne 2-door sedan. This particular example harbors the optional 425-bhp 409-cid V-8, 4-speed manual, tachometer, and radio delete. Wanna run?

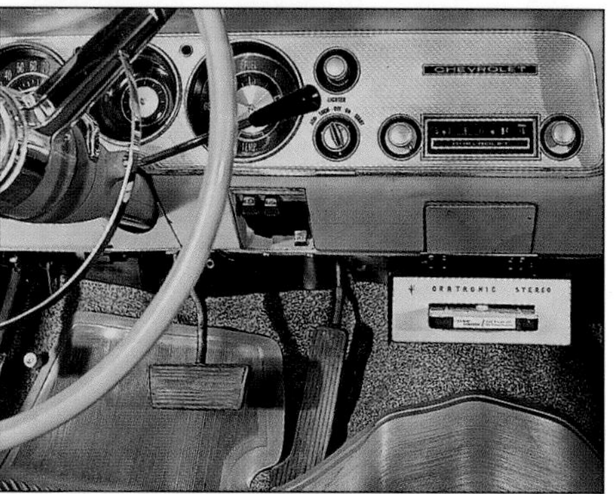

4

5

6

1

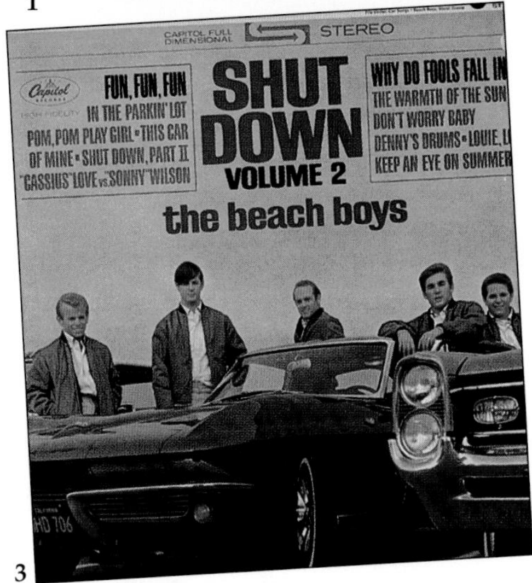

3

2

4

5

1-2. From most angles, the '64 Corvette was barely distinguishable from the ground-breaking '63, but it was easily identified from the rear, where the glass was now an uninterrupted span. Bowing to the argument that the '63's "split window" design was bad for outward visibility, Chevy eliminated the backlight's center spine. That improved visibility but also robbed the car of one of its more dramatic touches. **3.** Still, the 'Vette was plenty sexy enough to make the cover of this 1964 Beach Boys album—even though the featured tune, "Fun, Fun, Fun," was about a cool kitten gettin' her kicks until daddy took the T-Bird away. **4.** This experimental mid-engine "Corvette" featured 4-wheel drive, but the proposed 2-seat endurance racer never competed. **5.** Today, it's a collector's item. In '64, this 'Vette was a daily driver stained by salt and shorn of wheelcovers.

1964 Oldsmobile

1

2

3

4

Sales rose slightly to 494,000, but Olds slipped from fifth to seventh in the production race. **1.** More-conservative styling didn't help, though this Ninety-Eight ragtop didn't hurt for presence. **2.** Donna Axum, from El Dorado, Ark., copped the crown at the Olds-supported Miss America pageant. **3.** Ninety-Eights renewed their 126-inch wheelbase. This was the Custom Sports Coupe. **4.** Other big Oldsmobiles continued on a 123-inch chassis, and star of the bunch was the bucket-seat Starfire, back again as a convertible and this coupe. **5.** With sales of 147 new cars per dealer, Olds ranked ahead of only Cadillac (88) in GM.

5

1

3

2

4

5

1. Least-costly big Olds was the new Jetstar 88 series; here's the $2984 rag-top. **2.** Olds' top V-8 was the 345-bhp 394. It was available in all big cars save Jetstar. **3-4.** To confuse matters, the Jetstar I was a sort of cut-rate Starfire within the Dynamic 88 series. **5.** The F-85 ascended to GM's new 115-inch wheelbase and its highlight was the 4-4-2 option package. It stood for 4-barrel carb, 4-speed manual gearbox, and 2 (dual) exhausts, and included a 310-bhp 330-cid V-8. **6.** This shop gave S&H Green Stamps. **7.** Skylights came to the F-85 on the Vista Cruiser wagon.

6

7

1964 Pontiac

1

2

3

4

1. Tempest shelved its transaxle design for GM's conventional new intermediate chassis, then set the automotive world afire with the GTO. **2.** By stuffing its big 389-cid V-8 into a mid-size model, Pontiac created the first modern muscle car. **3.** It hoped to sell 5000 '64 GTOs, but the "Goat" struck a chord, and 32,450 were ordered. **4.** A GTO helped set a new Pontiac model-year production record.

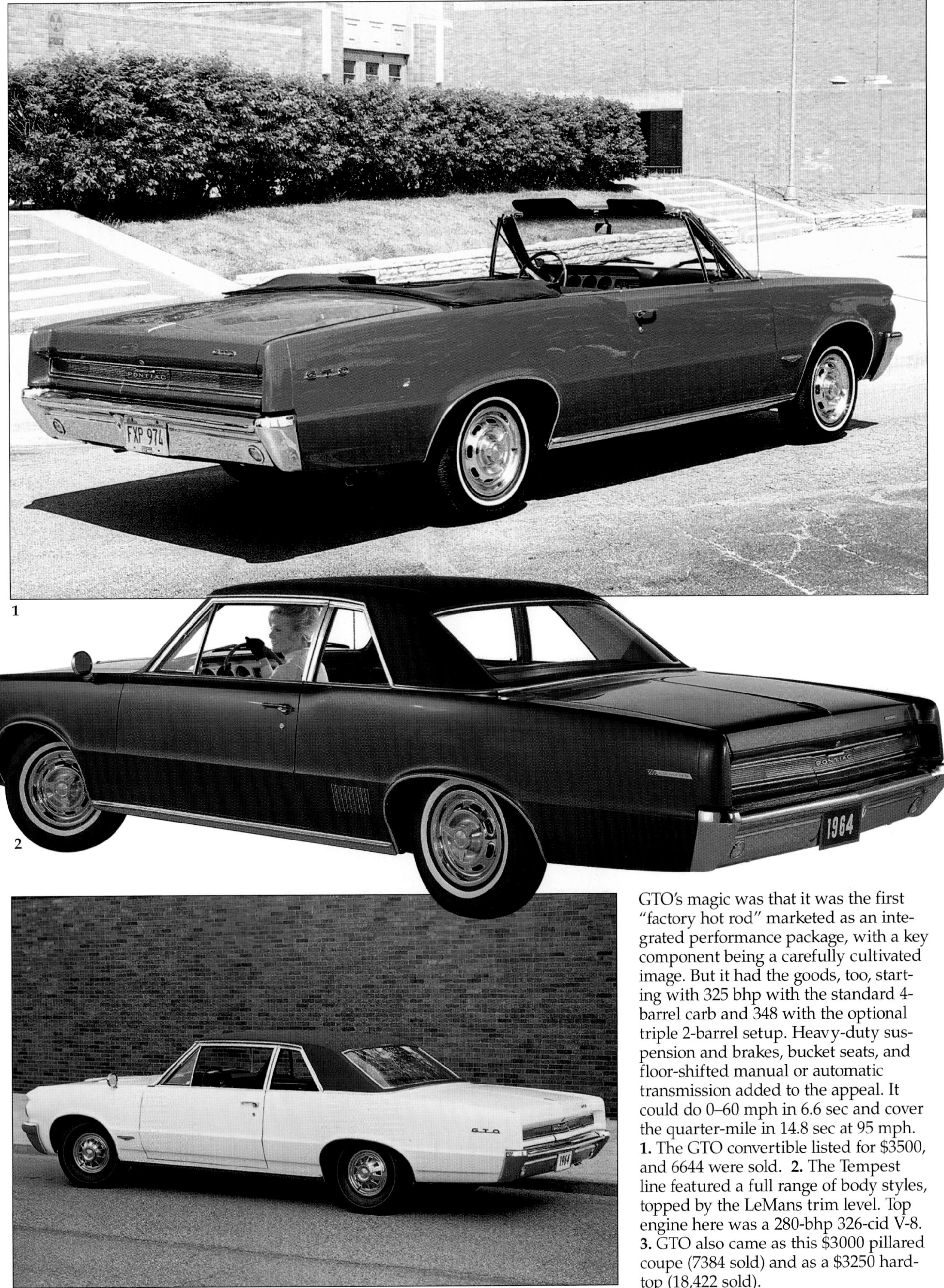

1

2

3

GTO's magic was that it was the first "factory hot rod" marketed as an integrated performance package, with a key component being a carefully cultivated image. But it had the goods, too, starting with 325 bhp with the standard 4-barrel carb and 348 with the optional triple 2-barrel setup. Heavy-duty suspension and brakes, bucket seats, and floor-shifted manual or automatic transmission added to the appeal. It could do 0–60 mph in 6.6 sec and cover the quarter-mile in 14.8 sec at 95 mph. **1.** The GTO convertible listed for $3500, and 6644 were sold. **2.** The Tempest line featured a full range of body styles, topped by the LeMans trim level. Top engine here was a 280-bhp 326-cid V-8. **3.** GTO also came as this $3000 pillared coupe (7384 sold) and as a $3250 hardtop (18,422 sold).

1964 Pontiac

1

2

3

1-2. Big Pontiacs got terrific new styling with stacked headlamps and a clean tail. All used a 389-cid V-8. This Catalina has the hot tri-carb version. **3.** A 20-percent jump in production, to 736,317, helped Pontiac strengthen its hold on third place in the industry. **4.** Very little was done to the already beautiful Bonneville ragtop to create the Club De Mer show car. **5.** No American automaker was doing a better job projecting a hip, young image in tune with the tone of the mid-1960s. **6.** Full-size models had a sophisticated-but-sporty cachet of their own.

4

5

6

Studebaker Corporation

The corporation is now in retreat; production shifts to the Canadian assembly plant, prestige models are phased out, morale fades

Production of '64 models splits between the South Bend plant and the Hamilton, Ontario, facility; total model-year output sinks 48 percent, to just 36,697

Assembly of Avantis, Hawks, Lark Challengers, and trucks is not shifted to Canada plant, so 1964 editions of these models are not built after late December '63

Brooks Stevens works his wizardry one more time, revamping the Lark again; in a desperate try to fashion a progressive image, Lark name is removed from all "Lark" models; public still calls them Larks, however

Avanti fades out of production with no break between the serial numbers of 1963 and 1964 models

Hawk gets detail changes and an optional half-vinyl roof for its swan song

The R1 and R2 289-cid V-8 engines from the Avanti are made available on all Studes

Andy Granatelli prepares a Daytona hardtop with the 335-bhp supercharged 304.5-cid R3 V-8; *Hot Rod* magazine gets 0–60 mph in "around six seconds flat," making it the world's quickest compact car

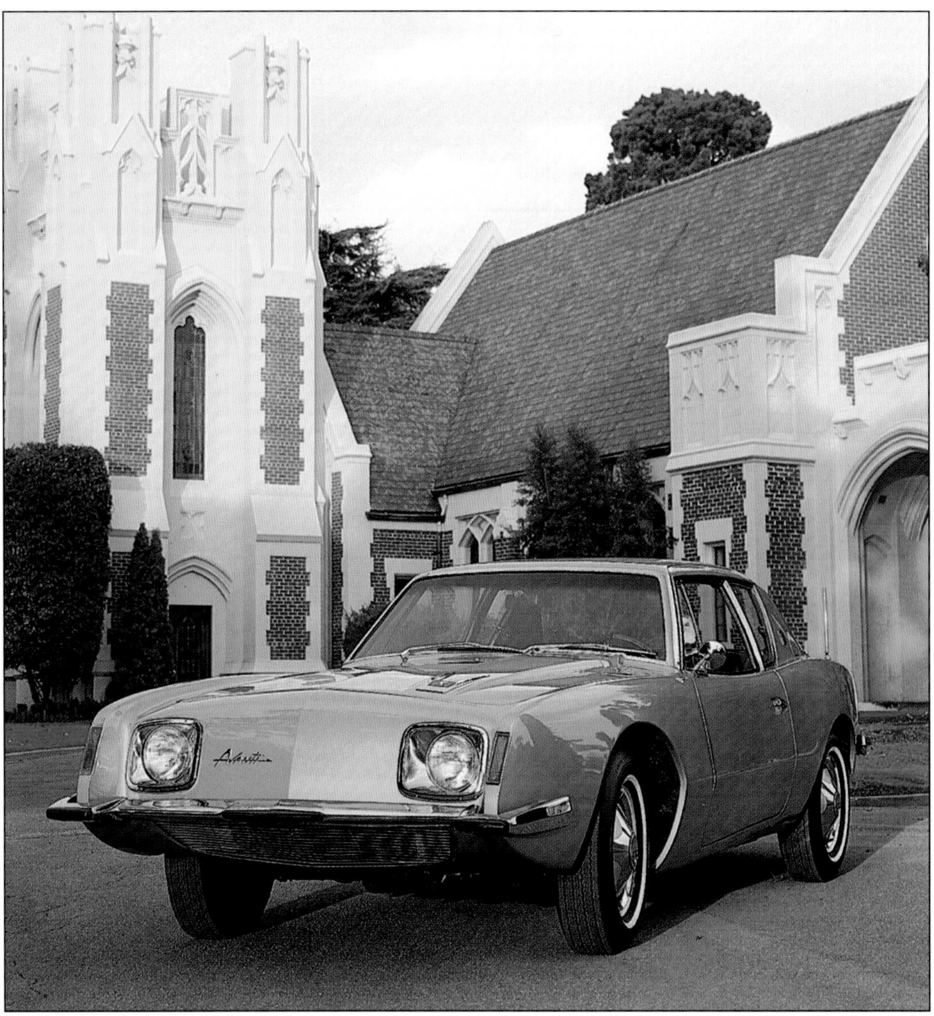

1

1-2. Avanti closed out its two-year Studebaker life in 1964. The company was loose with the car's model-year demarcations, preferring instead to institute running changes. For example, of the 809 built as "1964" models, about 60 had the round headlamp bezels associated with the '63s. Underhood, the 289-cid V-8 carried over in 240-bhp R1 tune and in optional supercharged 290-bhp R2 form. Nine '64s got the 335-bhp supercharged 304.5-cid R3 V-8. Engineer Andy Granatelli's R3 prototype did 168 mph on the Bonneville Salt Flats. Avanti's base price was $4445 for both of its Studebaker seasons. The R2 was $210 extra, a 4-speed manual added $188, and power steering $77. Studebaker ended Avanti production in late '63, but entrepreneurs would keep building the car in small numbers for years, usually with Chevy power and with little-altered styling.

2

1964 Studebaker

1

2

3

4

Larks got fresh bodywork but no longer wore the Lark name. They were instead badged by their trim-level designations: Challengers, Commanders, and Daytonas in 6- and 8-cylinder form, and the V-8 Cruiser sedan. **1-2.** The pretty Daytona ragtop cost $2670 with the 112-bhp six, $2805 with the 180-bhp 259-cid V-8. **3.** Most-expensive sedan was the $2603 Cruiser. **4.** This Daytona drag racer had the 290-bhp 289 R2. **5.** The Daytona 2-door hardtop came only as a V-8 model.

5

1

2

3

1-2. Four-doors and wagons used a 113-inch wheelbase, 2-door models a 109-incher. Here's the Daytona sedan, which started at $2318. **3.** Studebaker resurrected the Commander name for its mid-level compacts, an appellation last used in 1958. This is the 2-door version. **4.** The Granatelli-Paxton supercharger-STP connection led to an association with racing, though this Indy 500 roadster was powered by a Novi V-8. **5-6.** Hawk production totaled 79,615 since the sport coupe took wing in 1955. It ended with a final 1767 units for '64. The $2966 base price included a 210-bhp 289 V-8.

4

5

6

Etc.

Scientists in San Antonio predict that cars of the future will run on "gasoline bricks"

Richard Petty clinches his first NASCAR season championship in a year that claims the lives of three hero drivers: Fireball Roberts, Joe Weatherly, and Jimmy Pardue

SS Automobiles President Brooks Stevens unveils the Excalibur sports car, a Mercedes SSK replica built on a Studebaker Daytona chassis and powered by a Corvette V-8

The first Datsuns arrive in the Midwest, embarking at Muskegon, Michigan, for distribution through a 13-state area; body of the Datsun 410 sedan has been styled in association with Italy's famed Pininfarina design firm

At the Bonneville Salt Flats, Art Arfons aboard the Green Monster jet car sets a world land speed record of 536.7 mph; rival Craig Breedlove's Spirit of America loses steering and brakes at over 500 mph and rockets into a nearby lake; Breedlove extricates himself from the submerged cockpit unhurt

Porsche unveils its 911 series; the rear-engine design and basic styling would survive into the late 1990s as a sports-car classic

Top Toyota executives meet in Houston to discuss American-market expansion plans

1

2

1-2. Two from Hollywood's *The Lively Set*: hot rod trouble; the Chrysler Turbine goes racing. **3.** Surf's up for Frankie and Annette in *Muscle Beach Party*. **4.** Jaguar's 3.8S sedan used the XK-E's 6-cylinder. **5.** Excalibur Series I SSK was a retro Mercedes. **6.** Cheetah racers had Corvette running gear. **7.** LBJ and Lincoln, Phoenix. **8.** Stuffing a Beetle with college kids was good, clean '60s fun. **9.** The aluminum-bodied Apollo 3500 GT ran a Buick V-8.

3

4

5

6

7

8

9

1

2

1. A. J. Foyt ran a conservative pace and outlasted Rodger Ward's rear-engine racer to win at the Brickyard. Foyt's Offy-Watson was the last front-engine car to win the Indy 500. **2.** Lap belts were increasingly common as factory equipment in new cars, though shoulder belts were still somewhat of a novelty. Both were made mandatory by law in January 1968. **3.** Late in 1964, Jeep CJ-5s were shipped from Kaiser-Jeep's Ohio plant for January 1965 Inauguration duties in Washington. **4.** Porsche's mid-engine 904 GTS was designed as a race car but was legal for the street. It cost $7500 and used a 180-bhp 122-cid 4-cylinder to go 0–60 mph in 6.4 sec and hit 150 mph.

3

4

Etc.

The Indianapolis 500 suffers one of its most deadly crashes with a fiery collision at the end of lap 2; rookie Dave MacDonald's hard-to-control rear-engine racer hits the wall, triggering a 7-car accident that claims his life along with that of driver Eddie Sachs and seriously injures driver Ronnie Duman; it takes 1 hour, 45 minutes to restart the race

The Cord Sportsman bows in Tulsa, Oklahoma; the scaled-down replica of the classic Cord of the '30s has a plastic body of material made by the U.S. Rubber Co.

A three-wheel electric car manufactured in Long Beach, California, the Marketour, runs with six heavy-duty batteries that power a 36-volt motor; range is 35–40 miles

A baby Cobra, the Sunbeam Tiger roadster, debuts; the Anglo-American hybrid built by England's Rootes Group has a 260-cid Ford V-8 of 164 bhp; does 0–60 mph in 9.5 sec and costs $3499

Top 10 Selling Imports

1. Volkswagen 307,173
2. MG 24,128
3. Triumph 21,214
4. Renault 18,432
5. Volvo 17,326
6. Opel 14,077
7. Mercedez-Benz ... 11,234
8. Simca 9606
9. Fiat 8988
10. Austin-Healy 8397

Total import-car share of U.S. market: 6.0 percent

1965

Although car sales reached another all-time high—8.8 million units—General Motors was embarrassed during auto-safety hearings in Washington. GM chairman Frederic Donner and president James Roche appeared evasive and uninformed when Senator Robert F. Kennedy and other Congressional questioners accused GM of doing almost nothing to improve the safety of its cars. The hearings helped force GM and the rest of the domestic auto industry to commit massive resources to safety research.

Meanwhile, Washington's optimism that it could step out of Vietnam's civil war as easily as it had stepped in was shrinking. U.S. bombing of the North and of Viet Cong strongholds in the South did nothing to diminish the Communists' appetite for fighting. In November, 35,000 anti-war activists marched on Washington.

That wasn't America's only civil unrest. Rioting, looting, and arson tore open the predominantly black Watts section of Los Angeles, even in the wake of President Johnson's August 6 signing of the Voting Rights Act of 1965.

When government-mandated health warnings appeared on cigarette packs, smoking was suddenly a no-no. But a new technology, computer dating, was in. Kids loved the Super Ball and a simple board on skates, both introduced by the Wham-O toy company. Women's skirts got shorter, men's hair grew longer, and The Beatles were named to the Order of the British Empire for their contribution to the UK's economy. The Fab Four released *four* albums: *Beatles '65, Beatles VI, Help!* (the soundtrack from their second film), and *Rubber Soul*. Petula Clark scored with "Downtown," the Rolling Stones with "(I Can't Get No) Satisfaction," and James Brown with "Papa's Got a Brand New Bag."

Top films ran the gamut from the wholesomeness of *The Sound of Music* to the swingin' sexiness of *Darling;* the western comedy of *Cat Ballou* to the downbeat social drama of *The Pawnbroker*. James Bond's *Thunderball*, was a smash, as was *Repulsion*, a clever, disturbing thriller directed by Roman Polanski.

American Motors Corporation

The effects of Roy Abernethy's strategy to compete with the Big Three on all fronts takes shape

Ambassador is restyled on a longer wheelbase; adds a convertible body style

Ambassador sales reach an all-time high of more than 64,000 units

Classic is also restyled; wheelbase remains 112 inches, but body is longer and tail shows a squared-off profile similar to that of the larger Ambassador

Classic adds a convertible body style along with a larger optional V-8

All "high performance" V-8s are available with a 4-speed manual transmission

Intended to ride the wave of popularity enjoyed by a new breed of sporty cars like the Ford Mustang and Plymouth Barracuda, the Marlin boasts a fastback roofline and sporty touches

Rambler American earns top marks for economy in the highly respected Mobilgas Economy Run and Pure Oil Performance Trials

Despite record Ambassador sales, overall Rambler production is down significantly for the model year and profits tumble

1

1. Marlin was built on the 112-inch Classic chassis, losing some of the appeal of the similarly styled Tarpon show car, which used a 106-inch Rambler American chassis. **2.** Unlike most fastbacks, Marlin provided good rear-seat headroom for adults. **3.** Unusual two- and even three-tone paint schemes were available. The trunklid was very narrow—only the black-painted area opened. At $3100, Marlin was AMC's most-expensive car. Sales were a respectable 10,327.

2

3

1

2

3

4

5

1. Rambler tripled its convertible offerings with the addition of the Ambassador (foreground) and Classic (right) ragtops to the existing American (rear). Base prices were $2955, $2696, and $2418, respectively. **2.** Rambler's 1965 advertising slogan, "The Sensible Spectaculars," seemed almost contradictory—if not in terms, then certainly to the marque's image. **3-5.** Even the little American could be quite flashy in top-line 440 trim.

1

Selected 1965 AMC Engines

195.6-cid 6-cylinder

195.6-cid 6-cylinder (aluminum block)

327-cid V-8

3

2

1-2. To long-time customers who cherished Rambler's stodgy image, the company's foray into flash and dash didn't set well. Worse, trying to match the Big 3 model for model with dressier and more powerful offerings would prove impossible given AMC's limited resources. The restyled Classic was a case in point. Clean lines and the addition of a convertible did nothing for its popularity, and sales fell 4 percent in an otherwise robust market. Prices started at $2142 for a 550 2-door sedan. **3.** Through 1963, the Classic had been available only with 6-cylinder engines, the Ambassador only with V-8s. That changed in '64 when V-8s were available in the Classic, and changed again in '65 when a six was made standard in the Ambassador. Engines ranging from 128 to 270 bhp were offered in the Classic for '65. **4.** Traditional Rambler fare is represented by this Classic 770 Cross-Country wagon, the most expensive in the line at $2727.

4

1

2

3

4

5

1. Ambassador's redesign brought squared-up lines with stacked quad headlights—elements that also turned up on large Fords and Plymouths this year. **2.** Helped by roomier new packaging on a 4-inch longer chassis, Ambassador production more than tripled, to 64,145. **3.** The 5-millionth AMC—an Ambassador sedan—makes its way through the Kenosha plant. **4.** At $2970, the priciest Ambassador was the 990 Cross Country wagon. **5.** Two Ambassador hardtops were offered: the 990 at $2669 and the 990H for $2837. Still, AMC's foray into the sport/luxury field wasn't a successful one. **6.** The 990H's posh bucket-seat interior was indeed inviting, but only 5708 buyers accepted the invitation.

6

Chrysler Corporation

Chrysler and Plymouth sales soar on the strength of new designs; Dodge dips slightly, while Imperial drops about 20 percent

Chrysler brand records its highest annual production to date and passes Cadillac for the first time since the mid-1950s

Chryslers wear new slab-side, square-corner Elwood Engel styling

Famed Letter-series closes out its run with the 300L

Imperials get glass-covered headlights

Mid-size Dodges drop two inches in wheelbase and resurrect the Coronet name, last used in the 1950s

Full-size Dodges gain two inches in wheelbase and add a luxury Monaco model

Plymouth continues the Belvedere name—another 1950s moniker—for a line of restyled intermediates

Plymouth's redesigned full-size Fury paces the Indianapolis 500

Sporty Plymouth Barracuda adds a performance-oriented Formula S model

426-cid Hemi V-8 goes into "semi production," being offered in special mid-size Dodges and Plymouths built for drag racing

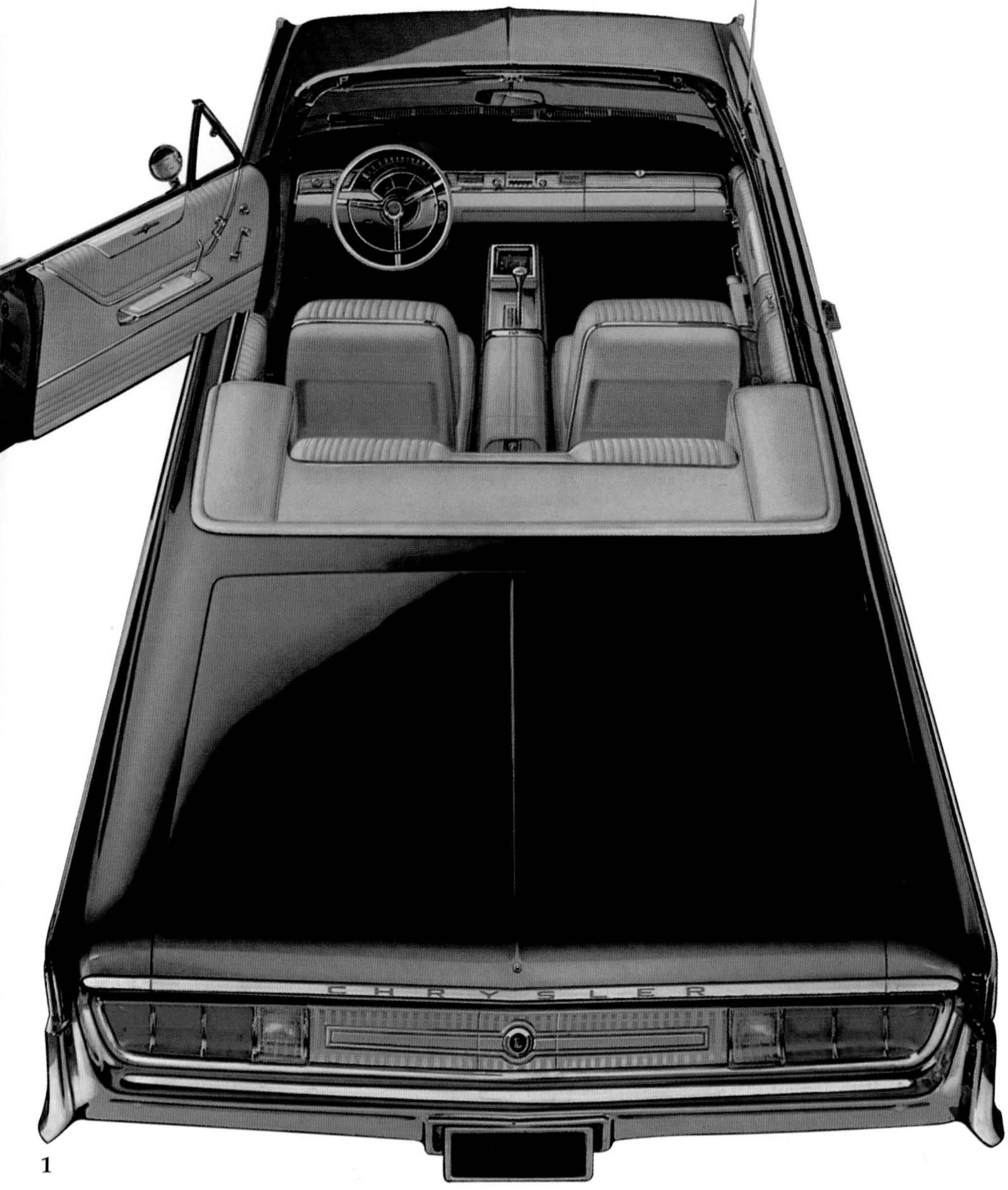

1

1. The last of the great Letter-series Chryslers was the 300L. By this time, Letter cars were little different than the far cheaper 300s; a 300L convertible like this commanded $4618, while a similar 300 cost $3911. As a result, sales of the 300L slipped to only 2845 units—of which just 440 were convertibles. Standard, and only, engine was a 360-bhp 413-cid V-8, which was optional on the 300 and New Yorker. **2.** A New Yorker unibody structure is lowered onto its powertrain/axle assembly. The Chrysler brand breached 200,000 in model-year production for the first time in history, good enough to finish ahead of Cadillac by 23,654 units.

2

1

2

1. Standard 300s wore the crosshair grille once exclusive to the Letter series. **2-3.** An *L* badge was about the only visual cue setting Letter models apart. **4.** Newport was the entry-level Chrysler, but the 2-door, here with optional vinyl top, didn't look chintzy.

3

4

1965 Dodge

1

Carrying the Coronet name last used from 1949 to '59, Dodge's new intermediate was only slightly smaller than the previous full-size Polara. **1.** Three convertibles were offered in the Coronet line: 6-cylinder 440 ($2622); 440 V-8 ($2718); and 500 V-8 ($2894). **2-3.** Badpoetrynotwithstanding, ads did a good job trumpeting the youthful image Dodge was attempting to portray with the Coronet. **4.** In top-line 500 trim, this sharp Coronet 2-door hardtop could be yours for just $2674. The mid-size rode a new 117-inch-wheelbase chassis. Regular-production engine choices ranged from the standard 225-cid Slant Six to the 365-bhp 426-cid Street Wedge V-8. **5.** Dodge had a strong presence on racetracks of all shapes, sizes, and scales.

2

3

4

5

1

2

1. Professional drag racer Bud Faubel behind the wheel of a lightweight, altered-wheelbase Coronet. Chrysler built six Coronets and six Plymouth Belvederes with Hemi V-8s and wheelbases shortened to 110 inches and axles that move radically forward. The idea was to move weight rearward for better traction off the line. **2.** Aluminum body panels were factory options for mid-size Mopars. The complete set cost $410 and weighed just 80 lb. **3.** Faubel's car, nicknamed "The Honker," is shown dressed for battle at the Chicago Auto Show **4.** Stock-car driver David Pearson hustles a Coronet up Pikes Peak. **5.** An old Crosley escorts a pair of Coronets driven by the Daredevils stunt team. **6.** Dodge Coronets and Belvederes shared an assembly line. **7.** Hot-rod artist "Big Daddy" Ed Roth shows off his "Hot Grandmother"—cartoon, that is. She's aboard a '65 Coronet.

3

4

5

6

7

1965 Dodge

1

2

4

3

5

1. California highway patrolmen could stand tall when their Polara packed the 426 Wedge. **2-3**. Dodge dressed up a 2-door hardtop Polara to create its personal/luxury entry, the Monaco. It used the Polara/Custom 880 121-inch wheelbase and retailed for $3355. Sales were relatively healthy, at 13,096. **4-5**. Top-trim full-size Dodges were called Custom 880s. They came as hardtops, wagons, a 4-door sedan, and these convertibles. Custom 880s outsold Polaras 44,496 to 12,705.

1965 Dodge Models

Dart 2dr sdn

Coronet 500 conv

Polara 4dr sdn

Dart 4dr sdn

Coronet 500 2dr htp

Polara 2dr htp

Dart 270 2dr sdn

Coronet 440 conv

Polara 4dr htp

Dart 270 4dr sdn

Coronet 440 2dr htp

Polara conv

Dart 270 2dr htp

Coronet 2dr sdn

Custom 880 4dr sdn

Dart 270 conv

Coronet 4dr sdn

Custom 880 2dr htp

Dart GT 2dr htp

Coronet 440 4dr sdn

Custom 880 4dr htp

Dart GT conv

Coronet 4dr wgn

Custom 880 conv

Dart 4dr wgn

Coronet 440 4dr wgn

Polara 4dr wgn

Dart 270 4dr wgn

Monaco 2dr htp

Custom 880 4dr wgn

1965 Dodge

1

2

3

1-2. The Charger II show car predicted the styling theme of the production Charger introduced for 1966. **3.** A glorious fall afternoon was a perfect time to enjoy the top-down pleasures of a Dart GT convertible—yours for just $2628. **4-5.** A Dart GT coupe cost $224 less than the ragtop, but this one is shod with genuine Cragar mag wheels—a factory option for '65. Even Dart GTs came standard with a humble Slant Six, but this example carries the top optional engine, a 273-cid V-8 with 4-barrel carb rated at 235 bhp.

4

5

1

2

1. Brontosaurus was Sinclair's favorite dinosaur, serving as the oil company's mascot and finding its way into millions of homes as inflatable green giveaways. **2.** The stunning Imperial Crown convertible sold for $6194, weighed 5315 lb and was a rare jewel; just 588 were built. The 4-door hardtop went for $5772 and was the line's top seller at 11,628 units. **3.** Production of the $5930 Crown coupe was 3874. **4.** Topping the regular-product line was the $6596 LeBaron, offered only as a hardtop sedan. All rode a 129-inch wheelbase and used a 340-bhp 413 V-8. **5.** Glass headlight covers were a new styling touch. **6.** Rear-seat occupants were surrounded by luxury, too.

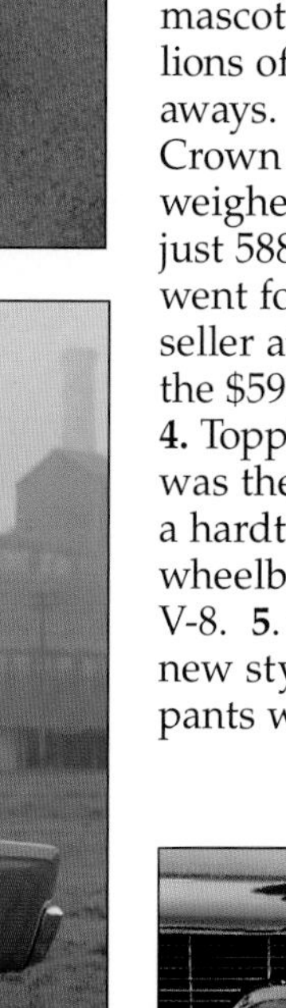

3

4

5

6

1965 Plymouth

1

1. Valiant got a new grille and a new option, the Commando 273, a hot version of the small V-8 with 235 bhp—55 more than the base 273. **2.** Dashboard push buttons gave way to column and floor shifters. **3.** The Valiant-based Barracuda lost all Valiant badging.

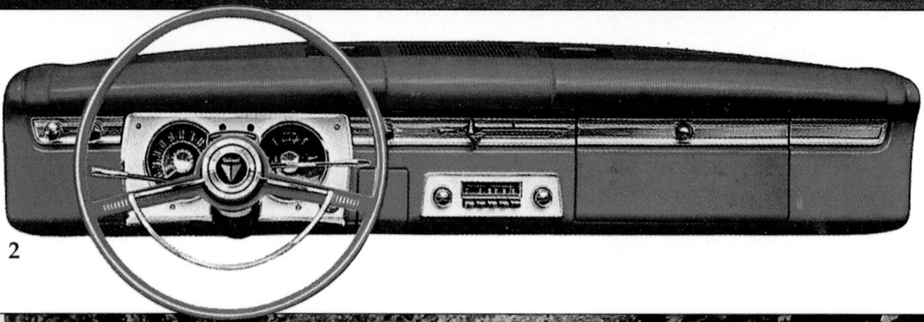

2

3

1. Barracuda's fold-down rear seatback created a cargo floor nearly 6-feet long. A trunklid behind the rear glass made it accessible from outside. **2-3.** A new option was the Formula S package. It added a tachometer to the gauge cluster, plus a beefed-up suspension, wider wheels and tires, and the Commando 273. With this engine, a Formula S did 0–60 mph in 8 sec. Barracuda sales nearly tripled to 64,596 in this, its second model year.

2

1

3

1

2

3

4

1-3. Plymouth's intermediates continued on a 116-inch chassis, but the Belvedere added a new sporty model called Satellite. It was available as a 2-door hardtop and a convertible with a standard 273-cid V-8. This example is fitted with the optional 325-bhp 383-cid 4-barrel V-8, TorqueFlite automatic transmission, and console-mounted tachometer. **4.** Belvedere 4-doors started as low as $2315, and fleet buyers surely paid less, making them fine taxi-duty values.

5-6. Fury was redesigned, gaining 3 inches of wheelbase, to 119, and new styling with vertical headlamps. Fury I, II, III, and Sport Fury models were offered; this is a Fury III 4-door hardtop. **7.** Chrysler Corporation President Lynn Townsend (right) and General Manager P. N. Buckminster seemed pleased with the new Fury. **8.** A '65 Fury is among cars vying for attention at a Standard—now Amoco—service station. **9.** Before in-dash cassette decks, the under-dash 8-track tape player provided personalized portable music.

5

6

7

STANDARD
STANDARD
ATLAS TIRES

8

Plymouth Fury. Pace Car.
This is the official Pace Car of the 1965 Indianapolis 500.
You can buy one just like it.
The car you see is a big, plush Plymouth Sport Fury Convertible.
It's not a race car. But it has power to spare. It can pace the pack to the starting gate at Indianapolis.
Plymouth Fury sets the pace off the track, too. It looks wonderful cruising along within the speed limit. Or even standing still at a stoplight.
Picture yourself in a Plymouth Fury. It's a snap. Just head for your nearby Plymouth Dealer's.
like zoom.
PLYMOUTH DIVISION
CHRYSLER
THE ROARING '65s
FURY
BELVEDERE
VALIANT
BARRACUDA
Plymouth

STEREO 8

9

Ford Motor Company

Introduced in spring 1964, the phenomenally successful Mustang scores a record 680,000 sales in its 18-month inaugural model year

Original Mustangs were titled as 1965s, though sometimes are called "1964 ½" models; a fastback body style is added at the start of the regular '65 model year

Mustang's success helps Ford surpass 2 million in model-year production for the first time in its history

Galaxie is restyled, adds a luxury model called LTD

Fairlane gets a larger new body of the straight-edge design school

Controversial overhead-cam 427-cid V-8 racing engine with 600-plus bhp debuts

Big Mercurys redesigned along Lincoln-like lines

Comets are also restyled, follow the crowd with stacked headlights

Lee Iacocca is named vice president of FoMoCo Car and Truck Group

Rear-engine Ford-powered Lotus driven by Brit Jim Clark wins the Indy 500

Chrysler boycotts NASCAR and Ford dominates, winning 48 of the season's 55 stock-car races

1

2

Mustang galloped into showrooms on April 17, 1964, and its appearance caused stampedes among eager buyers. Its long hood/short deck proportions and sporty looks gave birth to a new breed of compacts, nicknamed "ponycars" after the Mustang's equestrian logo. One of the car's attractions was its wide range of personalities, from flashy grocery-getter to roomy sports car. A $2368 base price—just $383 more than a strippo Falcon—didn't hurt. Initial offerings included a 2-door hardtop coupe and a convertible. **1.** Debuting at the start of the "official" 1965 model year in October 1964 was a fastback called the 2+2 to indicate its two front and two rear seats; no front bench seat was offered, as on the other bodies. **2.** At $2614, an impressive 101,945 Mustang convertibles sold during the '65 model year. **3.** Coupes attracted over *half a million* buyers that first year—a phenomenal accomplishment. Though a 101-bhp 170-cid six was standard initially, roughly three of four buyers chose the optional 164-bhp 260-cid V-8.

3

1

2

3

4

1-2. Fastbacks accounted for just over 77,000 sales in '65, not much more than 11 percent of total Mustang volume. But at $2589, it cost over $200 more than a coupe and just $25 less than the snazzy convertible. **3.** With the start of the '65 model year, Mustang's base six grew to 200 cid and 120 bhp, while the 260-cid V-8 was replaced by a 289 with 164 to 271 horses—which really put some kick in the young pony. **4.** Wire wheel covers, additional instrumentation, various luxury amenities, and such performance goodies as a 4-speed manual transmission and sport suspension were among the host of factory options. **5-6.** Professionally modified 2+2s were a drag-racing force. These track-only examples were fitted with Ford's awesome overhead-cam 427 V-8 and ran the quarter-mile in 10.9 sec at 128 mph.

5

6

1965 Ford

1

2

3

1-2. The big Fords' sharp-edged restyle included trendy stacked headlights. 3. Bucket seats, bright trim, and 4-on-the-floor shift helped make the 500 XL the sportiest Galaxie. 4. Ford pursued the law-enforcement market with a number of its vehicles, as this brochure cover shows. 5. Cheapest member of the full-size line was the Custom 2-door sedan at $2464. 6. Capitalizing on Chrysler's boycott of NASCAR, Ford dominated the stock car series. Here's road racer Dan Gurney on his way to victory at Riverside, California.

4

5

6

1

2

3

4

5

1. Topping the luxury end of the full-size line was the new Galaxie 500 LTD. Ford's comparison to Rolls-Royce raised eyebrows—and so it was effective advertising. **2.** LTD came as a 2-door hardtop or as this 4-door number, both with standard vinyl tops. **3-5.** Fairlane was restyled on a half-inch-longer wheelbase (now an even 116 inches, or 113 for wagons). Classiest of the intermediates was the Fairlane 500, here in 2-door hardtop form. Chrome accents and two-tone vinyl upholstery dressed up the inside. **6.** Even the Falcon wagon could have veneered bodysides if ordered in top-line Squire form. **7.** From over 20,000 in '64, Falcon convertible sales fell to under 7000 in '65. Blame the Mustang: Its ragtop cost only $133 more than the $2481 Futura. **8.** Futura coupe sales also dove, and for the same reason.

6

7

8

1

2

3

4

5

1. The Sport Roadster tonneau cover was a rarely ordered option on the $4879 Thunderbird convertible. **2.** In an effort to boost fluttering sales, the Limited Edition Special Landau hardtop joined the line at midyear. It had a parchment vinyl top and matching interior with either white or Ember-Glo metallic paint. It didn't help much. T-Bird production fell 19 percent for the model year, to 74,972. **3-4.** All T-Birds had a 300-bhp 390 V-8, buckets, and console. Prices started at $4486 for the hardtop. **5.** This show car had a mesh grille and rectangular lights.

1

2

1. What Lincoln ads called "refinements in styling" were primarily a bulged hood flowing to a flatter grille with wrap-around parking lights. Under the new hood, the 430-cid V-8 remained at 320 bhp. **2-4.** Some critics said four years of small annual changes had compromised Continental's classic '61 look. Agree? Neither did the public. Sales increased nearly 4000 units, to 40,180. **5.** Though described as hardtops, closed Lincolns actually had a vestigial center roof pillar.

3

4

5

1965 Mercury

1 2

1-2. Full-size Mercurys underwent an extensive revamp, shelving their 120-inch-wheelbase Ford-based chassis for a stronger, more exclusive 123-inch design. New bodies were larger with styling that intentionally mimicked Lincoln's—a fact the ads didn't hide. **3.** Big Mercs offered traditional and Breezeway rear windows; the latter's rear window again powered down for ventilation. **4.** Monterey was the entry-level full-size model and the best-selling big Merc. Its 2-door sedan was the line's cheapest at $2767 with a standard 250-bhp 390 V-8. **5.** The mid-level Monclair series offered a 2-door hardtop at $3135 and with yet a third roof style. **6.** A 14-percent jump, to 346,751, got Mercury past Rambler in model-year output. **7.** A Monterey is "road tested" on the chassis dynomometer. Buyers could get up to 427 cid and 425 bhp.

3

4

5

6

7

1

1. At $3599, the Park Lane convertible was the most-expensive Mercury and came with a 300-bhp 390 V-8. **2-3.** Comet went the stacked-headlamp route, dumped its base 170-cid six for a 200 six and its optional 260 V-8 for a 289, but still was the only Mercury line to lose sales volume. **4.** The $2664 Caliente ragtop shows off styling that belied Comet's compact-car origins.

2

3

4

General Motors

Record industry-wide sales carry every GM division to new production highs

Sporty Gran Sport editions added to Buick's Skylark and Riviera lines

Cadillac gets finless, sharp-edged restyle

Including trucks, Chevrolet builds a record 3 million vehicles

Chevrolet Corvair redesign brings sculpted lines, 180-bhp turbocharged engine, and new rear suspension

For the first time, Big Block V-8s are offered in Corvette

Chevelle Super Sport gains a big-block V-8 option, launching the famous SS 396

Oldsmobile sales hit 591,701, the highest in the division's long history; full-size models get pleasing new rounded-flank sheetmetal

An examination of Corvair's potentially dangerous handling characteristics forms the most-explosive chapter in Ralph Nader's best-selling book, *Unsafe at Any Speed*

In Washington, the Ribicoff Senate Committee is formed to investigate auto safety

GM executives admit to the committee that the corporation earned $1.7 billion in '64 but spent just $1.25 million on safety research

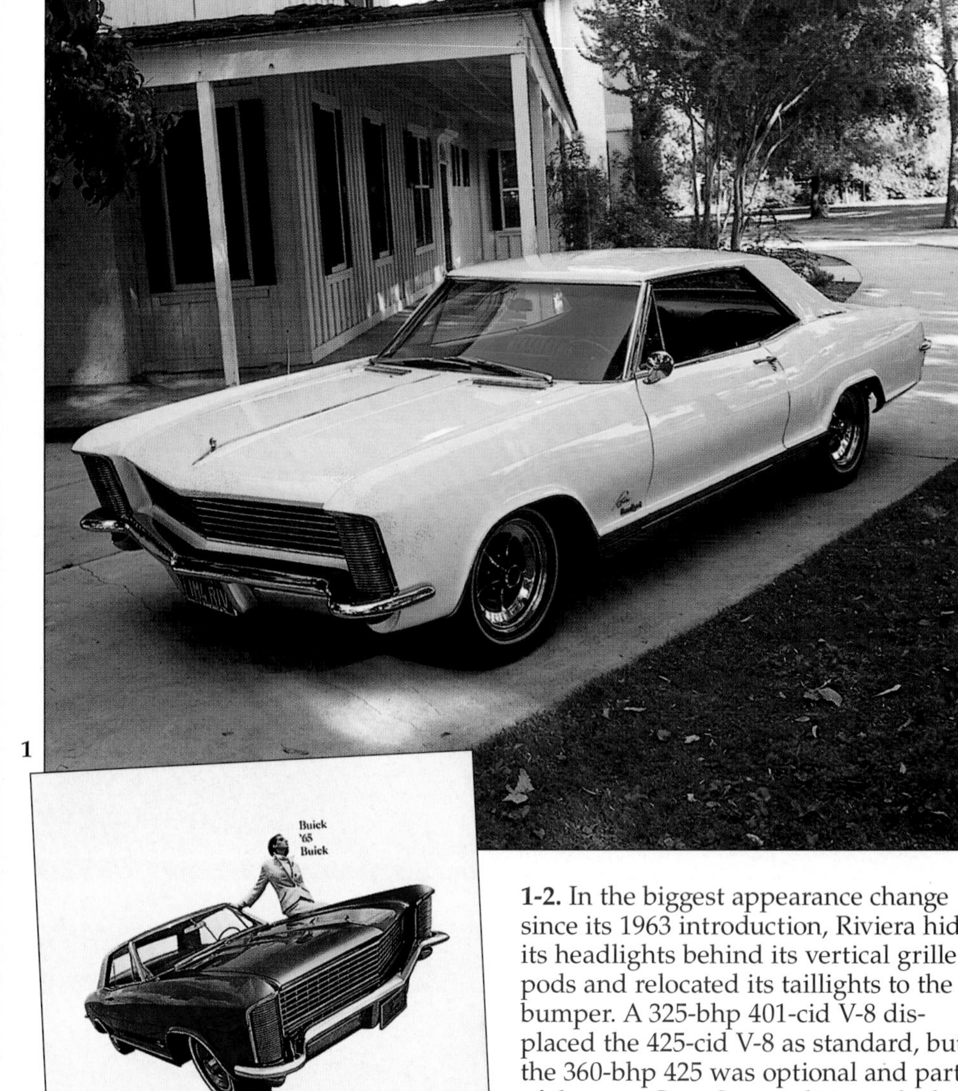

1-2. In the biggest appearance change since its 1963 introduction, Riviera hid its headlights behind its vertical grille pods and relocated its taillights to the bumper. A 325-bhp 401-cid V-8 displaced the 425-cid V-8 as standard, but the 360-bhp 425 was optional and part of the new Gran Sport edition, which also added the 5-spoke road wheels seen here. **3.** Buick was the U.S. source for the German-built GM Opel. Offered in four body styles, cheapest—and lightest—was the 2-door sedan (right), which weighed 1411 lb and cost but $1618. By comparison, Buick's next smallest car, the Special coupe, weighed more than twice as much and cost $2343. Opels were powered by a 60.6-cid 4-cylinder engine.

3

1

2

3

1. Never before—or since—had Detroit built so many convertibles in a model year, and Buick was on top of the trend with a ragtop in every series except Riviera. They were, (clockwise) Special, Skylark, LeSabre, Electra 225, and Wildcat. Prices ranged from $2605 for the Special to $4440 for the Electra. **2.** An Electra 225 4-door hardtop tipped the scales at 4284 lb, cost $4206. **3.** Ads touted the famous slogan, "Wouldn't you really rather have a Buick?" **4.** An Electra 4-door sedan saved $135 over the hardtop but sold in virtually the same volume.

4

1965 Buick

1

2

3

1. At 224-inches long and 4228 lb, the $4265 Electra 225 Sport Coupe was imposing in every respect. **2-3.** Wildcat graduated from LeSabre's 123-inch wheelbase to Electra's 126-inch span, but its body was some five inches shorter in length. **4-5.** Wildcat's style leader was Custom convertible, which included big bucket seats in its $3727 base price.

4

5

Buick 1965

1

1. Skylark, the upscale version of the Special intermediate, became a series of its own and cost about $200 more than comparable Special models. Here's the $2834 ragtop. **2-4.** Skylark Gran Sport was Buick's first modern muscle car. Though a "400" in ads, its engine was the 325-bhp 401-cid V-8. **5.** Note the Skyroof and fancier trim on the Skylark (left) versus the Special wagon. Skylark wagons had a 120-inch wheelbase, other bodies a 115.

2

3

4

5

1965 Cadillac

1

2

3

Cadillacs retained a 129.5-inch wheelbase but replaced a frame design that dated from 1957 and got new sheetmetal with vertical headlamps and finless rear fenders. **1-2.** DeVille convertibles tipped the scales at 4690 lb and cost $5639. **3.** Limos stayed on a 149.8-inch wheelbase and kept '64 bodies and '60-style roofs. **4.** New options included tilt/telescoping steering. **5-6.** The ever-popular Coupe DeVille went for $5419. **7.** Power again came from a 340-bhp 4-barrel 429-cid V-8.

4

5

7

6

1

2

3

4

5

Corvair's attractive redesign brought a fully independent rear suspension that addressed the original car's tricky handling. **1.** One step up from base models was the Monza. Its ragtop sold for $2493. **2.** Best-selling Corvair: the $2347 Monza coupe. **3-4.** All Corvairs had a 164-cid flat-6 engine. A $158 option for the line-topping Corsa was a 180-bhp turbocharged edition. Other versions had 95, 110, or 140 bhp. **5.** This go-cart's rear-engine chassis was a natural for a Corvair body.

1965 Chevrolet

1 2 3 4 5 6 7

1-3. In its final season was the Corvair-based Greenbriar station wagon. Just over 1500 were produced at a base price of $2609. **4.** Eating into Corvair sales was Chevrolet's own Chevy II, a much more conventional compact. This Nova Super Sport model carries the optional 283-cid V-8. **5.** Chevy II was in the third and last year of its styling cycle and sales fell 37 percent, to 122,100. **6.** Chevy's cheapest car was the Chevy II Series 100 2-door sedan at $2011. Base engine was a 90-bhp 153-cid 4-cylinder, but most carried one of the optional sixes. **7.** Most automakers built passenger vehicles ranging from compacts to full-size cars, but few could match the variety offered by Chevrolet. Not pictured here are the Corvette and assorted compact vans.

1

2

3

4

5

6

1-2. The Malibu Super Sport edition of the midsize Chevelle entered the model year with a hot 350-bhp version of the 327-cid V-8 as its top engine choice. At midyear, Chevy brought out what would become a legend among muscle cars: the Chevelle SS 396. Its 396-cid V-8 made a rousing 375 bhp and teamed with heavy-duty chassis pieces. It went 0–60 mph in 6 sec and cost $4100. Just 201 were built. **3.** A "regular" Malibu SS convertible started at $2750 with a 194-cid six. **4.** Chevelle wagons came with two or four doors. **5.** The attractive El Camino car/pickup continued on the Chevelle platform. Available with six or V-8 power, prices started at about $2300. **6.** Chevrolet displayed a chop-top El Camino called the Surfer I on the auto-show circuit.

1

2

3

1-2. Gracefully curved new bodies on the big Chevys created one of the '60's best looks. Top of the heap was the $3104 Impala SS convertible. This one has wider-than-stock whitewalls. **3.** SS coupes started at $2839. **4-6.** Chevy reached for the luxury market with the new $200 Caprice option package for the Impala 4-door hardtop. **7.** Can't afford genuine mag wheels? Try the factory optional mag wheelcovers.

4

5 6 7

1

2

3

4

5

1. Sales of nearly 2.4 million cars made this Chevy's best year of the decade. **2.** GM stylist William Mitchell with the Mako Shark show car, a forecast of the '68 Corvette. **3.** Fender gills were now vertical and 4-wheel disc brakes standard. **4.** Hood blister marks the presence of the newly optional 425-bhp 396-cid V-8. It furnished 0–60 mph in 5.7 sec. Next fastest: the 375-bhp fuel-injected 327, at 6.3. **5.** 'Vettes were fine road-race cars and here share the grid with Shelby Mustang GT-350s.

1965 Oldsmobile

1

2

3

4

1. The $4778 Starfire convertible was the priciest Olds. **2.** The 2-door hardtop cost $4138. The full-size models' top V-8 grew from 394 cid to 425 for '65 and Starfires had the top version, at 370 bhp. **3.** Ninety-Eights rode a 126-inch wheelbase; other full-size models a 123. The $4197 Ninety-Eight 2-door hardtop was outsold by 4-door models, 74,337 to 12,166. **4.** Olds continued its support of the Miss America pageant; 1965's winner was Vonda Kay Van Dyke of Phoenix, Arizona. **5.** Rounded new contours softened the big cars' look. Ninety-Eights came with a 360-bhp 425. The convertible cost $4493 and was the slowest seller, at 4903.

5

1

2

Olds Vista-Cruiser

carries more than 100 cubic feet of cargo

. . . the proudest family in town

. . . and a price that starts below 38 other station wagons!

You're looking at a wagon that's *loaded* with convincing reasons to go Olds in a big way.

- Like a cargo capacity over 100 cubic feet huge.
- And a Jetfire Rocket V-8 with up to 315 horses.
- A forward-facing third seat that makes back seat passengers part of the family.
- And a tinted-glass Vista-Roof that makes back seat riding part of the fun!
- But Vista-Cruiser's happiest surprise is this: For all its niceties, *prices actually start below 38 other station wagons!*

'65 OLDSMOBILE

Try a Rocket in Action . . .
Look to Olds for the New!

OLDSMOBILE DIVISION • GENERAL MOTORS CORPORATION

3

1. The rounded-flank new styling and fastback roofline were most pronounced on the volume big cars, including this Jetstar 88 Holiday 2-door hardtop. Golfer Betsy Rawls is aboard this Ladies PGA tour courtesy car. **2.** A Cutlass 4-4-2 concept car highlighted auto show displays. **3.** The Cutlass-based Vista Cruiser wagon shared its Vista Roof with Buick's Skylark Sportwagon. **4.** A V-6-powered F-85 does battle in the Mobilgas Economy Run. **5.** Dressed-up F-85s were Cutlasses; the ragtop cost $2983. **6.** The 4-4-2 option was now confined to F-85 and Cutlass 2-doors and convertibles and included an exclusive new 345-bhp 400-cid V-8. The name now stood for 400 cid, 4-barrel carb, and dual exhausts.

4

5

6

1965 Pontiac

1

1. Bonneville gained four inches of wheelbase, to 124 inches, and "extruded" new styling made it look even larger. The 4-door hardtop cost $3433 and weighed 3995 lb. **2.** The $3594 Bonneville droptop: the most expensive Pontiac. **3-4.** Ad lines were clever and confident. **5.** Catalina, the make's best-selling line, got new styling and grew an inch in wheelbase, to 121. **6.** The Catalina-based personal/luxury Grand Prix coupe cost $3498. Like all full-size Pontiacs, it came standard with a 389-cid V-8 but offered a 421 with up to 376 bhp as an option.

2

3

4

5

6

1

2

3

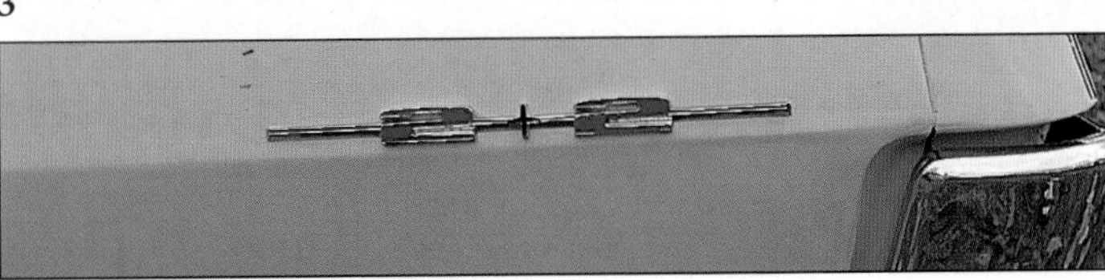

4

5

6

1-4. The 2+2 option package cost $244 and turned a big Catalina coupe or convertible into a fast tiger. It included bucket seats, heavy-duty suspension, and the 421 V-8. The 376-bhp version did 0–60 mph in 7.2 sec. **5.** A Tempest V-8 finishes the Mobilgas Economy Run in New York's Times Square. **6.** Division General Manager E. M. "Pete" Estes poses as the 10 millionth Pontiac—a gold Catalina—comes off the assembly line in Pontiac, Michigan.

1965 Pontiac

1

2

3

4

1-4. New bodies graced the mid-size Tempest and LeMans. The GTO was a $296 LeMans option package and made for a 2-door starting at $2751 or a convertible at $3057. This one has the optional 4-speed manual with Hurst shifter and 360-bhp tri-power (three 2-barrel carb) version of the 389 V-8. It did 0–60 mph in 6.1 sec. GTO sales more than doubled, to 75,352. **5.** LeMans ragtops started at $2797. Their top engine option was a 285-bhp 326-cid V-8. **6.** A tiger and a goat.

5

6

Studebaker Corporation

Canadian-built Lark-like sedans and wagons are only vehicles being produced by Studebaker

All Studebakers adopt engines built by General Motors of Canada; old Stude engine names are retained: Thunderbolt V-8 and Stovebolt Six

Commander line includes a 2-door sedan, 4-door sedan, and Wagonaire station wagon; Daytona line offers only a 2-door sedan and Wagonaire wagon; Cruiser returns as a 4-door sedan

Commanders and Cruisers available with either 6-cylinder or V-8 power; Daytonas are V-8 only

First introduced on the R3 Avanti, transistorized ignition becomes standard on Daytona Sport Sedans and optional on other models at midyear

Sales continue their downward spiral; fewer than 20,000 Studebakers are built for the model year

Former South Bend Studebaker dealers Nathan Altman and Leo Newman purchase assembly facilities, parts, and tooling for the Avanti and hire a small group of ex-Studebaker engineers; about 20 Avantis with Chevy V-8s are assembled by year's-end and sold independently as the Avanti II

1

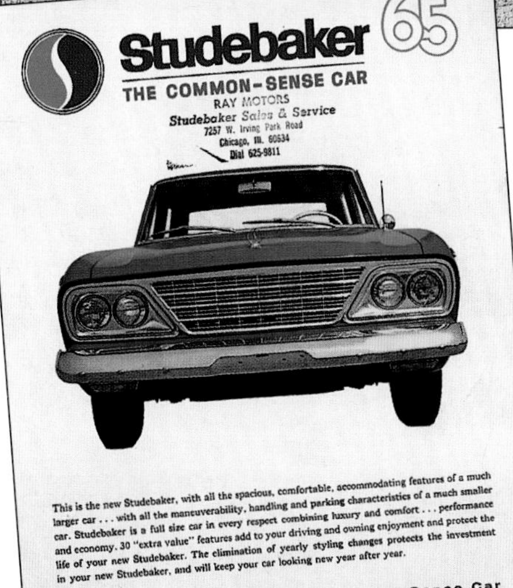

1. Daytonas came standard with a 283-cid GM-built V-8. Offered only with a 2-barrel carburetor, it made 195 bhp—somewhat less than Studebaker's old 289, and *far* less than the old high-performance "R" engines. The 2-door sedan went for $2565. **2-4.** Cruisers were available with either the V-8 or a 120-bhp 194-cid GM-built six. This stately Cruiser sedan sold for just $2470 with the six, $2610 with the V-8.

2

3

4

Etc.

Private automobiles log 877 million passenger-miles, accounting for 89.4 percent of all U.S. intercity traffic

U.S. and Canada remove tariff barriers, a move designed to create a common market for automobiles and parts manufacturing

Easy credit is blamed for increasing dollar losses in auto repossessions

Inventor C. W. Kelsey announces his intention to build and market a wingless flying automobile, the Skycar

The RRollway division of General American Transportation Corp. shows scale models of a RRollway Auto Ferry, which would run on railroad tracks at 150 mph and transport passengers in their own cars

FBI director J. Edgar Hoover warns motorists of the danger of giving rides to harmless-looking hitchhikers

Chicago Motor Club's *Motor News* asserts that, because of the increasing availability and popularity of options, "certain owners will never see an exact duplicate of their car anywhere else in the U.S."

The CBS television network airs the *National Drivers' Test*, a one-hour special designed to test viewers' judgment, knowledge of rules of the road, and ability to spot potential road hazards

1

2

1. Scottish Formula 1 champion Jim Clark's British-built Lotus, powered by a Ford V-8, is the first rear-engine car to win the Indy 500. Of 33 cars to start the race, just six are front-engine, and none finishes higher than fifth. Every winning car from here on has a rear engine. **2.** Ralph Nader's controversial *Unsafe at Any Speed* attacks what the consumer crusader claims is Detroit's long-standing disregard for automotive safety. It becomes one of the decade's key books, helping to launch the consumer movement, and hastening the demise of Chevy's Corvair. **3-5.** From *Red Line 7000*, director Howard Hawks's fictionalized look at motorsports: An MG 1100 Sports Sedan stops for a dumped Shelby Cobra coupe; a hot time in the infield; pit-stop action with a '64 Galaxie.

3

4

5

1

2

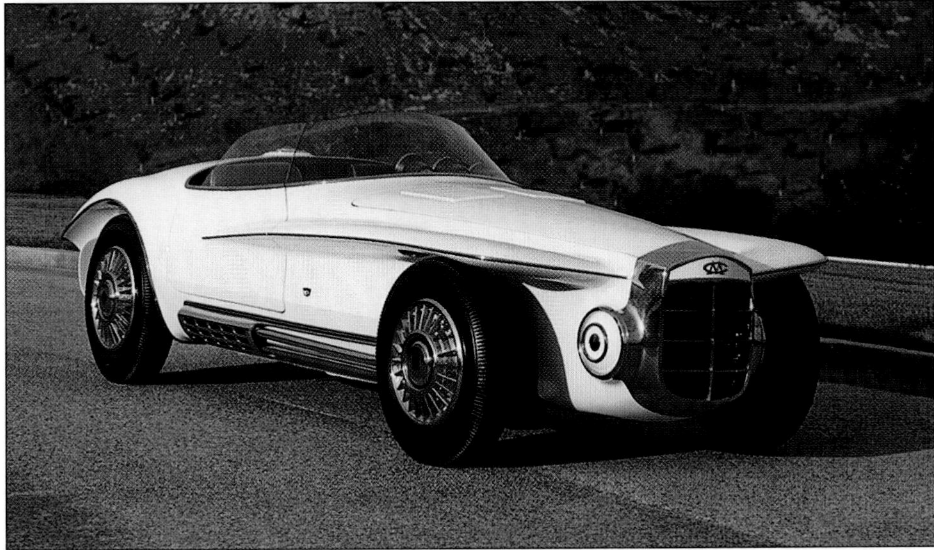

3

4

5

1. A 289-cid Ford V-8 gave the British Sunbeam Tiger its growl. **2.** It doesn't look it, but the Renault 8 Gordini 1100 was a popular European racing sedan in the mold of the Mini Cooper. **3.** Virgil Exner and his son, Virgil, Jr., designed the one-off Mercer Cobra to showcase its copper componentry. **4.** Presidential daughter Luci Baines Johnson smiles from her Corvette. **5.** The King Midget roadster had an 8.5-bhp 1-cylinder engine and got 60 mpg.

Etc.

Craig Breedlove and Art Arfons continue their world land speed record duel at the Bonneville Salt Flats; Breedlove's new jet car, the Spirit of America Sonic I, retakes the record at 555.1 mph; the next week, Arfons's Green Monster jet car runs 576.6 mph; eight days later, Breedlove recaptures the record with a run of 600.6, making him the first driver to top 600 mph

Station wagons and cars with front-wheel drive become increasingly popular in Europe

Exports of Japanese-made automobiles increase by 90 percent over 1964

C. Itoh & Company, Ltd., a mammoth, Tokyo-based trading firm, announces plans to market Japanese cars in the United States

Four young French women team-drive a pair of Renault station wagons from the southern tip of South America to Anchorage, Alaska, in 4 ½ months

Top 10 Selling Imports

1. Volkswagen 383,978
2. MG 22,322
3. Triumph 20,347
4. Volvo 18,115
5. Opel 16,216
6. Datsun 13,201
7. Simca 12,994
8. Mercedes-Benz 11,994
9. Renault 11,431
10. Fiat .... ,8194

Total import-car share of U.S. market: 6.11 percent

Safety was the key word—and the thorn in the side of Detroit—as automakers scrambled to meet tough standards set by a powerful new federal agency, the National Highway Traffic Safety Administration.

Inflation grew as President Johnson convinced Congress to appropriate still more billions of dollars to feed the unpromising U.S. military effort in Vietnam. In China, Chairman Mao was at the vanguard of his nation's "great proletarian cultural revolution," carried out by young Communist zealots waving the "Little Red Book" of Mao's musings.

The U.S. and Soviet space programs accelerated, with Russia's successful Venus 3 probe of our sister planet and with America's manned Gemini missions.

Summer riots struck inner-city Chicago, Cleveland, Atlanta, Brooklyn, Minneapolis, Omaha, and Dayton; National Guard troops were deployed to quell the unrest. Meanwhile, black voter registration continued to be violently resisted by some whites in the South.

Many universities instituted the simple "pass/fail" grading system, a relief to male students who might otherwise have been booted from college and sent to Vietnam.

Americans shopped for an intriguing new invention, freeze-dried coffee, and sipped Metrecal and other low-calorie food substitutes.

Fashion's latest word was the asexual Carnaby Street look from "swinging London." Women and men wore patterned pants, flowered shirts, and colorful caps. Boots, shoes, even skirts utilized plastic and vinyl for a wet, shiny look. Young women pierced their ears and ironed their hair into long, perfectly straight tresses.

Influential albums included the Beach Boys' *Pet Sounds,* and a pair by the Beatles, *Yesterday and Today* and *Revolver.* But the year's biggest single was Frank Sinatra's "Strangers in the Night." Other hits: Petula Clark's "I Know a Place," Dusty Springfield's "You Don't Have to Say You Love Me," and the Rolling Stones' "Under My Thumb."

The secret-agent craze brought *Our Man Flint* and *The Silencers* to theaters. Spies hit TV, too: *The Man from U.N.C.L.E., Get Smart,* and *I Spy,* the first series to feature a black actor (Bill Cosby) in a non-comedy starring role. Other notable shows included *Batman, Honey West, The FBI, Mission: Impossible,* and *Star Trek.*

In sports, the defending World Series champion Los Angeles Dodgers were swept in four games by the underdog Baltimore Orioles. Football's top dogs were the Green Bay Packers.

American Motors Corporation

AMC President Roy Abernethy's ambitious plan to abandon the make's compact-car image and tackle the Big 3 is symbolized in a name change

Abernethy believes the Rambler name will hurt the larger, more-expensive models he plans to develop

The full-size Ambassador and Marlin of 1966 are marketed not as Ramblers, but under the AMC badge

The compact American and Rogue models and the intermediate Classic and Rebel still sell as Ramblers—for now

Plush DPL model joins the Ambassador line to reinforce its upscale aspirations

Lukewarm acceptance of the Marlin in its debut year turns cold; sales slide more than 50 percent

Rebel name is disinterred for use on a new Classic hardtop

American series gets its own sporty hardtop under the new Rogue label

Rambler production totals 265,712; combined with production of AMC-badged cars, American Motors' 1966 output is 341,951, an increase of 17,282 units over 1965

1

1. Marlin was now an "AMC" and gained a slightly altered grille, a sway bar for 6-cylinder cars, and, as seen here, an optional vinyl section for its fastback roof. **2.** This was the second—and as it turned out, last—year on the 112-inch-wheelbase chassis of the Classic series. Base price was reduced by $499, to $2601, by deleting previously standard items, such as power brakes, but sales still were less than half the year before, at just 4547. **3.** AMC pictured itself a full-line rival for the Big 3, but among its handicaps was an inefficient factory system that had partially finished cars trucked between assembly lines in different buildings.

2

3

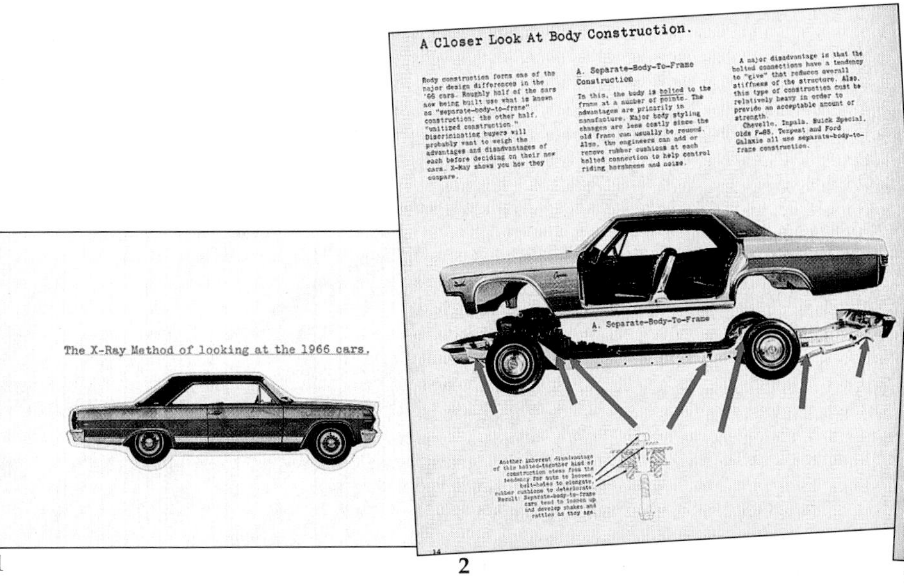

1

2

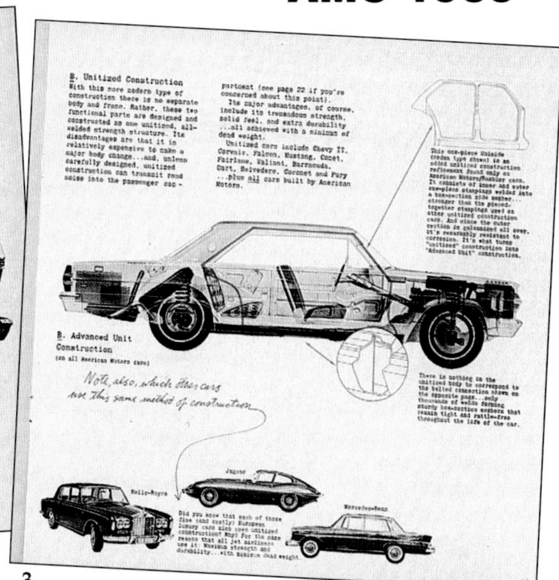

3

1-3. AMC couldn't compete on style or power, but it didn't hesitate to tout the advantages of its unitized construction. This ad spread compared bolting a body to a frame with the sturdy welds used by AMC and, as it noted, by Rolls-Royce, Jaguar, and Mercedes. **4.** Technically, the new DPL was a separate model, but it really was a high-zoot Ambassador 2-door hardtop with such perks as reclining bucket seats as part of the $2756 base price; seat-fabric-covered throw pillows were optional. **5.** Ambassador got a minor facelift and was back in 880 and 990 trim. The sole ragtop was a 990 and listed for $2968. **6.** The basic 2-door hardtop went for $2600. A 155-bhp six was standard in Ambassador/DPL and V-8s of 287 cid and 198 bhp, and 327 cid and 250 to 270 bhp, cost extra.

4

5

6

1966 AMC

1

2

Meanwhile, back at Rambler, the American got longer front fenders and a clean new grille. **1.** Racing stripes weren't offered, but the compact was for the first time available with a V-8. AMC's nifty new 200-bhp 290-cid unit was introduced at midyear and slid right into the engine bay. It teamed with a new manual gearbox—four on the floor—to give the American surprising go. **2.** As with the DPL, the new Rogue was technically a separate model but was really American's new upmarket entry. The heavily trimmed 2-door hardtop listed for $2370. **3-4.** Mainline Americans returned on a 106-inch wheelbase in 220 and 440 guise. The only convertible was the 440, and it started at $2486 and weighed 2782 lb. **5.** The 112-inch-wheelbase Classic series added a deluxe-level 2-door hardtop called the Rebel. This is the 770 wagon with the optional side-opening tailgate and third rear seat.

3

5

4

1

2

3

Not only was AMC venturing upmarket with models like the DPL, it also was eyeing the small, sporty-car field. In June 1966, it displayed a quartet of idea cars to gauge public reaction. **1-3.** The most-exciting was the AMX, for American Motors Experimental. It was a 2-seat fastback coupe with a "Ramble Seat," a modern take on the old rumble seat. The rear window flipped open to form a windshield for the seat. **4.** A straight hardtop interpretation of the AMX was the AMX II, one of the most beautiful cars ever from the AMC studios. **5.** Most innovative of the idea cars was the Cavalier. Its fenders were interchangeable diagonally, and the hood and trunklid and front and rear bumpers also could be swapped. **6.** The Vixen adapted the Cavalier's concept of interchangeable body panels to a semi-fastback coupe. Its windshield was moved back 12 inches and canted rearward for a sportier profile.

4

5

6

Chrysler Corporation

Chrysler Corporation's market share increases one point, to 16.6 percent

Chrysler models get mild facelift; 300 series stands alone as the sporty Chrysler

Chrysler introduces the industry's largest V-8, a 440-cid workhorse that debuts in New Yorker and Imperial, then as an option in other Chryslers

Dodge continues to bury its "retiree's special" image for one of high performance; sales surge, and '66 is among its best years ever

A fastback roof is slapped onto a Dodge Coronet to create the sporty Charger

Monoco 500 bows as Dodge's full-size sport/luxury entry

Competition from Pontiac and Dodge causes Plymouth sales to slip despite an attractive revamp of the Belvedere/Satellite line

Valiant is clothed in new sheetmetal; Barracuda now shares Valiant's grille

"Street" version of the mighty 426-cid Hemi V-8 bows as a regular-production option on mid-size Dodges and Plymouths

NASCAR reinstates the Hemi; Dodge and Plymouth dominate stock-car racing—helped by a boycott by Ford in protest of the Hemi

1

2

1. In a strong new-car market and amid renewed appreciation of engineering and sensible design, the formidable line of Chrysler, Dodge, Plymouth, and Imperial models was well received. **2.** Chrysler-brand production increased 22 percent, to 264,848, for its second-best year of the decade. The roster ascended from Newport through the 300 to the New Yorker models. Newports and 300s used a 383-cid V-8 with 270 or 325 bhp. New Yorker had the new 440 with 350 bhp. Highlighting this auto-show display is the $4157 New Yorker 2-door hardtop. **3.** Wagons rode a 121-inch wheelbase that, oddly, was 3 inches shorter than that of the other body styles. **4.** A vinyl rear-roof pillar insert was a popular New Yorker option. The series' best-seller was this $4233 4-door hardtop.

3

4

1

2

4

1-3. Demise of the letter-series left the 300 line as Chrysler's sporty leader. A 4-door sedan, 2- and 4-door hardtops, and a convertible were offered. All had front bucket seats and, at 222-inches overall, were Chrysler's longest cars, excluding Imperial. **4.** The Turbine experiment ended in '66. In all, 203 people in 48 states tested the pretty Ghia-built cars. Of 50 assembled, all but 10 were scrapped to avoid high import duties on the Italian-built cars.

"We do not intend to sell the vehicles. When we finish the testing program, we will destroy them."

—Chrysler Corp. vice president for product planning and development, on the fate of the company's 50 turbine test cars; April 1966

3

1966 Dodge

1

2

1-2. In the tumultuous '60s, an invitation to rebel didn't seem out of place, even when it came from Madison Avenue. **3-7.** The wedgy roof-pillar theme was retained, but the mid-size Coronet otherwise got a full sheetmetal redo to become one of the year's handsomest cars. The carried-over 117-inch wheelbase hosted a full range of body styles capped by the $2921 Coronet 500 convertible. **8.** Helped by a 17-percent increase in Coronet production, Dodge enjoyed a 23-percent jump in sales, to 632,658. That would be its high mark of the decade and boosted it from seventh to fifth in model-year output.

3

4

5

6

7

8

1

2

5

3

4

6

1-3. A fastback roof on the restyled '66 Coronet intermediate created the Charger. Hidden-headlamps and full-width taillamps were style spiffs. A common stand-in for the standard 230-bhp 318-cid V-8 was the optional 325-bhp 383. **4.** Four buckets, full-length console, and folding rear seatbacks were inside. **5-6.** The special-order 425-bhp 426-cid Hemi made the ultimate Charger. **7.** Was it revolutionary? **8.** Mag-look wheelcovers cost extra. **9.** Charging around the track.

7

8

9

1

2

3

4

1. Never before had a half-million Dodges been built for a single model year. **2.** Full-size models got only subtle appearance changes. Monaco was the up-trim series. **3.** Atop the line again was the $3604 Monaco 500 coupe. **4** Polara was the bread-and-butter big car. Here's the $2948 4-door hardtop. **5.** Dart was fully restyled.

5

Dart sedans, coupes, and convertibles retained their 111.0-inch wheelbase and wagons a 106-inch chassis, but all got sharp new sheetmetal. The bodies were slightly longer and wider and base, mid-range 270 series, and sporty GT models were again offered. Slant Sixes were back in 101- and 145-bhp form, as was the 273-cid V-8 in 180- and 235-bhp tune. Starting prices ranged from $2094 for the base 2-door sedan to $2828 for a V-8 ragtop. (Left) A GT ragtop, a flip hairdo, pink headband and matching lipstick, stretch pants, and vinyl boots—the '60s! Dart production was up by 16,703 units, to 209,376, making 1966 the car's best model-year of the decade.

1966 Imperial

The grille was now a series of mesh rectangles and the trunklid's pseudo spare-tire bulge was more subdued, but Imperial's styling was otherwise little changed. The Crown series of 2- and 4-door hardtops and a convertible continued, as did the flagship LeBaron 4-door hardtop, all on a rerun of the 129-inch-wheelbase body-on-frame platform. Prices ranged from $5887 to $6540, which was a reduction of about $60 from '65, despite presence of a new 350-bhp 440-cid V-8 in place of a 340-bhp 413. Cabins were as expansive and plush as ever. Behind the scenes, however, Chrysler was preparing to bring Imperial back into its mainstream unibody family.

1966 Plymouth

1

2

1-2. Barracuda had its best year yet, with 38,029 sales. The Formula S version had a 235-bhp 273 V-8 and a sport suspension. **3.** "Fireball 500" was a Barracuda-based George Barris-built show car. **4.** A mid-mounted Hemi got this famous exhibition-race wheel stander airborne. **5.** The Valiant Signet.

4

3

5

1

Plymouth spent most of its money on a restyled intermediate for '66; luckily, its full-size line didn't require much change. Fury I, II, III, Fury Sport, and VIP series made up the roster. **1-4.** VIPs were hardtops in $3069 2-door and $3133 4-door form. Tufted upholstery, fold-down armrests, and reading lamps were among the amenities. **5.** Sport Fury came as a convertible or 2-door hardtop. A 318 V-8 was standard on Sport Fury, but engines in the big Plymouths ranged from the 145-bhp Slant Six to the 365-bhp 440-cid V-8, the latter a $234 option. Even a floor-shifted 4-speed manual was offered. **6.** Eight-track tape players were just becoming factory accessories.

2

3

4

5

6

1966 Plymouth

1

Plymouth's revamp of Chrysler Corp.'s intermediate looked even cleaner than Dodge's effort. The lineup retained its Belvedere and Satellite badging and its 116-inch wheelbase except on wagons, which switched to a 117-incher. Belvederes came with the Slant Six or V-8s of 272, 318, 361, 383, or 426 cid. **1.** Satellites were 2-door hardtops and convertibles, all with V-8s. King of the hill was the new Street Hemi, an only-slightly tamed version of Mopar's racing 426-cid V-8. The street version used two huge 4-barrel carbs, and its output was underrated by the factory at 425 bhp. It went into 1521 '66 Plymouths, mostly Satellite hardtops, including this one. It added $908 to the price of a $2695 Satellite hardtop or $2910 convertible. With the optional automatic transmission, a Hemi Satellite did 0–60 mph in 5.3 sec and the quarter-mile in 13.8 sec at 104 mph. **2.** Weighing just 3095 lb, 160 lb less than a Satellite, the Belvedere 2-door sedan was an inviting home for the Hemi. Jere Stahl's winning example turned the quarter-mile in 11.7 sec at 119.6 mph.

2

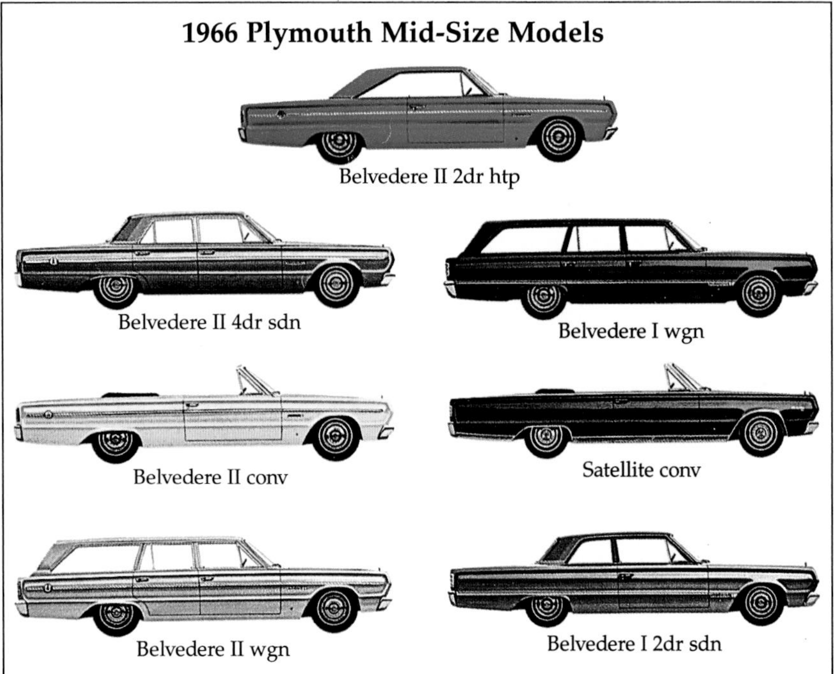

Ford Motor Company

Ford division notches its best year of the decade, building 2.2 million cars to edge Chevrolet by 6215 units for the No. 1 slot

Second-generation Fairlane debuts; finally has room for a large-displacement V-8

Falcon is upgraded from compact to near mid-size; shares some Fairlane underbody structure and continues to offer a V-8-engine option

In its sophomore year, Mustang changes only slightly; for comparable 12-month periods, the '66s actually outsell the "1964 ½" models by 50,000 units

Four-wheel-drive Ford Bronco debuts to compete with Jeep CJ and International Scout

Lincoln gets longer new sheetmetal and gains a 2-door hardtop body style; V-8 is enlarged to 462 cid

Mercury's Comet gets its first major redo, shifts from compact to intermediate size

Corporate big-block 428-cid V-8 is introduced; marketed as the 7-Litre engine

Marketers declare, "Ford has a better idea," revive the blue oval logo

Ford-powered Lotuses win second consecutive Indy 500; GT-40s finish 1-2-3 in the 24 Hours of LeMans, are first American winners

1

2

3

4

Still without any real ponycar rivals, Mustang changed little and remained a sales phenomenon. The 170-cid 6-cylinder was dropped, making the 120-bhp 200-cid six standard, and 289-cid V-8s of up to 271 bhp optional. **1-2.** Carroll Shelby-modified high-performance Mustang fastbacks were called GT-350s. They had 306-bhp 289s and for '66, got rear-quarter windows. This is one of about 1000 available for rental from Hertz. **3-4.** Convertibles started at $2653; this one has optional wheels and upgraded interior trim.

1966 Ford

1

"The median Mustanger is 31 years old, compared to age 42 for the median purchaser of the regular Ford car."

—Ford Division General Manager Donald N. Frey, on Mustang demographics; February 1966

2

3

4

1. Ford sold 499,751 Mustang hardtops, 35,698 fastbacks, and 72,119 convertibles for '66. The car had become an integral part of the '60s youth movement. **2-3.** Fairlane matured with a full redesign on a wheelbase longer by a half-inch, to 116 inches (wagons were at 113). Base engine was a 120-bhp six, but there now was room for Ford's new 390-cid V-8. This is a Fairlane 500. **4.** About 70 special-order 2-doors got Ford's 425-bhp 427-cid V-8; they did 0–60 mph in 6 sec, the quarter-mile in 14.5 at 100 mph. **5.** The GT coupe and convertible were new and used a 335-bhp 390. **6.** Four-door sedans like this 500 made up most of Fairlane's 317,074-unit production. **7.** Top wagon was the $2796 Squire.

5

6

7

1

2

3

4

5

6

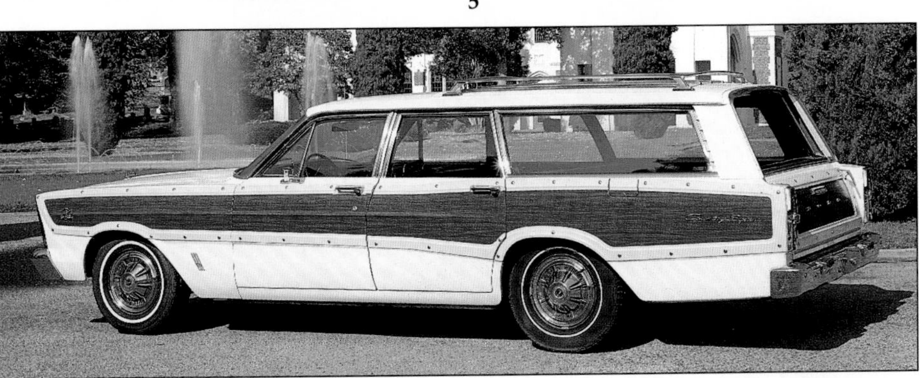

7

8

1-2. Pride of the fleet of facelifted full-size Fords was the new Galaxie 500 7-Litre, a bucket-seat $3872 convertible or $3621 2-door hardtop. Named for the metric size of the new 428-cid V-8 (345 bhp, or 360 in police tune), these cruisers did 0–60 mph in 8 sec. **3.** Ford briefly offered this limo through its dealers as a special-order item. It was built by an aftermarket coachbuilder on a lengthened production chassis. **4.** Plushest big Ford again was the LTD hardtop in $3231 2-door form or as this $3278 4-door. **5.** A big seller at 171,886 units was the Galaxie 500 4-door sedan. **6.** Ford's retort to Chrysler's Hemi was an overhead-cam 427-cid V-8. It was outlawed in stock-car racing but was a winner in drag racers, including this Galaxie. **7.** A family classic: the $3265, 4040-lb Country Squire. **8.** The Black Pearl LTD show car had no exterior door handles.

1966 Ford

1. Falcon gained 1.4 inches of wheelbase, to 110.9, and took on near-midsize airs, but was overshadowed by the Fairlane and sales dipped 15 percent, to 182,699. **2-5.** Full-width taillamps marked the '66 Thunderbird. Cruise control with steering-wheel buttons was a new option. Leather upholstery added $147, an 8-track tape player $82. The 345-bhp 428 was a bargain at $64 over the 315-bhp 390. The '66 ragtop listed for $4879 and was the last factory-built T-Bird convertible.

1

2

3

4

5

1

2

1. Bronco debuted for '66 as a compact 4-wheel-drive truck with a semblance of comfort—a preview of today's sport-utility vehicle. **2.** The open-top Bronco "Dune-Duster" and sybaritic Econoline "Apartment" were Ford show trucks.

1966 Lincoln

1

2

Lincoln updated the Continental while preserving the essential character of the classic '61. The '66 retained a 126-inch wheelbase but got new sheetmetal for a body length of 220.9 inches, nearly 5 inches longer than before. Curved side glass returned, and the 320-bhp 430-cid V-8, which dated from 1958, was replaced by a new 340-bhp 462. The changes were well-received. Model-year output jumped 17 percent, to 54,755, for Lincoln's best showing of the decade. **1-2.** The convertible was still America's only 4-door ragtop and now had a rear window of glass, not plastic. Base price was $6383, below '65's, but at just 3180 units, its share of Lincoln sales fell to 5 percent from 8.

1966 Lincoln

1

2

1. Lincoln offered a 2-door hardtop for 1966, its first since '60. Listing at $5485, it was the least-expensive model in the lineup, and the second-most popular: 15,766 were built. **2.** Lehmann-Peterson coachbuilders of Chicago stretched the new Continental into another of its elegant 7-passenger limos. **3.** The 4-door was sometimes called a "pillared hardtop sedan" because, although there were slim center roof pillars, there were no frames in the way when the side windows were lowered. The sedan, as always, was the best-seller, attracting 35,809 buyers. It listed at $5750. **4.** The Lincoln Continental Coronation Coupe show car had fat rear-roof pillars and a lower-body band of woodgrain framed in bright metal.

3

4

1. This show-car version of the full-size Mercury boasted experimental Twist-Wrist Steering. **2.** The new 428-cid V-8 was available in all big Mercs, including the Park Lane ragtop. **3.** Comet graduated from a compact-class car to an intermediate by taking up the Ford Fairlane's 116-inch chassis. The sporty Cyclone series added a GT coupe and convertible. The 390-cid V-8 was a GT standard and the drop-top GT paced the Indianapolis 500.

1

2

3

General Motors

Alfred P. Sloan, Jr., former GM chairman whose management practices shaped General Motors into the world's largest industrial corporation, dies of a heart attack at age 90

Despite initial denials, GM admits it used private detectives to investigate *Unsafe at Any Speed* author Ralph Nader; an embarrassed GM acknowledges nothing incriminating was found and issues a public apology

Most important new GM car of '66 is the Olds Toronado, the first front-wheel-drive American production car since the prewar Cord

Buick launches the second-generation Riviera; division slips from fifth to seventh in U.S. model-year production

Cadillac gets a subtle facelift; new top model is the Fleetwood Brougham

Chevrolet makes Caprice a separate model; Chevy II/Nova is reskinned and gets up to 350 bhp

Chevy loses model-year production leadership to Ford by a slim margin; it's just the second time Chevy would be outpaced by its rival during the '60s

Pontiac introduces the overhead-cam Sprint engine, America's first performance-oriented 6-cylinder since the Hudson Hornet six in the early 1950s

1

2

3

A crisp, new body graced the redesigned Riviera. Buick's personal/luxury flagship gained 2 inches of wheelbase, to 119, and 150 lbs. Headlights were now hidden behind a fresh grille, which was mirrored by the new taillamp design. Standard power was 1965's optional 340-bhp 425-cid V-8; an available 360-bhp dual quad version delivered 0–60 mph in 8.2 sec. **1.** The extra-cost Gran Sport package included heavy-duty suspension among its features. **2.** A bench seat was standard, but buckets and a center console were separate options. **3.** Base price was $4424, up just $16 from '65. Production jumped 24 percent, to 45,348.

1

2

3

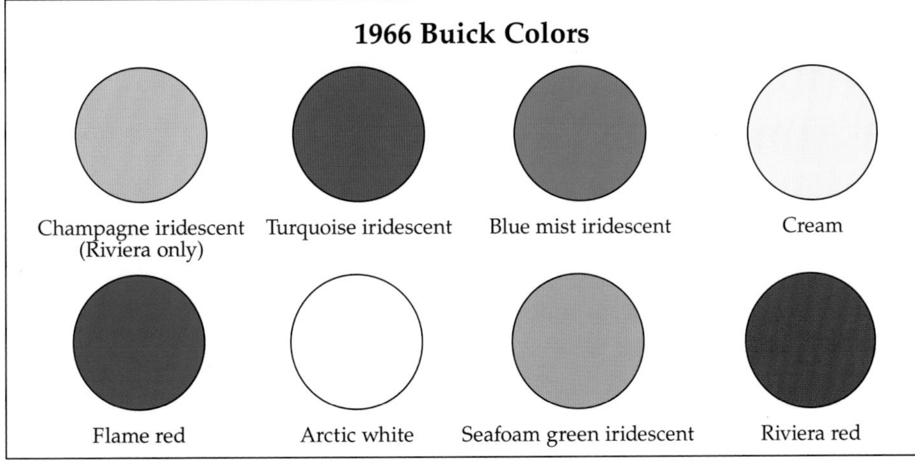

Changes in full-size Buicks ran to trim and equipment details—not enough to sustain the public's interest at 1965 levels. Model-year volume declined by nearly 50,000 units, to 553,870, and Buick relinquished its fifth-place standing to Oldsmobile. **1-2.** The Wildcat herd included convertibles and 2-door hardtops in base and Custom trim. Both could be fitted with the Gran Sport package, which included the 340-bhp 425. **3.** At $2942, the LeSabre 4-door sedan was the only big Buick with a sub-$3000 base price. It also was the make's single best-selling model, finding 39,146 customers.

1966 Buick

1

2

3

4

1. A distinguished nose, graceful new contours, and a tunnelled rear window highlighted style changes to the Special and Skylark. Here's a Gran Sport and a Skylark 4-door hardtop. **2-3.** Buick signaled its commitment to the muscle-car market by elevating the Gran Sport from a Skylark option package to its own series of 2-door sedans, hardtops, and convertibles. Its 325-bhp 401-cid V-8 delivered 0–60 mph in 7.6 sec; a quicker 340-bhp version was optional. **4.** Wagons continued on a 120-inch wheelbase (versus 115 for other body types). This is the Skylark Sport wagon. **5.** The basic 2-door hardtop was the best-seller.

5

SOME OF OUR BEST FRIENDS ARE CHAUFFEURS. And there are a number of reasons why: the car's exceptional comfort, its great interior luxury, its new smoothness and quietness of operation, the marvelous ease provided by Cadillac's new steering and handling, and, of course, the car's impressive new stature and beauty. No wonder that wherever you find Cadillac chauffeurs—professional or amateur—you find a solid body of praise for the 1966 Cadillac, the world's most highly regarded luxury car. Drive it soon at your authorized dealer's. You'll discover why Cadillac makes friends so easily.

New elegance, new excellence, new excitement!

Cadillac 1966

1

2

3

4

5

6

Presenting the nineteen sixty-six Cadillac

The finest of all Cadillacs is here! It greets you with an exciting new elegance, highlighted by a totally new split-level grille and new clean-swept body contours. Inside you'll admire breathtaking new leathers, fabrics and new appointments (with dramatic walnut paneling on all Fleetwood models). And Cadillac's traditional engineering excellence rewards you with a number of suspension, chassis, and acoustical advances providing a new realm of quietness and relaxation. You'll marvel at the alert response of Cadillac's new variable ratio steering and easier handling. Today, tomorrow or very soon . . . discover the unmatched excitement of Cadillac for 1966—now on display at your authorized Cadillac dealer!

New elegance, new excellence, new excitement!

7

1. Cadillac's new nose looked quite formal. This is the $5181 DeVille sedan. **2.** Rarest '66 was the $6631 Eldorado. All were convertibles and just 2250 were built. **3-4.** The other ragtop was the $5555 DeVille; 19,200 of these were made. New for all Cadillacs was speed-dependent variable-ratio power steering and optional heated front seats. **5.** Plenty of room for hats in the $10,521, 5435-lb Seventy-Five limo, which got its first redesign since 1959. **6.** Model-year sales were up 14,250 units, to 196,685. **7.** Fleetwood Brougham moved from the 129.5-inch wheelbase to the Sixty Special's 149.9.

1966 Chevrolet

1

2

3

4

Chevelle got the Coke-bottle contours given all 1966 GM intermediates. Chevelle 300 and Malibu lines returned, and Super Sport was now a series of its own. **1-2.** Super Sport ditched its 327-cid V-8 for standard big-block power and became the SS 396 with 325 bhp standard and 375 optional. The latter did 0–60 mph in 6 sec. **3.** El Camino had its own unique appeal. **4.** Chevelle sales rose 16 percent, to 412,000.

5-6. Besides squared-up sheetmetal—no aesthetic advance over the svelte '65s—big news for the big Chevys was the new Caprice. Elevated from a trim option to a series of its own, Chevrolet's new luxury leader was available as a 2- and 4-door hardtop and a wagon. All had V-8s, ranging from the standard 195-bhp 283 to the newly available 385-bhp 427. Caprice's first-season sales were a healthy 181,000.

5

6

1 2 3 4 5 6 7

1. Of nearly 1.2 million full-size '66 Chevys, 46 percent were Impalas. Here's the $3097 V-8 ragtop. **2.** Between Impala and the entry-level Biscayne was the Bel Air. A fine value at just $2542, this is the 6-cylinder 2-door sedan. **3.** Only Lincoln among modern American automakers built a 4-door convertible, but the Caribe concept car showed what a Chevy version might have been like. **4.** All but 900 of the 76,055 Impala Super Sports for '66 had V-8 engines **5.** Chevy built 2.2 million cars for the model year and still trailed Ford. **6-7.** Costliest non-Corvette was the $3413 Caprice Estate wagon.

1966 Chevrolet

1

2

3

Bad press and competition from the revamped Chevy II cut sales of Corvair by half, to just over 100,000. Even Chevy seemed to sense the party was ending, noting in midyear that the top-line Corsa and its turbo engine would be dropped after '66. **1.** Only change of note for '66 was standard front seatbelts. The Monza coupe was Corvair's most-popular model. **2.** A clean Corvair is a happy Corvair. **3.** The 4-door hardtop sold better in this Monza trim than in base 500-series guise. **4.** All ragtops were Monzas.

4

Electrovair II

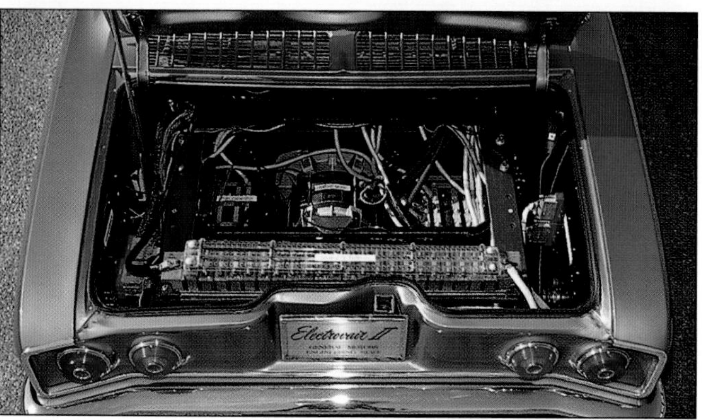

Electrovair II was a GM-built experimental '66 Monza. A standard 4-door was modified to accept a 100-horsepower AC electric motor. Silver-zinc batteries occupy the trunk and engine bay. The Marina Blue body was mildly modified to accommodate the conversion, and appropriate gauges went into the dashboard. It's on loan from GM to the Corvair Preservation Foundation Museum.

1

2

3

1. Corvette changed little outside, but sales rose to a record 27,720. **2.** The idea of the 'Vette as a lifelong object of desire was nurtured by promotions such as the 25-inch-long red plastic Kiddie Corvette. **3.** A "power bulge" hood indicated presence of the new 427-cid V-8 option. It had up to 425 bhp and replaced the 396. **4-5.** Chevy's compact kept its 100-inch wheelbase and full range of body styles but was reclothed in sharp new sheetmetal. New for the Nova SS was a 350-bhp 327. Chevy II sales rebounded to 163,300.

4

5

1966 Oldsmobile

1

2

3

Go ask 'em up on Pikes Peak what Toronado's front-wheel driving can do.

They found out, in the 44th annual test of machines vs. mountain, known as the Pikes Peak Auto Hill Climb.

Three privately-owned Toronados made their runs against the clock. So did the rest of the toughest competitive lineup ever brought together for the stock car class.

You know what? These front-wheel-driving cars finished 1-2-3 in the event sponsored by the United States Auto Club.

But, that's Toronado for you: a great luxury car, built on the superior traction and maneuvering capabilities of front-wheel driving.

It tracks where others can't. And in more normal driving, Toronado tends to its business with a response and obedience you didn't know a big car could have.

All the while, coddling you in comforts a limousine owner might envy.

Isn't it time you found out what front-wheel driving can do to spoil you for conventional cars? Your nearest Olds dealer would be more than happy to oblige.

Oldsmobile Toronado: For front-wheel-drive roadability.

4

1. A landmark automobile and one of the decade's most-important cars, the 1966 Olds Toronado re-introduced front-wheel drive to America and forecast the design revolution that would sweep the U.S. industry in the 1980s. **2.** Proud engineers and executives with the first one off the exclusive assembly line set up for Toronado. **3.** For a new design, the car was surprisingly trouble-free, thanks to exhaustive testing. Underhood was the most-powerful Olds V-8, a 425 with 385 bhp. It drove the front wheels via a segmented automatic transmission nestled around the engine. **4.** Handling was surefooted, traction unsurpassed, and acceleration a lively 9.5 sec 0–60 mph—good enough to snare the *Motor Trend* "Car of the Year" trophy. **5.** The 4300-lb coupe got 13 mpg on premium fuel in *MT*'s 2700-mile-long road test.

5

1

2

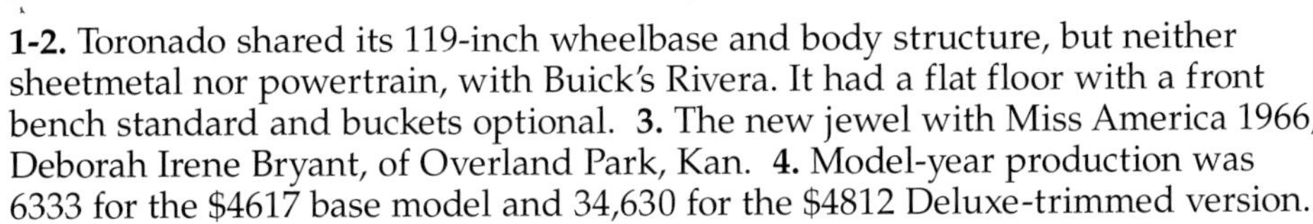

1-2. Toronado shared its 119-inch wheelbase and body structure, but neither sheetmetal nor powertrain, with Buick's Rivera. It had a flat floor with a front bench standard and buckets optional. **3.** The new jewel with Miss America 1966, Deborah Irene Bryant, of Overland Park, Kan. **4.** Model-year production was 6333 for the $4617 base model and 34,630 for the $4812 Deluxe-trimmed version.

3

4

1966 Oldsmobile

1

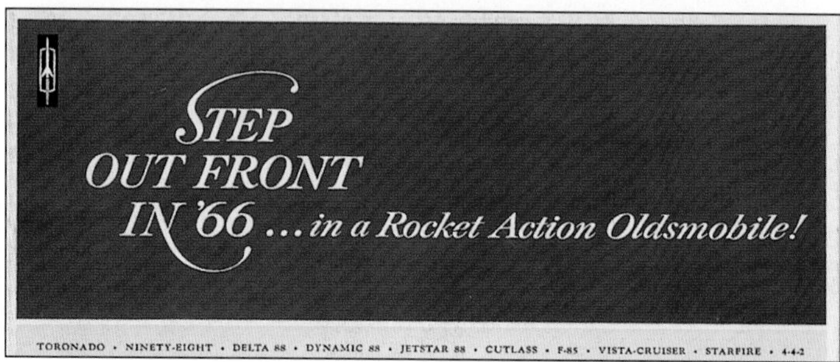

Model-year output fell 13,316 units, to 578,385, but Olds retained sixth place in U.S. production. **1.** Full-size cars got a minor facelift, as seen on this Dynamic 88 ragtop, which listed for $3404 with the standard 310-bhp 425 V-8. **2.** The mid-size F-85/Cutlass series was reskinned. Its 4-4-2 edition was more civilized than most muscle cars, but still did 0–60 mph in 7.1 sec with its standard 350-bhp 400 V-8. **3.** This exhibition drag racing version used two Toronado V-8s driving all four wheels. **4.** Division chief Harold Metzel with a model of the next year's auto-show display.

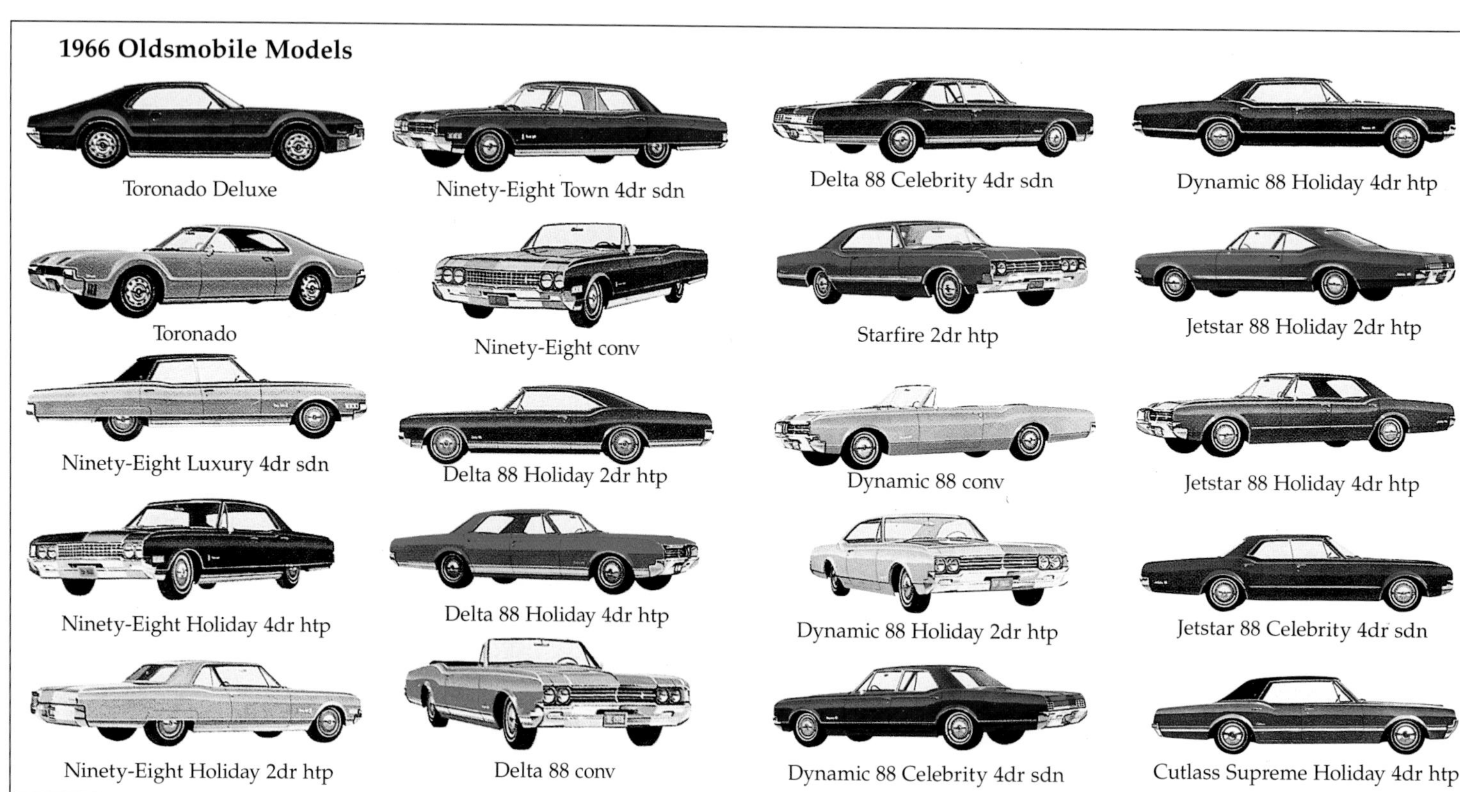

2

3

4

Cutlass Holiday 2dr htp

F-85 wgn

F-85 4dr sdn

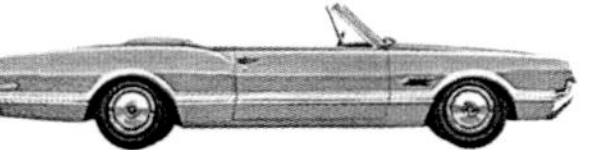
Cutlass 4-4-2 conv

Cutlass conv

F-85 Deluxe Holiday 2dr htp

Vista Cruiser Custom wgn 9 pass

F-85 4-4-2 Holiday 2dr htp

Cutlass Sports Coupe

F-85 Deluxe Holiday 4dr htp

Vista Cruiser wgn 9 pass

F-85 4-4-2 club coupe

Cutlass Celebrity 4dr sdn

F-85 Deluxe 4dr sdn

Cutlass 4-4-2 2dr htp

Vista Cruiser Custom wgn 6 pass

F-85 Deluxe wgn

F-85 club coupe

Cutlass 4-4-2 club coupe

Vista Cruiser wgn 6 pass

1966 Pontiac

1

2

3

4

5

Pontiac turned 40 years old in 1966 and in June built its 11-millionth car. Model-year production increased about 30,000 units, to 830,778, keeping Pontiac behind only giants Ford and Chevy among U.S. automakers. Much sales success was due to the redesigned compact line, but full-size models provided plenty of appeal. **1.** Grand Prix, a big coupe with lots of personality, listed for $3492 and weighed 4015 lb. **2.** This year's slightly revised styling looked good on the 124-inch chassis of the Bonneville and Star Chief. Here's the $3586 Bonneville convertible. **3.** Best-selling Bonne was the 4-door hardtop. **4-5.** Full-size performance cars were fading as mid-size muscle took over, but Pontiac held out with the 2+2. This Catalina-based 2-door hardtop and convertible became an independent series for '66 and was the only Pontiac with a standard 421-cid V-8. With up to 376 bhp in three 2-barrel form, a 2+2 could do 0–60 mph in 7 sec. **6.** John Z. DeLorean was one of the period's brightest and most-colorful automotive figures. He joined Pontiac as an engineer in the late 1950s and by 1965 was division general manager, an office he'd hold into 1969.

6

1

2

Taking its lead from the flamboyant DeLorean, Pontiac projected a brash image—and usually delivered on its bravado. Helping it back up any boast was a wide selection of engines. Of 11 V-8s, the smallest displaced 389 cubic inches, the largest 421, and just three had a single 2-barrel carburetor. The two 6-cylinder engines were advanced, performance-oriented overhead-cam designs. **1.** This brochure highlights not the wagons or sedans, but the excitement offerings, including the 2+2, GTO, and new overhead-cam Tempest. The tiger was the division's marketing mascot. **2.** "Arrogant split grille," is how this Grand Prix ad begins, in typical Pontiac fashion. The artwork is another in a series by master illustrators Van Kaufman and Arthur Fitzpatrick. **3.** Catalina was the "entry level" big Pontiac. It featured a full range of body styles. The 2-door hardtop listed for $2893 and pleased 79,013 buyers. Only the $2831 Catalina 4-door sedan, with 80,483 units, had a higher model-year production total for Pontiac.

1966 Pontiac Engines

230-cid ohc 6-cylinder, 165 bhp

230-cid ohc 6-cylinder, 207 bhp

326-cid V-8, 250 bhp

326-cid V-8, 285 bhp

389-cid V-8, 256 bhp

389-cid V-8, 290 bhp

389-cid V-8, 325 bhp

389-cid V-8, 333 bhp

389-cid V-8, 335 bhp

389-cid V-8, 360 bhp

421-cid V-8, 338 bhp

421-cid V-8, 356 bhp

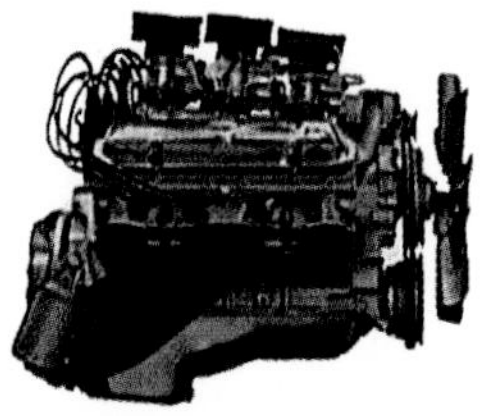

421-cid V-8, 376 bhp

3

1966 Pontiac

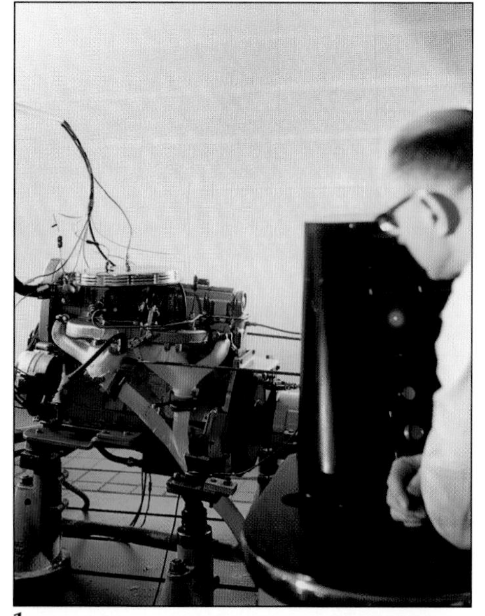
1

2

3

1-2. In a day of V-8 dominance, John DeLorean pushed for a new 6-cylinder engine of a sophisticated overhead-cam design. The result was Pontiac's 230-cid ohc six. It replaced a 140-bhp 215-cid overhead-valve six as standard in Tempest and LeMans and had 165 bhp in base form, 207 with the 4-barrel Sprint option. A 6000-rpm redline—nearly twice that of the V-8s—gave it a European feel and good acceleration. But it was not popular and would die after the '69 model year. **3.** Youthful and aggressive, Pontiac's revamp of its mid-size line was among the decade's best styling jobs. A 4-door was offered for the first time, but didn't quite fit into this Tiger-image ad. **4-6.** GTO became its own model line and sold 96,946 units, highest-ever one-year total for a true muscle car. Pillared coupe, hardtop, and convertible were offered, all with a 389 V-8; 360-bhp versions did 0–60 mph in 6.5 sec.

4

5

6

Studebaker Corporation

One-hundred and fourteen years of vehicle production ends as Studebaker stops building cars at its sole remaining plant in Ontario, Canada

Official announcement of the halt in automobile production comes on March 4

Final cars roll off the line on March 17; the last is a Cruiser V-8 in Timberline Turquoise; it's later put in the Studebaker Historical collection in South Bend, Ind.

Model-year volume totals only 8947, far below the 20,000 needed to break even

The end is preceded by innovative survival efforts; chief executive Gordon E. Grundy negotiates with Datsun for Studebaker to become the Japanese automaker's U.S. importer; Studebaker's board instructs him to approach Toyota instead, but the apparent indecision frightens off both foreign firms

As in 1965, the '66 line consists of Lark-based Six and Eight models; a General Motors 230-cid 6-cylinder is an option on automatic transmission cars

Studebaker itself lives on as a diversified investment and real-estate company

Avanti, too, survives as an independently built low-volume speciality car

1

2

3

The '66s were warmed-over '65s with a new twin-headlamp grille and air-extractor vents in place of upper taillights. **1.** The Cruiser 4-door sedan topped the line, at $2545 for the V-8 model. **2-3.** The Daytona was the sporty entry. **4.** Avanti—with a II suffix—continued production in low numbers. Hand-built under independent ownership, early IIs used a 327-cid Chevrolet V-8. Avanti was built into the early 1990s.

"While I sincerely regret the necessity of discontinuing production of Studebaker cars, the irreversible losses being incurred permit no other course."

—Studebaker President Byers A. Burlingame; March 1966

4

Etc.

The Michigan State Highway commission concludes that cars of the future will probably not be nuclear-powered because "the lead shield needed to keep radiation within the power pack would be far too heavy to be practical, and fear of radiation escaping would scare potential buyers"

United States Bureau of Public Roads reports that travel on interstate highways is approximately twice as safe as travel on conventional roads and streets

Dan Stafford, a salesman at Waters Buick in San Francisco since 1941, spends his 96th birthday working the showroom floor

The AAA auto club offers allergic motorists summertime routes to "hay fever relief areas"

A study by psychologists at the University of South Dakota suggests that nearly half of all drivers are incapable of safely executing passing maneuvers

A Chicago sheriff's department auction of confiscated automobiles nets $893; unfortunately, the department had spent more than $900 to store them

A Mercury dealer in Winnipeg, Manitoba, Canada, encourages sales by placing scantily clad "a-go-go" girls in his lot

CBS-TV airs *Crash Project—The Search for Auto Safety*

1. Those darling Monkees had their own GTO-derived Monkeemobile, but here pack an MG MGA Twin-Cam roadster. **2.** Burgers, dogs, fries, and shakes were wholesome food in the '60s. Just a speak into the "Teletray Microphone" at this drive-in restaurant, and they were yours. **3.** Here's the limited-production, oddly retro Duesenberg designed by Virgil Exner and built by Fred Duesenberg. **4.** The Italianate Bosley Mark II Interstate was designed and built in Ohio. It had a fiberglass body and a 345-bhp Pontiac V-8. **5.** A mess o' Bugs at Los Angeles Harbor. **6.** Imports dominate this parking lot's small-car-only section. **7.** The Griffith GT originated in New York State and was bodied by Intermeccanica of Italy.

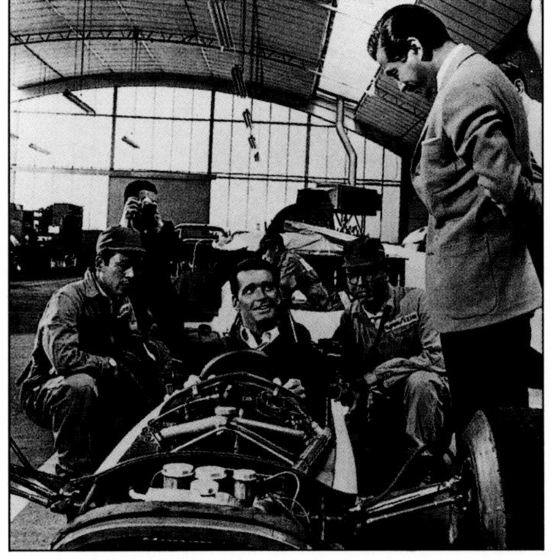

1

2

3

4

5

1. Actor James Garner gets comfortable in the apocryphal "Yamura" racer in *Grand Prix*. **2.** Paul Newman as anti-hero detective Harper snoops from between a Mercury Park Lane and a T-Bird. **3.** TV's the Girl from U.N.C.L.E., secret agent April Dancer (Stefanie Powers), sits in the U.N.C.L.E. car and brandishes an unidentified projectile. **4.** The obscure BMW Electric roadster was not made by Germany's BMW; the name is likely comprised of the maker's initials. **5.** Toyota's breakthrough sports car, the 2000GT. It had a 121-cid six, 150 bhp, and great handling, but cost $6800. This gaily decorated example was owned by Toyota president Suchi Hattori. **6.** When low oil pressure forced Jackie Stewart out of the Indy 500 with just 10 laps to go, his teammate, Graham Hill, drove this Ford-powered Lola to victory. Hill's average speed: 144.3 mph.

6

Etc.

The Batmobile, built by customizer George Barris on the carcass of the 1955 Lincoln Futura show car, debuts as the caped crusader's ride on ABC-TV's *Batman*

U.S. Congress legislates the first federal tire standards

Fifty-two import models available for the model year have list prices below the lowest-priced domestic car

Communist China updates its Red Flag sedan and claims it is comparable with "the best standards in the world"

Interior Secretary Stewart Udall predicts that by 1986, half the cars on the road will be electric-powered

Volkswagen Fastback and Squareback models debut in the U.S. market

Studies suggest many women drivers find antifreeze "mysterious"

Federal estimate of completion date of the interstate highway system is revised to 1976 from 1972

Top 10 Selling Imports

1. Volkswagen 420,018
2. Opel 31,555
3. Volvo 25,126
4. Datsun 21,726
5. MG 21,709
6. Triumph 17,184
7. Mercedes-Benz ... 16,081
8. Toyota 15,814
9. Simca 12,596
10. Renault 11,500

Total import-car share of U.S. market: 7.31 percent

1967

A crippling 61-day strike against Ford Motor Company was settled with UAW workers at the Big 3 winning a pay hike of about a dollar an hour phased in over three years. In America at large, there was no hint of a settlement over the Vietnam War. By year's end 475,000 American troops were in Southeast Asia; stateside peace rallies were multiplying; and boxer Muhammad Ali (the former Cassius Clay) was stripped of his heavyweight crown when he refused induction into the armed forces in protest of the war.

In the Middle East, the Six-Day War (June 5-10) pitted Israel against attacking Syria, Egypt, and Jordan. When it was over, victorious Israeli troops occupied key territory that would be fought over through the end of the century.

In what was becoming an annual summer ritual, inner-city America exploded in rioting; in Detroit, 40 people died, 2000 were injured, and 5000 made homeless when arsonists, looters, and gunmen took over the streets. It took 7000 National Guard troops to restore order.

A pencil-thin 17-year-old British model named Leslie Hornby called herself "Twiggy" and was a fashion sensation. The miniskirt continued to rule fashion's

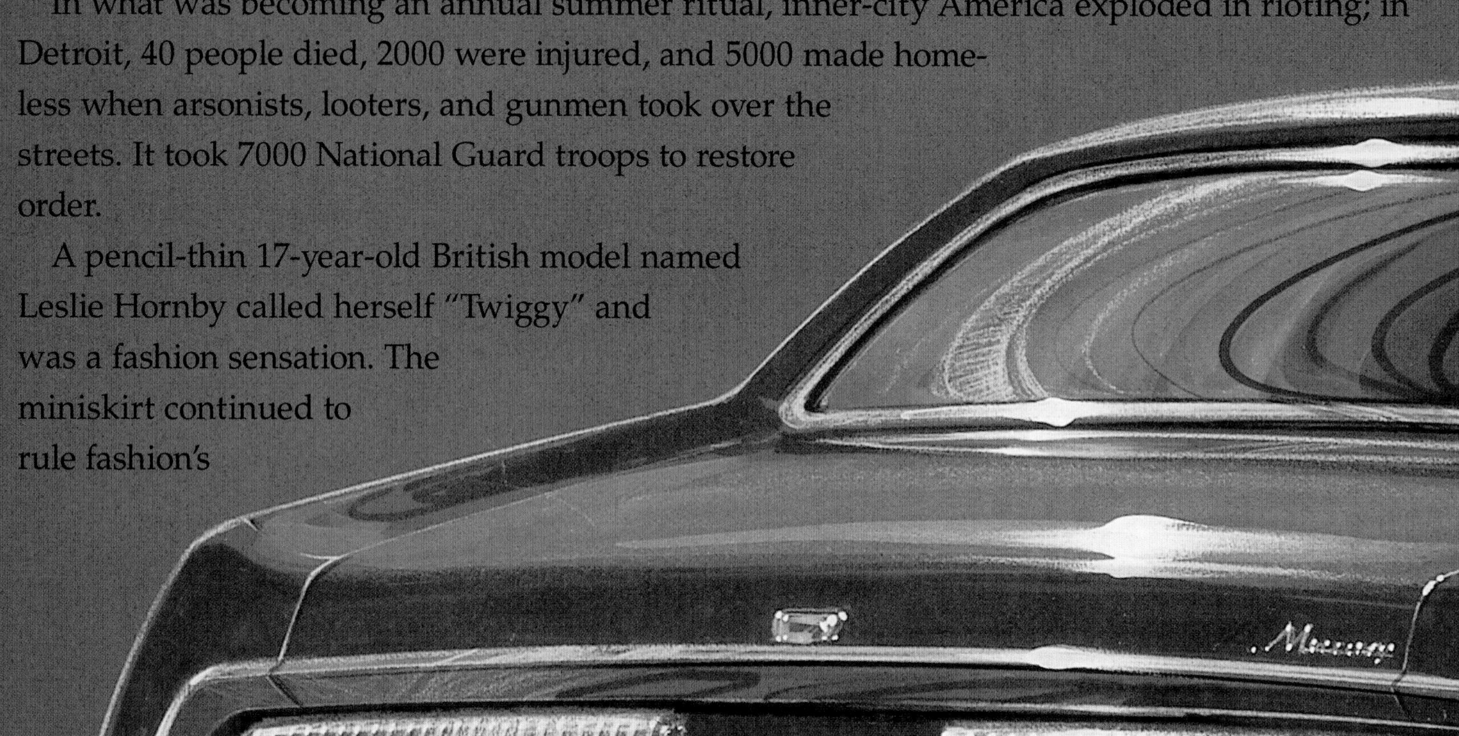

runways, and turtleneck jerseys and sweaters became popular with men and women. Paper clothing was a short-lived fad.

Singles bars, discotheques, and go-go dancers were new fixtures in cities and towns across America. Youth also was served by the Beatles, whose brilliant concept album, *Sgt. Pepper's Lonely Hearts Club Band,* took rock into the psychedelic future. Young people who thronged to San Francisco's Haight-Ashbury district for the "Summer of Love" got friendly, smoked pot, and grooved to the sounds of the Grateful Dead, Jefferson Airplane, Big Brother and the Holding Company with Janis Joplin, Quicksilver Messenger Service, and the Byrds. Top song, though, as chosen by the conservative Grammy Awards committee, was the 5th Dimension's "Up, Up and Away."

Moviemakers celebrated alienated youth in *The Graduate, Bonnie and Clyde,* and *Cool Hand Luke.* Other big hits were *Guess Who's Coming to Dinner, The Dirty Dozen,* and *In the Heat of the Night.*

Top TV shows included *The Wild, Wild West, The Fugitive* (which wound up its hero's four-year quest for justice with a widely seen two-part episode), and *The Dean Martin Show. The Monkees, Gomer Pyle U.S.M.C.,* and *Family Affair* were among the top-rated sitcoms.

Football was dominated by the Green Bay Packers, and baseball's World Series was won by the St. Louis Cardinals, who slipped past the Boston Red Sox, four games to three. Red Sox left fielder Carl Yastrzemski won the Triple Crown, batting .326 with 121 RBIs and 44 home runs.

American Motors Corporation

Besieged by mounting financial problems, AMC endures a pivotal year

As annual losses approach $76 million, an astronomical sum for the day, a desperate board of directors forces Roy Abernethy, president since 1962, to retire; William V. Luneburg replaces him

Unsold cars pile up on lots; AMC unloads 14,000 to rental companies at minimal profit; gets federal help when U.S. Postal Service buys 3745 Ambassador sedans

To meet payroll, AMC takes out emergency loans and prepares to sell the finance arm of its Kelvinator Appliances subsidiary

Combined Rambler/AMC model-year production drops 12 percent, to 302,945, a deceptively slight decline given the overall picture

Mid-size line is redesigned on a longer wheelbase; drops Rambler Classic title and joins new Rebel series

Ambassador is redesigned on a new, longer chassis; aspires to be taken seriously as a full-size luxury car

Fastback Marlin moves from the old Classic platform to the larger new Ambassador chassis

1

2

3

4

The compact American/Rogue line was the only AMC series that didn't undergo big change for '67. **1.** Biggest news was the addition of a convertible to the uplevel Rogue. The $2611 ragtop was taken home by just 921 buyers. **2.** Rogue's other car, a 2-door hardtop, cost $2426; 4249 were sold. Top engine option was a 225-bhp 290 V-8. **3.** A whiff of chrome and spiffier interior fabrics helped identify the American 440 series. Here's the $2259 4-door sedan. **4-5.** Americans were still tagged Ramblers and the base 2-door sedan lived up to the name's budget-value image. Most made due with the unexciting but economical 128-bhp 199-cid 6-cylinder that was standard.

5

Concept Electron

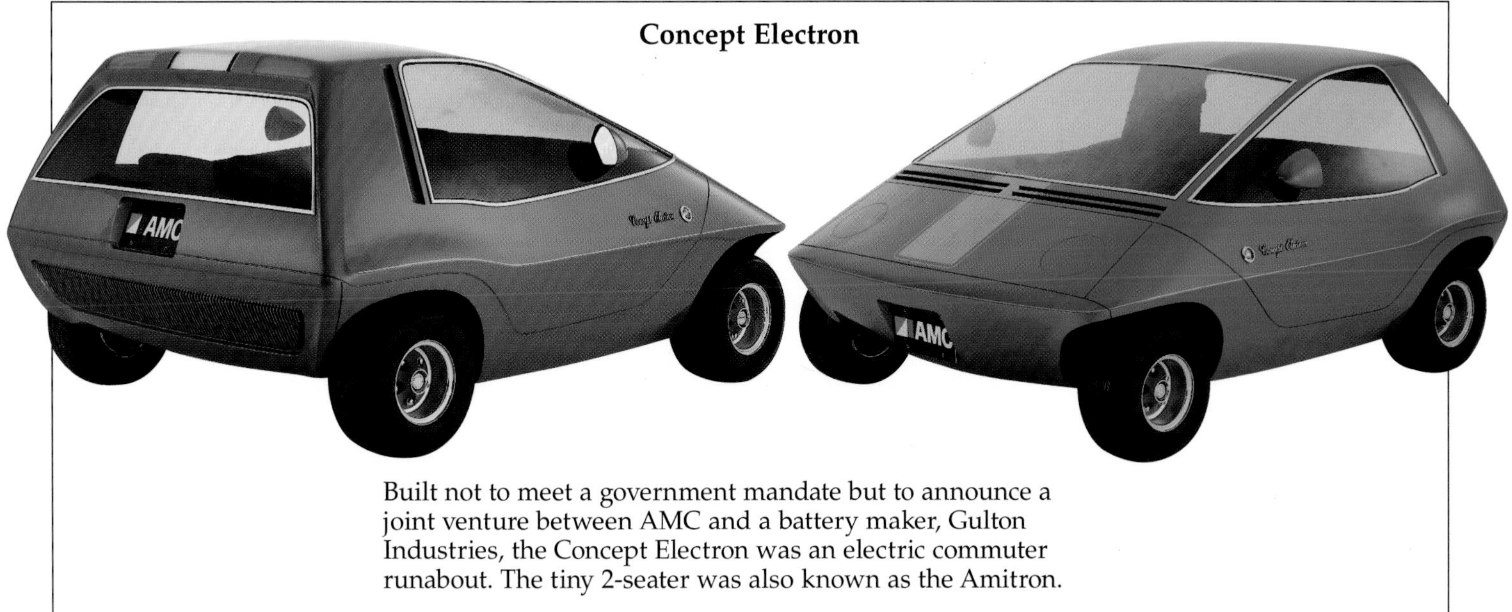

Built not to meet a government mandate but to announce a joint venture between AMC and a battery maker, Gulton Industries, the Concept Electron was an electric commuter runabout. The tiny 2-seater was also known as the Amitron.

1

2

1-3. Marlin kept its less-than-graceful fastback roof, but dumped the 112-inch chassis of the mid-size Classic for the new 118-inch wheelbase of the full-size Ambassador. It also adopted Ambassador's new stacked-headlamp nose. Weight ballooned by 300 lb, to 3342, and the car was 6 inches longer and nearly 4 inches wider. That was "plenty of room for six swingers," said AMC in its best wild-and-crazy-guy voice. But sales that had been halved for '66 fell by 50 percent yet again, to just 2545. A base-price hike of nearly $400, to $2963, didn't help, especially since the same 145-bhp 6-cylinder was expected to pull this heavier car. AMC's new 280-bhp 343-cid V-8 was optional, replacing the old 270-bhp 327. But a full-size AMC fastback answered a question nobody had asked. It wasn't nimble, or pretty, or fast. It would be replaced for '68 by something that was.

"If I don't double my business this year, I'll quit."

—American Motors dealer Ben Lindenbusch, anticipating strong sales of the 1967 AMC line

3

1967 AMC

Replacing the unpretentious Classic as Rambler's mid-size offering was the sleeker Rebel. Its 114-inch-wheelbase chassis was 2-inches longer than Classic's and it had more cabin room. **1.** Rebel offered a full range of body styles, but the only convertible was in the top-trim SST series. **2.** The other SST body was a 2-door hardtop. **3.** An SST ragtop helped celebrate a milestone in an otherwise dour year for AMC. **4-5.** The mid-line trim level was called 770. It included this rather stylish wagon, which rode the standard Rebel wheelbase. **6.** Four-door sedans were the line's bread and butter and came in base 550 and in this 770 trim. The 145-bhp six was standard in all Rebels, with the 280-bhp V-8 the top option. Prices ranged from the 550 2-door's $2319 to the SST ragtop's $2872.

1

3

2

4

5

6

1

2

3

4

The redesigned Ambassador symbolized AMC's questionable plan to meet the Big 3 head-on. **1-3.** Top-trim DPL series had the sole convertible. It came with a 200-bhp 290-cid V-8 that was optional on other Ambassadors. **4.** A 2-door hardtop was the other DPL. It came with Ambassador's standard 155-bhp six. **5-6.** This sedan and wagon belong to the best-selling mid-range 990 series. Base prices ranged from $2510 for the entry 880 series 2-door to $3143 for the DPL convertible.

5

6

Chrysler Corporation

Imperial's transition to a top-line Chrysler model is complete; it abandons body-on-frame assembly for a stretched unibody Chrysler platform

Chrysler slides a new series, the Newport Custom, in between Newport and 300; "semi-fastback" roofline debuts

Dodge drops from fifth to seventh in production despite restyled intermediates and compacts

Reskinned Dodge Coronet offers its first comprehensive muscle-car model, the R/T

Dodge Dart is restyled, scraps station wagon body

Plymouth stays fourth in production; unveils restyled mid-size lineup and its first muscle-car model, the GTX

Valiant and Barracuda restyled; Barracuda separates from Valiant stylistically, though it continues to share a platform

High-performance version of Chrysler's 440-cid V-8 is available in mid-size cars

Richard Petty and his Hemi-powered Belvedere rack up one of the greatest one-year performances in motorsports history, winning 27 NASCAR races, including 10 in a row; Petty and Plymouth run away with the stock-car crown

1

2

Much sheetmetal changed, but big Chryslers looked little different than in '67. The make's sales dipped slightly, though New Yorker was hit inordinately hard, dropping 17 percent to 39,457 units, its lowest ebb in the last half of the decade. **1.** The $4339 New Yorker 4-door hardtop was Chrysler's costliest model. It weighed 4240 lb and came with a 350-bhp 440-cid V-8. **2.** Elwood Engel had a distinguished design career, styling such notables as the 1960 Ford and '61 Lincoln, then succeeding Virgil Exner at Chrysler in '62, where he added the '63 Turbine car and '64 Imperial to his resume. That last set a pattern for big Chryslers that would extend through 1968. **3.** Slotted between the base Newport and the sporty 300 series was the new Newport Custom. It offered a pair of 4-doors and this 2-door hardtop.

3

1 2 3 4

1. Newport Custom echoed most 300 series body offerings but started under $4000. It used the 383-cid V-8 and wasn't eligible for the 440 that drove 300s and New Yorkers. **2.** Retailers were ahead of Detroit in offering wild colors and graphics. Chicago's Mel Wolff Chrysler-Plymouth tarted up a 300 coupe with a pop-art paint scheme. **3.** The Newport 4-door sedan was Chrysler's cheapest, best-selling, and arguably most conservative model, but that didn't stop wacky Wolff from offering one with floral-pattern paint. No word on how much these paint jobs cost or how many sold. **4.** A Newport Custom shows off this year's new semi-fastback 2-door hardtop roofline.

1967 Dodge

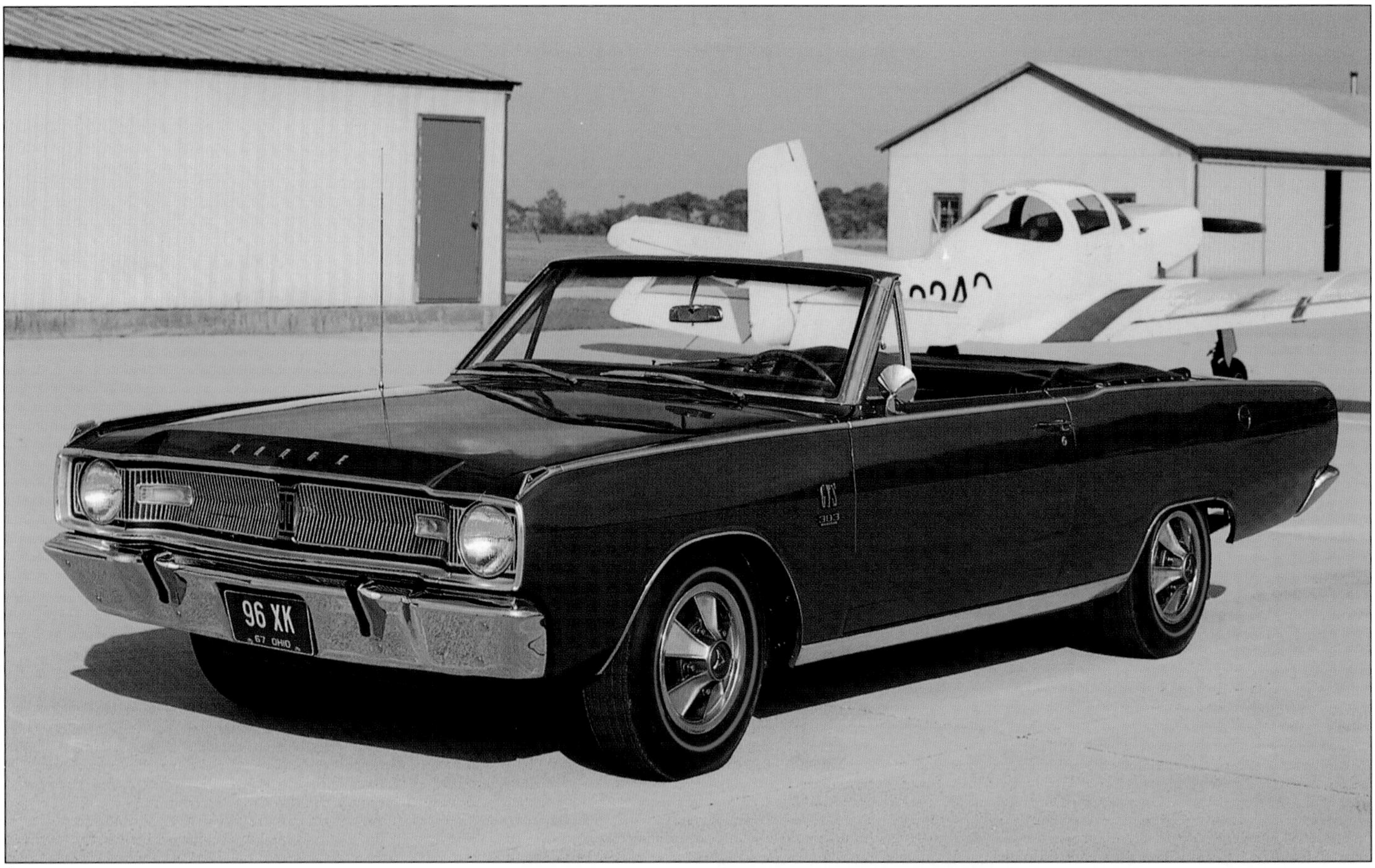

1

1-2. The compact Dart kept its 111-inch wheelbase but shed its wagon models for fully restyled sedans, hardtops, and convertibles that looked better than ever. Base, 270, and sporty GT series were offered with prices ranging from the base 2-door sedan's $2187 to $2860 for V-8 GT ratops like this. Engine choices carried over from '67, with 170- and 225-cid Slant Sixes, and 273-cid V-8s in 180- and 235-bhp versions. Despite the clean new sheetmetal, Dart sales declined 22,000 units, to 154,495, the lowest total since 1963. Competition from Plymouth's restyled Barracuda was partly to blame.

2

1967 Dart Models

GT 2dr htp

270 4dr sdn

Dart 4dr sdn

GT conv

270 2dr htp

Dart 2dr sdn

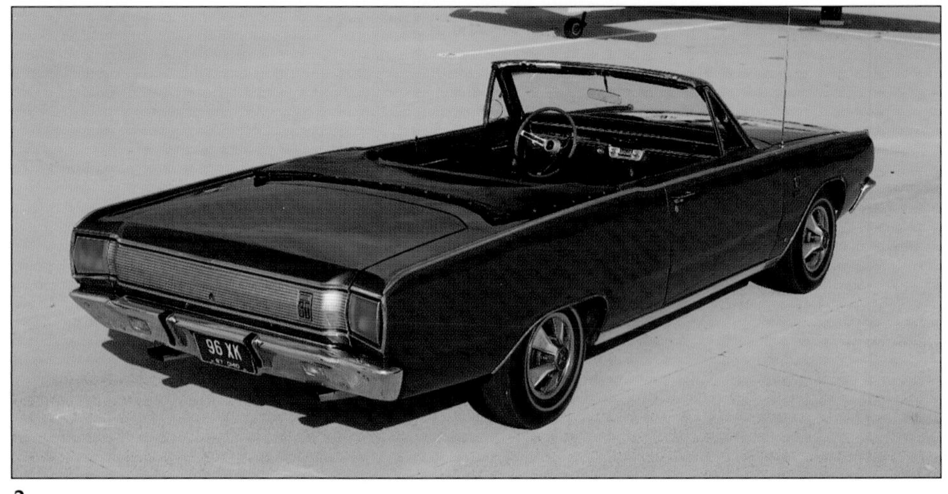

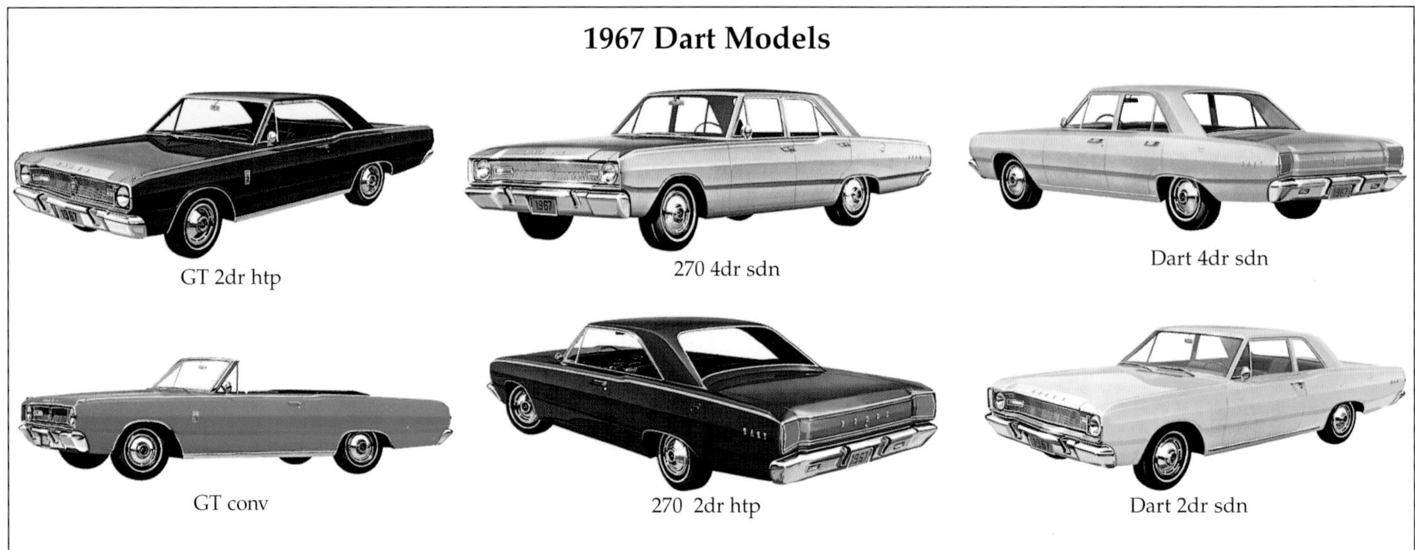

1

2

3

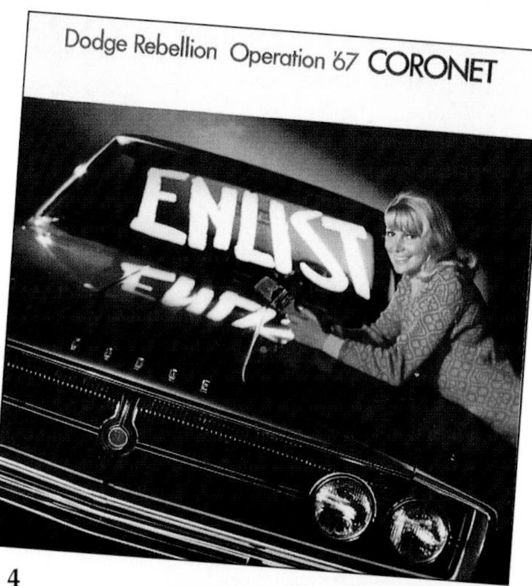

4

5

1-2. Charger was back for the last year of its original styling cycle. Buyers rebelled, and sales plunged by more than half, to just 15,788. **3-4.** Coronet could again be fitted with the 426-cid Hemi V-8, but even that powerhouse didn't lend much outward excitement to a run-of-the-mill Coronet 500 hardtop. **5.** Dodge solved that dilemma by building the Coronet R/T, its first comprehensively packaged muscle car. Standing for Road and Track, R/T models came as $3199 2-door hardtops and this $3438 convertible. They got an exclusive Charger-inspired grille with exposed lights, hood slats, R/T badges, bucket seats, and a heavy-duty suspension. **6.** Standard was a 440-cid V-8 tuned for 375 bhp and christened the Magnum. On the street, it was virtually as fast as the R/T's sole engine option, the 426 Hemi.

6

1967 Dodge

1

2

3

4

6

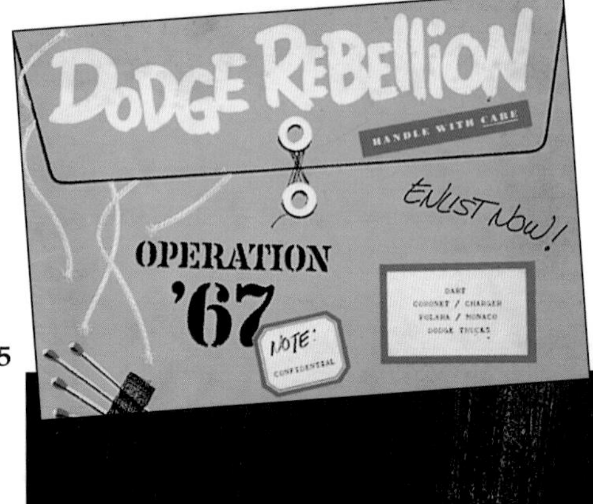

5

1-3. Of 9553 R/T hardtops and 628 convertibles, just 283 had the Hemi option. **4.** Racer Shirley Shahan was the "Drag-On-Lady." **5.** Dealer sales kits reflected the Dodge rebellion theme. Dodge sales plunged 26 percent, and the make slipped from fifth to seventh in model-year production rankings. **6.** Flower power! For $85, about $10 more than a single-color vinyl roof, Van Dyke Dodge in Detroit would apply this wildly printed substitute. It was available in six different patterns. **7.** The most-expensive Dodge of all was the $3712 Monaco 500. It came as a loaded 2-door hardtop only. A 383 was standard. Just 5237 were built.

7

1

2

A steady sales decline made sustaining exclusive body-on-frame construction untenable, so Imperial switched to the same basic unibody structure as other Chryslers. Wheelbase contracted 2 inches to 127, but that was still 3 inches longer than other Chryslers'. Imperial maintained its own sheetmetal, though unibody construction cut weight by about 100 lb. Sales rose 4000 units, to 17,620. **1-3.** The base series offered 2- and 4-door sedans, a 4-door hardtop, and these $6244 ragtops. **4-5.** Top-trim LeBaron model came only as a $6661 4-door hardtop.

3

4

5

1967 Plymouth

"We should get some of the sports-car business now."

—Oak Park, Illinois, Chrysler-Plymouth dealer Larry Stenson, on the 1967 Plymouth Barracuda

1

2

Barracuda was redesigned on a 2-inch-longer wheelbase, now 108 inches. A Euro-flavored hardtop and a convertible joined its fastback body and sales jumped 40 percent, to 62,534. **1.** The sporty choice was again the Formula S. **2-3.** There was now room underhood for the optional 383-cid V-8.

3

1

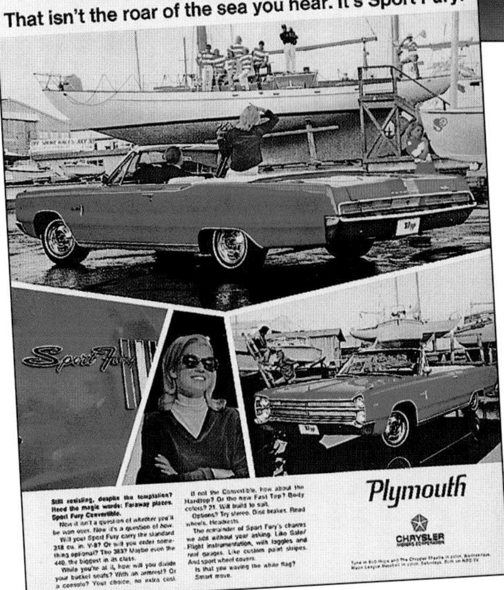

2

3

4

5

1-2. Big Plymouths got new styling in Fury I, II, III, Sport Fury, and VIP trim. These are Sport Furys, which came as 2-door hardtops and convertibles. The former offered traditional rear roof pillars or this semi-fastback. **3.** Cop tires, cop suspension, cop seats, cop engine—in this case, the nasty 440-cid V-8: the crime-fighting Fury Pursuit. **4.** Plymouth cribbed from the GTO for the name of its first comprehensive muscle machine. The GTX had fake hood scoops, but a very real heavy-duty suspension and a choice of 440 Magnum or Hemi V-8s. It came as a hardtop or convertible for about $3000. **5.** Richard Petty and his Hemi Belvedere were nearly unbeatable in '67. Mario Andretti won the Daytona 500 in a Ford, but Petty took the NASCAR crown in a runaway and earned himself a new title: The King.

1967 Plymouth

1

The New Belvedere GTX is out to win you over this year.

Supercar.

Supercar. And how! The standard GTX powerplant just happens to be the biggest GT engine in the world. At 440 cu. in., it pumps out 375 hp. and 480 lbs.-ft. of torque.

What's more, the GTX comes with a raft of equipment to complement its under-the-hood prowess: special suspension, brakes, and exhaust system—even a pit-stop gas filler and hood scoops.

Yes, the awesome Hemi is available. With 426 cubes. 425 horses and 490 lbs.-ft. of torque, no less. Still not won over? Come along quietly: we're going for a ride.

'67 Plymouth

PLYMOUTH DIVISION CHRYSLER MOTORS CORPORATION

2

3

1. A Hemi Satellite did 0-60 mph in 4.8 sec and the quarter-mile in 13.5 at 105 mph. **2-3.** The 440 GTX's times were 6.6 sec and 15.2 at 97 mph. **4-5.** Mel Wolff was at it again, this time with a Satellite ragtop and GTX coupe. **6-7.** Valiant: killed hardtops, soft tops, and wagons; kept 2- and 4-door sedans.

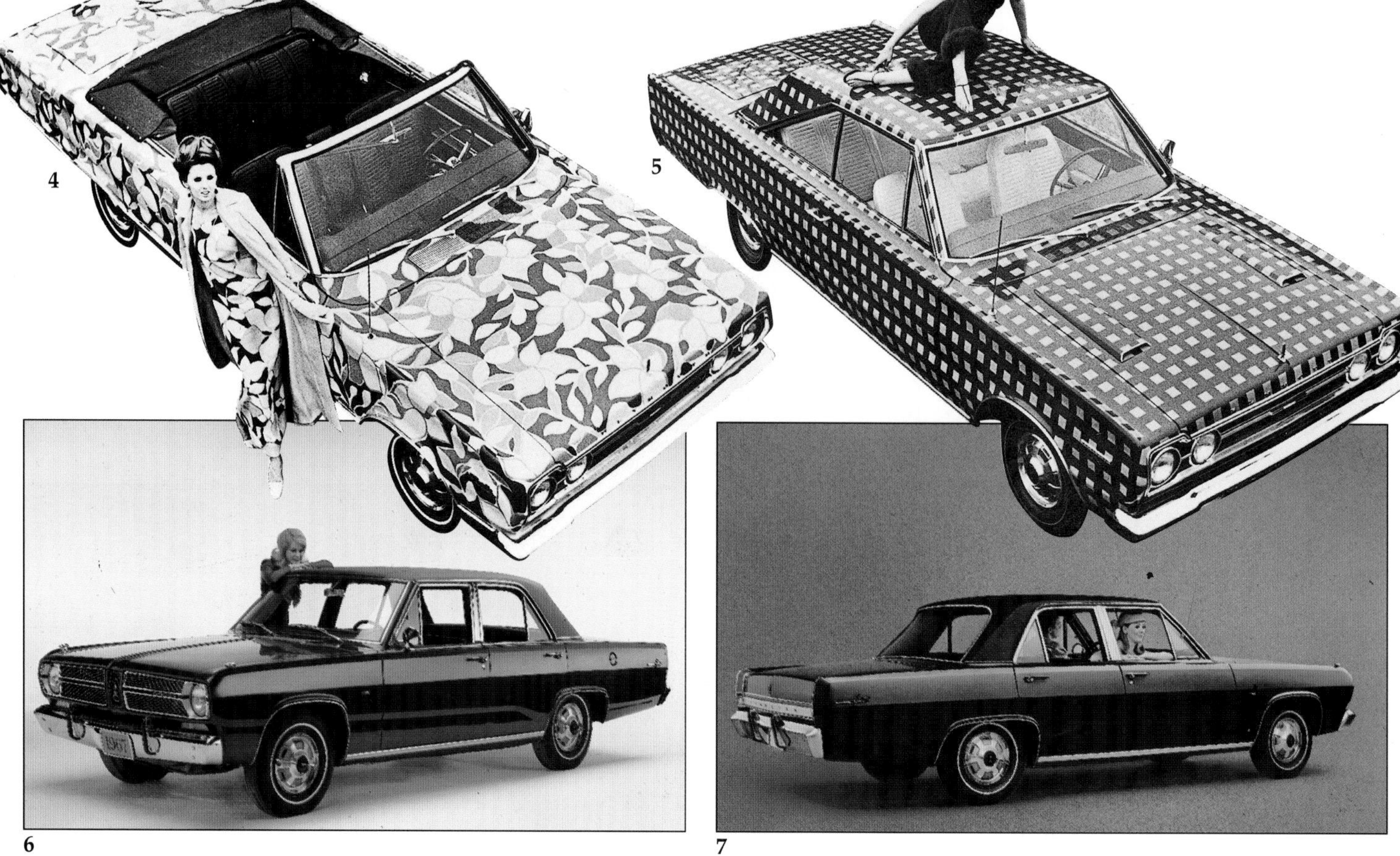

4

5

6

7

Ford Motor Company

Ford Division builds 1.7 million cars for the model year, down nearly 500,000 from '66, and relinquishes its first-place standing to rival Chevrolet

Thunderbird is redesigned; now a full-tilt luxury car; T-Bird offers its first 4-door body style

Full-size Fords enjoy a "mid-life" restyle

Mustang gains new lower-body sheetmetal and its first big V-8, a 390; Shelby versions go it one better, offer the 428-cid V-8

Little-changed Falcon suffers a 64.8-percent sales decline

Mercury gets its version of the Mustang, a slightly larger and upscale ponycar called the Cougar

Big Mercurys are facelifted; add the Marquis personal-luxury hardtop and full-luxury Park Lane Brougham

Shatter-resistant inside rear-view mirror, dual-circuit hydraulic brake system, and energy-absorbing steering-wheel hub are among safety features added to all FoMoCo products

Ford's a racing winner: Its engine powers the top five Indy 500 finishers; wins its second consecutive LeMans 24 Hours with the 427-cid GT40 Mark VI; takes the Daytona 500 checkered flag

1

2

1. With Mustangs and Fairlanes catering to the younger crowd, Ford felt a sport-oriented Thunderbird was no longer needed. Thus the fifth-generation turned fatter and softer. Convertibles were shelved in favor of 2-door hardtops on a 114.7-inch wheelbase (up 1.5 inches from '67). The line's first 4-door model, a hardtop with Lincoln-like rear-hinged back doors, premiered on a 117.2-inch chassis. A 390-cid V-8 or optional 428 returned underhood. Sales increased 21 percent, to 77,956, so somebody liked it. **2.** The mildly reworked Apollo was a T-Bird show car. **3.** Falcon changed little, and sales fell to an all-time low of 64,335.

3

1

2

3

Fairlane got only trim changes. **1.** The 390-cid GT (GTA with automatic transmission) was the main muscle offering, but was no match for GTXs and SS 396s. **2.** Ford's solution was to make the 427 V-8 a regular option for 500 and XL models. It was as fast as most any rival, but fewer than 200 were ordered. **3.** A Fairlane 500 wagon (with incorrect GT wheels). **4.** The 427 Fairlanes were fairly successful drag-racing mounts. **5.** This XL has the 390 V-8. **6.** Mario Andretti scored his only Daytona 500 victory in a 427 Fairlane.

4

5

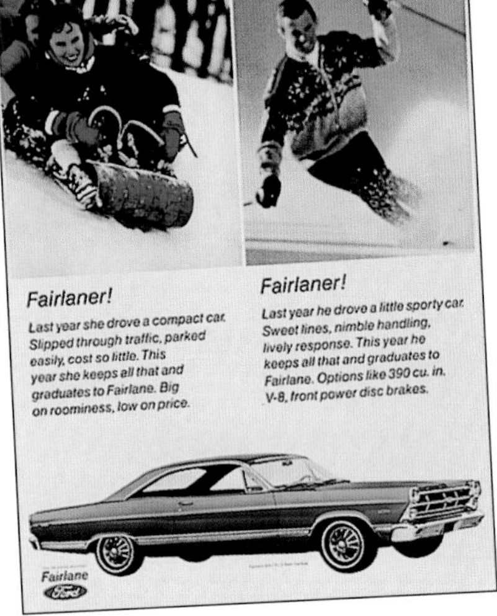

6

1

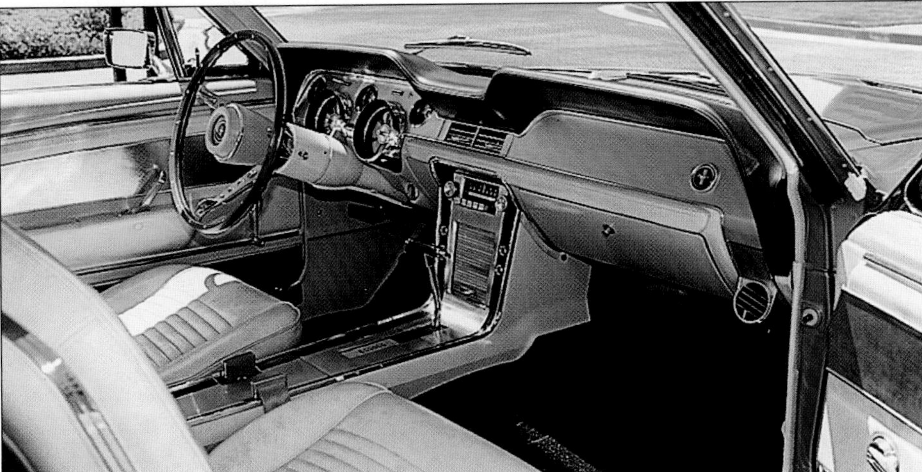
2

3

4

The 108-inch-wheelbase chassis stayed, but Mustang got its first significant styling changes. Coupes, ragtops, and fastbacks were back with a new nose and concave tail panel. Bodies were longer by 2 inches, and a wider engine bay held the big 390-cid V-8 option. **1.** Blending the GT package with automatic made the GTA. **2.** The dash was a new dual-cove design. **3.** A 120-bhp six was still standard, with a 289 V-8 (220-271 bhp) or the 320-bhp 390 extra. **4.** GTs added fog lamps, stripes, dual exhausts, and wide-oval tires. Overall, Mustang sales fell 25 percent, but Ford still sold 474,121 for the model year, making it by far the No. 1 ponycar.

1967 Ford

1

2

3

4

Ford called its restyled big cars "Luxury leaders of the volume car field." Chassis was unchanged. The 352-cid V-8 was retired, but engine choices again ranged from a 150-bhp six to the 345-bhp 428-cid V-8 and the now-rarer 425-bhp 427. **1-2.** Auto showgoers were spellbound by the Magic Cruiser fastback, which prestidigitated into a wagon with a rear-facing bench seat. Zounds! **3.** Highest base price, $3493, belonged to the 500XL convertible. **4.** Between the base Custom and posh LTD was the Galaxie 500 series. Its $2756 2-door hardtop was the most-popular big Ford (197,000 sold). **5.** Ford's 70-millionth U.S. vehicle was built on May 3, but big Ford model-year output fell 15 percent.

"In 1914, Ford made history by introducing the $5 day [for workers]. Right now, we are closely approaching the $5 hour."

—Ford Motor Co. Chairman Henry Ford II, on rising automotive production costs

5

Still with their '66 bodyshells, Continentals got a new horizontal-texture grille and matching rear panel appliqué. The sole engine was again the 340-bhp 462-cid V-8. The 2-door hardtop and 4-door sedan returned, priced at $5553 and $5795, respectively. But this was the final year for the convertible. Sales of the $6449, 5505-lb beauty would sink to just 2276, compared to 33,331 for the sedan and 11,060 for the coupe. Air conditioning and Interstate-highway cruising helped kill it, with a push from Lincoln's standard new Fresh-Flow system, which circulated air through the cabin even with the windows up. Overall, Lincoln model-year production slumped 17 percent, to 45,667.

1967 Mercury

Built on a Mustang chassis stretched three inches into a 111-inch wheelbase, Mercury's flashy Cougar was promoted as a "luxury sports car." Distinctive panels hid the headlamps and were mirrored by taillamps with three-element sequential turn signals. Cougar bowed as a 2-door hardtop that was 6.7-inches longer and 200 lb heavier than a Mustang. At $2851, base Cougars cost $350 more, too, but came with the 200-bhp 289. The $3174 GT added the 390 V-8. At midyear came the XR-7, with leather upholstery. Most XR-7s sold for around $3600.

Mercury 1967

1. Cougar sold a respectable 150,893 units in its first season and was named *Motor Trend*'s "Car of the Year." This "mod" paisley vinyl roof was a proposed Cougar option, but didn't make the catalog. **2-3.** Like other ponycars, Cougar went racing in the SCCA's Trans Am series. Despite some big-name drivers, it wasn't a big winner, but did spawn a special customer edition. **4.** Rarest of the big '67 Mercurys was the sporty S-55 convertible. Just 145 were built, at $3837. **5.** The 9-seat $3752 Colony Park was the costliest—yet most-popular—big wagon. **6.** The mid-size Comet Villager had fake wood, too.

1 2 3 4 5 6

1967 Mercury

1

2

3

4

Cougar's arrival diverted what attention there was in Mercury performance, but the Comet Cyclone didn't give up. **1.** Jack Chrisman put a fiberglass-replica Cyclone body on his supercharged 427-cid-V-8-powered funny car and hit 180 mph in the quarter-mile. **2.** Don Nicholson's similar mount had 900 bhp and did the quarter in 7.6 sec. **3-5.** The "tamer" 425-bhp 427 was now a regular-production option and this entry-level Comet 202 had one of the handful ordered. It looked like a Milquetoast, but did 0–60 mph in 6 sec, the quarter-mile in 14.3 at 102 mph. **6.** The $3294 Cyclone GT packed a 390 V-8 under its fiberglass hood.

5

6

General Motors

James M. Roche replaces Frederic Donner as GM chairman; Ed Cole becomes president of the corporation

Roche and a handful of nervous executives stand on the roof of the GM building and watch rioting in Detroit; stung by critics of its own racial policies, GM will begin to increase minority hiring

Chevrolet regains model-year production leadership from Ford

Chevy launches its belated answer to Mustang, the clean and curvy Camaro; it's a sales hit

Buick climbs from seventh to fifth in production; restyles its full-size models and unveils the muscular GS 400 intermediate

Cadillac transforms its personal/luxury Eldorado into a front-wheel-drive coupe

Oldsmobiles take on Toronado styling flavor; Starfire specialty coupe is dropped

Pontiac's Firebird is GM's second ponycar; built around the Camaro shell but with its own distinct Pontiac personality

Chevy and GMC pickup trucks get a facelift; bucket seats with an armrest that converts to a center third seat is a newly available option

1. Buick's prestige big car, Electra 225, got only detail changes and saw sales rise by about 12,000 units, to 100,304. This is the standard 2-door hardtop, which listed for $4075. Four-door sedans and hardtops also were offered. **2.** Custom was the uplevel 225 trim, but 4-door hardtops could also be ordered in Limited livery, which added posher cabin appointments and a vinyl top. **3.** Wildcats were the other models on Electra's 226-inch chassis. Two-door hardtops got this new swept-back roofline. **4.** More equipment meant more weight. Buick met the need for more power with a new 430-cid V-8. It had 360 bhp, 20 more than the 425-cid V-8 it replaced, and ran more smoothly. Wildcats, 225s, and Rivieras got it.

1967 Buick

1

2

1-2. Skylark's muscle edition dropped the Gran Sport tag for GS 400 in honor of its new engine, a 400-cid V-8 of 340 bhp, 15 more than the old 401. Ragtops cost $3271 and 2454 were built; hardtops went for $3127 and 10,743 sold. **3.** New for '67 was the GS 340, a junior GS hardtop with a 260-bhp 340-cid V-8. Buick made 3692 of them at $2845. **4-5.** Optional fender skirts made the Skylark 4-door sedan and 2-door hardtop look even lower. **6-7.** Sharp eyes noticed the new grille and taillight treatment, but Riviera's big change was adoption of the new 430-cid V-8. Model-year sales of the $4615 coupe increased about 13 percent, to 49,284.

3

4

5

6

7

1

2

ONE THING FOR SURE...IT'S A CADILLAC.

The Fleetwood Eldorado has earned instant acclaim as the newest idea in luxury motoring. Its unique combination of front wheel drive, variable ratio power steering and automatic level control provides incomparable handling and performance. Its five-passenger luxury, its many interior conveniences and its unexcelled safety features provide a sense of satisfaction totally new to personal cars. And while its poised elegance imparts an air of youthful dignity and daring, the Eldorado is completely a Cadillac in the way it performs, rides and looks. Drive the Eldorado. You'll soon learn what all the excitement is about.

GM

Fleetwood ELDORADO *by Cadillac*

WORLD'S FINEST PERSONAL CAR

3

4

1-3. Cadillac reserved the Eldorado name for a special car, and that surely described the totally new 2-door hardtop that bore the badge for 1967. Adopting the Olds Toronado's front-wheel-drive technology, Caddy fashioned a creased coupe on a 120-inch wheelbase (9 inches briefer than the rear-drive '66 Eldo and 1 inch less than Toronado). The $6277 Cadillac rode and handled better than the $4850 Olds, and its sales of 17,930 were just 4000 short of Toronado's. Like all '67 Caddys, the Eldo used a 340-bhp 429-cid V-8. **4.** Joan Klatil came on board this year as GM's first female passenger-car designer. She was assigned to the Cadillac studio. With her is Stanley Parker, Cadillac chief designer.

1967 Cadillac

1

2

3

For 1967... Surprisingly New! Superbly Cadillac!

Who else but Cadillac could introduce a
personal car as fabulous as the Eldorado
—and at the same time offer you eleven
more of the newest and most exciting luxury cars
ever created! There are dramatic new advancements
throughout, including a new padded instrument
panel . . . a more responsive Cadillac engine . . . improved variable ratio power steering . . . and a new
General Motors-developed energy absorbing steering column. The remarkably new Eldorado provides the spirit and action of a performance car
with the comfort and elegance of a luxury car. It is
the first car in the world to combine front wheel
drive, variable ratio power steering and automatic
level control for a totally new driving experience.
These are but a few of the many achievements that
make the 1967 Cadillacs incomparable in comfort,
unmatched in performance and unexcelled in safety and convenience. See
and drive the 1967 Cadillacs soon.

GM

And introducing ELDORADO World's Finest Personal Car.

4

5

Mainstream models got a forward-raked grille and fenders. Inside were mylar printed circuits for instruments, automatic level control (standard on Fleetwood and Eldo), cruise control, and a tilt wheel. **1-3.** This is the $5639 DeVille convertible. **4.** Tradition and innovation. **5.** Helped by the new Eldo, Caddy's sales were up slightly to 200,000 in a year most makes declined. **6.** The Seventy-Five limos started at $10,360 and could carry up to nine.

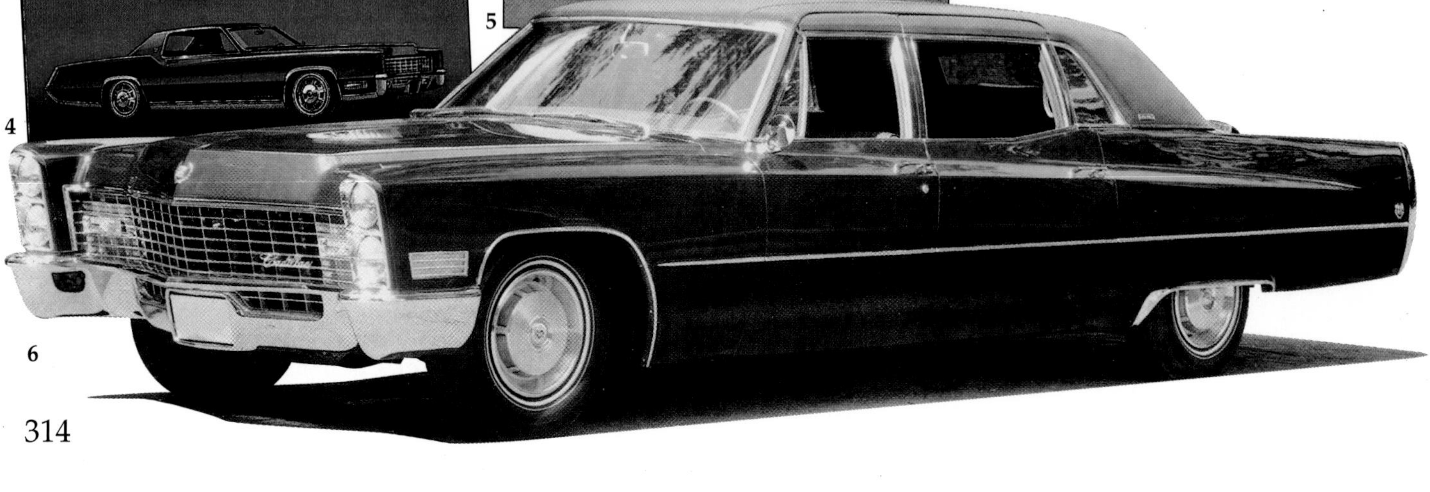

6

1

3

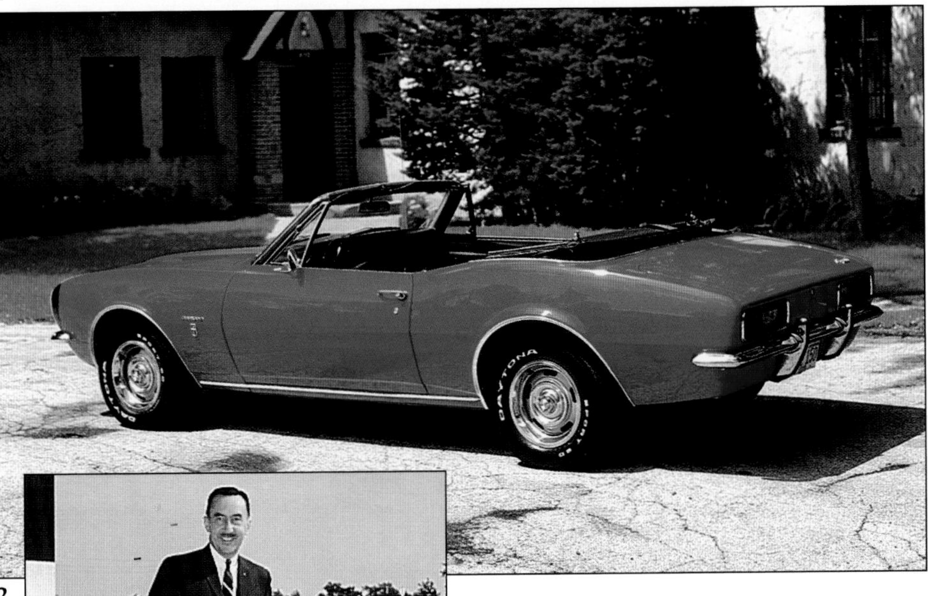

2

4

5

GM spotted Ford more than two years and 1.3 million Mustangs before answering the ponycar challenge. Camaro was Chevy's version and it followed the long-hood/short-deck 108-inch wheelbase formula that made Mustang a winner, though with svelter styling. **1.** The Z28 was a racing-type option package with a special 290-bhp 302-cid V-8. **2.** Convertibles complemented the coupe; unlike Mustang and Barracuda, Camaro didn't offer a true fastback. **3-4.** Super Sport versions used a 350- or 396-cid V-8 and could be combined with the Rally Sport option, which included hidden headlamps. **5.** Chevrolet General Manager Elliott "Pete" Estes was destined to be president of GM. **6.** Camaro went native with the Waikiki concept car. **7.** An SS 396 convertible paced the '67 Indy 500.

6

7

1967 Chevrolet

1

2

3

4

5

1. Pro racer Bill "Grumpy" Jenkins shot his Camaro through the quarter-mile in 11.5 sec at 115 mph. **2.** Here's how the RS's headlamps hid. **3-5.** Chevy sold 369,111 Chevelles for '67. Most were nice family sedans and wagons, but 63,006 were muscular SS 396 models. SS ragtops started at $3033, coupes at $2825. They had 325 bhp standard, 350 optional; the latter did 0–60 mph in 6.5 sec, the quarter-mile in 15.3 at 94 mph. **6-7.** The '67 drew the curtain on Corvette's classic era. Chevy's plan to retire this generation after '66 was thwarted by production delays. So the '67 carried on shorn of most badges and rid of some assembly problems. The yellow coupe has the base 327-cid V-8, but the blue ragtop packs the 435-bhp 427; it did 0–60 in 5.5 sec, the quarter in 13.1 at 106.

6

7

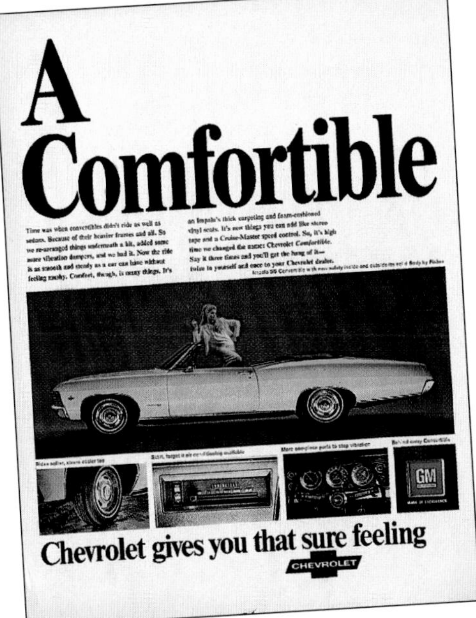

1

1. Super Sport Impalas could be had with a 6-cylinder engine, but this ragtop has the optional 396-cid V-8. **2-4.** "For the man who'd buy a sports car if it had this much room," was Chevy's spin on its new SS 427 Impala. It came with a beefed-up suspension and 385 bhp, hit 60 mph in 8.4 sec, and did the quarter-mile in 15.7 at 86 mph. An even stronger 425-bhp 427 was optional. Both manual and automatic transmissions were available. **5.** Chevy built more than 1 million full-size '67s. **6.** A Chevy marked a GM milestone.

2

3

4

5

6

1967 Chevrolet

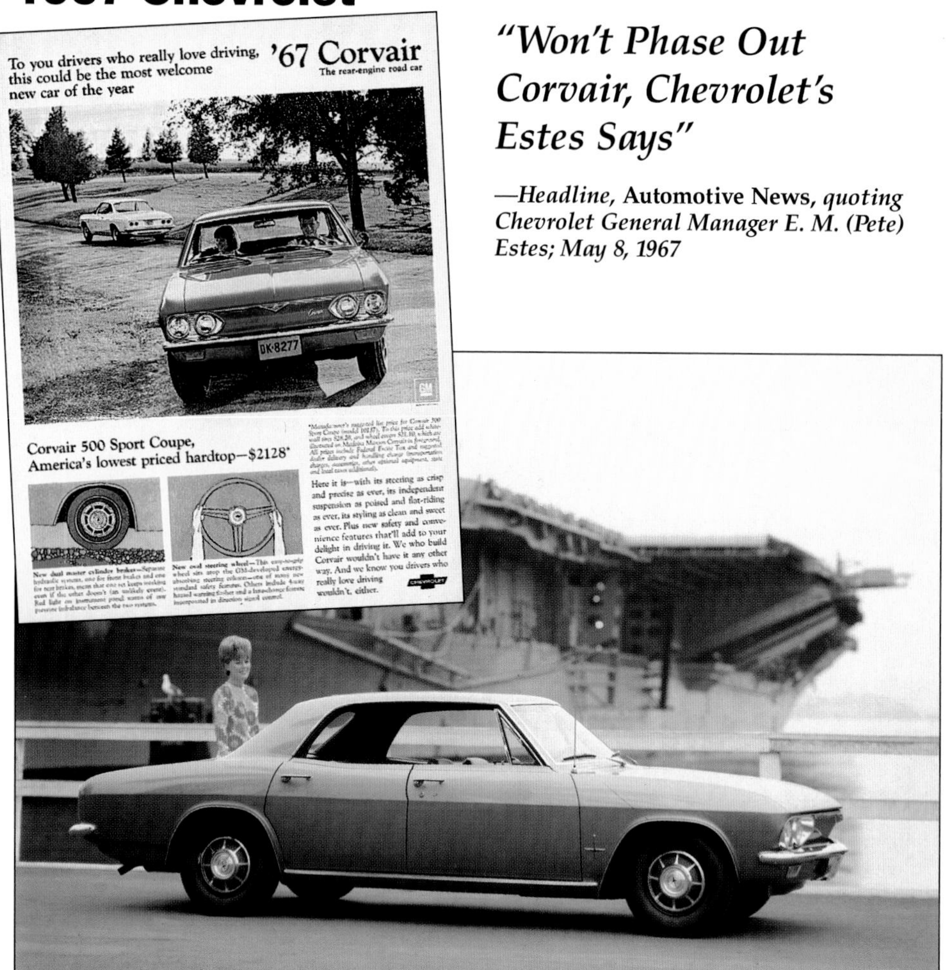

"Won't Phase Out Corvair, Chevrolet's Estes Says"

—Headline, **Automotive News,** *quoting Chevrolet General Manager E. M. (Pete) Estes; May 8, 1967*

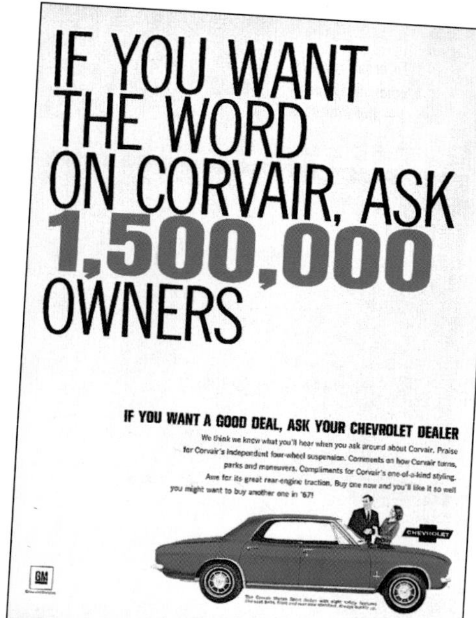

Chevy claimed 1.5 million owners couldn't be wrong, but bad publicity and the new Camaro meant Corvair's days were numbered. **1.** This was the last year for the 4-door body style, shown here in uplevel Monza form. **2-4.** The Chevy II was in the last year of its styling cycle and went out with a bang in the form of the Nova SS 327 models. The $2683 base price bought 275 bhp for a lightweight street threat.

1

2

3

4

1

2

3

1. Full-size Oldsmobiles got curvier and were led again by the Ninety-Eight series. Here's its $4498, 4271-lb convertible. **2-4.** Toronado was no longer America's only front-wheel-drive car. That didn't diminish its appeal, though second-year sales did drop 47 percent, to 21,790. Grille and tail were altered and the long, heavy doors opened easier thanks to a spring assist. Base models started at $4674. Deluxe versions sold for $195 more. Toronado shared with all big Oldsmobiles a 425-cid V-8, though it had 385 bhp to the others' 300–375.

4

1967 Oldsmobile

1. Now that's a gown. Miss America, 1967, Jane Anne Jayroe, of Laverne, Oklahoma, and the sponsor's Delta 88 Custom 4-door hardtop. **2.** Olds was not a high-volume police-car provider in these years, but the California Highway Patrol included the Delmont 88 in its fleet. **3-5.** Like other GM intermediates, the F-85/Cutlass line was in the last year of its styling cycle. The muscle model reflected Oldsmobile's level-headed values and so was more a well-balanced performance machine than barely tamed race car. That's not to say acceleration was ignored. Its 350-bhp 400-cid V-8 could be outfitted with the optional W-30 performance package. That put air-induction scoops in the headlamp housings and returned 0–60 mph in 6.7 sec, the quarter-mile in 14.9 at 95 mph.

1

2

3

4

5

1

1. Firebird hit showrooms months after Camaro and was saddled with its 108.1-inch wheelbase chassis and major body panels. Under Pontiac General Manager John Z. DeLorean, however, Firebird strove for its own identity, adopting the division's trademark split grille and GTO-inspired taillamps. Like Camaro, coupes and convertibles were offered, starting at $2666 and $2903, respectively. Engines were a 230-cid 6-cylinder and V-8s of 326 and 400 cid. **2-3.** The Sprint version used the 215-bhp overhead-cam six and did the quarter-mile in 17.4 sec. **4.** Pontiac's pony was positioned slightly upmarket from Chevy's, cost about $200 more, and its model-year production of 82,560 paled next to the 220,900 Camaros built. **5.** Firebird took its name from a series of 1950s GM idea cars, represented here by the original 1954 Firebird I. The red ragtop is a Firebird 400. It listed for more than $3800 with the optional Ram Air system, which breathed through the otherwise decorative hood scoops. It could do 0–60 mph in 6.2 sec and the quarter-mile in 14.7 at 98 mph.

2

3

4

5

1967 Pontiac

1

2

SUNOCO Special LONG MILEAGE MOTOR OIL 10W-40

NEW BREED OF OIL FOR THE NEW BREED OF CARS

Get more miles in every quart...more protection every mile...all year long!

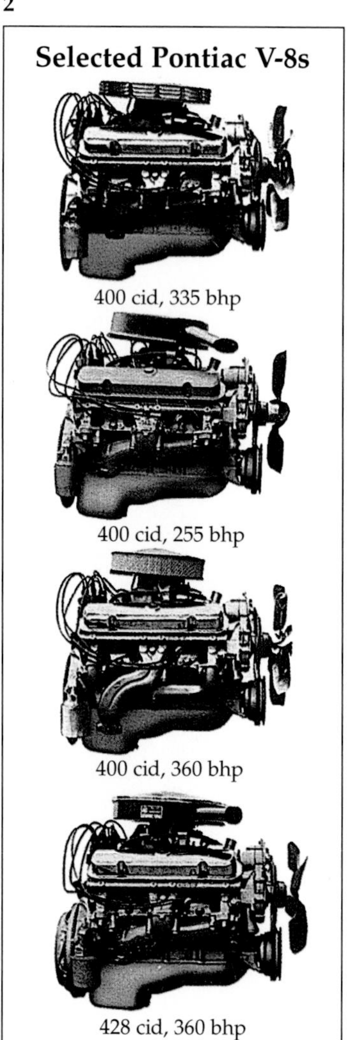

Selected Pontiac V-8s

400 cid, 335 bhp

400 cid, 255 bhp

400 cid, 360 bhp

428 cid, 360 bhp

3

1. Rivals now had specially badged muscle cars, and some were faster, but none had GTO's panache. **2.** All GTOs had a 389-cid V-8. The 360-bhp Ram Air version did 0–60 mph in 6.6 sec, the quarter-mile in 14.6 at 99 mph. **3.** Hollywood customizer Dean Jeffries used this rendering to create the GTO-based Monkeemobile for the wacky made-for-TV pop quartet. **4.** Of 782,734 Pontiacs built for '67, nearly 82,000 were GTOs.

4

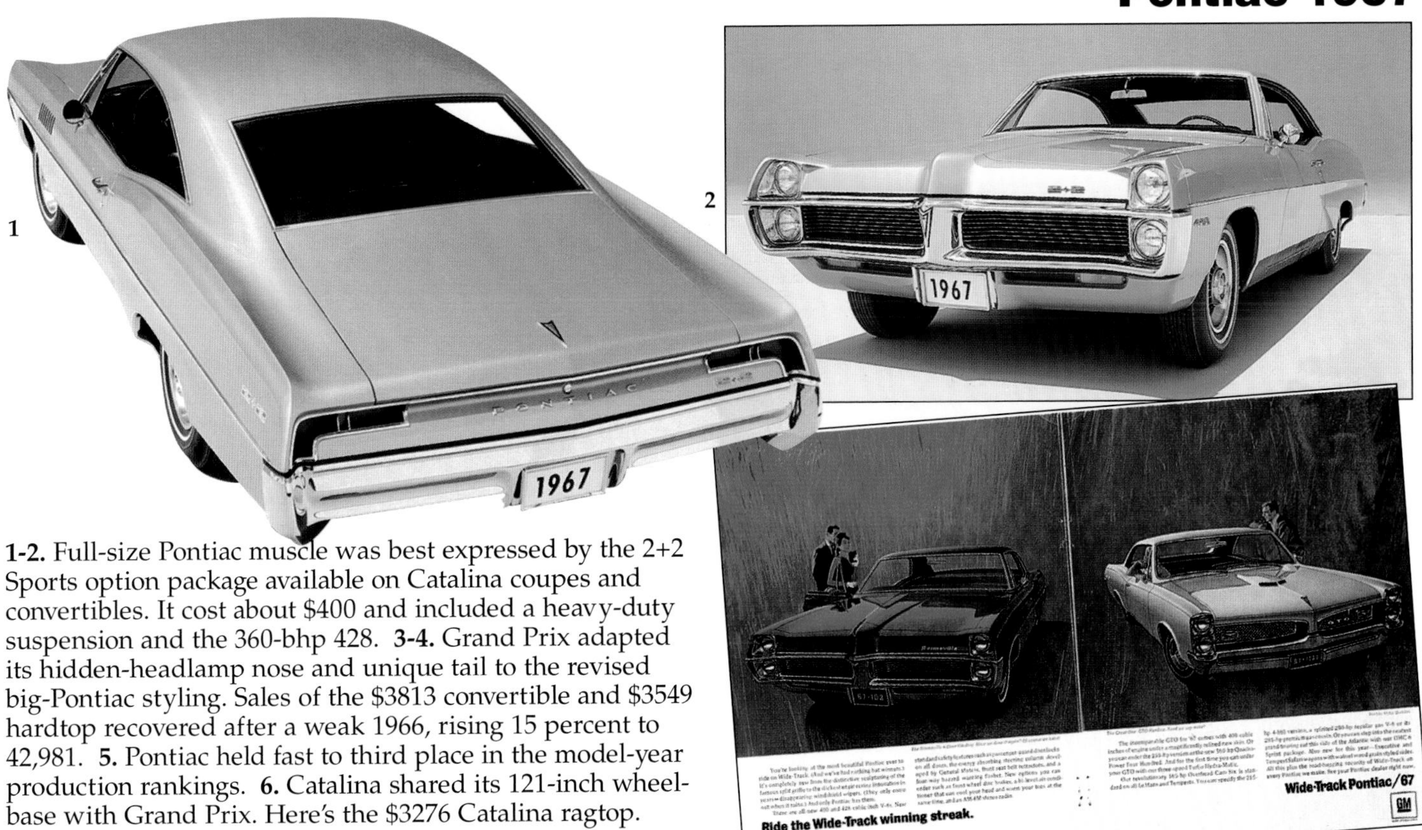

1 2

1-2. Full-size Pontiac muscle was best expressed by the 2+2 Sports option package available on Catalina coupes and convertibles. It cost about $400 and included a heavy-duty suspension and the 360-bhp 428. **3-4.** Grand Prix adapted its hidden-headlamp nose and unique tail to the revised big-Pontiac styling. Sales of the $3813 convertible and $3549 hardtop recovered after a weak 1966, rising 15 percent to 42,981. **5.** Pontiac held fast to third place in the model-year production rankings. **6.** Catalina shared its 121-inch wheelbase with Grand Prix. Here's the $3276 Catalina ragtop.

3

4

5

6

Etc.

Highway Research Record publishes a paper describing private research into "balloon-like air bags in front and back of car passengers that would inflate automatically if a collision were imminent"

General Motors Research Laboratories receives a $493,000 federal grant to evaluate and develop hardware for a "highway route-guidance system" that would direct motorists to their destinations without need for road maps or directional signage

Chicago Motor Club offers advice to passengers on vacation drives: "Never startle the driver. Don't irritate the driver. Talk with the driver, but don't argue, shout or anger him. Be helpful. Light [the driver's] cigarette"

Russian Communists announce from Moscow that the "capitalist, free market response to the automobile has been unscientific, even irrational"

Inventor Donald Dean devises a steering wheel that gives a sleepy driver mild, intermittent electric shocks

Chicago auto columnist Jody Carr urges women to learn more about their cars, but adds that "I don't propose that we discard our aprons for overalls"

The proposed 41,000-mile interstate highway system is 57-percent operational

The varied world of independent American automaking: **1.** Rohm & Haas Explorer IV. **2.** The Graham replicated its 1940 namesake. **3.** Ghia bodywork, DeTomaso hardware made the Rowan Electric. **4.** Westinghouse's Markette electric. **5-6.** Two fiberglass sportsters: Fiberfab's Chevy-based Valkyrie; Daimler-powered Panther.

1

2

3

4

5

1. A. J. Foyt threaded his Coyote/Ford through a four-car wreck on the last lap to win the Indianapolis 500. It was his third of four eventual wins at the Brickyard. **2.** Speed-crazed punks terrorized an innocent family in MGM's low-budget, terrifically named *Hot Rods to Hell*. **3.** Stock cars shared the big screen with other lively diversions in *Thunder Alley*. **4.** Hippies and boldly painted Volkswagen buses were essential elements of San Francisco's fleeting Summer of Love. **5.** Summer of Love, Kansas-style, with Dad's Buick at the local A & W.

Etc.

Datsun mounts its biggest-ever U.S. ad campaign, covering the country with massive 30-sheet billboards that say, "Drive a DATSUN then decide! Confident, aren't we?"

The number of import dealerships in the United States has increased by 30 percent since 1964; import registrations are at record-setting levels for the second straight year, while domestic registrations are down

At a stockholders' meeting in Germany, Volkswagen officials announce that the 20-year-old Beetle will remain in production despite a recent dip in sales

A 2-door-sedan, the 142-S, is added to Volvo's 140 Series

Chevrolet's service engineering department conducts a "powder puff" mechanics class for "girl warranty clerks"

The Cord Automobile Co. declares bankruptcy and sells its Oklahoma plant

Top 10 Selling Imports

1. Volkswagen 443,510
2. Opel 51,693
3. Toyota 36,002
4. Volvo 34,392
5. Datsun 33,275
6. Mercedes-Benz ... 20,691
7. Renault 20,218
8. English Ford 16,636
9. Fiat 15,932
10. Saab 10,755

Total import-car share of U.S. market: 9.32 percent

1968

Imports took 10 percent of U.S. car sales , with Toyota passing Datsun as the No. 1 Japanese make in America. But Detroit buzzed when Semon "Bunkie" Knudsen was named Ford Motor Company president just a week after quitting as GM's executive VP.

Springtime in America was horrifying. The Rev. Martin Luther King, Jr., was assassinated in Memphis on April 4, and Democratic presidential front-runner Robert F. Kennedy was mortally wounded in Los Angeles on June 5. The national fabric seemed torn. Massive anti-war demonstrations disrupted streets and campuses. Yippies and police clashed at Chicago's Democratic National Convention. Riots flared in inner-city Washington, Baltimore, Chicago, and Cleveland. The Black Panthers and other armed separatist groups grew more vocal.

In Vietnam, U.S. troops at Khe Sanh were assaulted on January 21 by withering artillery fire that did not let up for 10 weeks. January 30th's Communist attack on Saigon sparked the Tet Offensive. President Johnson brushed off the brazen, wide-ranging action, but it dealt a blow to American morale. LBJ announced in March he would not seek re-election and Republicans Richard Nixon and Spiro Agnew took the White House, narrowly defeating Hubert Humphrey and Edmund Muskie.

Pop culture reflected the year's tumult. Top movies included *Rosemary's Baby, Planet of the Apes, Bullitt, In Cold Blood, 2001: A Space Odyssey,* and John Wayne's *The Green Berets.* On TV, the satiric *Smothers Brothers Comedy Hour* and *Rowan & Martin's Laugh-In* shocked as many viewers as they amused. *Bewitched, Flipper,* and *Lost in Space* supplied the fluff. Rock hits included "Lady Madonna" and "Hey Jude" by the Beatles, "Jumpin' Jack Flash" by the Rolling Stones, and "MacArthur Park" by Richard Harris and songwriter Jimmy Webb. A leather-clad Elvis Presley made a high-energy comeback via a TV special.

Despite a flirtation with see-through blouses, the year's "look" seemed generally less radical than before; minis were joined by maxis and midis. Pop art looked to comic strips and commercial design for inspiration.

Pitcher Denny McLain put together an astounding 31-6 record for the Detroit Tigers, and helped lead the club to a seven-game World Series victory over the St. Louis Cardinals.

American Motors Corporation

All models wear AMC badging except the compact American/Rogue, which return as the sole entries with Rambler nameplates

Total AMC/Rambler sales rise a healthy 23 percent, to 446,781

AMC introduces its most-exciting automobile ever, the Javelin ponycar; follows it with the midyear introduction of the 2-seat AMX

An optional buzzer in AMC cars sounds when the lights are left on

Ambassadors are first moderately priced cars with standard air conditioning

Rebel offers AMC's only convertible, and just 1200 are built—it will be the last true AMC ragtop

Two-door sedans cut from the Rebel and Ambassador line; American is AMC's only 2-door sedan

Deciding to concentrate on cars, AMC sells off Kelvinator Division at a paper loss of $10.8 million, but in reality, the sale provides much needed capital for new-model development

Land-speed record driver Craig Breedlove runs Javelins and AMXs to class speed records on the Bonneville Salt Flats in Utah

1

1. The sporty iteration of the American was the Rouge. It shared the American's compact 106-inch wheelbase and Rambler badging. Rogue's convertible body style was shelved for '68, leaving this 2-door hardtop. It came with a 145-bhp 232-cid 6-cylinder. A 225-bhp 290-cid V-8 was optional, as were wire wheels. Base price was attractively low: $2244; but sales were unattractively low: 4765.

2

2. Starting at $1946, the American 2-door sedan was the only car made in the U.S. priced under $2000. Compared to the similarly priced Volkswagen Beetle, AMC noted, the American was 20 inches longer, 10 inches wider, and much roomier—with double the trunk space. "Yet it turns around in the same circle a Volkswagen does," bragged this brochure. Plus, the VW had a 4-cylinder engine of about 53 bhp, while the American came with a 128-bhp six. Still, the Beetle had a personality and image the American lacked, and VW was selling nearly 500,000 of them in the U.S. annually. AMC sold 76,216 Americans for '68. **3.** The costliest American was the $2426 wagon, which came in the uplevel 440 trim.

3

1. Putting an AMC badge on the Rebel was intended to remove the low-price stigma of the Rambler tag. With its 114-inch wheelbase, Rebel fit in nicely below the posh 118-inch Ambassador, but the name game wasn't a big success: Rebel sales fell 27 percent, to 73,895. **2.** Rebel's sporty SST model cost $2999 as a convertible, $2775 as this 2-door hardtop. **3.** Ambassador got into the SST act with a $3151 4-door sedan and this $3172 2-door. A 200-bhp 290 V-8 was standard.

1

2

3

4

1-3. AMC's Marlin was shot down by the Javelin, a hardtop coupe ponycar in base and SST trim. A 232-cid six was standard, but 390 V-8s were optional. **4.** AMC shortened the Javelin's 109-inch wheelbase by 12 inches to create the 2-seat AMX at midyear. **5.** The Javelin was AMC's entry into the Trans Am racing series. It competed against Camaros and Mustangs. **6.** Hot on the heels of the AMX show car was the ungainly 4-door AMX III.

5

6

1

2

3

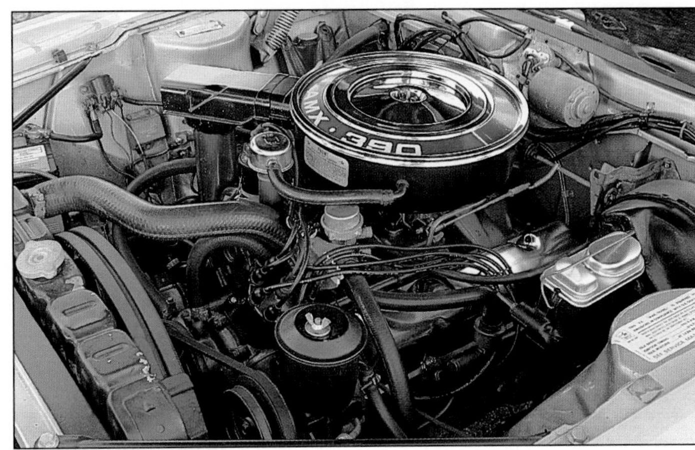

4

5

1-2. AMX was AMC's most exciting car ever. It used lots of Javelin tooling, keeping its base price at $3245, just $658 over the Javelin SST. **3-4.** AMX and Corvette were America's only true 2-seaters; full gauges were standard. Engine choices ranged from a 225-bhp 290 V-8 to a 315-bhp 390. The latter did 0–60 mph in 6.6 sec. **5.** Twin racing stripes and a luggage rack were among the options. **6.** Dick Teague designed both the Javelin and AMX, and his AMX GT show car's chopped hatch style foretold his '70s shapes.

6

Chrysler Corporation

Chrysler Corp's total car production rebounds from its 1967 decline, increasing an encouraging 24 percent

Chrysler brand moves up a notch in industry production standings, to ninth; Dodge does likewise, to sixth; Plymouth strengthens its hold on fourth place

Plymouth unveils a muscle-car classic with the Road Runner, a no-frills intermediate with big V-8 power; it starts off as a pillared coupe, but strong demand necessitates the midyear introduction of a hardtop

Dodge Coronets and Chargers earn a full redesign with trendy "Coke-bottle" body contours

Dart adds baby-muscle-car GTS with hot 340- or 383-cid V-8s

Prodded by the Road Runner's success, Dodge adds no-frills Super Bee muscle car to Coronet lineup

Dodge groups its high-performance Chargers, Coronets, and Darts cars under the "Scat Pack" banner, puts "bumble-bee" racing stripes around their tails

Imperial's final convertibles go on sale; only 474 are built

Chrysler corporation wagons introduce an optional tailgate window wiper/washer

1

2

1. "Sportsgrain" simulated-wood bodyside trim was a new option for Newport convertibles and 2-door hardtops but attracted only 175 and 965 buyers. **2.** A Chrysler 300 2-door hardtop cost $4010, against $4086 for the 4-door hardtop sedan, which sold almost as strongly: 16,953 versus 15,507. The most noticeable styling change to 300s was disappearing headlights—a first for the series. They hid behind movable doors that matched the rest of the 300's unique black-out grille. **3.** Standard power for the Newport was Chrysler's 290-bhp 383-cid V-8; however, buyers could option-up to the big 375-bhp 440-cid mill.

3

1

1. Chrysler trumpeted unabashed elegance for its top-line models, touting the $4523, 4410-lb Town & Country wagon as a "limousine" with "load-space." A unique T&C feature was an optional concealed tailgate window washer/wiper. **2.** New Yorker's line of 2- and 4-door hardtops and a 4-door sedan was little changed, but sales jumped 19 percent, to 48,143. **3.** The Letter series was just a memory, but the 300 gave a fine account of big-Chrysler style and performance. Offered were 2- or 4-door hardtops and this $4337 convertible, all with a standard 440 V-8. These cast steel wheels were a new option. Just 2161 buyers selected the ragtop. **4.** The 300's expansive interior featured "anthropometrically" designed buckets with stainless steel seatback panels.

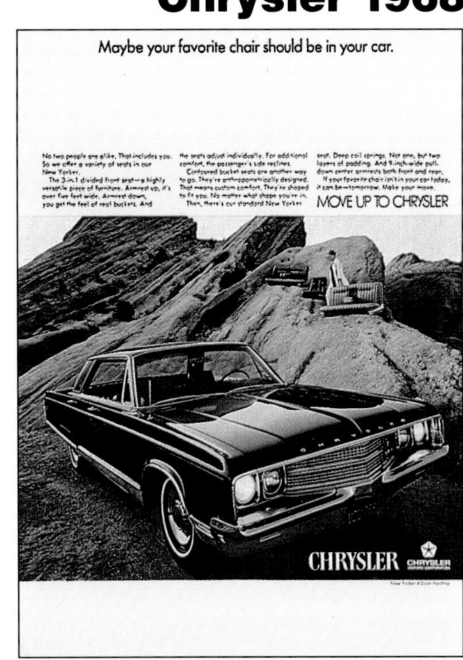

2

3

4

1968 Dodge

1

3

2

1-2. With its hidden headlamps, fulsome shape, and flying-buttress rear roof, the rebodied Charger was a sensation. This R/T model has the optional Hemi engine. 3. "Dodge Girl" Joan Parker lights one for drag racer Dick Landy. 4-5. Buddy Baker and Bobby Isaac ran new Chargers, but couldn't catch Ford for the '68 NASCAR title.

4

5

1968 426-cid Hemi V-8s

Street version used two 4-barrel carburetors

Street version was rated at 425 bhp

1

2

3

4

5

1. Baseball catcher-turned-broadcaster Joe Garagiola pitches a Charger. **2-3.** The experimental Charger III was called "the most aerodynamic car ever conceived and built by Dodge." It had air-brake flaps. **4-5.** Continuing on a 117-inch wheelbase (shared with Charger), the mid-size Coronet was reskinned and offered in every body style imaginable. It was Dodge's best-selling line, at 220,831 units. Low-priced versions came with a 6-cylinder engine, but the R/T—for Road and Track—ragtop and coupe came with the 375-bhp Magnum 440 V-8.

Professional drag racing version made well over 500 bhp

NASCAR version was limited to a single 4-barrel carb

1968 Dodge

1

2

3

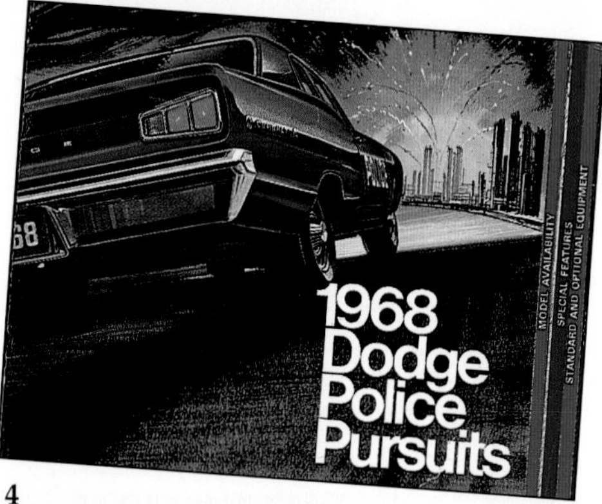

4

5

1-2. R/T hardtops started at $3379. The optional bumblebee tail stripes signified membership in Dodge's performance-oriented "Scat Pack." **3.** Stung by rival Plymouth's budget-muscle Road Runner, Dodge stripped down a Coronet, installed a 335-bhp 383 V-8 (426 Hemi optional), and created the Super Bee. This 3395-lb pillared coupe cost just $3027. **4.** Cities seemed aflame in fact and fancy in '68. **5.** An overdressed Super Bee made the show circuit. **6.** Dart returned as a basic 2- or 4-door compact with a convertible tossed in for spice. Slotted above the snappy GT was the new baby-muscle GTS hardtop (shown) and ragtop.

6

1

2

1-2. The $3189 Dart GTS hardtop and companion $3383 convertible came with a 275-bhp 340 V-8 and did 0–60 mph in 6.0 sec. **3-4.** The 383-cid V-8 was an option, but some aftermarket tuners went the factory one better, stuffing in 440s and even a few Hemis to create lightweight drag-racing terrors like this. **5.** Big Dodges returned little changed with the Monaco 500 2-door hardtop at the head of the class. Its $3869 base price included the 383, buckets, tape player, cruise control, and automatic temperature control.

3

4

5

1968 Imperial

1

2

1-2. Imperial wrapped a new grille around its fenders. The Crown 4-door hardtop was the best-seller, at 8492 units. Its 440-cid V-8 had 350 bhp, 360 with dual exhausts. **3.** This $6497 ragtop was Imperial's last convertible. **4.** Sales declined 13 percent, to 15,367.

3

4

Plymouth 1968

1. Plymouth put a hot 335-bhp 383 V-8 and fortified chassis into a no-frills Belvedere 2-door sedan, rented a cartoon name, and created the budget-muscle Road Runner. Starting at $2896, it did 0–60 mph in 7.1 sec and attracted 44,599 eager buyers. Its popularity fueled a 15-percent jump in Plymouth sales, to 747,237. **2-3.** The sole Road Runner engine option was the mighty 425-bhp 426-cid Hemi. It cost $714 (plus $139 for the mandatory heavy-duty axle) and brought 0–60 mph in 5.3 sec, the quarter mile in 13.5 at 105 mph. It was ordered by 1019 buyers. **4.** Hemi-powered mutants of the Road Runner soon saw drag strip duty. Sox & Martin's was among the best. **5.** Firestone trumpeted its new "Wide Oval" tires as similar to those on Andy Granatelli's 1968 Indy 500 STP turbine car. The turbine conked out, but Firestone won Indy in '69, '70, and '71.

1

2

3

5

4

1968 Plymouth

1

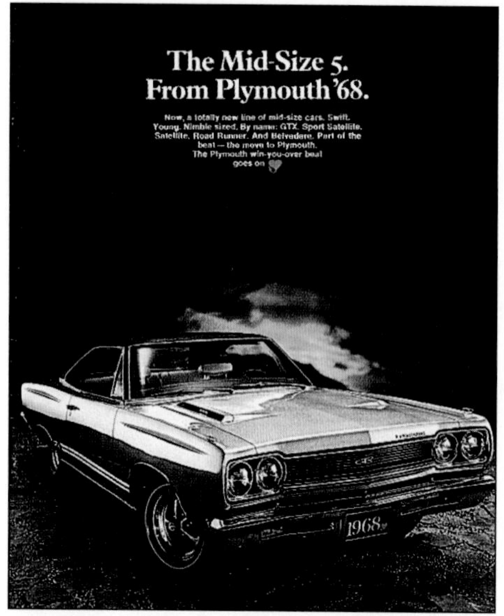

2

3

4

5

Mid-size Plymouths kept a 116-inch wheelbase but were restyled. A full range of body styles in Belvedere and Satellite trim was offered. **1-3.** Lushest performance model was the $3355 GTX 2-door hardtop and $3590 convertible, which had the 375-bhp 440-cid V-8 as standard and the Hemi as an option. **4.** Full-size models got only subtle appearance changes and offered engines ranging from the Slant Six to the 440. Of 26,204 Sport Furys, 35 percent had this "Fast Top" styling. **5.** Two doors or four, a 440-cid police-package Fury was a formidable traffic enforcer.

1

2

3

4

1. Getting the feel of this psychedelic thing, Plymouth offered Barracuda coupes with a new option called the "Mod Top," a vinyl roof covering with a "flower power" motif. It sold as a package with seat- and door-panel inserts of the same pattern. Coupes started at $2605 and 19,997 were sold **2.** Barracuda convertibles began at $2907 and 2840 were made. **3.** The $2762 fastback snared 22,575 buyers. **4.** Sox & Martin added a specially built Hemi Barracuda to their arsenal. **5.** Barracudas came from the factory with a Slant Six, a 318-cid V-8, or this hot little 275-bhp 340 V-8 **6.** Valiant soldiered on as the tame compact in 2- and 4-door sedan form with prices as low as $2254.

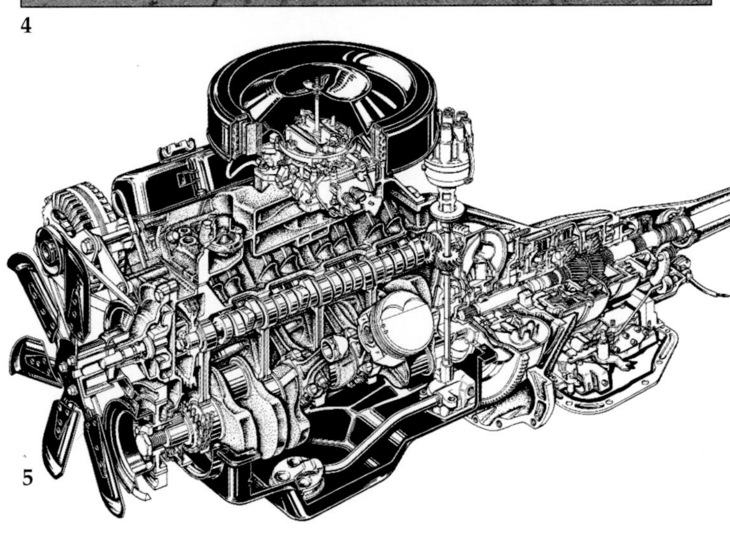

5

6

Ford Motor Company

Shocking the industry, Semon E. "Bunkie" Knudsen quits as executive vice president of GM and assumes presidency of Ford Motor Company

New corporate slogan says, "Ford has a better idea"

Mid-size models revamped, add Torino line that includes a rakish fastback

Ford output rises slightly, to just over 1.75 million cars, despite long labor strike

Ford still trails Chevrolet in car output, but races neck-and-neck for the truck title

Assembly of Shelby Mustangs shifts from Shelby shops to a Ford subcontractor in Michigan; a convertible model is added

Edsel Ford takes the wheel of a Torino GT to pace the Indianapolis 500

Lincoln Mark III coupe bows

Ford unveils high-mileage "clean air" experimental auto

Edsel Ford elected to Automotive Hall of Fame

Ford's GT40 becomes the first—and only—American car to win the international sports-car championship

Ford builds 50 Mustangs with the Cobra Jet 428; they clean up at the NHRA Winternational drag races

1

2

Square taillights and a new grille were the main Falcon changes. Sales of the compact rebounded, doubling to 131,389 **1.** Costliest Falcon was the $2728 Futura wagon. Wagons rode a 113-inch wheelbase, other models used a 110.9-inch chassis. **2.** Second priciest Falcon was the Futura Sport Coupe at $2541. Base power in the Falcons was a 100-bhp six, and buyers could option-up to a 230-bhp 302-cid V-8. **3-4.** With Mustang sales sliding, Ford tried to add a little luster to its ponycar with the Mach 1 show car. Based on a '67 'Stang, it sported a lowered roof, rectangular headlights, and big air scoops ahead of the rear wheels. Note the streamlined mirrors attached to the side glass. The Mach 1 name would soon show up on a regular-production Mustang model.

3

4

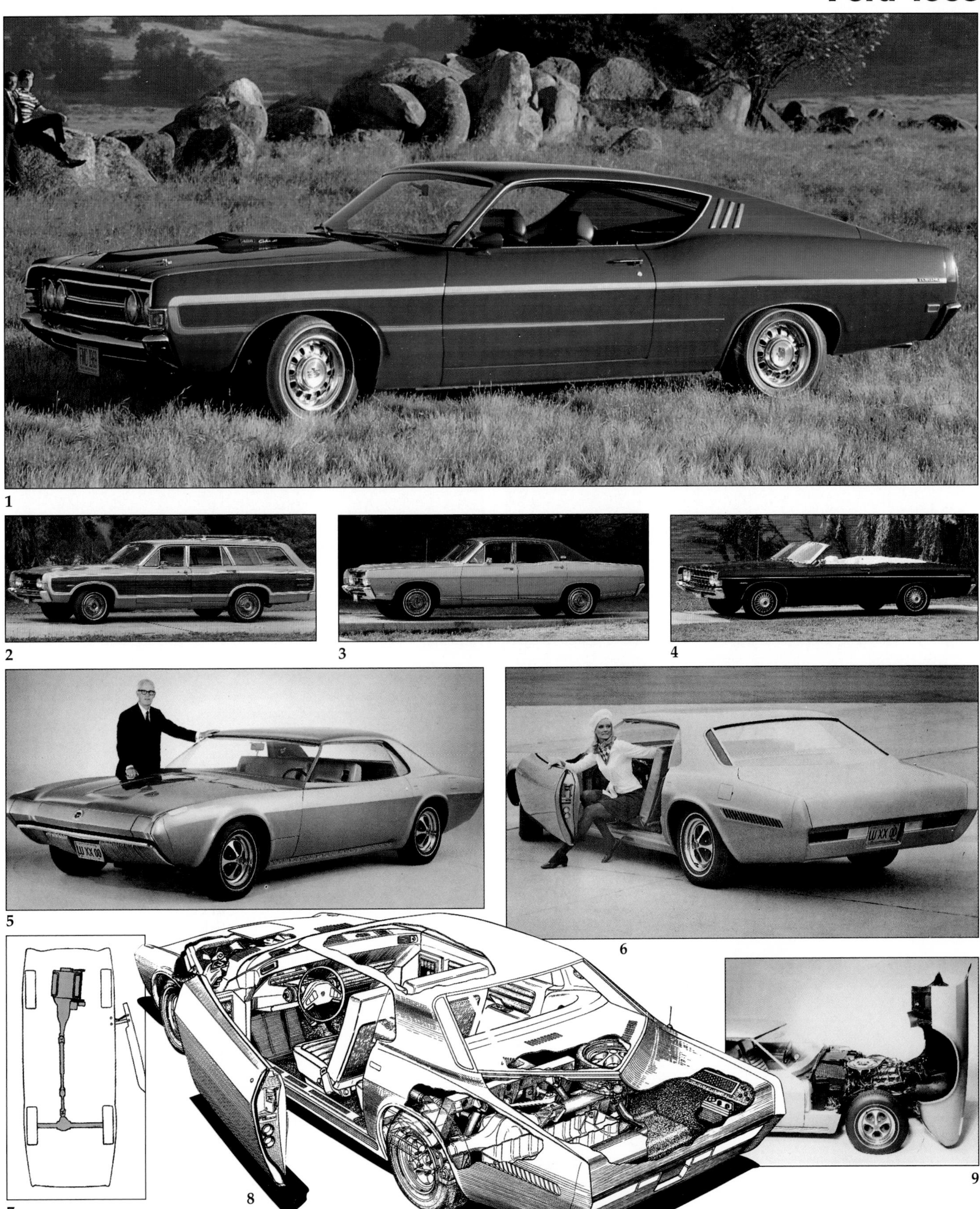

Mid-size models kept their 116-inch chassis but got new bodies. **1-4.** Sporty Torinos were added at the top of the Fairlane series and included racy new fastback coupes, plus the Squire wagon, a convertible, and a 4-door sedan. **5-9.** Techna, Ford Engineering's "experimental car of the future," put into practice more than 50 new ideas, including plastic bumpers, a roof-supporting windshield, and doors that opened laterally. Brake lights and tail-lamps flanked the rear window. The hood had a small "inspection hatch" for minor service but flipped up for big jobs.

1968 Ford

1

2

3

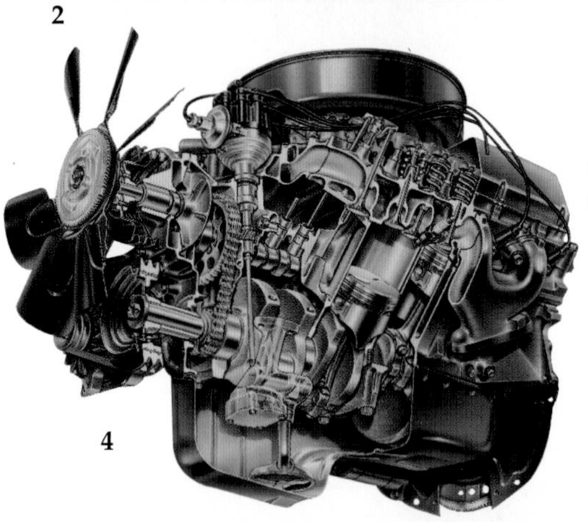

4

5

6

Big Fords got new, more-formal sheetmetal on carry-over platforms. **1.** The 500/XL coupe with its new fastback roof provided a dash of sportiness. Sales of the $3214 XL convertible rose slightly, to 6066, but the new fastback attracted 50,048 buyers, helping increase XL demand nearly three-fold. A 240-cid 6-cylinder was the standard engine, with V-8s of up to 429 cid available. **2.** LTD was back as the luxury model; this $3206 4-door hardtop was the series' best-seller at 61,755 units. **3.** The Custom 500 2-door sedan went for $2669. **4.** Arriving late in the year was Ford's new 429-cid V-8, a slow-revving powerhouse with 360 bhp. **5.** Replacing the big-cars' 7-Litre package was an XL-optional GT Equipment Group tied to the 390, 427, and 429 V-8s. **6.** A new underhood challenge was phased in for '68: federally mandated exhaust emissions gear.

1

2

3

4

5

6

8

7

9

Ford pushed 317,404 Mustangs out the door in '68, but that was a 23-percent drop from '67. **1-5.** Coupes, fastbacks, and convertibles returned. Two new big-block V-8s were available. The 427 cid thumped out 390 bhp but was replaced at midyear by a better-mannered 428 V-8 tabbed the Cobra Jet. It had about 410 bhp but was rated at 335 and made for one of the quickest Mustangs ever: 0–60 mph in 5.4 sec. **6-9.** The Cobra Jet, with its ram-air induction hood scoop, debuted for the winter pro drag races and helped Al Joniec snare the top spot with a quarter-mile run of 12.5 sec at 97.93 mph.

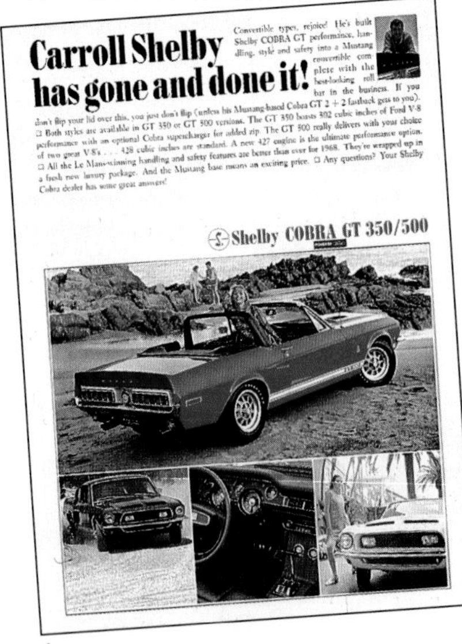

1

2

3

4

1. Carroll Shelby was losing full control over the GTs that bore his name, but that didn't stop the ad men. The ragtop was new for '68. **2.** The GT 500 had a 428, starting the year with the Police Interceptor version, then moving to the Cobra Jet. GT-350s adopted the new 250-bhp 302 V-8 but were outsold by GT-500s 2-1. **3.** Shelby-prepared 302 Mustang coupes represented Ford in Trans Am racing. **4.** The new ragtop came with a real roll bar. **5-7.** Other than a revised grille and trim touch-ups, Thunderbird was unchanged. Early '68s had a 315-bhp 390 V-8 or optional 360-bhp 429; the new 429 became standard midyear.

5

6

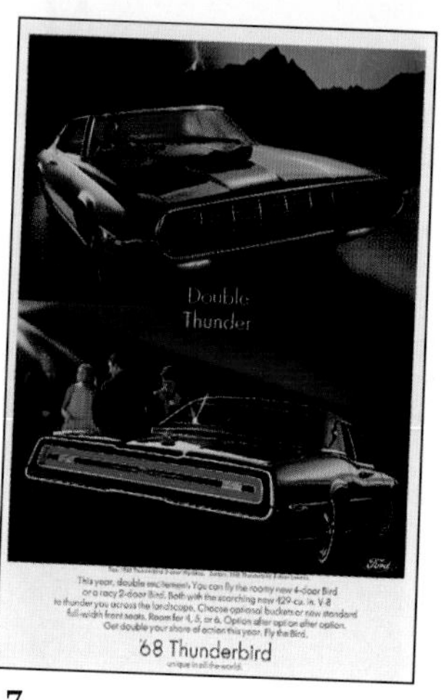

7

1

2

1-2. Lincoln resurrected its historic Mark name with a glamorous new 2-door hardtop, the Mark III. It rode its own 117.2-inch wheelbase, 8.8 inches shorter than other Lincolns, and had unique styling cues, including a formal roofline, "spare-tire" hump, and hidden quad headlamps. Starting at $6585, it was the most-expensive Ford product, but a success with 7770 sales. It weighed 4739 lb and used a 365-bhp 460-cid V-8. **3.** New Ford President, Semon "Bunkie" Knudsen, just over from GM, poses with the new Mark at the Chicago Auto Show. **4.** Lincoln built its one millionth car in '68, a Continental 4-door sedan. It's shown here with a 1925 Lincoln Town Car, which had a 90-bhp 357.8-cid V-8.

3

4

1968 Lincoln

2

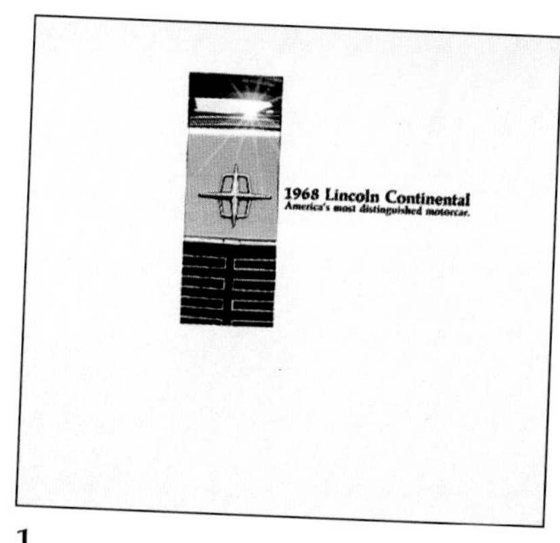

1

1. Continental lost its sexy convertible body style for '68 but got freshened front and rear styling **2.** The 2-door hardtop's revised roof was influenced by that of the Mark III. **3.** The $5970 sedan was again the top seller, at 29,719 units. Lincoln started '68 with leftover 462-cid V-8s but switched in mid-season to the new 460. **4.** The coupe cost $5736. **5.** Limousines were available from custom coachbuilders Lehmann-Peterson of Chicago.

3

4

5

1

2

3

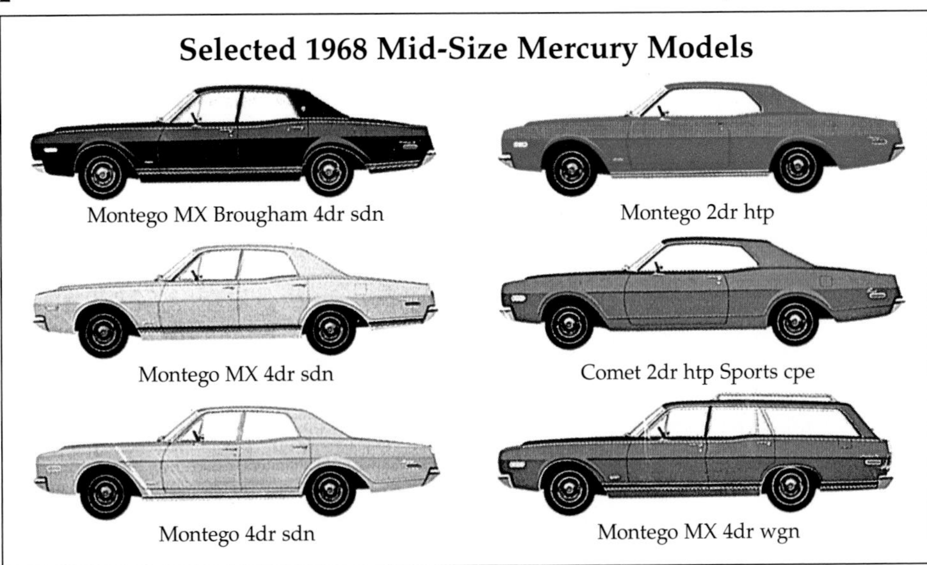

4

5

1-2. A step up from the Comet in Mercury's restyled mid-size line was the new Montego. It was available as a sedan, hardtop, wagon, and convertible. This 2-door hardtop and convertible are in the uplevel MX trim level. **3.** Cyclone became a stand-alone series offering 2-door hardtops and fastbacks. This is the $2768 base-level coupe, which came with the 210-bhp 302-cid V-8. **4.** The GT no longer included the 390-cid V-8 but did get stripes, heavy-duty suspension, and, like the Montego, could be optioned with the new 428 Cobra Jet. **5.** Cale Yarborough won the Daytona 500 in the Wood Brothers Mercury. A slight aerodynamic advantage made the fastback Comet faster than the Torino on NASCAR's long superspeedways, so it was raced in place of the Ford on those 185-mph tracks.

1968 Mercury

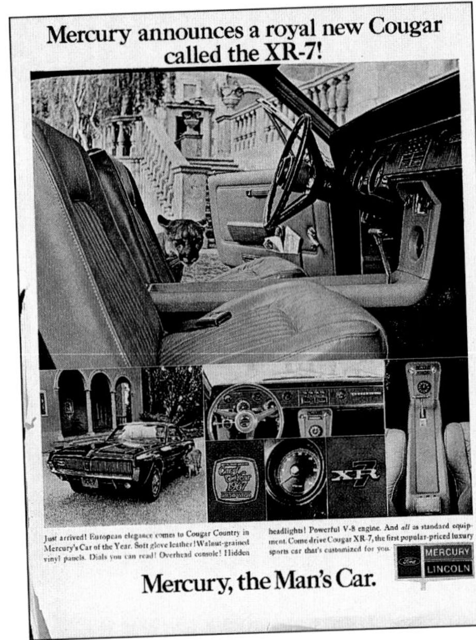

1

2

3

4

5

1. Ritzy XR-7s accounted for 28 percent of the 113,726 Cougars built for '68. They had leather seats and full gauges. **2-3.** Side-marker lights were new. These are XR-7 "G," or Dan Gurney Specials (that's racer Gurney himself) that added a vinyl top, hood scoop, and special wheels and tires. **4.** Gurney raced a Cougar in Trans Am. **5.** Drag racer "Dyno" Don Nicholson's "funny car" wore a fiberglass Cougar body replica over a tubular frame.

1

2

3

4

1. Big Mercurys looked Lincolnesque for '68. This Park Lane convertible sports a pseudo-wood bodyside appliqué, a new option. **2.** Monterey 2-door hardtops wore a new semi-fastback roof. **3.** Most Park Lanes were 4-door hardtops. **4.** Park Lane ragtops started at $3822—without fake wood.

General Motors

General Motors redesigns its mid-size cars, giving the 4-door models a longer wheelbase than the 2-doors

Hidden windshield wipers are seen on more GM cars; some adopt no-vent side windows

Chevrolet maintains its lead in model-year production, builds 2.1 million new cars

First restyled Corvette since 1963 appears; its wild new body is seven inches longer and sports vacuum-operated slip-up headlights

Chevy II, renamed Nova, grows from compact to near mid-size dimensions; hardtop coupe, convertible, and wagon are gone

Cadillac's new 472-cid V-8 is designed to meet tougher emissions standards

Buick's revamped mid-size Skylark enjoys record sales

GTO, companion to Pontiac's redesigned Tempest intermediate, gets a hidden-headlight option and an energy-absorbing, steel-reinforced, body-color rubber front bumper

Big Oldsmobiles have a new 455-cid V-8; mid-size Cutlass is redesigned and its 4-4-2 derivative spawns a limited-edition Hurst-modified car

Chevrolet shows off the radial mid-engine Astra II idea car; some observers see in it the future Corvette

1

2

3

1-2. The Gran Sport used the new 112-inch-wheelbase chassis and body of 2-door hardtop and convertible Skylarks but was now designated a separate model series. Like the previous year, the GS400 was powered by the 340-bhp 400-cid V-8 and cost $3127 in hardtop form and $3271 as a ragtop. These were relatively tame muscle cars, doing 0–60 mph in 6.8 sec but offering Buick-level comfort. **3.** Buick sales increased 89,316 units to 651,823. But the rest of the industry increased, too, so Buick held fast to fifth in the model-year production rankings. Its tagline was "Talking your language." **4.** Mid-size wagons rode a 121-inch wheelbase, up an inch from before. Buick sold the flashy glass-roof Sportwagon as a separate model. It cost $3341 with seating for six and $3499 with seating for nine, and 22,908 were built. Of those, 10,909 had the optional woodgrain siding. Power came from either 230- or 280-bhp 350-cid V-8s.

4

1

2

As on other GM intermediates, the Buicks gained an inch of wheelbase and far more rounded sheetmetal. A full range of body styles was available in Special and Skylark trim. **1-2.** Here's the new GS350, Buick's junior muscle car. It shared its shell and much trim with the GS400 but was fitted with the division's new 350-cid V-8, which effectively replaced the old 260-bhp 340-cid V-8. It sported a 4-barrel carburetor and had 280 bhp. Available only as a hardtop coupe with an initial list price of $2926, Buick sold a respectable 8317 GS350s for 1968. Yet a third iteration was the California GS, essentially a GS350 in 2-door sedan guise.

1968 Buick Mid-Size Models

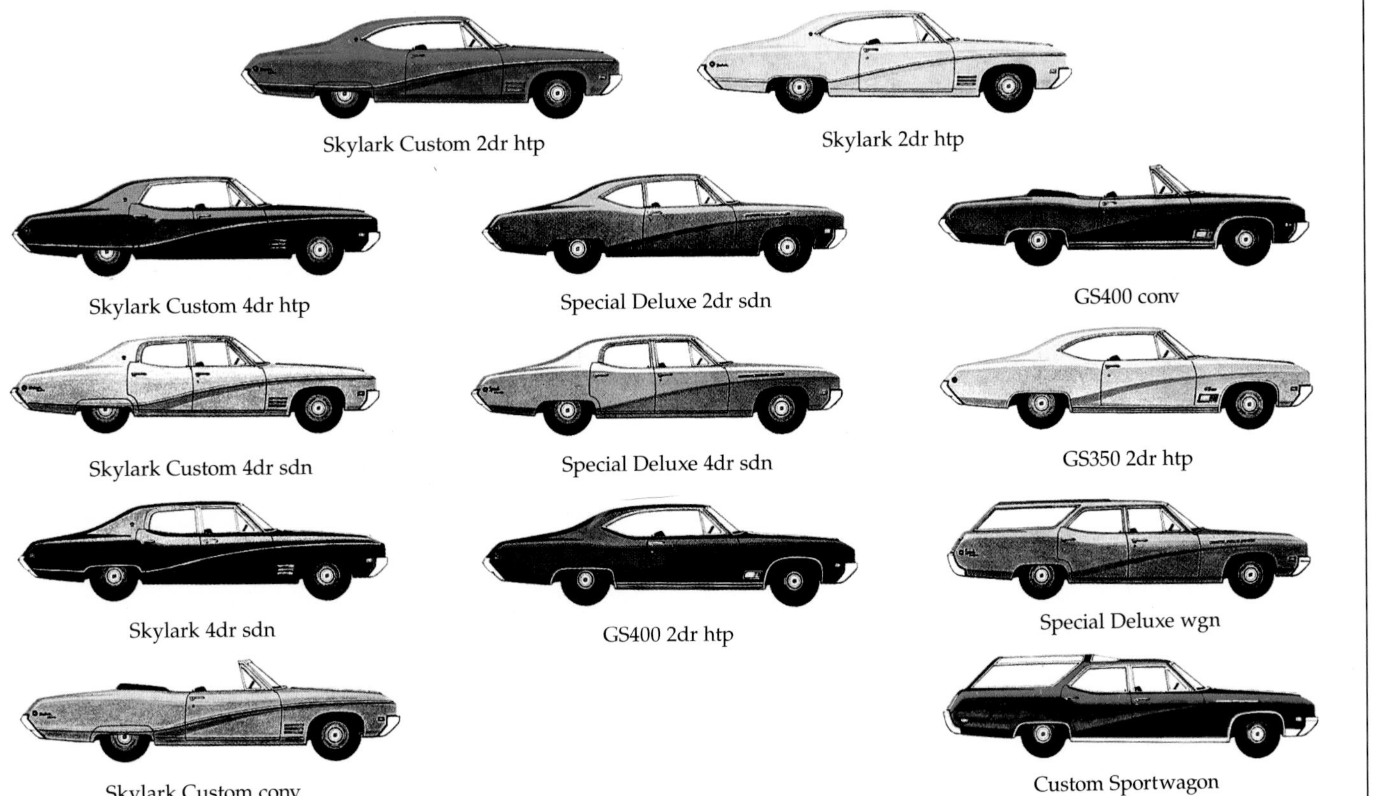

Skylark Custom 2dr htp

Skylark 2dr htp

Skylark Custom 4dr htp

Special Deluxe 2dr sdn

GS400 conv

Skylark Custom 4dr sdn

Special Deluxe 4dr sdn

GS350 2dr htp

Skylark 4dr sdn

GS400 2dr htp

Special Deluxe wgn

Skylark Custom conv

Custom Sportwagon

1

2

1. Riviera got hidden headlamps in a restyled grille. Still offered only as a 2-door hardtop on a 119-inch platform, its sales rose 14 percent, to 49,284. Base price was $4615, curb weight 4222 lb. It shared with Wildcat and Electra 225 a 360-bhp 430-cid V-8. **2-3.** The flagship Electra 225 retained its 126-inch wheelbase, formal look, and four stylized VentiPorts. Just 7976 of the $4541 convertible models were built. **4.** Buick's least-expensive full-size car, the LeSabre rode its old 123-inch wheelbase and came with a 230-bhp 350 V-8. Its convertible started at $3504, weighed 3966 lb, and found 5257 buyers. **5.** New were concealed parallel windshield wipers. They boasted an articulated driver-side wiper arm and a 20-percent greater wipe area.

3

4

5

1

2

Wildcat returned on the 126-inch wheelbase in base and Custom trim. **1-2.** The 2-door hardtop was available in both trim levels, but the 4-door sedan was only available in the base trim level. In addition, Buick offered a $3873 Custom Wildcat convertible. The line's only available engine was the 430-cid V-8. Wildcat sales held steady at around 70,000 despite deletion of the base-trim convertible. **3.** Evidence of Buick's big-car luxury image was the fact that its second-most-popular model was this $3375, 4007-lb LeSabre Custom 4-door hardtop, at 40,370 units. Not convinced? The single best-selling Buick of all was the even bigger Electra 225 Custom 4-door hardtop. It cost $4509, weighed 4314 lb, and satisfied 50,846 comfort-seeking buyers.

3

1968 Cadillac

1

1. Government-mandated side-marker lights were a subtle visual change for Cadillac's Eldorado. As in all Caddys, a new 375-bhp 472-cid V-8 replaced the 340-bhp 429. Base price rose $328 to $6605; sales jumped 37 percent to 24,528. **2.** The Fleetwood Brougham was again a member of the Sixty Special family and had a 133-inch wheelbase. **3.** Cadillac's hardtop Sedan DeVille rode on a shorter 129.5-inch chassis. **4-5.** For the auto show circuit, Cadillac created a special Eldorado called the Biarritz Towne Coupe. It featured a brushed aluminum grille, a landau-type targa roof, 20 coats of gold-flecked dark-olive Firefrost enamel paint, gold velour upholstery, mouton carpeting, and antique walnut trim accents. Wow.

2

3

4

5

1

2

3

1-2. Chevelle followed the other GM intermediates onto a new platform with a 3-inch-shorter wheelbase for 2-door models. With 325 bhp (375 optional), the SS 396 remained the line's top performer. Starting at $2899, the hardtop coupe captured 60,499 youthful buyers. **3.** The Chevelle lineup also featured the 300 and Malibu lines, plus Concours wagons, but only the SS 396 and Malibu offered a convertible. **4.** The experimental Astro II fueled rumors that a mid-engine Chevy sports car was near. It carried a Corvette V-8, and the rear half of the body could tilt up for engine access. Just one Astro II was built.

4

1968 Chevrolet

1

Corvette kept the '67 model's 98-inch wheelbase, chassis, suspension, even engines. But a completely new body reasserted its standing as America's one true sports car. **1.** GM styling chief Bill Mitchell used his 1965 Mako Shark II show car as the '68 'Vette's blueprint. **2.** The new interior had a prominent central tunnel and obligatory full instrumentation. **3.** The styling was controversial, but production set a new record at 27,134 (14,436 were ragtops). **4-5.** On the coupe, both the roof panels and the back glass could be removed for an open air feeling.

2

3

4

5

1

1. A 327-cid V-8 was standard. In optional 350-bhp guise, it did 0–60 mph in 7.7 sec. **2.** A hood bulge signals the 427 big-block V-8. It had up to 435 bhp and did 0–60 in just 5.3 sec. **3.** As in past years, the 'Vette's steel frame supported a fiberglass body. Coupes started at $4663, convertibles at $4320. **4.** Chevy didn't officially participate in racing, but "privateers" such as Tony DeLorenzo proved the new 'Vette a strong runner in SCCA competition.

2

3

4

1

2

1-2. The Z28 was again a $400 package that included a special 290-bhp 302-cid V-8, but it now wore fender ID badges. These cars have the hidden-headlamp Rally Sport package. **3.** Vent windows were out, side marker lights in. Biggest engine was still the 396, but this year it had 375 bhp. **4.** The "Caribe" show car was a sort of sporty/utility vehicle. **5.** Camaro started at $2588, but neither this yellow SS nor its Pontiac Firebird 400 companion are low-buck strippers.

3

4

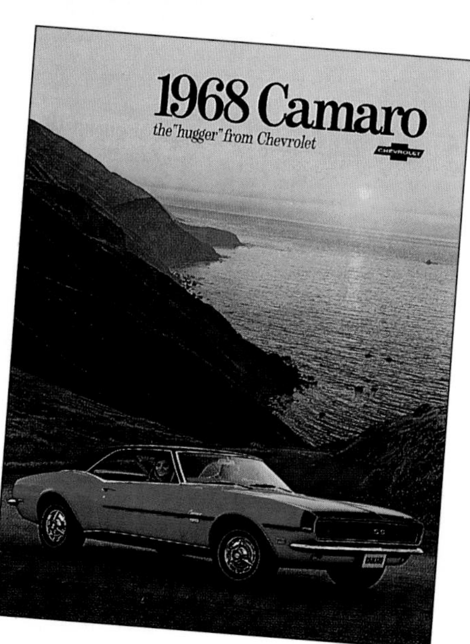

5

1

2

3

4

1. Concealed wipers, a fresh nose, and a new rear bumper with "horse-shoe" taillights were big-model style changes. **2.** Caprice was again the top-of-the-line series. **3.** This styling buck is fitted with an Impala vinyl front bench seat and a rear seat upholstered in Caprice's embroidered cloth. **4-5.** Full-size car sales increased 117,600, to over 1.1 million for '68 **6.** The compact Chevy II was redesigned, gaining an inch of wheelbase, to 111 inches, and a wider new body. All models wore the Nova name, and sales nearly doubled, to 201,000. **7.** Corvair dropped its 4-door body style, but engines and transmissions were unchanged. Production declined to 15,399. Rumors of its demise intensified.

5

6

7

1968 Oldsmobile

1

2

3

4

5

6

The restyled Cutlass and F-85 shared the same new mid-size platform with siblings at Buick, Chevy, and Pontiac. **1.** Powerhouse 4-4-2s came as this $3150 hardtop, a $3087 pillared coupe, or $3341 convertible. The 400-cid V-8 made 350 bhp, or 360 with optional W-30 hop-ups. **2-3.** Cutlass/F-85 sales rose 10 percent to 275,128. Overall, Olds sales increased by only 14,069, precipitating a slide from sixth place to seventh in the model-year production race. **4.** Olds teamed with the Hurst shifter outfit to create the first Hurst/Olds. It added $1161 to the price of a 4-4-2 coupe or hardtop and 515 were built. They had a special 390-bhp 455 V-8, automatic transmission with Hurst Dual Gate Shifter, heavy-duty everything, and this special paint job. **5.** Saying it did not make it so, but Olds was trying to change its image. **6.** Local promotional tie-ins were part of the program.

1968 Mid-Size Oldsmobile Models

4-4-2 2dr htp

Cutlass Supreme 2dr htp

4-4-2 2dr sdn

Cutlass Supreme 4dr htp

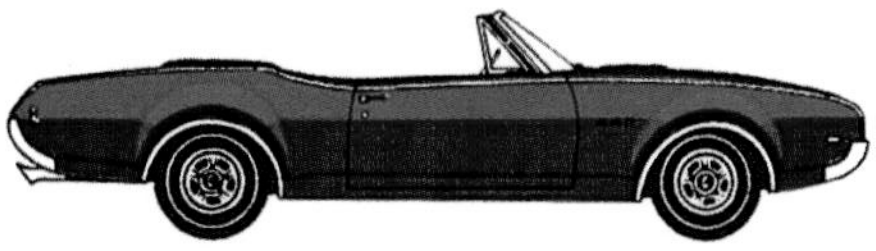

4-4-2 conv

Cutlass Supreme 4dr sdn

Cutlass 2dr htp

F-85 2dr sdn

Cutlass 2dr sdn

F-85 4dr sdn

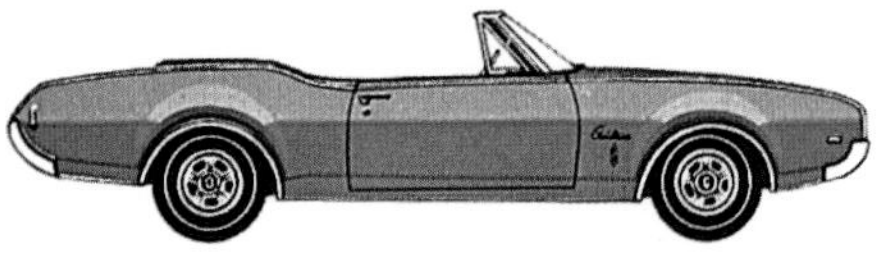

Cutlass conv

Cutlass Vista-Cruiser wgn 6 pass

Cutlass 4dr htp

Cutlass Vista-Cruiser wgn 9 pass

Cutlass 4dr sdn

Cutlass wgn 6 pass

1968 Oldsmobile

1

2

3

4

5

1. Ninety-Eights saw little change. Rarest was the convertible, with just 3942 built. Its $4618 base price included 2-way power seats, power windows, cut pile carpeting, dual exhaust, and a vinyl coated fabric top with glass rear window. **2-3.** Delmonts were now grouped under a single Delmont 88 line featuring new front and rear styling. These were the least-costly cars on the 123-inch wheelbase and the best-selling big Oldsmobiles, at 121,418 units. **4.** Delta 88's most popular model was the 4-door sedan with 33,689 sold. The standard engine on all full-size Olds cars was a 455-cid V-8 of between 310 and 365 bhp, depending on model. **5.** Service bays are timeless; only the cars change. **6.** The Toronado got a new split grille and America had a new ideal, Debra Dene Barnes of Moran, Kansas.

6

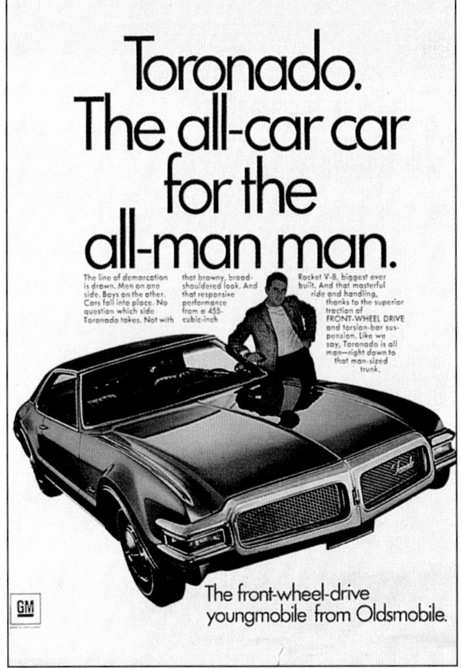

1

2

1-2. Toronado again had exclusive use of a 119-inch-wheelbase front-wheel-drive chassis, but 1968's restyle, with its gaudier nose, seemed to sully the classically clean original 1966–67 design. Still, sales were up nearly 5000 units, to 26,521. The price rose $76, to $4750 for the base hardtop, which attracted just 3957 buyers. In contrast, the $4945 Custom model drew 22,497 takers. Standard Toro power came from a 375-bhp Rocket 455. However, a 400-bhp unit with forced air induction and dual exhaust was optional. **3.** Oldsmobile engineering shops built this shortened Toronado as an emergency vehicle for proving-ground usage. The front and rear bumpers were made of wood coated with rubber for "tug-boat" duties.

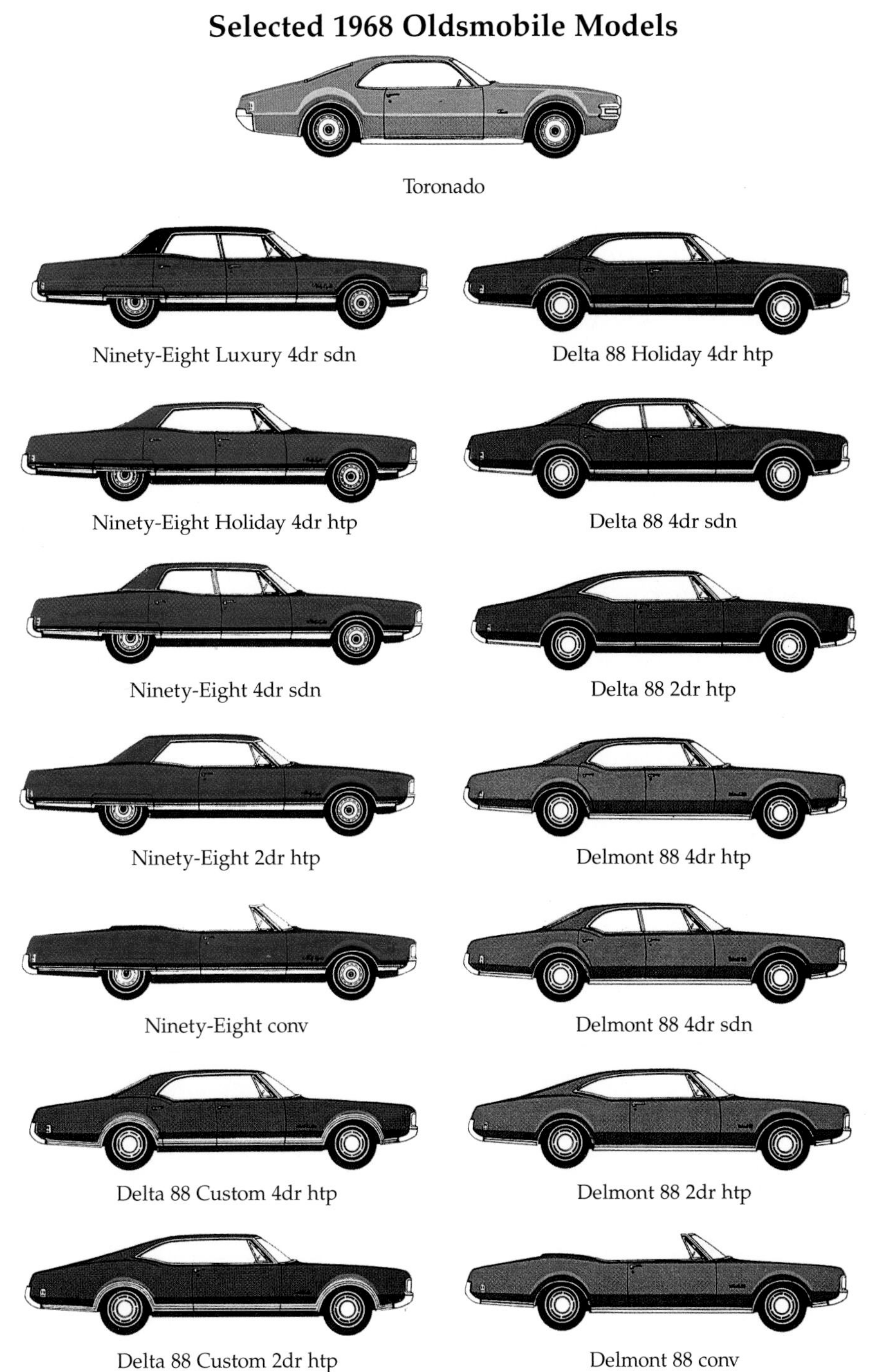

3

1968 Pontiac

1

2

3

4

5

Shades of Edsel—or so some said of Pontiac's new big-car "face." **1-2.** Hardtop and convertible Bonnevilles were joined late in the season by the line's first 4-door sedan. **3.** In Canada, Bonneville-size Pontiacs were Grand Parisiennes and had hidden headlamps. **4-5.** Catalinas could be equipped with a Ventura option package that included specific badges.

1

2

3

4

5

6

1. Pontiacs sold in Canada, including the Parisienne 2+2, featured Chevrolet engines and running gear. **2.** The Executive was the least-expensive series on the big 124-inch Bonneville wheelbase. **3.** Skirted wheels and a heavier look marked Grand Prix. It continued as a $3697 coupe, but sales declined 26 percent to a new low of 31,711. **4-6.** Pontiac sales as a whole jumped 15 percent. **7-8.** Catalina held down the 121-inch chassis and offered the widest range of body styles. A 400-cid V-8 was the smallest engine available in full-size Pontiacs.

7

8

1968 Pontiac

1

2

3

4

5

Once you've tried Wide-Tracking in a LeMans you'll understand why we call it LeMans.

And once you take our LeMans out of the garage, your days in motoring anonymity end. Magnificently.

LeMans' scintillating lines hold attention the way Wide-Track holds to a highway.

And when you're inside, you're held by the likes of bucket seats so comfortable you might want to take them home to meet the family. Especially since they're covered in fully expanded Morrokide. And it's all complemented by liberal samplings of walnut-grain styling.

On the road, LeMans lives up to its name with engines available up to 320 hp. And transmissions that get you through gears as smoothly as LeMans gets through tight corners.

For more reasons why we call a LeMans a LeMans, see your Pontiac dealer. Or your nearest "S" curve.

Wide-Track 1968 Pontiacs

6

1. Firebird's appearance changed little, but V-8 choices were shuffled to include new, more emissions-friendly 350- and 400-cid V-8s. **2.** This convertible has the high-output "Sprint" overhead-cam 6-cylinder with 215 bhp. **3.** The 400 was the hot model, its 330-bhp 400-cid V-8 taking it to 60 mph in 6.2 sec. **4.** The 400 HO added 5 bhp and subtracted a half-second 0–60 mph. **5-6.** Mid-size models moved to the new 112-inch wheelbase and got curvaceous new styling. The convertible is a Tempest; the coupe is a part of the higher-trim LeMans series.

1

2

3

4

5

6

1. Wagons, here a Tempest, rode a 116-inch wheelbase. **2.** A 4-door hardtop returned to the LeMans line but sold only 9002 units, compared to 110,036 for the 2-door hardtop. **3-6.** GTO put its own spin on the new styling with its Endura front bumper, a dent-resistant plastic unit color-matched to the body. Hidden headlamps were popular options, and bucket seats were standard. A 400-cid V-8, now at 350 bhp, was standard, with 265- and 360- bhp versions optional. The last did 0–60 mph in 6.4 sec. Sales rose by about 6000 units, to 87,684. The $3101 hardtop accounted for 77,704, the $3227 convertible making up the balance.

Etc.

TALUS (The Detroit Regional Transportation and Land Use Study) concludes automobiles still will be the major form of transportation in America in the 1990s

Motor News notes the following shortcomings of women drivers: "Over cautious. Indecisive. Drive so near the curb you think they're parking. React slowly in a crisis. No mechanical knowledge. Swing wide on right turns"

SANIBAT (Sanitary Battery) spokesman Calvin C. Cable declares, "A dirty [car] battery is a blight on our society"

Florida-based Horseless Carriage Corp. produces the Ford 1901, a three quarter-scale replica of "the 1901 Ford" (interestingly, regular Ford production did not begin until 1903)

Westinghouse's Marketeer I electric car, designed for urban delivery, is powered by 12 six-volt, heavy-duty lead-acid batteries; it has a range of 50 miles and a top speed of 25 mph

The Taylor-Dunn electric car (top speed, 12 mph) ceases production after 20 years

Jim Clark of Scotland, former Indy winner and two-time Formula 1 champion, is killed at Hockenheim, West Germany, when his Lotus Formula 2 race car loses air pressure in one tire and strikes a tree

1-2. Steam-powered fiberglass roadsters: the Keen Steamliner, and the Williams. **3.** Bobby Unser won the Indy 500 when leader Joe Leonard's turbine car failed with nine laps to go. **4-5.** Two from *Speedway:* Elvis, Bill Bixby, and Nancy Sinatra check out the King's Charger; Bill and Elvis compute the chemical formula for Nancy's eyeliner. **6.** The uncharacteristically dour Clampetts step up to Olds power in this publicity still from TV's *The Beverly Hillbillies.*

1

2

3

4

5

6

7

8

9

10

1. TV's *Green Hornet*, Van Williams, with Bruce Lee and the Black Beauty, a George Barris-touched Imperial. **2.** *Adam-12:* Kent McCord, Martin Milner, and Plymouth Belvedere. **3.** Stock car heroes (from left) Richard Petty, Cale Yarborough, Lee Roy Yarborough. **4.** Richard Nixon campaigns with with wife Pat. **5.** The Spook Electric had a 36-volt DC ball-bearing motor. **6.** Feed me. **7.** Family, fried chicken, and Ford's Econoline. **8-9.** Two from Datsun: Fair Lady 1600; 510 wagon. **10.** Fabian is race-ready!

Etc.

Lotus and STP get together to create six turbine racers for this year's Indy 500

Datsun restyles the Bluebird 1300; establishes a regional sales office in Detroit

Mazda introduces a small pickup, the 1000, to its line of U.S. commercial vehicles; the $1030 truck runs with a 1000-cc four that generates 48 bhp; Mazda's RX-97 and RX-85 coupes are powered by NSU/Wankel twin-chamber rotary-piston engines

The Subaru 360, a tiny, 2-door sedan with a 20-bhp 2-cycle, 2-cylinder engine comes to the U.S. market; Subaru of America president Malcolm Bricklin aims for eventual 30-state coverage

A California woman who does not know how to drive redecorates a Culver City Toyota dealer's showroom (in a Japanese motif, of course) in exchange for driving lessons, so she can enjoy the Corona she wants to buy

Top 10 Selling Imports

1. Volkswagen 582,009
2. Opel 84,680
3. Toyota 71,846
4. Volvo 40,810
5. Datsun 40,760
6. Fiat 30,521
7. Mercedes-Benz ... 24,553
8. English Ford 24,402
9. Renault 20,504
10. Saab 12,191

Total import-car share of U.S. market: 10.2 percent

1969

New energy-absorbing frames, front headrests, and side-impact door beams protected consumers' bodies, while their wallets were cushioned by the new federal Truth-in-Lending law, which for the first time required auto dealers to state costs, terms, and conditions of sale in a uniform manner.

One of humanity's highest achievements occurred on July 20, when American astronaut Neil Armstrong became the first human to set foot on the moon, answering a challenge posed early in the decade by John F. Kennedy.

Back on earth, U.S. casualties mounted in Vietnam, mammoth anti-war rallies disrupted cities across the country, and the cars of many political conservatives bore bumper stickers that read "America—Love It Or Leave It."

In July, a sedan driven by Senator Ted Kennedy plunged from a small bridge at Chappaquiddick Island, Massachusetts, drowning his passenger, 28-year-old Mary Jo Kopechne, a campaign worker. Kennedy swam to safety and did not report the accident until the following morning; he was not held legally responsible in the death.

The Beatles' *Abbey Road* album went to No. 1 and produced the hit single "Come Together." Other pop hits: The Doors' "Touch Me"; the Band's "Up on Cripple Creek"; the 5th Dimension's "Aquarius/Let the Sun Shine In"; Led Zeppelin's "Whole Lotta Love"; the Temptations' "I Can't Get Next to You"; and Frank Sinatra's "My Way." Janis Joplin released a live album, *I Got Dem Ol' Kozmic Blues Again Mama!* Impressionist David Frye mimicked Richard Nixon on a Top 20 comedy LP, *I Am the President.*

For some, the '60's defining cultural event was the Woodstock Music and Art Fair, held at the New York farm of Max Yasgur August 15–17. More than 400,000 young people grooved, tripped, got mellow, played in the mud, and took off their clothes. The Who, Jimi Hendrix, Ten Years After, Crosby, Stills, Nash & Young, Arlo Guthrie, and others supplied the music.

Military jackets ironically decorated with peace signs and other symbols of the counterculture were "in," as were wild hair, headbands, and wall posters.

The year's two most significant films were Dennis Hopper's anti-establishment biker parable, *Easy Rider;* and Sam Peckinpah's bloody, revisionist western, *The Wild Bunch. Midnight Cowboy, True Grit, They Shoot Horses, Don't They?*, and *Butch Cassidy and the Sundance Kid* were among other major pictures. TV junkies gorged on *Mayberry R.F.D., Here's Lucy, Marcus Welby, M.D., Hawaii Five-O,* and *The Carol Burnett Show.*

Sports took a major step into the modern age when renegade playboy quarterback "Broadway" Joe Namath guaranteed that his New York Jets of the upstart AFL would win Super Bowl III, and then guided them to a 16–7 upset of the NFL's Baltimore Colts. And baseball fans were astonished when New York's "Miracle Mets" defeated Baltimore's favored Orioles four games to one in the World Series.

American Motors Corporation

Compact American series enters its last model year and is shorn of its American badge to be sold simply as the Rambler series; all other models wear the AMC label

Rambler series includes the American and its spiffier Rogue version and is spiced up by the additon of the wild SC/Rambler, a junior muscle car nicknamed the Scrambler

Built in conjunction with Hurst Performance Products, the Scrambler packs AMC's 390-cid V-8, 4-speed manual floor-shift transmission, and patriotic paint scheme

Ambassador wheelbase grows by four inches to 122, topping that of the full-size entries from Chevy and Ford

Convertibles are absent from AMC/Rambler lineup for first time since 1960

Javelin, AMX, and Rebel continue with few changes

The AMX GT show car previews a chopped-off tail that later turns up on the new-for-1970 subcompact Gremlin

After a rousing 1968, AMC production dips 4 percent to 309,000 worldwide sales

Final Rambler-badged car comes off the Kenosha assembly line on June 30, 1969; it's the last of 4.2 million Ramblers built since 1950

1

2

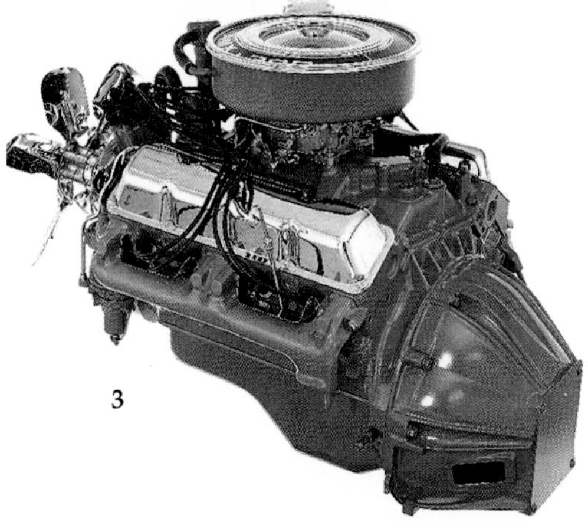

3

1. The last cars to wear the Rambler name, the former American line lost its top-line Rogue convertible. This $2296 2-door hardtop was the only surviving Rogue. **2.** AMC plunged into the muscle-car game with the wild Hurst SC/Rambler. Priced at just $2995, it really stood out with its "snorkel" hood scoop and eye-catching red, white, and blue paint treatment. **3.** Powering the "Scrambler" was a 315-bhp 390-cid V-8 hooked to a 4-speed manual transmission **4.** Built only in '69, production totaled just 1512 units.

4

1

2

3

1-2. AMC products weren't known for their performance, but that began to change in the late '60s. AMX (shown) and Javelin were offered in bright, "Big Bad" orange, blue, and green colors. The 2-seat AMX started at $3297 with the standard 225-bhp 290 V-8, but most buyers opted for the 343- or 390-cid V-8s. **3-4.** The mid-engine AMX/2 show car was a dream that never came true. **5.** Ambassadors were redesigned on a 122-inch wheelbase in base, DPL, and SST trim. Air conditioning was standard on all. The SST 4-door sedan cost $3605. **6.** An SST 2-door hardtop was $3522. **7-8.** Ambassador wagons featured a new two-way tailgate.

4

5

6

7

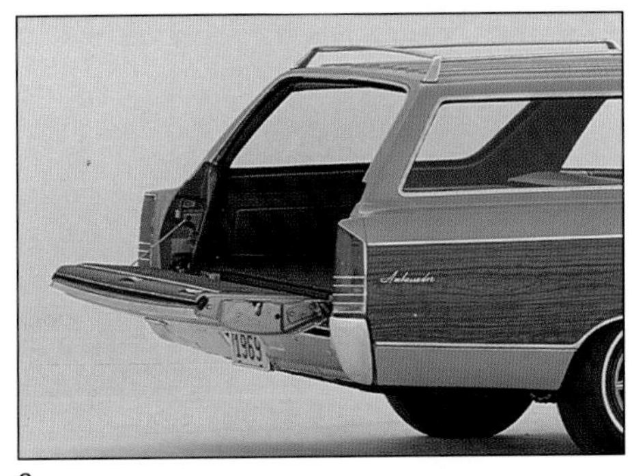
8

1

3

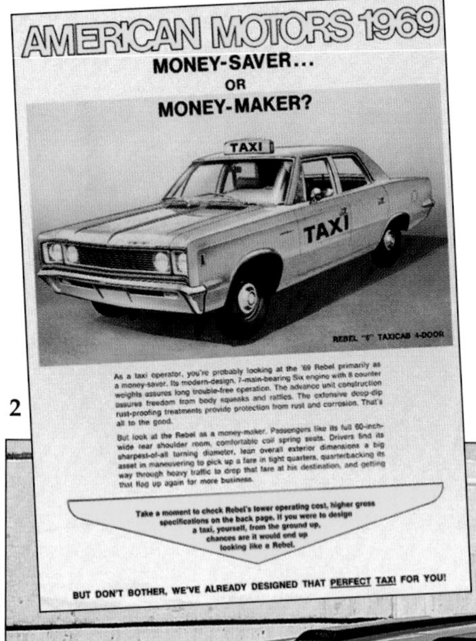

2

4

5

6

7

8

1-2. The mid-size Rebel was little changed. The base 2-door hardtop cost $2496, while the $2484 sedan was an attractive fleet buy. **3.** Stocked with the new Ambassador and sporty Javelin and AMX, AMC dealers were happier than they'd been in a long time. **4-6.** Like other ponycars, Javelin offered a wide range of engines. This racy-looking example has the thrifty 145-bhp 232-cid six, but the 315-bhp 390 V-8 was a new option. Prices started at $2512. **7.** AMC promoted the Javelin by sending it out to set long-distance speed records. Behind the wheel is Craig Breedlove, who knew a thing or two about Bonneville. **8.** Javelins could be dressed up with a rooftop spoiler, dummy hood scoops and fake side exhaust outlets. Bumper hues matched the body on cars with "Big Bad" colors.

Chrysler Corporation

Full-size Chryslers, Dodges, and Plymouths adopt curvey new "fuselage" styling

Bodies of full-size Chrysler-brand models grow 5.5 inches in length but retain the same 124-inch wheelbase as in '68

Full-size Dodge continues on 122-inch wheelbase

Front disc brakes offered for the first time on full- and mid-size Dodges

Dodge builds slick Charger 500 for NASCAR racing, then builds outrageous Daytona

Wild, winged Daytona helps Dodge to numerous NASCAR victories

Dart Swinger introduced as a lower-priced version of the GT/GTS

One of the fiercest muscle-car engines ever makes its appearance when engineers put a trio of 2-barrel carburetors on the big 440-cid V-8 to create the 440 "Six Pack"; it's available on special mid-size Dodges and Plymouths

Imperial grows by five inches, still on a 127-inch wheelbase; convertible is dropped

Big Plymouths ride a new 120-inch wheelbase, up from 119, and adopt horizontal headlights

Convertible added to Road Runner line; 'Cuda gets optional 440-cid 4-barrel V-8

1

2

1. Newport, Chrysler's least-expensive and best-selling series, offered a $3823 convertible. Next rung up the ladder was the Newport Custom; this is its $3730 4-door hardtop. **2.** Newports came standard with a 290-bhp 383-cid V-8, but options ran up to a 375-bhp 440. **3.** Chrysler's most popular car—the $3414 Newport 4-door sedan—weighed in at 3941 lb and sold more than 55,000 copies. **4.** Chrysler's new fuselage styling resulted in a wider, roomier interior.

3

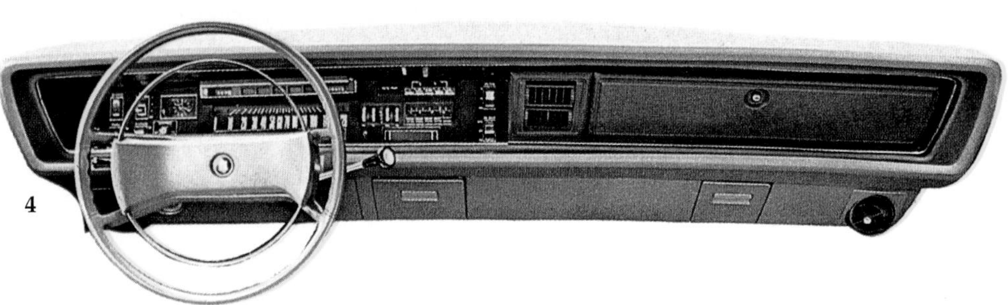

4

1969 Chrysler

1

2

3

1-3. The sporty Three Hundred series included 2- and 4-door hardtops and a convertible. They were the only Chryslers with hidden headlights. The $4450 ragtop is striking and rare; just 1933 were built. **4.** Three Hundreds shared with the New Yorker a standard 350-bhp 440 V-8 and offered a 375-bhp version as an option. The styled wheels depicted in this brochure artwork were recalled shortly after introduction because they tended to crack.

4

1

1. Concept 70X was a radical show car with sliding front and rear doors on the driver's side and a single sliding door on the passenger's side. Note the high-mounted brake lights below the rear window. 2. The 70X got top billing at Chrysler's auto show displays, including this one in Chicago. 3. The flagship New Yorker went for $4539 in 2-door hardtop form. 4. It was outsold 16,075 to 7537 by the Three Hundred coupe, which started at $4104. 5. A Newport Custom cost about $170 more than a comparable base Newport. From the rear, a Custom could be identified by its vertically segmented taillight panel. 6. Chrysler sales slipped 4000 units to 260,773, but the brand retained ninth place in model-year production. This is a Newport convertible.

2

3

4

5

6

1969 Dodge

1

2

3

4

5

6

1. Charger returned with only minor changes. A split grille graced the front, and the rear replaced round taillamps with elongated lenses. Sales dipped 7 percent, to 89,700. **2-3.** The recessed grille and tunneled rear window were aerodynamically inefficient on the big NASCAR tracks, so Dodge came up with the Charger 500 and built about 500 street examples to qualify the slippery shape for competition. It featured a flush-mounted grille with fixed headlights and a rear window that followed the contour of the roofline. The 375-bhp 440 Magnum V-8 was standard. The optional 426 Hemi V-8 furnished 13.7-sec quarter-mile times. **4-5.** A Propane-fueled Charger 500 is shown competing at California's Irwindale Raceway. California was a leader in emissions legislation, having stiffer regulations than the rest of the country. Due to its fuel source, the Propane X was promoted as a "clean air car." **6.** Joanie Parker, Dodge's popular spokesperson in the swingin' late-'60s, gets ready to do her thing for a television commercial.

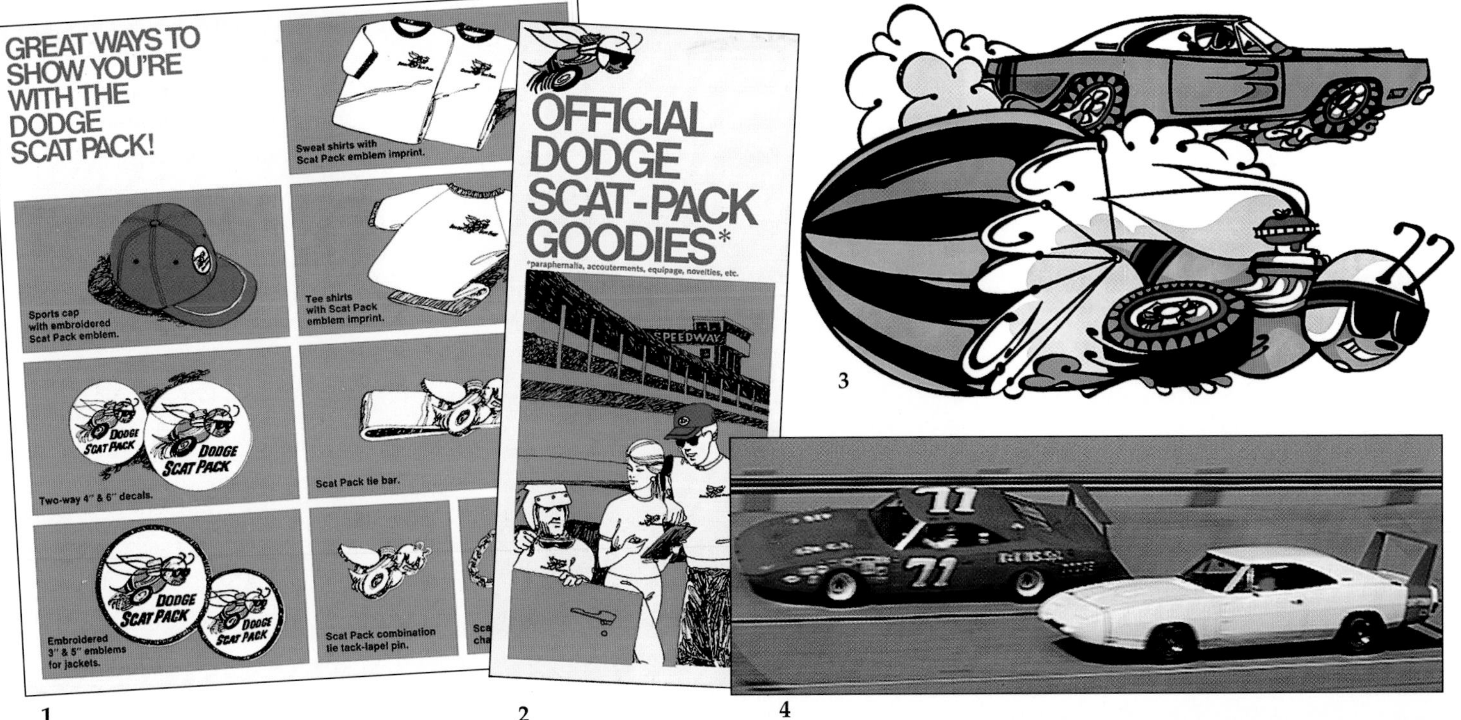

1 2 3 4

5

6

1-3. Sporty Dodges were members of the Scat Pack and diehards could show their loyalty with a host of wearable accessories. **4.** When even the sleek Charger 500 proved ineffective on the stock-car circuit, Dodge pulled out all the aerodynamic stops and created the wild Charger Daytona. Grafting a pointed snout and tall rear wing onto the Charger 500 body resulted in odd proportions but a wind-cheating profile. **5.** This design also had to be produced in limited numbers to qualify as a "stock" car, and Dodge dutifully built 505 for street use. **6.** Driver Charlie Glotzbach poses with his No. 99 Daytona at the car's namesake track in Florida. These Chargers still couldn't unseat Ford for the NASCAR title.

1969 Dodge

1-2. Five versions of the Coronet were offered, from the base $2554 Deluxe to the flashy R/T coupe. The R/T cost $3442 with its standard 375-bhp 440 V-8. **3.** A $2692 Coronet 440 is treated to a front-end alignment. Base and 440 Coronets came standard with the 225-cid Slant Six. **4-5.** A 275-bhp 340-cid V-8 in the lightweight Dart produced mid-14-sec quarter-mile times—an impressive performance from such an innocent-looking car. This would be the last year for the top-line GTS, though the 340 would remain available in lesser Darts. A GTS convertible went for $3419. **6-7.** Optional in the GTS was a 383-cid V-8. It had 330 bhp, but the engine's extra weight upset the Dart's balance and the extra power went up in smoke—rear tire smoke—so the cars were no faster than the 340s. The GTS coupe started at $3226.

1

3

2

4

5

6

7

1

2

1. Base Dart coupes were called Swingers, and when fitted with the 340-cid V-8 they became—you guessed it—Swinger 340s. At $2836, they were budget bullets. **2.** Many police officers still claim that the '69 Dodge Polara with a 440 V-8 was one of the finest patrol cars ever built. **3-4.** "You in a heepa trouble, boy." That was the signature line of fictional Southern sheriff Joe Higgins, another Dodge pitchman. Entertainer Dean Martin looks troubled. Insert your own punchline. **5.** With this face mask, anyone could play 'ol Joe. **6.** Well, almost anyone.

5

3

4

6

1969 Imperial

1

2

1. Chrysler's new fuselage-styled bodies were shared by Imperial. Imperial, however, continued on a 127-inch wheelbase, 3 inches longer than the Chrysler's, and had unique front and rear styling. These luxo-cruisers looked massive and were: The $5592 Crown 2-door hardtop weighed 4555 lb. Still standard was the 350-bhp 440 V-8, but the optional 360-bhp version was dropped, as was the convertible body style. **2.** A 2-door hardtop joined the existing 4-door hardtop in the flagship LeBaron series. LeBarons cost about $360 more than comparable Crowns, but looked nearly identical. **3.** Priciest Imperial was the LeBaron 4-door hardtop at $6131.

3

1

2

3

1. Barracudas were back in coupe, convertible, and fastback body styles, and were little-changed in appearance. Top engine option was the 330-bhp 383 V-8, and those Barracudas so equipped could get a bold side stripe and small "383-S" badges on the front fenders. **2-4.** A similar stripe adorns a convertible that carries the 275-bhp 340 V-8. Bucket seats and woodgrain trim highlight the interior. **5-6.** A new performance package for fastbacks and hardtops was introduced under the 'Cuda tag. It was available with the 340 or 383 V-8, and in a bow to overkill, at midyear was expanded to include the monster 375-bhp 440-cid V-8. Plymouth now had bragging rights to the ponycar with the largest engine of the day, though the big V-8 left no room for power steering or power brakes. Too much rear-wheel spin off the line kept quarter-mile times to a middling 14 sec.

4

5

6

1

2

1-2. Joining the Road Runner line was a $3313 convertible. It accounted for just 2128 of the 84,000 Road Runners built. **3.** The muscle-car market was reaching its zenith and Plymouth intermediates were in the thick of it. The GTX on this brochure was basically a dressier and more expensive version of the Road Runner: The coupe started at $3416, the ragtop at $3635. Combined production was less than one-fifth of Road Runner's. **4.** Photos taken at sanction drag strips made good PR, but most drag racing was done on the street. **5.** A hardtop had joined the original Road Runner pillared coupe in mid-'68. All featured the unique "beep-beep" horn that sounded like the cartoon character.

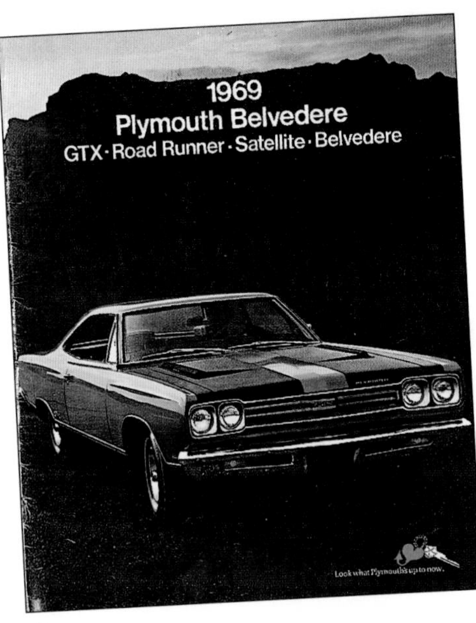

3

4

5

1

2

3

4

5

1-2. Road Runners continued their stampede on the muscle market despite some new bargain-priced competitors such as the Ford Cobra. Cheapest Road Runner was the pillared coupe at $2945, but it was outsold by half by the $3083 hardtop. Total Road Runner production nearly doubled that of '68. **3.** Standard in the flashier GTX but not offered in the Road Runner was the Super Commando 375-bhp 440-cid V-8. It delivered 0–60 mph in 6.4 sec and the quarter-mile in 14.3 sec at 98 mph **4.** Road Runners continued with a 335-bhp 383 V-8. It powered the 3450-lb car to mid-14-sec quarter-miles. Midyear brought the 440 6-barrel option, but the ultimate was the Hemi, which ripped to 60 mph in 5.3 sec and through the quarter-mile in 13.5 sec at 105 mph. **5.** The influential Road Runner was *Motor Trend*'s "Car of the Year," and Glenn White (left), Chrysler-Plymouth general manager, accepted the trophy from *MT* publisher Ray Brock.

1969 Plymouth

1

2

Furys were redesigned on a 1-inch-longer wheelbase (now 120) and wore "fuselage" styling like other full-size Chrysler products. Five trim levels were again offered: Fury I, II, III, Sport Fury, and VIP. Prices ranged from $2701 to $3502. **1.** The Sport Fury hardtop coupe was priced at $3283. **2.** Driver Art Pollard at the wheel of the STP-Plymouth Super Wedge Indy car. The radical racer was powered by a stock-block 305-cid Plymouth V-8 but failed to qualify for the big race.

1969 Plymouth Models

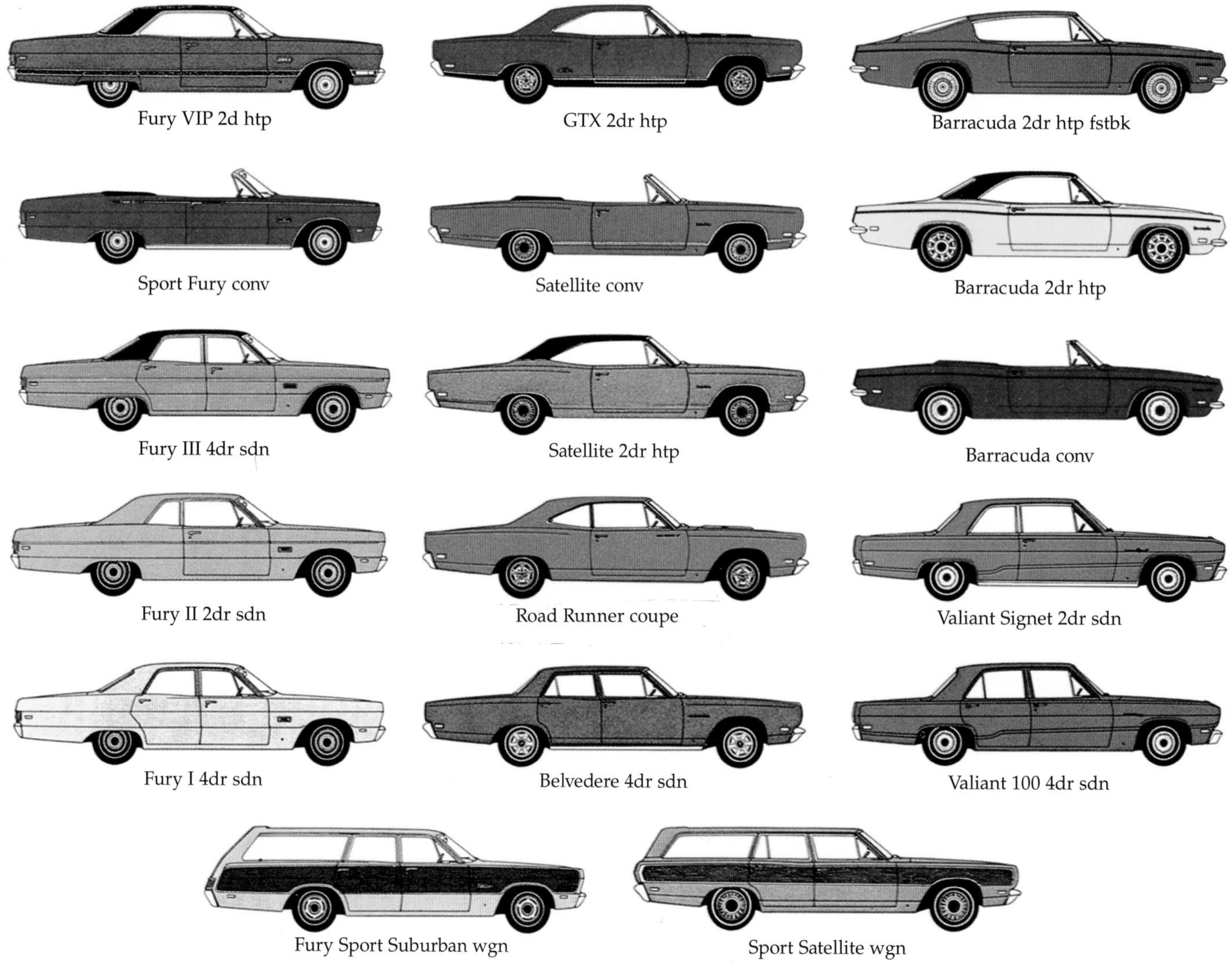

Fury VIP 2d htp

GTX 2dr htp

Barracuda 2dr htp fstbk

Sport Fury conv

Satellite conv

Barracuda 2dr htp

Fury III 4dr sdn

Satellite 2dr htp

Barracuda conv

Fury II 2dr sdn

Road Runner coupe

Valiant Signet 2dr sdn

Fury I 4dr sdn

Belvedere 4dr sdn

Valiant 100 4dr sdn

Fury Sport Suburban wgn

Sport Satellite wgn

Ford Motor Company

In the year's biggest auto-industry story, Semon E. "Bunkie" Knudsen, named president of Ford Motor Company in 1968, is sacked by Henry Ford II after just 19 months in office

Full-size Fords are redesigned on a longer chassis

Low-buck Cobra muscle car and race-inspired Talladega aerodynamic fastback are added to the Fairlane line

Mustang gets its first significant restyling; gains a longer nose and quad headlights

Three high-performance Mustangs are added to the lineup: Mach 1, Boss 302, and Boss 429

The famous Shelby Mustangs are now built alongside standard Mustangs, but not for long; this would be their last year of production, with leftovers sold as 1970 models

The 351-cid V-8 is introduced while the venerable 289-cid V-8, a Ford workhorse since 1965, is put out to pasture

Full-size Mercurys get redesigned on two wheelbases: 121 and 124 inches; novel Breezeway-roof model is eliminated

Cougar gets new styling and flashy Eliminator model

Ford GT40 nets its fourth straight victory in the LeMans 24 Hours, after which it is retired from racing

1

2

3

4

1. Full-size Fords, represented here by a $2649 Custom 2-door sedan, were redesigned on a 2-inch-longer wheelbase (now 121). **2.** Falcons changed little. This Sport "Coupe" cost $2598. **3.** Cheaper yet—and the cheapest Ford—was the base Falcon 2-door sedan at $2283. When the Maverick bowed in April 1969 as a '70 model, it carried a $1995 sticker, and Falcon sales took a dive. **4.** The 4-wheel-drive Bronco lost its convertible body style but gained its first V-8 option, the 302 cid. **5.** English-built Ford Cortinas began appearing in the U.S. around 1963. By 1969, the sporty GT version carried an economical 1600-cc 89-bhp 4-cylinder and cost around $2300. About 21,000 Cortinas were imported this year.

5

1

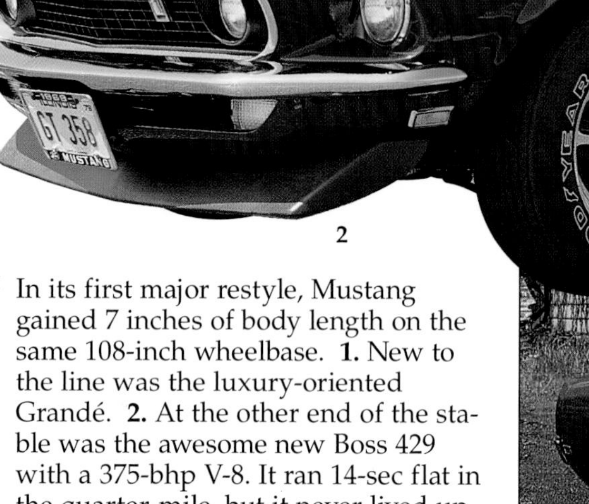

2

In its first major restyle, Mustang gained 7 inches of body length on the same 108-inch wheelbase. **1.** New to the line was the luxury-oriented Grandé. **2.** At the other end of the stable was the awesome new Boss 429 with a 375-bhp V-8. It ran 14-sec flat in the quarter-mile, but it never lived up to its straight-line performance potential. **3.** Most popular of the performance Mustangs was the new Mach 1. Engines ranged from a standard 250-bhp 351 to the 335-bhp 428. **4-5.** The Boss 302 held a 290-bhp 302-cid V-8 and a special handling suspension.

3

4

5

1

2

3

1-2. One of four specially built rumble-seat Mustangs, this Playboy Pink convertible was intended for parade use. **3-5.** Shelby Mustangs lost some individuality by being incorporated into regular Mustang production. GT-350s carried the new 250-bhp 351-cid V-8, while GT-500s continued with the 335-bhp 428 Cobra Jet. With less-costly Machs and Bosses eating into sales, demand for Shelbys fell to 3150. After about 600 leftovers were sold as '70s, the line was discontinued.

4

5

1

2

3

4

5

6

7

1-3. Ford's answer to the budget-muscle Plymouth Road Runner was the Fairlane Cobra. Though it cost about $220 more than its Plymouth rival, the Cobra came standard with a 335-bhp 428-cid Cobra Jet V-8. Here's the $3189 fastback SportsRoof. **4.** A 2-door hardtop, at $3164, was the other Cobra body style. These cars did 0–60 mph in 5.5 sec and the quarter-mile in 14.4 at 101 mph. **5.** Ford made its own aero-wonder for the stock car circuit, grafting a slick new nose on a Cobra SportsRoof to create the Talladega. It was so good it enticed Plymouth racer Richard Petty to defect to Ford. This is one of 745 built for street use. **6.** A. J. Foyt's Talladega in battle dress. **7.** Putting a fiberglass shell over a single-seat tube frame created a "funny car." Phil Bonner's Torino ran 7.8-sec quarter-miles, but was not a title winner.

1

2

3

4

1-4. Lincoln's Mark III continued for its second season with few changes, though at midyear it offered the optional Sure-Track Braking System, an early form of anti-lock brakes. It was the priciest Lincoln at $6758. **5.** Continentals received only minor front and rear styling updates. The 2-door hardtop cost $5830. **6.** Tipping the scales at over 5000 lb, the $6063 4-door was the heaviest—and most popular—Lincoln, at 29,719 units. All Lincolns carried a 365-bhp 460-cid V-8. **7.** Lehmann-Peterson-built stretch limos didn't come only in black. **8.** The Town Sedan show car had open chauffeur seating, a closed rear cabin.

5

6

7

8

1

2

1-3. Full-size Mercurys were redesigned, gaining an inch of wheelbase, to 124 inches. The sporty new Marauder, however, was built on a 121-inch span. The 2-ton-plus coupe was too heavy to be a muscle car, even though the top-line $4091 X-100 (shown) came with a 360-bhp 429 V-8. X-100s were identified by their bucket-seat interiors and matte-black tails. **4.** Apollo 9 astronaut Col. James A. McDivitt sits at the wheel of a special Marquis convertible equipped to monitor body responses. Behind him is Ford safety manager, Fletcher N. Platt. **5.** Though kissing cousins on the production line, the Ford Talladega and similar droop-nose Mercury Cyclone II were fierce competitors in stock-car racing. Special Cale Yarborough (white/red) and Dan Gurney (white/blue) commemorative editions were offered to the public. **6.** The $3224 Cyclone CJ came standard with the 335-bhp 428 Cobra Jet V-8. **7.** Some "normal nose" Cyclones got the Spoiler (no "II") name and the same Yarborough/Gurney treatments.

3

4

5

6

7

1

2

1. Cougars received their first styling revisions and added a convertible body. A ragtop was the official pace car of the Michigan International Speedway.
2. Both base and XR-7 Cougars were offered as 2-door hardtops and convertibles. Base soft tops started at $3382, XR-7s at $3595. **3-4.** Added midyear was the high-performance Cougar Eliminator, Mercury's answer to the Mustang Mach 1. Decked out in scoops and spoilers, it offered an array of engines: 290-bhp 302; 290-bhp 351; 320-bhp 390; and 335-bhp 428. **5.** Hot Mercs were cleverly billed as "sweet streepers."

3

4

5

General Motors

Full-size cars from Buick, Chevy, Oldsmobile, and Pontiac are redesigned on longer wheelbases

Much to the dismay of thousands of owners—especially smokers—GM deletes the vent windows on many models; decision is a combination of styling and cost-saving considerations

Cadillac reverts to horizontal headlights and builds its 4-millionth car

Cadillac kills "small" Series 61

Camaro is restyled; the line includes the last Camaro convertible until the '80s

Corvair is laid to rest

Stingray name returns to the Corvette; coupe outsells convertible for the first time

Four-wheel-drive sport-utility vehicle debuts as the Chevy Blazer and JMC Jimmy

Big Oldsmobiles redesigned on a 1-inch-longer wheelbase, but styling changes little

Pontiac Grand Prix sales triple with downsized redesign

Trans Am version of the Firebird is quietly introduced

General-manager shakeups move John Z. DeLorean from Pontiac to Chevy, E. M. "Pete" Estes from Chevy to GM corporate, and install Lee N. Mays at Buick and George R. Elges at Cadillac

1

2

3

4

1. Electra's restyle was most evident in front, though its body lines were sharper and straighter than before. This Custom 4-door hardtop started at $4611, but carries the optional Limited package. **2.** Wildcats, formerly based on the larger Electra, were now sportier versions of the smaller LeSabre but still carried the Electra's 360-bhp 430-cid V-8. A Custom 2-door hardtop went for $3817, about $430 more than a comparable LeSabre. **3.** The biggest seller in Buick's line was the LeSabre, which also was redesigned. And the biggest-selling LeSabre was the $3450 4-door hardtop. LeSabres came standard with a 230-bhp 350 V-8. **4.** Buick was again fifth in model-year volume.

1 2

3

4

5

1-2. Rivieras didn't change much, yet at nearly 53,000 units, sold better than ever at $4701. **3-4.** Special Deluxe, Skylark, and Gran Sport models also returned with few changes, though GS 400s got functional hood scoops. Both the convertible and coupe shown are fitted with the optional Stage 1 package, which boosted the 400-cid V-8 from 340 bhp to 345—on paper. The actual increase was probably more. A Stage 1 could cover the quarter-mile in 14.4 sec. **5.** A Special Deluxe 2-door sedan listed for $2562. **6.** A sleek Skylark convertible started at $3098.

6

1

1-2. Sportwagons rode their own 121-inch wheelbase, 5 inches longer than the Skylark sedans. Exterior wood-look trim was optional. Six- and 9-passenger models were offered; a handy step was built into the rear bumper to assist passengers entering the rear seat. 3. The $3151 Skylark 4-door hardtop wasn't very popular, accounting for only 9609 sales—less than a tenth of Skylark production. 4. Attending to points and condenser ignitions was a tune-up routine. Here, a technician hooks a diagnostic unit to a Riviera. Note the Riv's headlights in their "hidden" position behind the grille. 5. Though the block letters on the rear fender say "BUICK," this space-aged Century Cruiser concept car didn't look like anything else from Flint—or from this century. It's pictured at the 61st Chicago Auto Show.

2

3

4

5

1

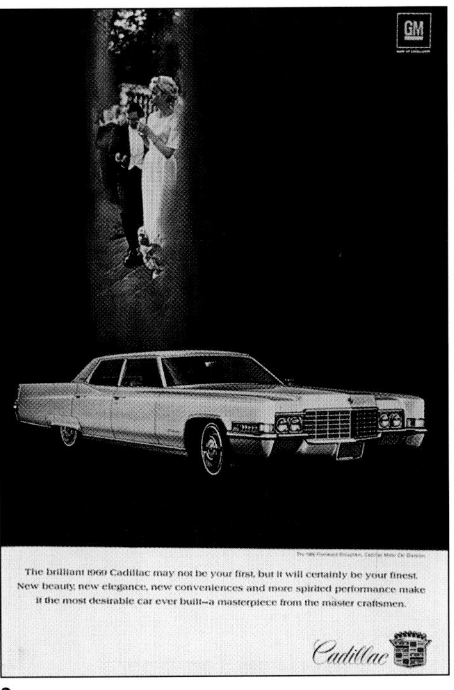

2

3

4

5

6

7

8

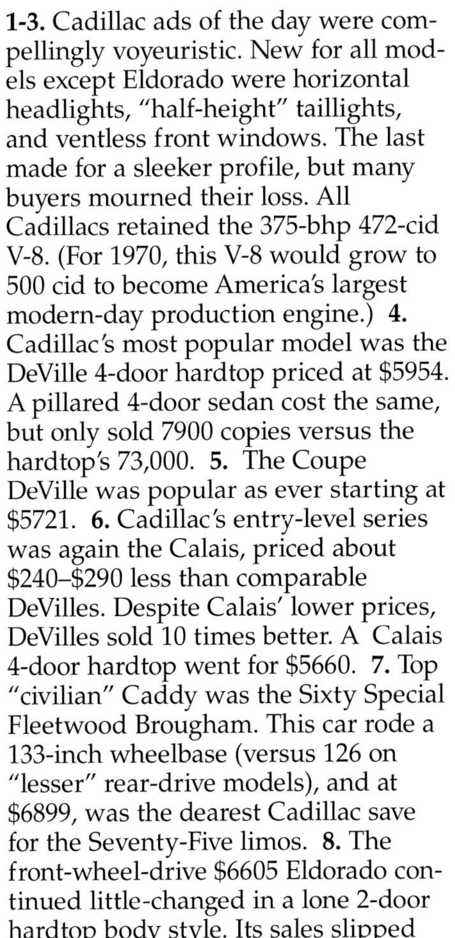

1-3. Cadillac ads of the day were compellingly voyeuristic. New for all models except Eldorado were horizontal headlights, "half-height" taillights, and ventless front windows. The last made for a sleeker profile, but many buyers mourned their loss. All Cadillacs retained the 375-bhp 472-cid V-8. (For 1970, this V-8 would grow to 500 cid to become America's largest modern-day production engine.) **4.** Cadillac's most popular model was the DeVille 4-door hardtop priced at $5954. A pillared 4-door sedan cost the same, but only sold 7900 copies versus the hardtop's 73,000. **5.** The Coupe DeVille was popular as ever starting at $5721. **6.** Cadillac's entry-level series was again the Calais, priced about $240–$290 less than comparable DeVilles. Despite Calais' lower prices, DeVilles sold 10 times better. A Calais 4-door hardtop went for $5660. **7.** Top "civilian" Caddy was the Sixty Special Fleetwood Brougham. This car rode a 133-inch wheelbase (versus 126 on "lesser" rear-drive models), and at $6899, was the dearest Cadillac save for the Seventy-Five limos. **8.** The front-wheel-drive $6605 Eldorado continued little-changed in a lone 2-door hardtop body style. Its sales slipped slightly to 23,333.

1969 Chevrolet

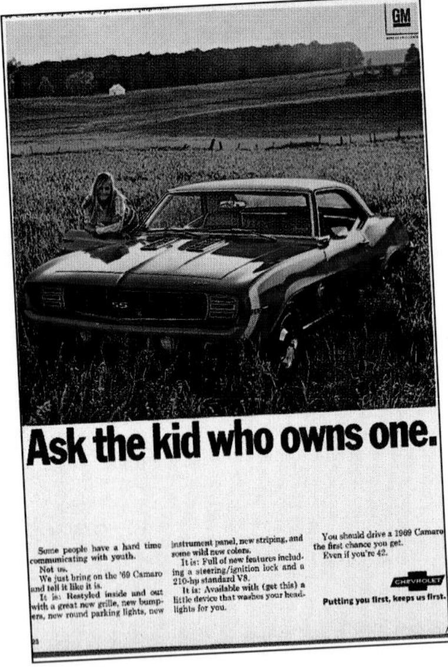

1

2

3

4

1-2. Camaro was reskinned on the same 108.1-inch wheelbase. This styling would serve for the '69 model year only. **3-4.** The Super Sport package was one of many options returning. Top engine was the 375-bhp 396-cid V-8. **5.** A Camaro paced the Indy 500, and Chevrolet issued 3675 replica coupes and convertibles. **6.** The Penske/Sunoco Z-28 driven by Mark Donahue captured the Trans Am championship for Chevrolet's second consecutive title. **7.** Street Z-28s cost $3184 and again carried a 290-bhp 302 good for low-15s in the quarter-mile. **8.** The popular RS option package hid headlights behind windowed louvers.

5

6

7

8

Chevrolet 1969

1-3. Biggest V-8 officially offered in the Camaro was a 396, but a few thousand 427s were fitted via special order. Just 69 of those were aluminum racing 427s coded ZL1. Cost was $4160 for the engine alone. Rated at 430 bhp, it really had over 500 bhp. A ZL1 Camaro like this did the quarter-mile in 13.1 sec at 110 mph. **4.** Chevelles, especially the SS 396, appealed to the young and young at heart. **5-6.** The popular Malibu 2-door hardtop started at $2601. **7.** The SS 396 was no longer a separate model but a $348 option package that turned a base Chevelle or Malibu into a 14.5-sec quarter-miler. A '69 SS 396 ragtop was a muscle classic.

1

2

3

4

5

6

7

1

2

3

1-3. Corvettes changed little after being restyled for 1968, yet managed to sell a record 38,762 copies—a 35-percent increase over the year before. Prices started at $4438 for the ragtop, $4781 for the coupe. Previously, convertibles sold far better than coupes, but that trend was reversed this year, due at least in part to the coupe's removable T-tops. Base engine was now a 300-bhp 350-cid V-8 (which replaced a 300-bhp 327), but this example sports the optional 435-bhp 427, which cost $437 and took it to 60 mph in 5.3 sec. **4.** This dark blue coupe has the legendary L88 engine. This was a 427 with weight-cutting aluminum cylinder heads. It was a $1032 option and just 116 were ordered. Its 430 bhp rating was conservative.

4

1

2

3

4

5

The much-maligned Corvair breathed its last gasp, with production ceasing after a run of just 6000 model-year '69s. **1-2.** Only 521 Monza convertibles were sold at $2641, making them the rarest of all Corvairs. **3.** The $2522 Monza hardtop coupe was outsold slightly by the cheaper 500 coupe. **4.** Chevrolet's popular compact dropped "Chevy II" from its name to become simply the Nova. Engine offerings included a 90-bhp 153-cid 4-cylinder, a pair of sixes, and V-8s up to 396 cid and 375 bhp. The last was offered in the Nova SS and did 0–60 mph in 5.9 sec, the quarter-mile in 14.5 at 101 mph. More user-friendly was this garden-variety $2405 Nova V-8 2-door sedan with its standard 200-bhp 307 V-8. **5.** Topping Chevy's extensive line of station wagons was the $3565 Kingswood Estate.

1969 Chevrolet

1

2

3

4

5

Big Chevys got less-curvaceous sheetmetal on the same 119-inch wheelbase. A 327-cid replaced the 307 as the base V-8. **1-3.** An era would end after '69, the last year Chevy offered a full-size big-block Super Sport. Just 2455 Impala SSs were built for '69, and all had a 390-bhp 427 V-8. This SS convertible listed for $3683, including the $422 SS 427 package. **4.** Helped by prices as low as $2645 on full-size models, Chevrolet closed the decade with its eighth straight year of 2-million-plus sales. **5.** Chevy answered the Ford Bronco with the larger, more-luxurious Blazer 4x4. Based on the full-size General Motors pickup trucks, Blazers and the companion GMC Jimmy were offered with a removable hardtop. **6** Among the wildest GM show cars of the era was the turbine-powered, three-wheel Astro III, which featured a power-operated lift-up canopy for access to the interior.

6

1

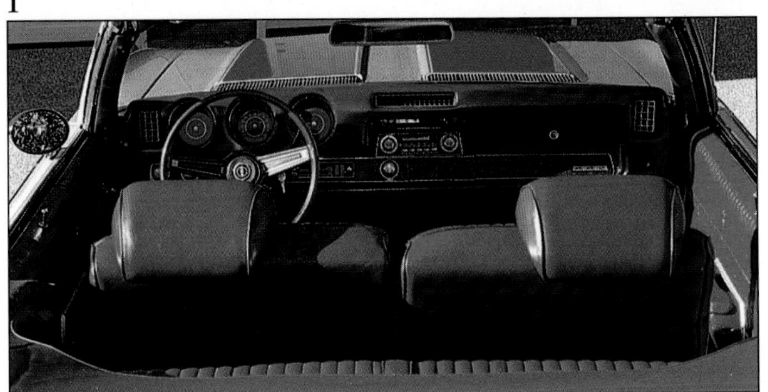

2

3

4

5

6

1-3. Oldsmobile's Cutlass got a modest facelift and was again keynoted by the sporty 4-4-2, which cost $3395 in ragtop form. **4.** Fictional Dr. Oldsmobile was a mad scientist of Olds performance. Here the lab-coated nut shares an auto-show stage with a couple of misfit assistants. **5.** A Ford and an Olds: Miss America, Judith Anne Ford of Belvidere, Ill., with a 4-4-2. **6.** One of every two new cars sold was a GM product, so they seemed everywhere.

1

2

4

3

5

1-3. The Cutlass-based Hurst/Olds with its 455-cid V-8 returned, though horsepower fell from 390 to 380. Huge hood scoops replaced the former subtle under-bumper scoops, and a heroic airfoil graced the tail. Available only with a Hurst-shifted 3-speed automatic transmission, it did the quarter-mile in 14 sec. The Hurst/Olds partnership would fade out after this year but return in the '70s with more focus on luxury. **4-6.** Toronado changed only in detail and was still Oldsmobile's only front-wheel-drive car. Offered as a base and Custom 2-door hardtop, it had a 375-bhp or optional 400-bhp 455 V-8. Prices started at $4835.

6

1

2

1-2. Though redesigned on a 1-inch-longer wheelbase (now 124 inches), the full-size Delta 88 didn't look much different than before. The convertible moved from the departed Delmont 88 series to become a $3590 Delta 88. Base engine was a 250-bhp 350 V-8; options ranged to a 390-bhp 455. **3.** The $3600 Delta 88 Custom 4-door hardtop. **4.** Costliest 88 was the new Royale 2-door hardtop at $3836. **5.** Ninety-Eights were also redesigned and rode a 1-inch-longer (127) wheelbase. A 2-door hardtop was $4461. **6.** The $4692 Ninety-Eight Luxury 4-door hardtop.

3

4

5

6

1969 Pontiac

1

2

3

1-6. Bucking an industry trend, the redesigned Grand Prix shrunk 3 inches in wheelbase (to 118 inches) and lost 360 lb (now 3715). Yet the trimmer GP sported one of the longest hoods in autodom, and with V-8s up to a 390-bhp 428-cid available, it combined muscle-car go with luxury-car comfort. As per tradition, there was one body style, a $3866 2-door hardtop. Standard equipment included the industry's first concealed antenna (in the windshield). A hood-mounted tachometer was optional. At 112,486, production more than tripled 1968's.

4

5

6

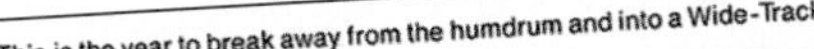

How come Pontiac engineers never seem to let great enough alone? Our even-plusher-than-usual Bonneville causes us to ask the question. Bonneville's wheelbase is longer—now stands at a luxurious 125 inches and rests on new, wide-tracked, 15-inch wheels for '69. Bonneville's 428 V-8 can be ordered up to 390 horsepower along with 3-speed Turbo Hydra-Matic. New energy absorbing material protects its new bumpers front and rear. And the interior accommodations? Rest easy, friends. That great Bonneville magic abounds. You can select from a dazzling array of cloth and expanded Morrokide, or all-Morrokide (or all-leather in the convertible). And rich-looking inserts touch up the doors and instrument panel. We can't think of any better way to put something great between you and the highway. Your Pontiac dealer will gladly handle the introduction.

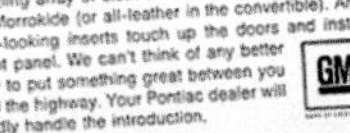

The year of the great Pontiac break away.

1

2

4

3

Pontiac's full-size cars were redesigned but looked very similar to the '68s. Catalinas rode a 122-inch wheelbase, while Executives and Bonnevilles had a 125-inch span—both one inch longer than before. **1.** Bonneville's ragtop started at $3896. **2.** Bonneville 4-door hardtops listed for $3756. **3.** Catalina 2-door hardtops proved popular at $3174. **4.** The $3872 Executive wagon featured a dual-action tailgate and built-in rear bumper step. **5-7.** The division demonstrated an experimental air bag in these promotional photos.

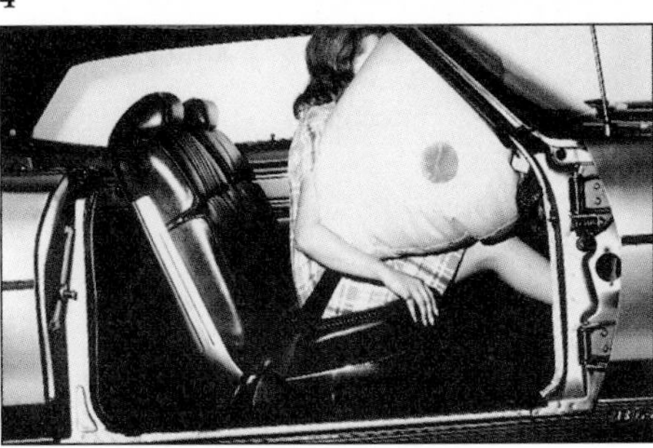

5

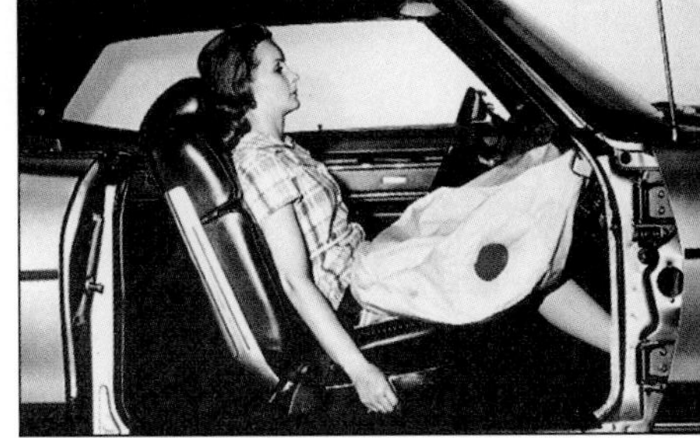

6

7

1969 Pontiac

1

2

3

It's the official car of the U.S. Ski Team. But don't let that snow you.

The year of the Great Pontiac Break Away.

4

5

6

1. Pontiac's mid-size cars changed little. This $3064 LeMans convertible sports the optional hood-mounted tach and wire wheel covers. **2.** A Tempest sedan was Pontiac's cheapest 4-door at $2557. **3-4.** With its standard 350-bhp 400, a GTO started at $3156. **5.** Arnie "The Farmer" Beswick drops the gavel on his GTO Judge at the NHRA Winternationals. **6.** The first Trans Am debuted at the Chicago Auto Show.

1

2

3

1-3. Arriving at midyear was a special $332 option package for GTOs called The Judge. It came with exposed headlights, a rear-deck spoiler, and op-art graphics. Early examples were painted Optic Orange, but later models offered a choice of colors. Standard equipment included a 366-bhp Ram Air III 400-cid V-8 that furnished mid-14-sec quarter-mile times. **4.** Even considering its midyear debut, first-year production of the legendary Trans Am was minuscule at only 897 units, including just eight convertibles. Included in the $725 Trans Am option package was a 366-bhp Ram Air 400 and heavy-duty suspension. All were painted Polar White with blue racing stripes. Despite humble beginnings, the T/A would go on to become one of Pontiac's top sellers in the '70s. **5-6.** Firebird convertibles started at $3045, but this one has the optional Sprint package that added sporty touches and a hotter 230-bhp version of the standard 175-bhp 250-cid overhead-cam inline-6-cylinder engine.

4

5

6

Etc.

Two Yale University professors predict that America's central cities will have to outlaw automobiles within the next few years if the cities are to survive

President Nixon proposes a $10 billion program of urban mass-transit development

Big-brained stylists at Firestone Tire & Rubber come up with "his" and "hers" tires: "his" has a bold tread design and plain sidewall; "hers" is decorated with a flowery stripe molded in the sidewall and colored plastic traction studs implanted into the tread surface

Representatives of the Big 3 admit at a Washington, D.C., meeting hosted by the National Highway Safety Bureau that air-bag development has a long way to go

V-8 engines are installed in 77 percent of new American cars; in 1960, it was 52 percent

Hardtops, with nearly 4.8 million registrations, are the year's most popular body style

The typical U.S. autoworker earns $170.97 a week

A long-haired blonde woman imitating Lady Godiva rides a horse into a Tampa, Florida, dealership to protest poor service; she declares that the horse is the only working transport she owns

1

2

3

4

1. The bad guys' Charger gets air on a San Francisco hill in *Bullitt.* **2.** Gridlock at Woodstock encouraged this couple to turn their Fairlane into a crash pad. More than 400,000 descended on the New York State farm community for the music and art fair, and far too many drove. **3.** Shovel-nosed Delta from General Electric. As with numberless other electric autos, the Delta's practicality was severely limited by battery technology that meant modest speed and range. **4.** Debbie, are you in there? Thirty-one junior high-school students from Fullerton, California, cram themselves into a VW Beetle to set a new Bug-packing record.

1

2

3

4

5

6

1. Toyota's U.S. sales were on the rise; a big reason was the reliable, economical Corona. **2.** Datsun's 510 sedan started at $1996. **3.** The Italia Spyder, built by Italy's Intermeccanica, had a fiberglass body and a 302-cid Ford V-8. **4.** The XJ6 was the last Jaguar body style for which company founder Sir William Lyons was primarily responsible. **5.** Inspector Lewis Erskine (Efrem Zimbalist, Jr.), of ABC-TV's *The FBI,* and his Mustang. **6.** Legendary racer Mario Andretti started 29 Indy 500s but registered his only win in this STP-sponsored Hawk III-Ford V-8.

Etc.

A Ford study during development of the Maverick compact shows import-car buyers tend to be young, college educated, with above-average income

Datsun unveils a 2-door companion for its remarkable 510 4-door sedan; the 510 has dull styling, but, with its 4-wheel independent suspension and tough 96-bhp 4-cylinder, captures a cult following that consideres it a baby BMW

Triumph's TR-6 sports car has handsomely squared bodywork by Germany's Karmann; U.S. list: $3275

Senate Commerce Committee sees crash-test film in which a VW Beetle fares better than a Subaru 360 and a King Midget; in a 30-mph crash, though, the Beetle is demolished by a '57 Ford

In the American Northeast, representatives of 11 Volvo dealers attack a Volvo with sledgehammers to demonstrate the make's durability

Top 10 Selling Imports

1. Volkswagen 548,904
2. Toyota 127,018
3. Opel 93,520
4. British Leyland ... 68,066
5. Datsun 60,872
6. Fiat 41,549
7. Volvo 36,146
8. English Ford 21,496
9. Mercedes-Benz ... 21,466
10. Renault 18,536

Total import-car share of U.S. market: 11.23 percent

INDEX